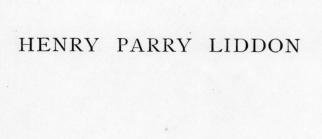

HENRY PARRY LIDDON

H P Liddon.

Emery Walker, ph. sc.

(Engraved 1890)

Life and Letters

of

Henry Parry Liddon

D.D., D.C.L., LL.D.

CANON OF ST. PAUL'S CATHEDRAL, AND SOMETIME
IRELAND PROFESSOR OF EXEGESIS IN THE UNIVERSITY
OF OXFORD

BY

JOHN OCTAVIUS JOHNSTON, M.A.

PRINCIPAL OF CUDDESDON THEOLOGICAL COLLEGE

WITH A CONCLUDING CHAPTER

BY

THE LORD BISHOP OF OXFORD

WITH PORTRAITS

LONGMANS, GREEN, AND CO.
39 PATERNOSTER ROW, LONDON
NEW YORK AND BOMBAY
1904

PREFACE

To-day is the fourteenth anniversary of Dr. Liddon's death; and some explanation of the long delay in the appearance of this volume may rightly be expected.

When the work was entrusted to me in 1890, there was every reason to suppose that I should be at liberty to begin it very soon. But unforeseen changes caused me to have a larger share than was intended in completing and editing the "Life of Dr. Pusey." Before that work was finished in 1898, other changes had deprived me of much of the leisure in which this book was to have been written; and it has been only possible to prepare it as opportunities arose at long intervals during the last six years.

The story of Dr. Liddon's life has been told so far as is possible from his letters and diaries. A selection of letters, on general subjects not directly connected with the events of his life, has been placed in the Appendix to each Chapter. The letters which he received and preserved—a very great number, and many of them deeply interesting—have not been used, except in very rare instances: they belong properly to the lives of the writers.

It remains for me gladly to express my grateful acknowledgments to the many friends without whose generous help this book could not have been written; and especially to all those who have entrusted me with their letters, or given leave for the publication of documents, particularly to the members of Dr. Liddon's family ; to Dr. Edward Liddon and the Rev. T. Vere Bayne, for allowing the reproduction of the portraits in their possession, and to Messrs. Graves & Co., for permission to use their engraving ; to the Rev. E. F. Sampson, for the account of Dr. Liddon's life at Christ Church ; and, above all, to the Bishop of Oxford, not only for many valuable criticisms and suggestions, but also for supplying one of the great wants of the volume by the sketch of Dr. Liddon's character and personality in the concluding Chapter.

J. O. JOHNSTON.

CUDDESDON,
September 9, 1904.

CONTENTS

CHAPTER VI. 1870–1871.

CHAPTER VII. 1872–1875.

CHAPTER VIII. 1876–1878.

CHAPTER IX. 1870–1881.

CHAPTER X. 1879–1883.

CHAPTER XI. 1883–1885.

LIST OF ILLUSTRATIONS

LIFE OF
HENRY PARRY LIDDON

CHAPTER I.

EARLY YEARS—SCHOOL DAYS—UNDERGRADUATE LIFE—
SCOTCH TOUR—FOREIGN TOURS—VISIT TO ROME—
ORDINATION.

1829–1854.

HENRY PARRY LIDDON was born on Thursday, August 20, 1829, at North Stoneham, in Hampshire. He was the eldest son of Captain Matthew Liddon, R.N., and of his wife Ann, daughter of Samuel Bilke, a Justice of the Peace for the county of Surrey.

His father's ancestors had been settled in the south of England for many generations. There is reason to believe[1] that a Ledun, from Lidon, near Saintes in Aquitaine, settled in England at or soon after the Conquest. In the thirteenth century, one Henry Ledun is mentioned as inheriting some property in Wiltshire. In later centuries the name in its modern spelling is found widely spread throughout the southern counties; and members of the family are frequently mentioned in wills and other records in various parts of Wiltshire, Dorsetshire, Somersetshire, and Devonshire.

In the early part of the eighteenth century a branch of the Liddon family migrated from Delford, near Broad-hembury, to Axminster; and there Matthew Liddon was

[1] See "The Norman People" (Henry S. King & Co., 1874), p. 311.

B

born in 1791. In 1804, at the age of thirteen, he entered the Navy, and enjoyed to the full the abundant opportunities of active service which were afforded by the exciting events of the following ten years. He is repeatedly mentioned in despatches ; for instance, at the age of fifteen, when serving in the West Indies, although only a midshipman, he was placed in charge of a prize, but was unfortunately captured by two French privateers and sent as prisoner with the rest of the crew to Cumana, in Venezuela. With about twelve others he planned his escape ; at dead of night they swam out to a schooner which was anchored in the harbour, and, having overpowered the crew, returned in triumph with their new prize to Jamaica. In 1807 he was present at the storming of Monte Video, and took part also in a number of detached engagements in the Mediterranean. Four years later, as a lieutenant, he gained great distinction during the operations on the North American coast, and kept till his death the sword of the captain of a privateer, the *Dolphin*, which he captured in the Rappahannock. Three times he is mentioned for jumping overboard to save lives, once in mid-ocean whilst the ship was under full canvas in half a gale of wind.

After the Peace he soon wearied of the uneventful routine of service ashore, and gladly accepted the position of Second - in - Command in the expedition which the Admiralty was sending out under Lieutenant (afterwards Sir Edward) Parry to attempt to discover the North-West Passage. The expedition sailed on May 19, 1819, Lieutenant Parry commanding the *Heckla*, and Lieutenant Liddon in charge of the *Griper*. Almost from the moment of starting Liddon was laid up with a very severe attack of rheumatism ; but he refused to be relieved of his duties, and continued to manage his ship from an invalid chair on deck, even when in most critical positions among the ice. As they sailed for the first time through Barrow Strait, Parry named the land on the north-west shore "North Devon" in memory of the county where Liddon was born. The expedition managed to penetrate as far as lat. 113° W., but the terrible pressure of the ice prevented them from passing beyond the large island which they called, after the First Lord of the Admiralty, "Melville Island." Their furthest point was a large bay in the west of "Melville Island," which Parry named "Liddon Gulf, after my esteemed friend and brother officer," the first association of these two surnames which have been so intimately connected with the pulpit of St. Paul's Cathedral. The ships returned to England in November, 1820, but Liddon's health had suffered so severely that he was obliged to give up all hopes of further active service.

In 1828 he married. His wife, Ann Bilke, was directly descended from a branch of the Churchill family, which had for some time been settled at Weycroft, near Axminster, whence her father had in early life removed to Surrey. She was a good linguist and a voracious reader, and was equally at home in English, French, and Italian literature. In religious matters her sympathies were deeply enlisted in the cause of the Evangelical school. They made their first home at North Stoneham, in Hampshire, in a house which stood on part of the site now occupied by the Eastleigh and Bishopstoke Station on the London and South-Western Railway. Here their eldest son was born.[1]

He was baptised on September 26 by the Rev. Frederick Beadon, the rector of the parish.[2] He was called Henry Parry, after his two godfathers—his mother's brother, Henry Bilke, and his father's friend, Sir Edward Parry. His godmother was Miss Louisa Liddon, his father's sister, who exercised a profound influence over his life from his

---

[1] The children of the marriage were: 1, Ann (died in infancy); 2, Henry Parry; 3, Edward (M.D. Edin.); 4, Annie (married R. Poole King, Esq.); 5, Katharine (married C. Davenport, Esq., M.D., the Carabineers); 6, John (M.A., Christ Church, Oxford); 7, Louisa Gibson (married Colonel Ambrose, C.B., the Buffs); 8, Mary (died in childhood); 9, Fanny (died in infancy); 10, Matthew (Captain in the 8th Liverpool Regiment).

[2] He had succeeded his father as Rector of North Stoneham in the year 1810. His father had been rector from 1740, and he himself continued to be rector until 1879, when he died at the age of 101 years. The father and the son were incumbents successively for 139 years.

earliest childhood till her death in 1858. She combined far more than average intellectual power with very deep religious feeling. Like her sister-in-law, she also had been trained in the strictest Evangelical school.

In 1832 Captain Liddon removed with his wife and their young family into Devonshire, and settled at the Grove, Colyton, which was their home for twenty years. Here Henry was sent to his first school; it was kept by a Mr. Tett, who gave some elementary teaching to the children of the young farmers in the neighbourhood. When he was ten years old, he was sent as a boarder to a proprietary school at Lyme Regis, kept by Mr. Roberts, well known in his neighbourhood for his wide and accurate learning. Little is recorded of Henry's work at that school. A story is told of his frank request to Mr. Roberts in open school, "Please, sir, may I leave off learning Greek? I am sure I shall never understand it." In the playground he is remembered for his courage in many a boyish battle. "I have seen him fight many a good fight, and come out smiling," writes one of his schoolfellows.

Military life had a great attraction for him; he read and discussed eagerly the details of Cæsar's campaigns in Gaul and of Napoleon's battles. Mr. Roberts, a good geologist himself, gave him an interest in geology; and the collection of coins which Liddon bequeathed at his death to Keble College was begun whilst he was at school at Lyme. Here, too, he wrote several plays: one of them—" Napoleon "—was acted by the boys in the early winter of 1843. In sending the manuscript to his aunt Louisa, he described it as " an historical drama rather than a tragedy," and as exhibiting " vices to be avoided rather than virtues to be imitated." Napoleon is portrayed throughout as a monster of selfishness, cruelty, and ambition. The performance was said to be successful; the author himself acted the part of Napoleon, and also, although he had never been inside a theatre, was stage manager.

During this time the religious side of his life was far from being neglected; he had already all the earnestness about personal religion which would be the natural result of an early Evangelical training. But he was beginning to feel the need of some fuller teaching. It is difficult to trace the influence that caused this. The only religious instructions which he received were the vigorous and impressive anti-Roman discourses with which Dr. Hodges, the Vicar of Lyme, tried to protect his flock each week from one of the least imminent of their dangers. Henry had himself begun to compose sermons—carefully written and expressed with all seriousness. There are still five of them, in a copy-book, which he wrote when he was fourteen and sent to his aunt Louisa, marking them, " My first attempt at sermons." They are on "various religious subjects "—chiefly the more usual subjects of Evangelical discourses—such as " Reading the Scriptures," " The Danger of Procrastination," " Preparation for Judgment," with strong anti-Roman passages, suggesting the influence of Dr. Hodges, and with not a little depreciation of the Sacraments. In the year 1844 he wrote many sermons, of which about ten survive. They are less strictly Evangelical in tone, and greatly improved in style. Some of these were shown to his father's friend, Dr. Barnes, who, besides being Canon and Sub-dean of Christ Church, was also their Vicar at Colyton. He was greatly impressed by the promise displayed in these youthful compositions.

In the autumn of 1844 he was sent to London to enter King's College School. He lived in the house of one of the masters, Mr. Hodgson, at 17, James Street, Buckingham Gate. Mr. Roberts' teaching had been so thorough that he was soon placed in the upper school under Dr. Major, the head master, for whom he always retained the deepest regard. His diary, which he continued until his death, begins with January, 1845 ; but at first it is a bare record of letters, visits, and constant ill health, and throws little light on his thoughts, except by showing the strength of his home affections.

To the last he was grateful for his intellectual training at King's College School ; but he often said that the school trained its pupils in only one half of its motto

"Sancte et sapienter." Like many other schools, in spite of a large quantity of Biblical instruction and of the high character of the teachers, it exercised practically no religious influence. The boys were taught Bible and Church history, dates, facts, doctrines, but all the while the imagination and the heart were left untouched by the truths with which the mind was thus familiarised.

"I can never forget," he said, when preaching at the re-opening of King's College Chapel on November 9, 1873,[1] "the two years which I spent as a schoolboy in the vaults beneath this chapel, some twenty-nine years ago. There was indeed teaching for the intelligence in abundance and of the best kind. The 'sapienter' was well provided for ; but what of the 'sancte'? Well (I must dare say it), if, after leaving the school, I had not come into contact with other influences, I should have shrunk to the end of my life from the religious truths which now have a first place in my heart."

Mr. Frederick Harrison was then a junior boy at the school ; at the time of Liddon's death he sent to the *Pall Mall Gazette* some reminiscences and impressions of Liddon's school days at King's College.

"I sat beside Liddon more than forty years ago in the Sixth Form at King's College School, for a year or two. He was three years my senior, and the gulf that exists from fourteen to seventeen among schoolfellows is not easily passed. But I sat in form next to him, and as in the Sixth we did not change places, I was his daily companion.

"I was fond of all sorts of games ; he of none. I read all sorts of books ; he had even then his own fixed line of thought and of study. He was much my senior, and very old for his years, so there was no kind of school intimacy between us. He always seemed to me an elder brother who wished the young ones were more serious. But, different though our interests and habits were, I always found him friendly, gentle, and considerate. What was Canon Liddon like as a boy of seventeen? Well, so far as I can remember, he was at seventeen just what he was at twenty-seven, or thirty-seven, or forty-seven— sweet, grave, thoughtful, complete. Others perhaps may recall growth, change, completeness gradually coming on him in look, form, mind, and character. I cannot. To me, when I heard him preaching in St. Paul's, or heard him speak at Oxford of more recent years, he was just the same earnest, zealous, affectionate, and entirely other-world nature that I remember him at seventeen. The lines in his face may have deepened ; the look may have become more anxious of late years ;

[1] Cf. "Sermons preached on Special Occasions," by H. P. Liddon, D.D. Sermon xiii., pp. 286–303.

but as a schoolboy I always thought he looked just what he did as a priest. There was the same expression of sweet, somewhat fatherly, somewhat melancholy interest. He would reprove, exhort, advise boys just as a young priest does in his own congregation. We expected it of him, and it never seemed to us to be in any way stepping out of his own business when he gave one of us a lecture or a sharp rebuke. He seemed to feel that this was what he was there for. He was entirely a priest among boys. I do not think that he ever joined in any game or even looked on at any game ; I am sure that he never took part in the rough-and-tumble horseplay common amongst boys ; and I am certain he never returned a blow or a practical joke at his expense. Nor had he any occasion to do so, for neither blows nor horseplay was ever practised upon Liddon. There was, I fancy, a kind of silent understanding that to treat Liddon rudely, even without intending it, would be unmanly, like striking a priest with his robes on. I distinctly remember the howl of indignation which rose when a boy, mistaking him for another, once roughly struck him from behind in a rude jest. When he turned with a look of sorrowful expostulation, without a sharp word, we felt somewhat ashamed of our companion, who, I think, was carried off and judicially pommelled. I lived with my own family, while he lived in a boarding house, so I cannot say much about his life out of school hours ; but I remember a legend that on the occasion of some violent outbreak in his house, a sort of barring-out or breaking-out, which had been planned without his knowledge, Liddon interposed with his personal influence, and by remonstrance and advice induced the house to surrender, or give up the plot, before much harm was done. His school work was always well done and adequate ; but I do not remember that he won prizes or cared to win any. His interests even then were entirely with Theology, the new Church Movement, and the preaching and teaching of the day. At seventeen Liddon was just as deeply absorbed in Dr. Pusey and his work as at twenty-seven." [1]

Apparently he was confirmed on May 29, 1846, during his last term at school. In his diary he baldly records the fact, " Could not go to college. Confirmation."

Before he left school, Henry had refused a cadetship in the East Indian Service because he wished to be ordained ; and Dr. Barnes, the first clerical reader of his sermons, had promised him a nomination to a Studentship at Christ Church, Oxford. At Colyton, however, in Dr. Barnes' absence, the curate-in-charge, an earnest but very bigoted person, did his utmost to prevent the acceptance of the offer. Only in the preceding October Newman had seceded to

[1] *Pall Mall Gazette*, September 13, 1890.

Rome, and it was represented to Mrs. Liddon that she
would seriously imperil her son's soul if she allowed him to
go within reach of the Romanising influence of Puseyism.
The whole Oxford Movement was vehemently denounced,
and Dr. Pusey himself was described as a false teacher, as unscrupulous, and as a wolf in sheep's clothing.   Mrs. Liddon
was seriously affected by such warnings from one whom
she had good reason to hold in high esteem, but Captain
Liddon's practical common sense and breadth of character
prevailed against any such narrow counsels.

On June 3, 1846, Henry went up "in a great fright" for
the Matriculation Examination at Christ Church, and was
matriculated on the following day.   Dr. Major wrote him
a parting letter, expressing his appreciation of "your
amiable disposition, your humility and untiring application," and added "I will, as a friend, urge you not (as in
most cases is necessary) to exert yourself to gain distinction, but to be careful not to task your mental powers to
the neglect of your health."   He went into residence on
October 15, and after the necessary residence for one Term,
he was, with eight others, admitted on Christmas Eve as
a Student of Christ Church.   Among those who were
admitted on the same day were R. M. Benson, the founder
of the Order of St. John the Evangelist, Cowley, G. W.
Kitchin, the Dean of Durham, and G. Ward Hunt, afterwards Chancellor of the Exchequer.

At Christ Church, he did not attempt to take any leading part in undergraduate life.   He only once mentions
being present at a debate at the Union ; and that with the
remark "Disgusted."   His leisure time was spent with his
intimate friends in long country walks (including a bathe, if
possible), in music and talks.   Amidst a host of acquaint-
ances, his chief friends amongst his contemporaries were
Alfred Bailey, R. M. Benson, H. N. Oxenham, and Edwin
Palmer.

Among the senior members of the University, Dr.
Barnes was always ready to welcome him ; in gratitude he
made it his first duty to call on him at the beginning of

each Term. His other great friends among the senior residents were the Rev. R. W. Church (afterwards the Dean of St. Paul's), the Rev. C. Marriott of Oriel College, and Mr. Manuel Johnson, the Radcliffe Observer, who had been most intimate with Newman. It was at Mr. Johnson's house, only three months before Liddon matriculated, that Newman had sadly taken leave of all his Oxford friends. Here Liddon spent almost every Sunday evening : "Dined at the Observatory ; very jolly evening." "Called on Johnson, and afterwards dined with him. Saw the moon, Jupiter, and Venus through his telescope. Saw also four illuminated Missals."

The few sermons which he wrote as an undergraduate betray clearly a great change in religious thought. They deal with the side of Church teaching which Dr. Pusey was at that time setting forth : "The Communion of Saints," "The Terms of Penitence," "Crucifixion to the World." In his diary he soon begins to note Saints' days and Fast days and Vigils. On November 5, 1846, he writes "Gunpowder Plot, University sermon. No Dr. P. in church." On November 5, 1847, the entry is "Papyst Conspiracy. What awful Services ! How very painfully unchristian !"

In the mean time he had made Dr. Pusey's acquaintance, and was constantly at his house, a perilous adventure in those gloomy and suspicious days. He notes on one occasion that he was seen on Dr. Pusey's doorstep by the son of one of the Canons, "*forsan omnia omnibus relaturus.*"[1] This suspicion was justified, for two days later Dr. Barnes interviewed him and spoke "very kindly about many things, *de doctrinâ aliisque.*" He is thoroughly interested in ecclesiastical architecture, in the Breviary Services, and especially in the work of a small Brotherhood among undergraduates, founded in 1844 by Alexander Forbes, afterwards Bishop of Brechin. This was the society which, when remodelled in 1852, was called by the name it still bears, the Brotherhood of the Holy Trinity. He is greatly impressed by reading Keble's sermons : "What a beautiful

---

[1] Latin sentences frequently occur in his diary.

mind is K.'s! Not unlike one's notion of St. John the Evangelist." As a tribute, he sends a donation to the restoration of Hursley Church, and carefully treasures the tardy acknowledgment of it.

Among the undergraduates there were many stories current, no doubt more or less exaggerated, of his manner of saying Compline in his rooms on Fridays with some of his friends, and of the large number of candles which were supposed to have been lighted on these occasions.

Early in 1848, he had already serious thoughts of devoting himself to Christ by taking a vow never to marry. But he postponed a decision until he had time for more mature thought.

"The poor Church of England," he explained to his aunt Louisa, "wants men of decided and earnest cast to serve her, quite disentangled from the work of this world. . . . It would be to me a blessed consciousness to feel that I was at least in part to live for Him Who redeemed me."

This change in his religious attitude caused no little difficulty at home, and he was greatly grieved at the partial alienation which resulted from it between him and his parents. Not long before her death his mother had a serious talk with him about it. "Inter alia dixit, 'You may be a good scholar, a good Churchman, and yet not a good Christian. You must conquer self.' Nec hæc mihi inepta." But this did not mean that there was on either side the least diminution of affection. His diary when at College gives the daily report of his mother's failing health; and in the Vacation before she died he has carefully recorded, "On Sunday morning, December 31, 1848, my dear mother went to church for the last time. She received the Holy Communion. I helped her with my arm up to the Altar, and she went in close to the eastern wall on the north side. I knelt next to her. She walked home leaning on my arm." About a fortnight later he saw her for the last time, when he was leaving home for Oxford. Confidence was entirely restored between them. "She kissed me and said, 'Good-bye, Henry; I know that you have stood temptation.

I have no fear for you.'" She died just a month later, on February 20, 1849.

Many years afterwards he notes in his diary on the anniversary of her death, "My dear mother's death seventeen years ago. Requiescat in pace, dulcis anima! How often do I think of her words during the last Oxford vacation that I spent with her!—"You may become a great scholar, but will you become a true Christian?"

His last Long Vacation as an undergraduate he spent with a reading party at St. David's, under the tuition of Mr. William Stubbs, Fellow of Trinity College (afterwards Bishop of Oxford). His own diary is a tantalisingly dry record of Cathedral Services, "delightful" walks, and bathing. But a common diary kept by the whole party gives many interesting details. The party is represented as a monastic community, of which Stubbs is Lord Abbot, Oxenham is Lord Prior, and Liddon is Coquinarius. There is another member of the party, John Burd of Christ Church, who is always called "The Hermit," as he had to find lodgings in another house. The common diary is supposed to be the chronicle of this old English monastery. It is chiefly written by the Lord Abbot, but the others contributed to it as they pleased.

"*September* 2.—Thys daie mie Lorddys went to yᵉ Masse in Welshe, and aftyr Mr. Coquinere ande mie Lorde Abbat to yᵉ Bauthe. Mr. Heremite of Sayncte Catherine dydde dyne wythe yᵉ Commuenytye. In yᵉ even yᵉ Brethren dydde disporte yᵐselves inne yᵉ fieldes and wente evyn soe farre as toe Sayncte Davydde his hede : Botte itte cayme to passe as we returned yᵗ Mr. Coquinere and me Lordde Preyoure dydde faulle oute bye the waye, and Mr. Coquinere dydde seese yᵉ stick and bellayboure my Lordde Preyoure wythyn one ynch of hisn lyfe ; and dydde seese my Lordde Preyoure hisn hatte, and place the sayme on an hege in such wyse yᵗ mie Lordde could no wyse fynde yᵗ agayne, and soe dydde get hym home bayrehedded. Natheless my Lordde dydde forgive Mr. Coquinere yᵗ and moche more."

At the end of the first month, a note in Stubbs' writing sums up their experience—

"Forasmoche as yᵉ brethren have been now settlyde in yᵉ house ane full month, I, William, Abbat, do deme it right to recorde our thankfulnesse for ye fine temperies of ye weather and chepenesse of provisionnes which hath so farre attendyd us. For albeit the first week of our visitacioune were somewhat inclement, it hath been repaid and over, by ye fine weather whiche we have been sithence favoured withal, insomoche that scarcely a daie hath passed on which we could not go to ye bath : albeit sometimes ye waves were horrible large and threatenyd to overwhelme us hadde we not swom, for ye which and for his other oblygeing conduct in ye mattyr of podynges we do returne our humble and heartye thankys to Master Coquinarius ! "

This last passage is the only allusion to the special duties which belonged to the "Coquinarius." There are other allusions to Liddon's swimming, and it was well known that on one occasion the future Bishop of Oxford owed his life to his pupil. The diary records the event very briefly—

"*September* 30.—Mie Lorddes dydde bathe with Mr. C., and mie Lordde Abbat was well nigh drowned, but Mr. Coquinar dydde hymme pulle oute."

A year or two before his death, when speaking of this reading party, Bishop Stubbs said very emphatically, " he was a splendid swimmer."

He took his degree in the summer of 1850, being placed in the Second Class in the Final Classical School ; and then he had more than two years to wait before he could be ordained. He detailed his plans for reading in a letter to his college tutor.

To the Rev. G. Marshall.

" Colyton, near Axminster, June 25, 1850.

" . . . Your letter gave me great pleasure both at the time of my receiving it and often since when I have read it. Let me again give you my very best thanks both for it and all that preceded it. I can only fear that I have not said enough to convey to you what I trust is a lasting sense as well of your uniform kindness as of your efficient direction and assistance, to which, beyond any aid derived from other quarters, and still more, any endeavours of my own, the late satisfactory results of my examination seem attributable.

" Your recommendations to idleness have been hitherto literally complied with ; indeed, I have had but little choice in the matter, as my friends seem determined to enforce them. I hope, however, before long to take to some general reading. As you observe, modern society demands much more than is comprised in one's University course. As to Divinity, I fear the prospect of my seriously reading it with a view to Ordination is as yet but slender. I cannot be ordained until Christmas, 1852, and though I hope seriously to keep that time in view before beginning deliberately to prepare for it, yet I would rather for the present engage in some definite occupation of a more secular and less painfully interesting kind. If you should hear of a foreign tutorship of any kind, I should be greatly obliged to you for letting me know ; as if I succeed in getting nothing of the sort I shall return to Oxford next Term (and in any case hope not to give up my rooms) ; but I would, for many reasons, gladly spend this next year in such a capacity."

He spent a good deal of time in reading for the Johnson Theological Scholarship, to which he was elected in 1851, and for the Ellerton Prize Essay, which he failed to win in 1852. Unfortunately, his diaries for these two years are lost, and it is not possible to reconstruct at any length the line of study on which he was engaged. But the positions which we soon find him taking in ecclesiastical discussions give some clear indication of their general direction.

The questions about the English Church which had been pressed upon Liddon's attention from different sides ever since Dr. Barnes proposed that he should go to Oxford, reached their acutest form during the years immediately following his degree. To that period belong the Gorham Decision and the days of agonising anxiety for High Churchmen that succeeded it ; the panic of popular excitement about the so-called Papal Aggression ; the secession of so many who had taken a prominent part in the High Church revival outside Oxford, especially of Archdeacon Manning and Archdeacon Wilberforce ; and the informal but widely known inhibition of Dr. Pusey by Bishop Wilberforce. It was a time of the most painful sifting of all who were connected with the Oxford Movement. Excited controversialists, Roman and Evangelical, had long ago decided, with the characteristic vehemency and inaccuracy of such prophets, that the Church of Rome was the only logical and possible goal of " Puseyism ; " and for the moment events seemed to justify them. As an under-graduate, Liddon had been brought into the closest inti-macy with the leaders in Oxford: Dr. Pusey, as well as those whom he met at the house of Manuel Johnson, were his friends. Several of his younger friends went over to Rome in the midst of this distress. But at this moment the comparative leisure of graduate life gave him the oppor-tunity of studying in detail the great questions at issue. Could the Church of England appeal to her children with all the strength which belongs to the Catholic Church of Christ? Had she ever in the past, or present, by any act of her own, forfeited her claims to true Catholicity? What had the Church of Rome to offer which the Church of England had not already? Liddon's diaries at this time show that he was steadfast in his allegiance to the English Church, not because he did not feel most keenly her diffi-culties, nor because he failed to recognise the force of many of the arguments which Roman Catholics alleged against her. But it is evident that under Dr. Pusey's guidance he had carefully studied Theology and History, and had so mastered the facts about the English Church, that, in spite of the widespread unsettlement, and amid great emotional excitement and the most alluring appeals from his Roman Catholic friends, he kept quite a clear head, and remained in unshaken and well-reasoned loyalty to his mother, the Church of England.

The diaries of the long tours that he made in Scotland and on the Continent give the clearest insight into his state of mind at that time. Of necessity, they contain very much besides; for few people enjoyed travel as thoroughly as he did. He notes everything that he sees and hears: history, geography, geology, scenery, stories, antiquarian notes, and conversations fill his pages. The following very characteristic extracts, however, are selected chiefly, though not entirely, with reference to his thoughts at this critical moment in his own life and in the history of the English Church.

His Scotch visit in July, 1851, made him see the great

distinction between the English Church and the Presbyterian body. Whilst travelling he met and discussed Theology with many Calvinists, and so came to realise what their creed meant. His host (he was staying with Mr. and Lady Louisa Oswald at Auchincruive, in Ayrshire) led him into a long discussion on Episcopacy, and then took him to see Edinburgh. Here he visits St. Giles' Cathedral.

" St. Giles is now cut up into three meeting-houses, belonging to the Scotch Establishment. Of these the eastern one is the largest. All are furnished with very capacious galleries, the whole arrangements centering towards the pulpit—the Kebla of Presbyterian devotion. We passed the tomb of Montrose : his aisle has been fitted up to make a comfortable vestry for the minister of the central church. Several Presbyterians went round with me ; they seemed to think the whole affair a due blending of the beautiful and the useful. The men did not take off their hats, and seemed surprised at my doing so. I could not forget that in past ages the Shekinah of the Catholic Church had rested beneath that roof. I left the church feeling a deep and unutterable aversion for a system whose outward manifestations are so hatefully repulsive. I thank God the Church of England *is* very different from the Kirk of Scotland."

He greatly displeases his Edinburgh guides by his "lukewarmness" about John Knox. At Stirling Cathedral he says—

" I proposed to the exhibitor the thesis that John Knox did a great deal of mischief—a thesis to which he assented. His assent must have been professional rather than otherwise."

Stirling Castle, however, delighted him from another point of view. "It is so strikingly mediæval. I shall never forget it. It is quite a realisation of one's earliest dreams of fortified prosperity."

In the following month he is travelling on the Continent with his friend and pupil, Charles Bridges. Everywhere he notices with interest the Church life. He attends the High Mass at the Cathedral at Ghent on St. Bartholomew's Day.

" The Service was very imposing ; the people uniformly devotional. In saying this I am only adding my testimony to a point on which those

who hold opinions diametrically opposite on the subject of the Roman
Catholic Church are agreed. But I will say more—it was more than
imposing: it had about it a winning awe, which was distinct from
poetry ; it must have conveyed to the most uninitiated a semblance of
the Supernatural. With the details of the ceremonial I was far from
familiar, and, had my own taste been consulted, should have curtailed
it considerably."

He gives a minute description of High Mass at Cologne
Cathedral. But he was far from praising the Services of
all foreign churches ; he frequently complains of the per-
functory way in which they were performed.

The whole account of the tour is most graphic ; a few
selections only can be given. He thus describes the guide
who took them over the field of Waterloo.

"About a mile before our getting there, we were joined by a guide.
He called himself Jean Jacques Pierson. He had, he said, guided the
French battalions in their march from Quatre Bras to the heights of
Waterloo. On the day after the battle he had assisted in tending the
wounded and burying the dead. He had seen Napoleon take snuff, at
a spot which he pointed out to us, and had heard him say that he
intended to sup in Brussels and give up that city to pillage. He professed himself intimate with the Duke of Wellington and Jerome
Buonaparte. The former had, ten years after the battle, given him a
five-franc piece, on which account he made a point of never taking anything less. The latter had wept bitterly at the thought of the ruin of
his brother consummated on that plain, and had made Jean Jacques
Pierson his *pro tem.* confidant."

Between Basle and Neufchatel, they find some of the
difficulties of *char-à-banc* travelling.

"We changed *char-à-bancs* at most of the villages ; at Delemont
we were detained some time in procuring one ; at last it was forthcoming, and a shady affair it was. Something like an old hansom
patent cab—minus a seat behind, minus, indeed, any seat at all, for it
had had one before, which was not. The deficiency was remedied by
an awkward and dangerous contrivance. The cloth was put up over our
feet, and on it was put a sack of oats or chaff ; on this sat the driver.
The seat was obviously too low for him to have any command of his
horse. Nor was the driver at all calculated to meet the difficulty by
any especial skill ; he and the seat might have changed places. Well,
we set out. The road, on leaving Delemont, runs along a bank raised
about five feet above the fields. The driver let us run down this bank ;
seemed surprised at my remonstrating ; explained : ' Hier das Pferd

arbeitet.' We jumped out, and for some minutes refused to get in. We abused the horse ; he was unfit for his work, etc. This the peasant never forgave us. He only wanted us to get in. At last he succeeded ; we got in. He set off. We could not stop him ; we tried bribery, threats, persuasion. Nothing would do. The excellence of his horse had been impugned, he would at once defy us, and prove 'a contradictory.'

"We passed through towns, villages ; we called to the peasant to stop our horse, Bridges in French, and I in German. The more we called, the more he lashed the horse and the by-standers. He was very angry and looked intensely sulky. To attempt to seize the reins would have been useless ; the struggle which would have ensued would have inevitably led to an accident. At last we praised his horse, and as we were now entering the hilly country, with rocks on one side and defiles on the other, we persuaded him to keep the inside of the road. At last we caught up the diligence ; he could not pass this. At the next stopping-place I complained to the conducteur."

At Lausanne he visited some of the many sights, including the Cathedral of Notre Dame.

"The Cathedral of Notre Dame is now appropriated by the State Calvinistic-Protestant Church. It is finely situated above the town. The architecture is what we should call first pointed, or Early English ; the clustering of the arches in the nave, the apsoid termination, and the southern doorway were particularly fine. It has two western towers, like those at Exeter, although smaller. The Calvinists have not done so much mischief as some people in the north, who ought to have known better. For instance, the bending figures in the entrance arches have been suffered to remain unmutilated, and so has the old painted glass in a St. Catherine's wheel window in the south transept. Instead of a ' table,' which might retain or recover the idea of an Altar and of a sacrificial Eucharist, they have put two, thereby irrevocably securing the symbolism of the place from any approximation to the Catholic truth. I asked the verger why this was. He had evidently been asked the question before, and was nettled by it. He said, ' When we have communions, which is only four times a year, everybody comes ; we want to get it over quickly, and so we spread two tables instead of one.' "

He was venturesome enough to attend the Service here on Sunday morning.

"I went to the Cathedral at 9 o'clock. Service was just beginning. This consisted of (I) a portion of Scripture read out by what I suppose was a deacon ; he was in a smart get-up—cut-away coat, etc., and pointed beard. His reading was like that of a fast scholar in an Oxford College chapel. Then a burly minister—a M. Coutin—in a gown and

C

cassock ascended the pulpit, read out a notice for communion, also an invitation to subscribe to a society for promoting missions in the Catholic Cantons. It may be imagined that when the man came round for money I did not give anything. I looked sternly at him ; he went away, thinking me, no doubt, an unconverted beast. God knows I may be that. . . . Well, then came the sermon ; the text was, 'Think ye that these men were sinners above all Galileans ? I tell you, Nay ; but except ye repent, ye shall all likewise perish.' I heard out two heads of the discussion ; went away before No. 3 commenced."

At Geneva he fell into discussion wherever he went. At the Cathedral he had to defend the memory of St. Francis de Sales against the attack of a Calvinistic verger, whose three arguments against the character of the Saint were that he wished to convert Geneva ; that he was a pupil of the Jesuits ; and, last of all, that it cost 200,000 francs to get him canonised. The next day he attended the English Church Service, which it was then the custom to hold in a Calvinistic chapel.

" At the end of the chapel was the pulpit. In the sounding board was a hole, through which light fell from a screened window upon the preacher's head. The material illumination implied no intellectual or spiritual correlative. The sermon was on the use of the Bible ; and among a series of other commonplaces, the improbable hypothesis that none of the Thessalonians were ever without one. A more serious error was his omission of the Athanasian Creed and the Collect for St. Matthew's Day."

On the following day he fell into conversation with a learned bookseller, who, after discussing the Oxford Movement, offered to introduce him to the clergy of St. Germain's. This he could only accept on condition that it was not to be for the purpose of controversy. But the first priest they met was anxious to know all about Oxford, for he had read all Newman's works that had been translated, and Dr. Pusey's condemned sermon. Then, after discussing the difference between Pusey and Newman, he passed to discuss the barriers on the way to Reunion.

" 'The Puseyites,' he continued, 'appear to me to agree with the Church in several doctrines rejected by Continental and other Protestants.' To this I energetically consented. He instanced confession, the Eucharist, Baptism. I agreed. 'One point,' he said, 'you do not admit—the supremacy.' 'No,' I said, 'we do not. We—I think it contrary to the facts of history, opposed to the organisation of the ancient Church. We reject the supremacy,' I continued, 'because we submit to the principle of authority.' 'Ah,' he said, 'Jesus Christ said, *Docete omnia quæcumque mandabo;* if you leave out *one* point, we have no guarantee that you will not omit three or four.' 'True,' I said : 'you will like to hear what has been said by a Catholic-minded writer in England, Mr. Keble. Mr. Keble says that we agree with the Romish Church in matters of principle, and that our differences with her are on matters of fact. Now,' I added, 'the doctrine of Sacramental grace is a matter of principle, so is the Eucharistic Presence, so is our Lord's Divinity; while the doctrine of the supremacy is a matter of fact. We reject it because we do not think it warranted by the testimony of history. We do not consider you heretics for believing it ; nothing of the kind. Our position is essentially defensive ; we merely maintain that we have history on our side, while we decline to admit its necessity or truth. Further than this,' I added, 'that while we rejected the supremacy, we distinctly recognised the primacy.' He replied, 'The doctrine of the Papal Supremacy seems to be a little matter to disagree about when we agree in so much.' I consented. 'And yet,' he added, 'in practice it makes all the difference ; it determines you—as you believe or reject it—to submitting to or denying the claims of the Roman Catholic Church.' I again agreed. 'Practically,' I said, 'it determined that point.' 'Now,' he continued, 'you have not the evidence of history.' I thought otherwise. Here we came to proofs."

Then follows a long historical argument with quotations and references on both sides. Liddon thus reviewed the conversation—

" We had set out with the intention of only conversing ; here we were controversing. He had some religious duties at 8 o'clock, which interrupted our discourse somewhat abruptly. I promised to come to him at 1 o'clock on Wednesday, with a view to reading the passage he had alluded to in St. Chrysostom. He concluded by saying that prayer was *the* remedy for disagreements. I agreed.

" His manners were very winning and nice ; his reading had evidently been sound and general ; his statements were apparently characterised by fairness and candour. Nevertheless, he does not seem to me to have proved the point. The blow may come from another quarter, *e.g.* the final acquiescence of the Church of England in the Gorham Decision, or any other soul-destroying heresy. Still, she seems to me to be strong in her historic attitude towards Rome, when the question is one of the supremacy of the Pope and the teaching of the early Catholic Fathers.

" *Fiat lux.* If I had sinned less grievously against Baptismal

grace, I should see my way more clearly. Even now I am in bondage
to sin. *Libera, miserere, Jesu.* Make me ever ready to know Thy Will,
and at all times diligent to perform it."

But he was not let off with only one discussion.

"*Friday, September* 26.—. . . In the evening I called on the Abbé
Mermillod ; he introduced me to the Curé and three other priests. . . .
We had a good deal of conversation. I sat between the Curé and
Abbé Mermillod. The Curé supposed I had never been in such a
circle of Catholic clergy before. I agreed I had not. The conversation
at once fell into *the* track. It opened by a comparison of Newman
and Dr. Pusey. The Curé thought Dr. Pusey a Roman Catholic at
heart, but held back by some considerations. I agreed as to his being
a Catholic, but added, in explanation of his non-submission to Rome—
(1) his rejection of the supremacy ; (2) his critique upon the practical
hyper-dulia of St. Mary. About the supremacy we again went through
the whole question. I took my stand on the Greek Church. 'The
Greek Church never denied it,' said the Curé, 'before the Photian
Schism.' ' C'est un fait, un fait pareil à la Divinité de N. S. J. C.' I
demurred.

"Abbé Mermillod here suggested that there had been no *Father*
in the Greek Church since the time of Photius. I met the objection
by observing that this was true of the Roman since the Council of
Trent. They were much amused. I continued my view of the Greeks.
I emphasised their success in the Kamchatka Missions. The Abbés
seemed surprised. Abbé Mermillod merely remarked that the
' sterilité Grecque' was proverbial. Proverbs, I observed, were the
offspring of fact ; fact may modify proverb. The Curé then changed
the subject. He advanced the cultus of St. Mary. I explained the
English Catholic position. We admitted the intercession of the
Blessed Virgin Mary ; denied the invocation. I adduced Bishop
Andrewes' prayer. ' Invocation,' said the Abbé Mermillod, 'is not a
point of faith. The Council of Trent merely recommends it.' I then
observed that, for a doctrine so theoretically unobtrusive, it occupied
a singularly prominent place in the practice of the Roman Church.
I illustrated it by a dissertation on the 'Zend' tradition of Austria
and Bohemia. ' That is local,' said they. ' Very well,' I added,
' granted. But since you advance locality as a plea for customs of a
very practical import, you have no right to deny us the benefit of the
plea when we urge it in behalf of omissions or peculiarities attendant
upon Anglicanism.' ' They are inherent,' said the Curé, ' and essential.'
' They are ephemeral,' said I, ' and *passagères*. The English Church
is in a clearly transitional state. At present it is difficult to divine an
issue ; she contains the elements, first, of a complete disorganisation,
and secondly, of a Catholic reconstruction. We are waiting in England
for Convocation, and we shall get it in time.' ' Convocation will be

against you,' said the Curé, 'on the subject of Baptism.' I thought
not. 'A majority of the Episcopate will.' I reminded him of the
Lower House. 'The Archbishop of Canterbury is against you at any
rate.' He is. 'That comes, you see, of giving the jurisdiction of St.
Peter into the hands of the Queen. *La Reine est papesse.*'

"In answer to this, I observed, first, that a similar fact was
observable in Russia. We believed the Greek Church to be a branch
of the Catholic Church, yet it was at the mercy of Nicholas. Secondly,
that in the English theory there existed two effectual checks upon
Royal Prerogative.

"First, Convocation—in matters of doctrine.

"Secondly, Chapters—in Episcopal elections.

"Thirdly, I observed that the condition of the English Church
was clearly transitory and unsettled—we were living in an *avenir
d'espérance.*

"'If you placed yourself under the guidance of the see of St. Peter,
all these difficulties would vanish.'

". . . Would they?[1]

"I returned to the Hotel des Bergues. I there read in Galignani
that the Hon. and Rev. Chancellor Law of Wells has seceded to the
Church of Rome. . . . A letter from Aunt Louisa received to-day
mentions the death of Mrs. ———. She, at any rate, now knows the
true solution of the problem of the Catholic Church of Christ.

> "Deus, Deus meus, ad Te de luce vigilo,
>   Sitivit in Te anima mea.
>   Emitte lucem Tuam et veritatem Tuam
>   Ipsæ me deduxerunt et adduxerunt in
>   Montem sanctum Tuum et ad tabernacula Tua
>   Et introibo ad altare Dei, ad Deum, Qui
>   Lætificat juventutem meam."

In the summer of 1852, after another stay in Scotland,
where he again acted as tutor to Mr. Oswald's son at
Auchincruive, Liddon started alone for Italy. He visited
the hospice of St. Bernard on the way, drove across the
Simplon, stopped a while at Milan and Pisa, finding it hard
to believe he was really in Italy, and at last reached Rome
by diligence from Civita Vecchia on September 21. The
whole city was so full of interest that at first it deprived
him of the power of criticism. His diary is crowded with
an account of all he saw. On September 27 he tried to be
present at a Consistory in the Sistine Chapel, but found it

---

[1] There is no omission. The diary is written as above.

was private. However, he made his visit an opportunity for presenting a letter of introduction which he had to Monsignor Talbot, who, having joined the Church of Rome in 1847, was now a chamberlain of the Pope, with great influence at the Vatican.

"He was excessively polite. We discussed secular topics, and gradually ascended to ecclesiastical. I soon found that he wished to secure a convert; of course he was quite right to do so. He kindly pressed me to stay to luncheon. He gave me several most useful admits to the Quirinal, some mosaics, etc."

Two days after he describes his first impression of Pope Pius IX., who at that date was still the temporal Sovereign of the Papal States.

"*Wednesday.*—Feast of St. Michael the Archangel. Hotel Minerva. After breakfast I accompanied my French friends, the two Lyonnais Abbés and ladies, to San Michele to see the Pope, who there heard a low Mass. We had some difficulty in passing the outside barrière, which was guarded by French sentinels. I was assisted by the Abbé, however, and this was surmounted. I proceeded at once to the church, which was nicely decorated: the walls were hung with a red and white drapery, which had a very good effect, and the Altars were brilliant with lights. I got possession of a seat in the front row, close to the High Altar. We waited an hour, when the pealing organ and simultaneous discharge of cannon on the Tiber announced the approach. [The Pope] entered accompanied by two Cardinals and a crowd of Monsignori in purple, besides courtiers, wearing old court dresses, frills, lace, etc., of the sixteenth century. They all knelt at *prie-dieus* in front of the Altar. A distinct accompaniment was played by the organ the whole time. This finished, the Pope moved into the chapel of San Michele, and then left the church in procession; he blessed 'the Navy' from the balcony of the Hospital overlooking the Tiber, and then re-entered his carriage, amid band, cannon, etc. I had a capital view of him; his face wears an expression truly beautiful, and I think the most ferocious Protestant could not but appreciate it."

Later in the same day he had a second interview with Monsignor Talbot.

"Hence I proceeded to the Vatican and called on Monsignor Talbot. He renewed the controversy. He considered that the invalidity of Anglican Orders did not depend upon the Nag's Head question, but upon the following argument, which I record as curious :—

"'Our Lord instituted Sacraments, first, *in specie*, *i.e.* Baptism and the Eucharist, where He gave the words conveying the essence of the Sacramental Action ; and secondly, *in genere*, where He instituted the Sacrament, but left it to the Church to define its essential character or symbol. Of this nature are the five others. The Church, invested with this power, may exercise it discretionally, *i.e.* may make certain acts essential to a Sacrament at one period, and others at another.

"'Now with regard to Orders : in early times the rites varied indefinitely, as is proved by the writer of *De Ordinationibus ;* but at the Council of Florence, Pope Eugenius IV. defined the essence of the Sacrament (when administered for the priesthood) to consist in the words, "Take thou the power to consecrate the Lord's Body, and offer it for the Christian people," etc. Obviously the English Ritual does not contain this, though composed after the Council of Florence ; therefore Anglican Orders are invalid.'

"Now to my apprehension, this proves only so much, that they are invalid if the existing Roman discipline be considered, but not absolutely, as numbers of priests had been previously ordained without the use of the formula of Eugenius.

"Mons. Talbot took me into his oratory, which was beautifully lighted up, and begged me to be admitted into the Roman Catholic Church. I felt that all this was an appeal to my imagination and feeling rather than to conviction, and accordingly declined. But I give him credit for the most pure and disinterested motives. He gave me several controversial books to read, and begged me to dine with him to-morrow, holding out the prospects of an interview with the Pope. I rather dread the repetition of to-day, but I trust in Him Whose guidance, wherever it may in the end lead me, does not, if it lead me at all, point Romewards now. He offered me rooms in the Vatican."

The next day was yet more eventful.

"*September* 30.—After breakfast I proceeded with the Comte de Begiami to St. Peter's. It was certainly a feat, this ascent of the dome. After signing a document, promising to behave well, and to be solely responsible in case of accident, we ascended the first staircase, which led to the roof of the church. With this roof I must confess myself on the whole disappointed. After Milan, where, in the most remote and unfrequented corners of the exterior, one had met with works of art of surpassing beauty, it was disappointing to find at St. Peter's sheds and tiles evidently never meant for the eye, and seriously interfering with preconceptions of finished grandeur to be met with in such a building. From the sides, a pavement slopes down towards the centre of the roof. The central roof, which is apparently inhabited, and runs nearly the whole length of the building, rises from the lowest point of declivity ; it has walls, windows, doors, etc. The figures on the end of the basilica are truly colossal ; that of our Blessed Lord is said to be 30 feet. We ascended the dome easily. There are two interior galleries, or rather three, if one includes the apertures above the cupola ; from them one gets a capital view of the mosaics, while the pavement and baldachino beneath appear ridiculously small. I went up into the ball, touching the top ; it was, however, so heated by the sun that I could not bear to stay there above three minutes. The view from the exterior gallery was magnificent : all between Soracte and the Sabine Hills on one side, and the Mediterranean on the other. On descending the dome we visited the manufactory of mosaics in the Vatican : they are now making the heads of the Popes, which are to be placed round the Basilica of St. Paul. It takes a year to make a single head. The number of colours, or rather shades, there, we are told, is not less than 20,000. The difference between ancient and modern mosaics seems to be chiefly this—that in the former the material is natural, in the latter artificial or composition. There were about fifteen or seventeen artists at work when we visited this most interesting manufactory. From this I adjourned to the church and convent of San Onofrio, to see the bedroom and tomb of Tasso.

" From this I proceeded to the Hotel Minerva, and dressed in black and white tie for my 'audience.' I reached the Vatican at two ; found Count Campbell Smith there and Monsignor Talbot. We at once proceeded to dinner. The conversation was at first quite general, and happily continued so during a great part of the day. At three I proceeded with Monsignor to see His Holiness. We passed through a great number of antechambers, well stocked with guards and attendants. At length I was desired to wait while Monsignor went on to arrange ; in a few minutes he returned, and conducted me through three other chambers, in the second of which I committed a ludicrous mistake in genuflecting to a Monsignor. At length I reached the apartment in which the Pope was sitting. He was at a desk, writing, surrounded with books and papers. I knelt first on entering the room, and a second time to kiss his feet. He was anxious to talk, and spoke for some minutes. He spoke in French ; said that he hoped I had enjoyed Rome—of course I had—and then went on to express his hope that I should pursue my studies with constant recourse to prayer to God, without Whose aid nothing would be obtained, and Who would ultimately lead me into the Truth. *Ainsi vous viendrez à la lumière.* He spoke about five minutes. I proffered some *objets* to be blessed, and then knelt and left the apartment. The apartment in which the Pope was sitting was very plain and unadorned, with a brick floor, and it contrasted strangely with the magnificent antechambers through which I had to pass to reach it.

" What a wonderful day in my life ! The first time I ever found myself in the presence of Royalty ; strange that this should have been in the court of the successor of Peter ! On returning to the hotel, I accompanied some French friends to see the sun-set from the tower of the Capitol. It was a grand sight, which I shall not easily forget. The

Ave Maria struck up in harmony with one's feelings, as the dark night veiled beneath one's eyes the city of the Popes and the city of the Cæsars."

Two or three times he met Monsignor Talbot in the street, and was at once taken off to a lunch and engaged in controversy. At length, on the day before he left Rome, a final effort was made to win him.

"*Monday, October* 11.—I drove to the Vatican to dine with Mons. Talbot. After we had been a short time at dinner, Stanley, of University College, Oxford, came in ; he brought an introduction from Ward of Balliol. The conversation immediately became general, and I own this somewhat relieved me. Stanley left a few minutes before I did, and Mons. Talbot accompanied me downstairs. He urged me with much importunity instantly to take the step. He had told the Holy Father, he said, that he was going to make a last attempt, and the Pope gave his blessing. What could I do ? I dared not, with strong convictions against the claims of Rome. 'Oh, but all that would vanish, when one got real faith through the medium of Sacramental Grace. You must make the venture,' he said. I *still* held out. I felt that my vanity was appealed to. He concluded by reminding me of that sorrowful look which our Blessed Lord cast on the young man who did not give up all to follow Him. 'You are that young man.' . . . He disappeared; he would not say good-bye. I was to come to him at 7.30 to-morrow morning. I caught up Stanley in the piazza, and walked with him to the Bridge of S. Angelo. I then went to the Zecca and met the Pope's carriage ; he was driving out. I had another, a last, view of Pio Nono, and his blessing. Thence I walked to S. Maria in Via Lata and S. Martino, to see the crypts ; in both cases I was unsuccessful. The Church of St. Martin is very fine ; it is adorned by some paintings of Poussin's. The pillars are evidently taken from an ancient temple. In this church it was that S. Silvester held the first Roman Council. After this I had a walk with Mr. Barnes. I was quite distressed at the conversation I had had with Mons. Talbot. Never do I recollect having felt so much affected by a few words. They quite suspended my power of thought ; they left me with ideas on *the* question in hopeless confusion. They did not illumine and direct by a *coup de main;* they only gave me a quite terrible feeling of the distance which exists in spirit between the Church of Rome and other bodies.

"*Tuesday, October* 12, 1852.—The day for my leaving Rome. Alas that it should have arrived, and so soon !

"Got up early after a sleepless night on account of toothache and thought. A tremendous thunderstorm. I walked to the Vatican at 7.30, where I found Mons. Talbot saying Mass.

"After Mass we breakfasted. I presented him with a note which I had written to close the controversy; he was very melancholy, but quite touchingly gentlemanly about it."

Liddon returned home through Vienna, Florence, Bologna, and Venice, writing elaborate accounts of all he saw on the way, and reached his uncle's house in London on November 5. On that day he ends his diary—

"It is a most Protestant proceeding coming to England on the day of Dutch William's landing; happily, however, too late for the solemnities which are celebrated in the National Church. It is nine weeks to-day since my leaving (September 3), but of these more than two were spent on this side of the Alps. I am thankful to have seen so much, and to have returned in safety. At present it seems impossible to disengage, from the various detailed reminiscences, still so vivid and delightful, the total impression produced on my mind by this tour. Should I not be pretty nearly true in saying that on the most important of all questions I return with much the same feelings as those with which I set out for the capital of Christendom? I knew what the Roman system was : that it was not what Protestants represented it to be ; that it was nevertheless a totally new development, it may be an inevitable one, upon the principles of antiquity. Such as I had expected I found it. I know it now, not merely by books, but experimentally."

The lengthy quotations from his diary at Rome show that the carefully planned appeals to his imagination and his "self-love," as he calls it, had for the moment produced an emotional impression, but without the slightest approach to any corresponding intellectual conviction. In fact, the impression itself was, at least on one occasion, one of recoil rather than of attraction. He soon realised that he had returned to England more convinced than ever that, so far as he could see, the Church of Rome, with all its interests, and the fascination of its history, organisation, and worship, had no claim on his allegiance. His friends at the Vatican still pressed him with letters ; they frankly acknowledged that they were uneasy about his return to the influence of Christ Church, and they tried to convince him that it was neither theology nor history but attachment to Dr. Pusey that caused him to leave Rome "without submitting to the Church." They argued that it was "no light thing to have

been in this city in your search for Truth, to have seen the
Vicar of Jesus Christ, and have been spoken to by him on
this very subject, and in every way to have been brought so
very near indeed, without accepting the Roman obedience."
The very urgency of their insistence suggests the conviction that, if all that had happened at Rome had in no way
drawn him to enter what they called "home," the question
of his conversion was practically hopeless.   This was
indeed the case; there is no sign that his intellect was
ever at any moment of his life in the least inclined to
recognise Roman claims; and his character was too well
balanced for him to be caught by the emotional methods
of Monsignor Talbot.

Liddon now knew that the Roman Church did not call
him with the Voice of God; but he was anxious to consult
one whom he could trust about the serious difficulties
through which the Church of England was then passing.
Just a week after his return to England he had his first
interview with Bishop Wilberforce, to consult him about
his Ordination.

"*November* 13.—Went to Eaton Place, and after two ineffectual
attempts succeeded in obtaining an interview with the Bishop of
Oxford.   I stated to him my difficulty about the Supremacy Oath.
Did the Reformation give the Queen that power or jurisdiction in
ecclesiastical matters which had previously belonged to the Pope?
The Bishop said decidedly 'No.'   The Reformation principle (he
conceived) asserted only that just independence of the Papacy which
the kings of England had continually struggled for in earlier days;
and the Oath of Supremacy was rather negative than positive—it
denied the power of the Pope more than it asserted that of the Crown.
The Judicial Committee was an abuse and an anomaly.   He did not
consider the Church of England compromised by the Decision of the
Gorham case; as he should still consider the law of treason the
law of the land if a guilty man had been acquitted.   He was far from
wishing to see the Evangelicals turned out of the Church of England.
They were to the Church of England what the Jansenists were to the
Church of Rome.   Each was an inevitable necessity.   A large class
of minds could not but adopt a theory which would have the appearance of being anti-sacramental.   They would dwell on the Omnipotence
and Omniscience of God, and on the resulting doctrine of human
Predestination to the seeming denial or at least exclusion of those
particular agencies in the Sacraments which were equally matter of

Revelation with the Attributes of God. The Church could only demand from them the profession of acquiescence in a formula ; they were, to be sure, inconsequential in signing it, but that could not be helped. He should be very sorry if the 'comprehensiveness,' which was the grace and boast of the Church of England, were narrowed by the exclusion of the Evangelical party."

He was ordained deacon in the Cathedral at Oxford on the Fourth Sunday in Advent, December 19, 1852, intending to work as curate at Wantage under the Rev. W. J. Butler, whom he had met in France in the preceding year. His first sermon was preached on the following Tuesday, St. Thomas's Day, at the Church of St. Thomas the Martyr in Oxford. He spent Christmas at Ardington with the Rev. Ralph Barnes, the son of the Canon of Christ Church who had nominated him to his Studentship. Here he preached both on Christmas Day and the Sunday following. Before going to Wantage, he had a month's holiday ; and on January 29 he went to live in lodgings at Wantage with Alexander Heriot Mackonochie, afterwards Vicar of St. Alban's, Holborn, who was then one of Mr. Butler's curates.

His diary describes his holidays rather than his work, so that there is little record of his daily life in the parish. Evidently from the first he was remarkable for his preaching. Mrs. Butler, who was no mean judge of sermons, is reported to have said to her husband, after she had heard Liddon's first sermon at Wantage, " That young man preaches better than Archdeacon Manning." At first he wrote out all his sermons, but soon after he was ordained he asked Dr. Pusey whether it was necessary that he should always write his sermons in full and preach from the manuscript. Dr. Pusey replied with some useful rules.

From Dr. Pusey.

" January, 1853.

" There can be no ground against your preaching extempore. I wish the gift was more cultivated. It is essential to missionary work in the Church. Only you should prepare for it well ; know accurately what you should say ; pray for God's Holy Spirit ; say nothing about which you doubt, nothing rashly. Labour for accurate thought altogether, that you may not overstate anything."

By the following Easter it was clear that he was not strong enough for parish work, if it was, as he desired it to be, combined with study ; and on March 30, when he had been at Wantage exactly two months, he had to leave it.

In May he was well enough to take the light charge of the parish of Finedon, in Northamptonshire, for a few weeks, but he gave up all hope of regular parochial work.

He was ordained priest on December 18, 1853. He records it in his diary.

"This morning I was ordained priest by the Bishop of Oxford, and carried the chalice after him at the Celebration. May God strengthen me for that to which Thou hast called me—most unworthy that I am ! Eighty-one priests and deacons were ordained at the same time. Oxenham, a deacon. I cannot speak with sufficient warmth of the Bishop of Oxford's paternal kindness."

CHAPTER II.

CUDDESDON.

1854–1859.

WHEN Liddon was at Cuddesdon Palace during the week before his ordination as priest, Bishop Wilberforce proposed that he should be the first Vice-Principal in the Theological College which he intended to open in his palace grounds the following summer.

The plan of this institution had long been in the Bishop's mind. At last on April 7, 1853, the foundation stone of the College was laid, and it was arranged that the first Principal should be the Rev. Alfred Pott, who for seven years had been the Bishop's curate at Cuddesdon, and was made Vicar in 1852, when the vicarage of Cuddesdon was separated from the see of Oxford. But the Bishop was still looking for a suitable Vice-Principal. In those days it was not so easy to find, from among the younger Oxford graduates, a man who would combine great ability with Churchmanship of a type which the adversaries of the new institution would consider moderate. The Vicar of Wantage suggested Liddon for the post. When the Bishop mentioned it to him, Liddon told him frankly his theological position, and, on December 28, after consulting his friends, he wrote to the Bishop to accept the post. But Liddon's account of himself had caused the Bishop to change his mind, and to withdraw the offer. In commenting on the Bishop's reply, Mr. Benson, the Vicar of Cowley, writes —

FROM THE REV. R. M. BENSON.

"New Year's Eve, 1853.

"The Bishop's letter is very nice. I am extremely glad he made you the offer, and I scarcely think he could with ordinary discretion have urged the office on your acceptance. It is part of the penalty we have to pay for past excesses that they do for a considerable time shut us out of many channels of usefulness. I find this in many, many ways. Would that they were all as innocent as any little ritual frivolities which may have marked your career at Oxford. . . . I am sorry the matter is broken off. . . . I am sure your health is not up to Wantage 'requirements.'"

In a few days, however, negotiations were reopened, and Liddon had to write a long account of his practice and teaching on the subject of Confession, after studying the Bishop's Charge of 1851 on the subject. The Bishop wished him to say whether he would consider it necessary to recommend confession to the students at the College indiscriminately. Without hesitation he said that of course he should not ; but that for himself he could not discontinue the use of confession at intervals. The Bishop did not object to this, but demanded that if Liddon came to Cuddesdon, Mr. Keble should be his spiritual adviser, and not Dr. Pusey, apparently basing his right to make this arrangement on the ground that Canon Law had made the Bishops the confessors of their clergy. Dr. Pusey gladly made this delicate change as easy as possible.

FROM DR. PUSEY.

"June 19, 1854.

"There is no matter of principle involved in exchanging me for Mr. Keble, brass for gold. I should like to take the opportunity of explaining to the Bishop, if his communication is not confidential to you. The Bishop of N[ew] Z[ealand] misapplied the Canon Law. When confession was compulsory, priests were required to confess to the Bishops, for fear they should connive at each other's sins. The English Church, which has abolished compulsory confession, cannot hold by that old law."

When the change was proposed to Mr. Keble, his first impression was to have nothing to do with it, but at last he consented under some very strict conditions, which the Bishop accepted; and Liddon was appointed Vice-Principal at the beginning of August, 1854.

The first Principal, the Rev. Alfred Pott, has kindly supplied the following account of the beginning of the College, and of its early difficulties :—

"It was, I think, in the year 1851 that Bishop Wilberforce proposed to me the building of a Training College for candidates for Holy Orders at Cuddesdon, and that I should be the first Principal.   Our experience in the examinations for Holy Orders of the very imperfect preparation of men direct from the Universities, had in part impressed upon the Bishop's mind the necessity for some such institution.   But there were other considerations also.   The want of clerical tone, and of religious habits, which the Bishop noted in his personal intercourse with some of the younger clergy, had a great deal to do with his proposals. Residence in such a College as he contemplated would, in his judgment, do much to foster such a tone and habit as he desired to see.   I well remember his developing his plan to myself in the course of a ride over Shotover.

"It is difficult, at the present day, to realise the difficulties which stood in the way of carrying out such a scheme.   The immediate vicinity to Oxford ; the jealousy stirred up in that University among its older members, of any proposals which suggested the smallest slight upon the perfection within the University itself of the facilities for preparation for Orders ; yet more the want of sympathy which the Bishop encountered on the part of many valued clergy of his own diocese ; and, further, the strong *odium theologicum* manifested by another section of his clergy, who could not divest themselves of the belief that any such institution must lead to the diocese of Oxford being sown broadcast with a body of Romanising young clergy ;—all these things, independently of financial hindrances, made the Bishop's work very arduous.   The next two years—1851 to 1853—were spent in raising funds for the intended building, and procuring the necessary legislative powers ; for an Act of Parliament was required.

"On April 7, 1853, the first stone of the building was laid ; and on June 15, 1854, the College was dedicated.

"The question of officers was one of most vital importance.   Liddon had been known alike to the Bishop and myself as a young preacher who had developed very unusual powers in the pulpit, notably at Wantage, as well as a man of much theological learning and deep personal piety.   The late Dean of Lincoln (then Vicar of Wantage) had a good deal to do with his selection as first Vice-Principal of Cuddesdon.   With this small staff (myself and Liddon) work began in the autumn of 1854.   I note in my diary that he joined us on Saturday, October 7.

" From that day until Easter, 1859, we worked together in close friendship, amid many difficulties. The opposition from without did not cease with the completion of the building. I remember one Head of a House calling a probationer Fellow of his College into residence in order to prevent his joining our party. We received, as a rule, only members of one or other of the Universities, the exceptions being very rare. Again, we had to make all our own rules, and organise all our own discipline. We had nothing to guide us. The older College at Wells was on a different basis, its internal organisation being altogether different from our own, and the same was the case with Chichester. And we were both of us young and inexperienced in dealing with younger men fresh from the University. Liddon, living in College and among the men, was brought into closer and more frequent contact with the other inmates than myself, as I had charge of the parish, and was also Rural Dean. We had to deal with students of very varied temperament and attainment, some coming to us very uncultured and devoid of all clerical instinct. I soon found out that the Vice-Principal's power of dealing with such men was far greater than my own. His chapel addresses and his private intercourse with individuals had much more influence, in all probability, than his direct theological teaching. The lectures were divided pretty equally between us. Both of us, it may be, aimed at too high a standard of theological teaching— at least, higher than we should do if we were to begin again. The great work done then, and since, was to form character and mould habits. In this work, during the latter time of our residence at Cuddesdon, we had great help from the Rev. Albert Barff, now Rector of St. Giles, Cripplegate, and the Rev. Edward King, now Bishop of Lincoln, successive Chaplains at Cuddesdon.

" Happy as those days were, it was no peaceful, halcyon time. There were troubles both within and without. ' Without were fightings, and within were fears.' Loyal and hearty as most of our students were (the College filled rapidly), there were some to whom the high standard of the priestly life set before them at Cuddesdon was not acceptable ; some, again, whose minds were set more eagerly upon the externals of ritual than upon the cultivation of the interior religious life. And from without, attacks and misrepresentations were continuous. The Church at large during those years was in a state of excitement and ferment. The ' Papal Aggression ' movement (as it was called), and the action of the then Government thereon (1850), had stirred up a good deal of mud, which took a long time subsiding. And every act of the Bishop was the object of calumny and suspicion. The College at Cuddesdon was of course looked upon with no favourable eye, and this for many different reasons, some connected with, and some quite apart from, theological bias. Liddon was not a man ready in any way to compromise his own judgment, or to give way to clamour. His error lay rather in the other direction."

The first Term was altogether one of experiment : the

officers had almost everything to learn. The aim of the College, from the first, was to supply that devotional preparation for the clerical life which the Universities do not profess to give. The complete system of the College life was very slowly built up with the greatest caution, and with abundant explanation at each new step. The notices that were placed on the College notice-board were somewhat homiletical and extremely deferential to the students' opinions, except when the Bishop now and again delivered some authoritative mandate through the Principal. Every effort had been made to fill the College; and residence was made attractive by offering exemption from the obligation to attend the lectures of the Theological Professors at Oxford, and from passing the Voluntary Examination at Cambridge. These very early tentative days are described by Liddon to Mr. Keble.

To the Rev. J. Keble.

"November 7, 1854.

"We have eight men here at present, three from Cambridge and five from Oxford. There is a promise of some more at Christmas, when six of our present staff will leave. At starting the Bishop dispensed with the rule about residence in the College for an entering candidate. . . . We have a weekly Celebration in the Bishop's chapel, but it is very difficult to give a markedly religious direction to the general tone of the place; there is the danger of forfeiture of influence if too much is attempted, which, I fear, makes us unwisely timid. The Bishop put smoking down summarily at the beginning of Term; and as to outward matters, with the exception of dress in one or two cases, we have nothing very unclerical to deal with. We hope to induce the Bishop to sanction a Midday Service in the chapel; it would be a great help to forming the men on a truly Christian type."

Before the Term was over, the midday Service was allowed, and Compline was also said three times a week; and the Vice-Principal had distributed and talked much about " Rules for Meditation." Only very gradually the devotional system grew up under great difficulties. The Services in the College chapel and Bishop's chapel and the parish church had to work the one with the other; and for some time the spiritual requirements of Ordination candidates were in danger of being subservient to the many unavoidable absences of the Bishop, and the scanty Services which were held in the parish church. For more than two years Liddon kept a copy of every notice that was issued, and recorded every arrangement made for the students ; and before he left, the devotional arrangements of the College had practically become what they have ever since continued to be.

Liddon's diary records all the shades of College life during those days ; a few extracts will here describe his life and work then.

"*January* 15, 1855.— —— thought we ought to moderate æsthetic tendencies above all in chapel, etc., as Cambridge High Churchism is much less patient of such than Oxford.

"*January* 21.—Baron and Lady Alderson in chapel. . . . In the evening went to palace after Compline, and was set upon by the Aldersons and Andersons about Gregorian music. Lady Anderson particularly attacked Helmore. It seems to be a question between fine and devotional chaunting. Anglican chaunts are the former, so say all musicians ; that Gregorians are the latter seems to be the verdict of religious Christendom.

"*March* 6.—Walked with Z. to Nuneham, Sandford, etc. A very interesting conversation with him. He seems greatly in earnest, but quite ignorant of the scope of religious life. He said that giving himself up to the work was quite a new view to him ; his friends had looked forward to his being a gentleman.

"*March* 9.—We certainly appear to have entered on a crisis in the internal history of the College. In consequence of the representations of Sturges and King as to the effect produced upon the Haseley and Wheatley people by our men wearing fez caps, coloured ties, and smoking short clay pipes on the ice, the Principal spoke to the men about it after the morning lecture. X. treated the communication *en souriant*—rather grumbled ; Z. was downright angry. . . . There seems to be an active dissatisfaction among the men. Walked with —— to Horspath and Garsington, and had some earnest talk, which I hope our Blessed Lord will vouchsafe to bless, about purity of soul and the motives for taking Holy Orders. He complained of the disadvantage of his education, and said that he had never had earnestness of life forced upon him in such a way as by the system of the College here. He had some difficulties concerning the necessity of such purity of motive.

"*April* 26.—My first lecture on the Prayer-book. Would that God would vouchsafe to enable me to touch the hearts of the men in lectures. Arrival of Mr. ———, of Trinity College, Cambridge, whose father wishes him to be utterly 'unbiassed' here in the matter of religious convictions.

"*August* 16.—Certainly the system here has now acquired considerable traditionary impetus, and appears capable of impressing itself upon each man who comes. The influence of adverse individual character is no longer felt, and we even defer to what is established and accepted as unquestionably right. We ought to thank our dear Lord for blessing in this unmerited way the work of our hands, and making rough places, as they seemed, smooth and plain."

But with much general happiness, and with a very great deal of spiritual work in the College, there were indications now and again of troubles from without, because of such matters as ritual and decoration. In 1856 a large party of Bishops, staying at the Palace, visited the College. One of them thought the cross over the altar might cause trouble. Another of them liked the College, but complained of the general appearance of the chapel. Soon afterwards the Bishop sent an ominous notice that he would attend a celebration of the Holy Communion in chapel on Sunday morning. Liddon thus recorded the visit—

"Everything in the chapel and sacristy was scrupulously done as usual. The Bishop made no objection to celebrating with his face to the Altar. He only required (1) the disuse of the music used at the time of administration ; (2) making less ceremony about washing out the vessels ; (3) printing a little book of prayers for before and after the Blessed Sacrament, which should leave out the matter of which he disapproves in Mr. Richards' book."

A year after this last meeting of Bishops at Cuddesdon, another was held, and the College chapel came in for far more censure. Two days before the Lent Term began, some changes have to be made.

"*February* 2, 1857.—After chapel, went over to the Palace, where the Bishops of London, St. David's, Llandaff, Salisbury, Glasgow, Chichester were dining. . . . After they had gone to their rooms, remained to have a long talk with our Bishop. The Bishops of Glasgow and London have represented to him in the strongest terms the necessity of making the chapel less 'gaudy.' Accordingly (1) the Cross has been removed ; (2) the white and green Altar cloths are forbidden ; (3)

T. & R. Annan & Sons. Pho. Sc.

Henry Parry Liddon

(1856)

the painted figures on the wall are to be covered over ; and (4) the celebrant is to stand at the end, not in front, of the Altar. This last change I feel to be the most important ; it is doctrinal. The Bishops wish to abolish the early Communions on Sundays, but these happily have been saved. The Bishop was very kind, but very decided. He objected to a difference between our chapel services and those in the parish church. This was the principle of the alterations.

" It is not impossible that this lost ground, for such it is, may be recovered. If by a loss of external aids man is driven more and more back upon the interior life, it will be well."

But there were far graver anxieties for the College than the decisions of any merely trifling questions about details of ornaments and ritual. Liddon had for himself faced and answered the most vital questions about the Church of England. In Rome itself, and within the walls of the Vatican, he had definitely refused to admit that any of the temporary difficulties of our Church impaired her essential Catholicity. Not a few of the Cuddesdon students in the early days of the College, were in their turn facing the same question ; and few men were so well qualified as the Vice-Principal to help them, or in the event so successful in guiding them, to reasonable and assured loyalty to the Church of their Baptism. But two or three of these students were under other influences, more potent in their case than anything that the College offered. At first they were not discernible from the others, and when their special weakness was seen, they were still allowed to stay, in the hope that with the rest they would gradually settle down.

Even when common sense suggested grave fears about the result, it was very difficult to know the best course. To retain men who were tempted Romewards was to incur certain misrepresentation, if they at last seceded ; to send them away was practically to compel their secession. To one of these students Liddon wrote the following letter :—

" Cuddesdon, October 21, 1857.

" If I am right in understanding you to look forward to returning after Christmas, it is clear that I am still in a relation towards you which entitles me to offer, and you to respect, some advice as to what to do in the interval.

" I would, then, very earnestly advise you (1) to return to Brighton as your natural residence. Your being at Canterbury is of itself suggestive of, as it expresses, an unhealthy excitement. (2) To read regularly for at least *five hours* a day Pearson, and St. Paul's Epistles, taking with the latter Bengel's notes and St. Chrysostom. (3) To avoid as a matter of conscience all intercourse with Roman Catholics. In your present state of mind this is clearly a duty. To this I would add—all intercourse with English clergy or others whom you know to be unsettled. Unhappily there are such in London at present. You would be unable to reply to the doubts they might suggest. You have no right knowingly to go into the way of temptation. (4) Try to get employed at Brighton in regularly visiting the poor, or teaching in a school. This is what you peculiarly need.

" If you take my advice, you will do a great deal which you do not like. Many persons, otherwise good, are grievously self-indulgent here. Do not read only such books as *you like*. Do not allow yourself to get into trains of thought which give you that ' sickly ' feeling you describe. Pray at such times resolutely, and you will find that God will help you.

" I hope that you are mistaken as to divergences between myself and Mr. Burgon. There are, of course, many minor matters in which difference is unavoidable, and legitimate. Much must be allowed too for different intellectual moulds. I think that I should agree with him in an honest and hearty wish to teach everything that the Church of England holds, and no more ; if I have conveyed to you a contrary impression to this, I am very sorry for it, and it has been quite unintentional. Of course, an individual who is obliged to say a great deal must make mistakes. But the Prayer-book as embodying Scripture and antiquity, and Scripture and antiquity as illustrating the Prayer-book with that atmosphere of thought which at any rate lights it up with most light and meaning, seem to me, as they have seemed to thousands before, a sufficient guide by which to live and die.

" I cannot at all accept your statement that Church principles ' clearly go beyond the Prayer-book.' This would be utterly to abandon any possible system of English Church authority, and I cannot admit that those who are heartily wishing to comprehend and to submit to the formularies of the English Church are quite guilty of such an abandonment of that which is the life of their religious endeavours.

" I do not think that the difference between, *e.g.*, Andrewes and Archbishop Sumner is greater than the chasm which separates Bossuet from Faber.

" You will I am sure feel it to be a duty not to communicate your doubts and distresses to those here, whom they might harass very seriously. Those who are in perplexity themselves are no fit guides for them."

In the next year the external troubles took a definite

shape. In September, 1858, frequent complaints were made to the Bishop about the system pursued at the College by the Rev. C. P. Golightly, a clergyman resident in Oxford, who claimed to speak in the names of the senior members of the University, the nobility and gentry of the diocese. The Bishop understood the attack to be made upon the Vice-Principal more than upon any one else, and most generously defended him. He admitted that there were some things that he could wish otherwise [1]—

"But men must work by instruments of the greatest possible excellence in fundamentals; it would in my judgment be clearly wrong to cast them away for non-essentials. I think my Vice-Principal eminently endowed with the power of leading men to earnest devoted piety, but with such a man I do not think I ought to interfere except as to anything substantially important. I have a strong conviction that Cuddesdon College is doing God's work for men's souls aright."

At Christmas, 1858, Liddon was spending the vacation in Bristol and Taunton. Whilst at Taunton he found that a man whom he had known as butler in a friend's house was under sentence of death, and would not listen to the exhortations of the prison Chaplain. At the request of the Chaplain and the Sheriff, Liddon went to see him.

"*January* 1.—Accompanied my uncle Henry to the gaol to see Beale, who is lying under sentence of death. Spent some time with him. The conversation mainly on his situation. I endeavoured to turn his thoughts away from the legal aspect of his case, on which he seemed disposed to dwell, and to fix them on the impending eternity.

"*January* 3.—In the evening saw Beale for an hour and a half. He seemed to join with me earnestly in prayer. He said that he was 'sold' by his attorney.

"*January* 4.—Saw Beale twice to-day. Went through the account of the Passion in St. John's Gospel. He was much touched by our Blessed Lord's Sufferings.

"*January* 5.—Saw Beale twice to-day. He seems to be getting on. I went through the history of the Passion in St. Matthew and St. Mark with him.

"*January* 6.—Saw Beale twice. In the morning very hopeful. In the evening he seemed to be greatly disturbed by a visit from Mr. ——. This sadly checked the spiritual tone of the conversation.

[1] "Life of Bishop Wilberforce," ii. 360.

"*January* 9.—Saw Beale for two hours. He touched freely enough in the way of conversation on his past life. We went through the Communion addresses in the Prayer-book, and he observed that he never before understood how solemn a thing it was to communicate.

"*Sunday, January* 10.—Saw Beale. . . . Said prayer preparatory to Communion. The best and only thing to do under the circumstances to produce, if possible, an act of contrition. In afternoon at gaol preached on Eccles. xii. 7, 'The spirit shall return,' etc. (1) Soul made for God, (2) its separateness, (3) its immortality, (4) its preciousness. Deduction as to nature of death. The people seemed touched by God's mercy. Saw Beale in the evening for one hour and a half. Told me that he had wept bitterly after afternoon service.

"*January* 11.—Beale would not confess. 'God knows all, and no good could come of it, and it is such a task.' Yet he prayed most earnestly. . . . Unable to do anything for thinking of poor B. It is terrible to think that to-morrow those eyes will be closed and that hand cold and stiff. *Deus misereatur.* . . . At 10 p.m. went again to the gaol. Went through the Passion according to St. John and the Burial Service. Poor Beale overflowing with expressions of gratitude. He told me that my coming had prevented his attempting self-destruction.

"*January* 12.—At 6 a.m. I was again at the gaol, engaged in prayer with B. until 7.15. The service in chapel and Holy Communion was at 8. B. communicated with much devotion. He had thanked me very warmly, and said that I had saved him. O my Saviour, grant that he may be right. At 9 I went with Uncle Henry to the scaffold, when B. gave me the manual and his wife's last letter. . . . He seemed to die without any severe struggle. Mr. Oakley thought it undesirable that I should preach to the people outside the gaol.

"*January* 13.—. . . In the *Times* to-day *full* account of Beale's execution, with a series of unfortunate references to myself. . . . Give me grace, O my Saviour, utterly to neglect what is said of me by man." [1]

In the same month the *Quarterly Review* openly attacked Cuddesdon College. The article was not from Mr. Golightly's pen, nor was it written in communication

[1] A fortnight later a West-country paper reported a "Flagrant Tractarian Scandal." After repeating some story about the convict's conduct in prison, the writer added, "And yet will it be believed that the hardened and miserable man had the Sacrament administered to him before his execution, either by the Principal or Chaplain of Cuddesdon, it is not ascertained which. There is something awful in so flagrant a prostitution of the most sacred of all the ordinances of religion. . . . The circumstances caused a most painful sensation in Bristol and Clifton. . . . Both the rev. gentlemen are Puseyites. We need say no more as to the character and tendency of Tractarianism—that class of opinions of which the Bishop of Oxford is the great prelatic champion."

with him, but it played into his hand completely, by charging the authorities of the College with having Romish ornaments and ceremonies in chapel, and using a Romish Service-book. Mr. Golightly at once took it up, and tried to rouse the whole diocese against the College, with no little success. A perfect hailstorm of letters and pamphlets followed, and early in February the Bishop, in self-defence, issued a Commission to the Archdeacons of the diocese to inquire into the facts and report to him.

In the midst of this anxiety Liddon was called away to visit his aunt and godmother, Miss Louisa Liddon, in a sickness which, according to her own presentiment, proved to be her last. The strong tie between them dated from his earliest years at Stoneham; in her he had always found the truest sympathy in all the highest aims of his life, and he felt that he owed her a debt which he could never repay. "To me," he writes to Mr. Keble, "she had given all that is best worth having." But at that moment he could not stay away from Cuddesdon; he had to hurry back from her bedside for the meeting of the Commission on February 6.

In after-years he delighted in telling the story of that Inquiry. When writing Dr. Pusey's life, he would relate scraps of it in connection with Mr. Golightly's action in 1844 and 1845; he would detail the scene, the gestures, and the words with his own inimitable humour, and would end by renewing his determination to write an account of "The Cuddesdon Row," if ever he lived to finish the Doctor's life. As it is, we have only the account in his diary.

"*February* 6.—At 12 the three Archdeacons and Golightly arrived to sit in commission on the College. Sat until 4 p.m. Commission read. Golightly inquired whether its powers were limited to the *status quo.* It was decided that they were, but that the past might be investigated, to avoid annoying G. G. would not come to chapel at 1 (to Sext), afterwards he was entirely foiled as to genuflexion and ' ceremonies.' He made a great set on our book of prayer. Thought that no liberty should be allowed to Principal or Vice-Principal or to individual Bishops to draw devotions from Romish sources. His improvisations addressed to the Commissioners were exceedingly amusing, and reminded me of Newman's 'Frisby' in 'Loss and Gain.' In afternoon went to Oxford and Deddington with Risley. Found that Golightly's letter had been placarded all over Deddington, in anticipation of my preaching there to-morrow.

"*February* 7. *Sexagesima Sunday.*—Preached at Deddington for the Spiritual Aid. Very good subscription, by God's mercy ; doubling what was expected."

The Archdeacons' report was sent in on February 10, and was regarded by the Bishop as negativing completely every charge brought "by my gossiping friend ;" although he instructed the Principal to weigh carefully its strictures on the "too great ornament" of the walls of the chapel, and on the College book of prayer. So the "ornaments" on the walls of the chapel were covered with panelling and the Service-book revised ; and it was hoped that all might again go on quietly. But the *Record* and the *English Churchman* and Mr. Golightly combined to frustrate such hopes.

These anxious days were broken for Liddon with hurried visits to Taunton to see his aunt ; she rapidly grew worse. After each visit he carefully notes the words which she had said. Under her nephew's influence she had entirely passed out of the narrow school in which she had been trained ; the fuller faith in the Sacraments was in her last days mentioned by her as a special blessing. On March 30 she passed away ; to Liddon the loss was very great.

"Felt all day a dreadful blank. Life without my dearest aunt ! My one great correspondent—perhaps the person who loved me and whom I loved best in this world. A love of twenty-eight years, ended till we meet hereafter. O my God, give me strength to live that I may die as she died ! "

During all the next Term, the College lived on under suspicion, newspapers openly attacking it, and friends only timidly supporting. The Chaplain, the Rev. A. Barff, had to leave, and the Rev. Edward King, the Curate of Wheatley, was appointed in his place. The annual festival was shorn of most of its simple ceremonial, because of Mr. Golightly's remarks upon it.

But, early in October, one who had been a Cuddesdon student some time before, and whom Liddon had done his best to guide, was admitted into the Roman Church. It was an unusually unfortunate moment for such an act ; and opponents knew how to make use of it. There was, however, another side to it, in which they little believed. Early in November, Liddon received from his late pupil a letter, dated from the Brompton Oratory, full of the usual arguments, and, with the best of intentions, warning him of his great spiritual peril if he continued in his present work.

" Such men as *you*, dear Vice-Principal, and Dr. Pusey, and a very few others are the monuments of Anglicanism, who prevent many men from doing what their conscience tells them is the right thing, viz. to join the Catholic Church. . . . You have been near the Church once, I am told, so I hope you will come at last."

Liddon replied—

To _____.

" November 9, 1858.

" I thank you for telling me how and where you are. . . . That you are able to conquer sins and temptations which have harassed you in past times is matter for much thankfulness to God. It is not a very cogent argument for the Roman Church, and reminds me of what the Dissenters used to say about 'going where one gets most good.' It seems to me lamentable beyond description thus to measure the limits of the Kingdom of Grace by the weakness of our own conscience—a process, however, which would by no means constantly tell in one direction.

" Thanks for your kind expressions as to myself. I can in no way reciprocate them, it being my present and constant prayer that I may live and die a true son of the Church of England. Men only need fear the future when they play tricks with their consciences and convictions, and turn their backs upon the light which God in His love and mercy has shed around them. As to being once 'nearer the Church' than now, it is, of course, one of the phrases which sound well on the Roman hypothesis. I certainly have endeavoured to look the Roman arguments in the face. And one result is that I am ' certain,' upon historical grounds, that portions of the modern Roman Creed were no part of the Creed of the ancient Church."

The health of the Principal had been so broken before

this growing trouble that he had repeatedly asked the Bishop to allow him to resign. At last, in November, the Bishop consented to his leaving. The choice of a successor was no light task. The Bishop found it so difficult that Liddon offered to resign the Vice-Principalship if such an act would make it easier to find another Principal, although he himself did not wish to leave. The Bishop, in reply, mentioned several very trifling matters in which he wished Liddon to make a change, but he hoped he would not leave the College. However, ten days after this, on December 3, one of the students suddenly announced that his whole conviction was unsettled in the direction of Rome. He was immediately sent from the College, and put under the care of Mr. Benson, of Cowley ; but he left him abruptly, and was received into the Roman Church on December 11. This seemed to justify all the worst suspicions of the opponents of the College, and just after Christmas the Bishop sent Liddon a letter from one of his clergy, which directly urged the dismissal of the Vice-Principal as the only hope of retaining the confidence of the diocese in the College. Liddon replied by putting his resignation in the Bishop's hands.

To the Bishop of Oxford.

"December 29, 1858.

"I beg you to act with respect to myself as seems to you best for the College, and for your own most important work in the diocese. My resignation is in your hands whenever you desire it. It will be to me a source of heartfelt satisfaction if I can help to relieve you of the weight of your present anxieties by leaving my post in the College *whenever* and *as* you think fit."

Evidently pressure was being brought upon the Bishop from more sides than one to get rid of Liddon. It came not only from the party represented by Mr. Golightly, for to them alone the Bishop would not yield; but from many persons whose position and influence lent great weight to their undue suspicions of the College, and fears for the Bishop. For some time the Bishop tried to satisfy them without acting on their advice. One important change after another was demanded in the internal arrangement of the College, each of which was calculated to diminish the influence of the Vice-Principal, and to change the character of his work. Liddon would far rather have been allowed to retire than thus surrender the system which he had so greatly helped to build ; and it was only Keble's influence that induced him to remain.

"I should not wish to retire," wrote Mr. Keble on December 31, 1858, " until I had found by actual trial that the standard of earnestness and efficient preparation was so lowered as to make it plain to me that I could not be responsible for the state of things. I own that in this conclusion I am more or less influenced by my deep heart's wish that you, and in my degree I, may go on with him as long as we can. I really think it a sacred duty."

An anxious correspondence with the Bishop, Pott, and the Vicar of Wantage was kept up through the whole of the Christmas vacation. The Bishop complained some-times of matters of doctrine, sometimes only of "tone." But when Liddon came back at the end of January, he found a letter awaiting him, which showed that the Bishop had so far accepted the position of the critics of the College that the separation was inevitable.

From the Bishop of Oxford.

[*Private.*]

" January 26, 1859.

" My very dear Friend,

"I *must* open my grief to you. I see in your reply to my last two letters difficulties which make me fear that I must use your tendered resignation, and yet really I know not how to make my mind up to the sacrifice it implies—of actions, ministries of love, and of all that I believe you have long done and are capable of doing in the special work of our College. Nor is the sacrifice made lighter by my belief that *really* the differences of actual belief between us are not such as require the separation. It is rather my growing conviction (1) that there is a certain tone about our very best men which I have felt to be a slight drawback from their excellence, and expected to see lessen, and which I now cannot but see is what you aim at forming in them as an excellence, and *will* continue to form in them. (2) That that discrepancy between me and *them* implies not *only* that from the College men will be sent not (as I think) ripe for that full measure of usefulness to which they might otherwise attain (for, if this were all, I might most properly set against it the risk of my losing something of those very highest qualifications which you have been the instrument of developing in so many, and, please God, might be in so many more, by any change which might put another in your place), but what is of far wider significance, that (as Leighton and others tell me who are well qualified to judge) my whole usefulness in the diocese has been greatly impaired, and is threatened still more by the perceived differences between our best students and myself in tone, etc. For men say, ' The Bishop preaches and ministers and celebrates one way, and yet these young men come from his College all doing the opposite ; and that shows that the Bishop really holds to the same and wishes to get it to pervade the diocese, and only does not venture to manifest openly in his own practice what he is endeavouring to get current through them.' Thus an impression of insincerity is created which would utterly mar my usefulness.

"I have a long and detailed letter put by in my pigeon-holes at Cuddesdon, urging on you the necessity of altering these points. I withheld it through the fear of paining you, and now in this correspondence these very points have come out as being in your mind of first importance. I have communicated freely with our dear friend Butler on this point, also with the Warden of All Souls, with Sir G. Prevost, with our Principal, and less fully with Milman ; and I find all in the same mind. Nothing can injure our love ; nothing can more grieve me than that we should part at this time, when it will seem like a triumph to Golightly and Co. ; and yet what can I do ? There is but one favourable circumstance ; it will seem a natural arrangement following the enforced resignation of the Principal, and have less the look of any decided difference between us."

Considering the wide difference of age and position between the Bishop and Liddon, the frankness and affection of this letter are remarkable ; but it was, evidently, one of the cases where by universal consent a certain step had to be taken, although the reasons for it did not admit of being satisfactorily put down in black and white. It only remained to take every precaution that no one should suffer. Liddon broke the news to the students with great care a few days later, and then wrote to Mr. Keble.

To the Rev. J. Keble.

"February 7, 1859.

". . . I have just gone through the painful scene of announcing it to the men. . . . And as matters are at present arranged, I leave the College at Easter. . . . The dear Bishop evidently acted under pressure, as at the last he seems quite undecided as to the ground of our parting. But he pressed me on *the* point of Eucharistic Adoration. Of his kindness throughout I can never say enough, and I shall do all in my power to avert any jar of feeling which may follow on my leaving the College on the part of our old men. And I am deeply thankful to God and to your kind advice that the momentum came from without, and that I have no choice in the matter."

The same evening he spent at the Palace at Cuddesdon, and the Bishop took the opportunity of showing his confidence in him by asking him to preach one of the sermons in the special Lenten course which he was arranging for Oxford churches. A few days later, Liddon incidentally dropped an allusion to their changed relations ; it greatly pained the Bishop. "Are you not," he eagerly asked, " and will you not *for ever* be my dearest friend ? "

Of course, Liddon's resignation had wider aspects than the personal, or even the diocesan. It was connected with the attitude of the Bishops generally to the whole High Church Movement. To this Mr. Keble refers, in returning to Liddon the correspondence that had passed.

" These papers," he writes, " do indeed fill me with anxious thought ; yet, far unlike many others that one has had the misfortune to see of late, one sees that it is 'the wounds of a friend.' What most perplexes me is some names in the list of those who have warranted this step. They are on the spot, and ought to know ; else I should have thought it one of the most ill-advised things that a good and clever man could do, especially just now."

Liddon felt the severance of his connection with the College most acutely. "I do not see any future whatever," he writes in his diary. "My first great attempt at work in life has failed. This is, no doubt, good for my character ! "

In the disappointment of the moment it was characteristic that he should be despondent. But not even a naturally sanguine person could have imagined that those five years of planting at Cuddesdon would have yielded so rich a harvest. To the present day, the special features of Cuddesdon College are due, under God, chiefly to the work of its first Vice-Principal. Without the wisdom and patience of his more immediate successors, his work would perhaps have been a failure, as a constructive effort; but they would be the first to admit that they were only building on his foundation.

CHAPTER III.

ST. EDMUND HALL.

1859–1862.

As soon as it was settled that Liddon was to leave Cuddesdon, his first plan was to go out to India. The recent annexation of that country by the Crown had drawn the attention of Churchmen, not only to the great missionary work that lay before the English Church, but also to the need of clergy there to minister to our own countrymen. This plan, however, was finally set aside when his medical adviser told him that with his constitution he could not live in India for twelve months; and a wish to see Palestine was postponed for financial reasons.

Many suggestions of work came in from various friends : a curacy at St. Paul's, Knightsbridge, the chaplaincy of Lancing College, and similar offers were declined because his chief advisers thought that he ought to be in Oxford, and have leisure to study. Personally, he dreaded living in College, lest he should come to acquiesce in the general tone of Oxford life, and he desired to continue the kind of work which he had done so happily at Cuddesdon.

At that moment the Vice-Principalship of St. Edmund Hall was vacant ; and after it had been refused by the Rev. W. Bright, Fellow of University College, it was offered by the Principal to Liddon.

" It seemed right," he wrote to Mr. Keble, "to accept it : (1) as coming unsought, and (2) as affording more of a recognised position for working, as far as may be possible, among undergraduates than

E

would be afforded by the mere fact of residence for purposes of reading."

One of his great hopes in returning to Oxford was that he would be able to study Oriental languages, and to write a portion of the Bible Commentary which Dr. Pusey was so anxious to complete. It was part of a great scheme [1] for making the Bible more intelligible, and so meeting a great deal of the Negative Criticism of the day, and of the Evangelical opposition to Tractarianism. Pusey was busy at his own share, the Minor Prophets, and had had many friends at work on other portions for twelve years. Liddon, at his urgent wish, undertook to write on the Pastoral Epistles, and worked at them carefully for many years. The materials he collected were used for his Lectures in later life, and the Analysis that he made of the First Epistle to Timothy was published after his death.

The opportunity of working among undergraduates is what chiefly attracted him to St. Edmund Hall. To some of his friends among the younger graduates, it was a matter of great amusement that he should undertake what appeared to them to be only a kind of second-rate tutor-ship among passmen. But to him the spiritual side and not the intellectual was most prominent. By talks and walks and addresses, and by throwing himself heartily into every effort that was calculated to promote the spiritual life of those around him, especially by the work of the "Brother-hood of the Holy Trinity," he aimed at religious influence on all around him. He went into residence on May 5, 1859, and in the first three weeks of his residence he notes in his diary, "We discussed the possibility of a Prayer Associ-ation." "Very interesting meeting of the Brotherhood. A proposition that something should be done with College servants in Oxford was very favourably received." "Dined at Ch. Ch. ; ——'s rooms afterwards. A conversation in which I tried to persuade him that we are really answerable for the souls of the undergraduates." "A painful feeling

---

[1] See a detailed account of the plan in Liddon's "Life of E. B. Pusey," vol. iii. pp. 149–158.

that I have done no *real* good to-day to any one. If my Oxford life is to be like this, I cannot go on. It is not saving souls. It is a waste of strength." Entries of this kind occur again and again in his diary at this time. He devotes himself to any one with whom he comes in contact. On one day, when he had taken the train to Wantage to see a dying man, he notes about other people whom he met. "Gave X. a 'Steps to the Altar,' an 'Invitation;' and a porter at Didcot[1] a copy of the Vicar of Wantage's sermon and a Ridley's 'Holy Communion;' and a 'Lyra Innocentium' to ——. O Lord, I thank Thee." As Proproctor he avails himself of the opportunities of his office to speak to those whom he arrests about their souls, as he did to all others about him. "Saw the messenger and had a talk with him about his prayers, etc., which led me to see how very much there is to do." "A long talk with our Hall messenger boy about his soul. He is sadly ignorant of Divine Truth."

In trying to help undergraduates, he began his Sunday evening Lectures for any who would come. The plan originated in a conversation, after a lunch at Cowley Vicarage, with the Rev. R. M. Benson, at the end of the first Term at St. Edmund Hall in 1859. He began the Lectures the following Term on November 6: "My first Lecture: Prolegomena on Epistle to the Hebrews; seven men present. No S. E. H. men." His diary records anxiously the numbers each week, and often adds a note of the presence or absence of a man about whom he is anxious. The attendance increased steadily but slowly. Before he left St. Edmund Hall, he had to lecture in the dining-hall, because his own room was not large enough to hold the forty or fifty men who attended. In 1865 the Provost of Queen's College suggested that he should move to the hall of his College; Liddon was very greatly pleased at this recognition and help. Bright wrote of it on March 24 to a friend:

---

[1] His frequent changes at Didcot for journeys to the West of England allowed him to know the railway officials well. In his last illness, he was greatly pleased to receive a letter of sympathy signed by all of them.

"Is not this grand? Liddon calls it the Feast of the Translation. His face was quite radiant on Sunday evening."[1]　He continued the Lectures, so far as he was able, up to the end of his life, and in his later years he would have an audience of four hundred men in Christ Church hall.

In his diary for 1860 are two Papers which show the aims and motives which underlay this work.　The first is a set of questions which he constantly put before himself ; and the second a statement of motives.

"1. Do I endeavour to teach my pupils the Religion of our Lord more earnestly and constantly than anything else ?

"2. Do I walk and talk with them as often as possible with this view ?

"3. Do I conscientiously prepare my Lectures ?

"4. Do I allow the work of the Hall to interfere with—

(1) The Commentary.
(2) Midday prayer.
(3) Sympathy for old Cuddesdon men.
(4) Spiritual reading.

"Motives for exerting myself at Oxford to save souls and in the Commentary—

"1. My Ordination vow.

"2. The Day of Judgment—account of time.

"3. The heartiness with which X. and Y. exert themselves for earthly ends.　Cannot I do as much for Jesus Christ ?

"4. The efforts of Bishop Wilson of Calcutta in my very position. I have just been reading his life by Bateman.　With nothing beyond the light of Evangelicalism, how much he did !

"5. The weakness of the Church cause."

During his residence at St. Edmund Hall, Liddon came to be widely known as a preacher.　Attention was drawn specially to him by the place which, from 1858, Bishop Wilberforce regularly assigned to him in the Lenten courses of sermons in Oxford ; it was an honour not shared by any other young man.　His Oxford reputation soon caused him to be busily employed in preaching or refusing invitations to preach all over the country.　Besides his regular

---

[1] " Letters and Memoir of W. Bright, D.D.," p. 2.

work and preaching at St. Edmund Hall during 1860, he delivered forty-two sermons in different places. In the vacation he is constantly on the move from place to place to satisfy his many friends ; and even during Term time he rushed about in a manner which would have made his other duties a conscientious difficulty to a less active man. The trouble that oppressed him just before leaving Cuddesdon—" God seems to have made preaching much more difficult to me of late "—soon passed away.

The sermons preached in St. Edmund Hall Chapel were mostly written out, like his earlier Cuddesdon addresses. But for most of his other sermons he made a few notes on an ordinary sheet of note-paper, and delivered them without any external aids to his memory. In 1861 he began the habit of writing out, at the earliest opportunity after delivery, a minute analysis of each sermon that he preached. There are two or three note-books full of these analyses, written out in his clear handwriting, without any erasures. The elaborateness of the arrangement of these sermons, the fulness of the thought, the wealth and range of his illustrations, the simple and ungrudged outpouring of his learning, the deep knowledge of the Bible and the clear grip of its inner meaning, and the fervour of his exhorta-tions, strike the mind even more readily in looking over these analyses than in reading his printed sermons. As compared with his later work, they, of course, show some of the defects of youth ; they are, perhaps, in parts, unduly rhetorical and full of startling statements and of descrip-tions of difficulties which are made clearer than their solu-tion ; but they possess the excellence as well as the defect of this period of his life. Even the analyses cannot obscure the fire which characterised them, and which was passed on from the preacher to his hearers.

Liddon's extempore preaching was no device for avoid-ing hard work. To the hearers it may have sounded like the natural, easy onflow of the full tide of the preacher's great gifts ; but the style, as well as the matter, was the result of exacting work—page after page of these analyses is planned out with most elaborate detail, as if his sermons had been cast in an iron mould. They are all written out under headings more or less after the following plan :—

Introduction.

Part I.

Objection I.
Answer I.
Objection II.
Answer II.

Part II.

Division 1.
,, 2.
,, 3.
,, 4.

Part III.

[Digression.]
Appeals.
Consolations.
Exhortation.

These sketches show on every page signs that Liddon already felt that preaching was to be the great work of his life, and that he was devoting all his energy to perfecting himself in it.

Little jottings at the end of the analyses and in his diary now and again give light on his own feelings about his sermons. After a sermon at St. Paul's, Bedminster, for the Bristol Infirmary, on September 1, 1861, he says, " In preaching this sermon I hesitated twice, more than I have done for five years. O Lord, pardon me." His diary on that day adds the prayer, " Make me, O Lord, humble for this ; and to desire only Thy glory and my own confusion. 'Ad Dei gloriam et nostri abjectionem.'" Another is noted " 1 hour;" another, " 1 hour 25 minutes ;" the next, " 1 hour 20 minutes." In his diary he notes, " Sermon more than an hour—could see that this disgusted Dr. ——. '1 hour 20 minutes, φεῦ.'"

From 1861 he frequently preached in Westminster

Abbey at the invitation of Dean Trench, and he was appointed Select Preacher before the University of Oxford in November, 1862. His first sermon at St. Paul's Cathedral was on April 19, 1863, at the invitation of Dr. Tait, the Bishop of London. It is thus described in the diary—

"*April* 18.—Left Oxford 1.55. A long talk in the train with a Particular Baptist, who seemed to be sincerely in earnest about his salvation. . . . Feel very unequal to preaching at St. Paul's to-morrow, both spiritually and physically. O Lord Jesus, help me—a poor sinner.

"*April* 19.—Early Communion at All Saints [Margaret Street]. Felt very unwell during the day. Mr. Headland [a medical man] came, and I was fortified with mutton chops, sal-volatile, and sherry. At special Evening Service, St. Paul's Cathedral, commended myself to God. Did as well as I could ; but feel that the sermon was a mess. The Dean told me that it was 1 hour 10 minutes, and that I exerted myself too much to be heard."

Other members of the congregation consoled him more than the Dean; but the exertion made him seriously unwell for six and thirty hours afterwards.

Sermons preached at Oxford before the University caused many anxious entries into the diary. While he had the opportunity, he nearly always submitted them to the Principal of St. Edmund Hall before they were delivered. One series of entries is very like another. In May, 1860, he was preparing the well-known Ascension Day sermon, which is the eleventh in his first volume of " University Sermons."

" *May* 7.—Have not done anything to my Ascension Day sermon.
„ 8.—In a great fright about my sermon engagement.
„ 9.—In evening tried to do something to my sermon.
„ 10.—Did a little sermon.
„ 11.—Wrote a little sermon.
„ 12.—Wrote sermon.
„ 13.—. . . Left for St. George's in the East. . . . After sitting more than half an hour in the vestry of St. George's, Mr. Dove decided that there should be no Service, on the ground that the Choir seats had been occupied by the mob. [This was during the riots there.]
" *May* 14.—Returned to Oxford ; two lectures ; wrote six letters. Wrote some sermon.
" *May* 15.—The Principal cut my sermon utterly up.

"*May* 16.—Spent afternoon in reconstructing sermon.

    „   17.—Preached before the University at Christ Church on the Blessings of the Ascension.

"*May* 18.—Published my sermon at Bright's suggestion. Mr. Parker [the publisher] very dignified."

On Low Sunday, April 7, 1861, he preached a sermon at St. Mary Redcliffe, Bristol, which was described at length in the *Bristol Journal* on the following Saturday.

"The Vice-Principal of St. Edmund's Hall, Oxford, whose reputation as a pulpit orator now stands very high in that famous University, preached at St. Mary Redcliffe, on Sunday evening last, in aid of the District Visiting Society. The reverend gentleman took his text from Saint Paul's Epistle to the Philippians, chap. iii. verse 10 : 'That I may know Him, and the power of His resurrection, and the fellowship of His sufferings, being made conformable unto His death,' on which he delivered a discourse marked by great earnestness and persuasive power. Mr. Liddon is an extempore preacher, and his sermons have, therefore, the fervour and spirit about them which only one out of a thousand can import into the reading of a composition, however eloquently worded. He at once strikes his hearers with an entire forgetfulness of self, thinking only of his great theme and of them, as he argues and strives and, as it were, wrestles with them—to convince, to influence, to affect them. His personal appearance, too, is calculated to add to the impression which his serious, eager manner makes upon a congregation. A keen-eyed, dark, slightly made man—some thirty years old, we believe, though looking ten years older, and worn with study and work—holding a little black Bible in his hand, and energetic and rapid ; his zeal and intense anxiety to reach the hearts of those who hear him are certain to secure at least their attention. This conscientious intensity—as it is, we believe, part of the character of the man—is also of his pulpit style the most prominent characteristic ; for, though his language is fluent, expressive, and perspicuous, it is by no means ornate, and force rather than fancy—as if he were too busy, too much in earnest, to stop for ornament—is observable in his sermons. Indeed, this quality of force, this feeling of power, or powerful feeling, which is exemplified in the text, appears to be that which he would have us to attain to, and the absence of which, in modern Christians, he deplores. 'We want more force in religious matters,' was the burthen of no inconsiderable part of his discourse—more force, more faith, the will and the purpose to do and to suffer for Christ. And as he extolled this force with an energy and yearning after it, and with a voice and action into which his whole soul was thrown, he was himself a good illustration of the earnest quality which he commended, and which he contrasted with the listlessness and lassitude that characterised our prayers, our devotions, our exertions in behalf of the Gospel, our alms, our duty to

God and our neighbour, and which was so unlike the resolution and the enterprise with which we pushed and prosecuted trade, science, and politics, and material movements. He showed how, in other subjects —metaphysics, mathematics, etc.—it was enough to apprehend them— to understand; in religion, however, there must be more than speculation—to know the doctrine was not enough ; it must be felt in the heart, and bring forth fruit in the conduct. It was in this sense that St. Paul, the master, the great missionary, teaching others still strove to bring further and closer to heart the 'power of His Resurrection,' the love of Christ, Who gave Himself for sinners ; and in this way, the confessedly High Church preacher continued, in a discourse deeply and beautifully Evangelical, to urge upon his hearers to realise the wonderful Sacrifice made for them, and return to some extent the great love Christ had shown for them. The preacher made a striking and most happy use of the manner in which our Lord spent the time between His Resurrection and Ascension, in retired meditation and visits of comfort and encouragement to His disciples, and wished it to be considered as an indication of how the Christian's time on earth should be spent ; for, as two-thirds of the iceberg are under water and unseen, so a large proportion of the life of the devout Christian, his communings with God and his kind offices to man, are in secret— withdrawn from view, or unobserved by others, though at times their light so shone before men that they, seeing their good works, glorified their Father Who was in heaven.

" We do not pretend to give even an imperfect plan of the discourse of the Vice-Principal of St. Edmund Hall, but it was an example of how the fire of earnestness will burn through ordinary studious reserve, and the feeling and fervour of the moment supply language, clear and coherent, and rapid as any to be attained by previous preparation ; while that freedom from the strict letter of a written composition gives scope for a rhetorical *abandon* which, when not abused, is one of the most effective instruments for arresting and engaging the attention and breaking through the 'indifferent crust' of commonly careless congregations.

" The fine old Church of St. Mary Redcliffe, was quite filled, and in the lights and shadows of tall piers and pointed arches, and the ' dim vista of far-receding aisle,' the dark-eyed and studious but vivid preacher, as he reasoned entreatingly and searchingly with his hearers on the great truths of the Redemption—voice, hand, and heart going together—was not only a picturesque object in the ancient building, but the apparent impersonation of that earnestness—that longing aspiration for religious force—which he so passionately enjoined."

In his diary the sermon is recorded thus—

" Prepared sermon for St. Mary Redcliffe, Visiting Society during the afternoon. Preached on Phil. iii. 10 : ' The power of the Resurrection Life.' Felt that I was unable to really gain the attention of my audience, and had a bad headache."

But although he preached so frequently, he shrank from conducting Retreats; he said that "it was quite out of his power." Still, Mr. Swinny, Principal of Cuddesdon College, repeatedly pressed him to conduct the July Retreat for Clergy at the College in 1862; he unwillingly consented, but was at the last moment prevented by news of the death of Colonel Ambrose, who had married his sister Louisa only five months before. The following year he had to fulfil his promise; he, however, never again attempted this kind of work. The late Dean of Chichester (the Very Rev. R. W. Randall) has given an account of that Retreat in the preface to his volume of "Addresses and Meditations for a Retreat." Alluding to two of the meditations contained in his volume, he says—

"The meditations in this volume on Life, and on the Most High God, are the expansion of very short notes of two addresses by Dr. Liddon, given in the course of a Retreat at Cuddesdon. It is impossible to mention these addresses without adding something about the character of the Retreat. It is needless to say that it was marked by all that intense earnestness, that directness of practical teaching, and accuracy of theological statement which characterises all Dr. Liddon's writing and preaching. There was all this in the schemes of meditation, but there was something more than this in them. There was a restraint of oratorical power which makes one feel how much more there was behind the words than the words could tell out. The meditations were concise, clear, vivid, full of a force and power which made them take hold of the hearer, or, rather, enter into him and possess him. The truths contained in them seemed first to live before the hearer, and then to begin to live in him. They were instinct with life. And the manner of presenting the truths made one understand what the conductor said about meditation. 'In meditation you are to set yourself down before a truth and wait to see what that truth says to you.' I can never forget the tone and manner with which one of the subjects was given out, 'We will meditate on the Most High God.' We seemed at once to be placed in the sight of that tremendous Presence. God was there, and we were face to Face with Him. Never were meditations better planned for use in the hours of retirement. Never was the spiritual and searching force of Divine Truth, and its claim upon heart and mind, more brought home. And yet the conductor, I believe, never gave another Retreat. He was reported to have said at its close, 'I ought never to have given a Retreat. I shall never give another; this has been so great a failure.' He little knew what it had pleased God to do through him, and how his words in the Retreat would live on in the memories of all those whom he so marvellously helped."

During this time old friendships were being deepened and new relationships were being formed which greatly influenced his after-life. When he left Cuddesdon, Dr. Pusey again becomes an important force in his life. Bishop Wilberforce's objection to Liddon's intimacy with him had naturally separated them a great deal in the years of trouble at Cuddesdon ; so much was this the case that Pusey first saw Liddon's resignation of the Vice-Principalship in the newspapers, three weeks after it had happened. But now in Oxford he was constantly with him, working for him and with him in all matters of theological, ecclesiastical, and academical interest. Only on one occasion, quite early in his Oxford life, he separated from him, and with disastrous results. Dr. Stanley had proposed to increase the endowment of the Greek Professorship, which was held by Mr. Jowett ; and although the proposal was in itself just, it was difficult to pass it without appearing to give some sanction to opinions held by Mr. Jowett, from which many Churchmen entirely dissented. To avoid all appearance of injustice, Pusey proposed, on May 7, 1861, in the height of the excitement about "Essays and Reviews," the simultaneous increase of the stipends of several inadequately endowed Professorial Chairs, including that of Greek, and found much influential support in his politic suggestion. But Bright, Liddon, and several others, who as a rule voted with Pusey, now went against him, and defeated his scheme. It was a most unfortunate mistake. Two days later, Pusey spoke and wrote to Liddon very strongly in condemnation of his vote ; and Keble also wrote in a tone of unusual sternness in defence of Pusey's action.

"All of us," Keble said, " are bound in equity to consider the pressure which lies upon persons trusted with government, and which, in more cases perhaps than not, forces them to adopt the least of two evils instead of what is abstractedly best. (N.B.—This will apply to W. E. G. as well.) . . . Whatever you do, beware of taking towards him [Pusey] a suspicious and aggrieved tone. I am sure you will repent of that sooner or later. As things are, the grievance, I should say, is much more on *his* side."

Liddon never forgot this rebuke ; he often spoke of it in later years, for he knew what such words meant from Mr. Keble. But at the moment he was quite ready to defend his action.

TO THE REV. J. KEBLE.

"St. Edmund Hall, Oxford, May 15, 1861.

"You may easily suppose that it was not without great doubt and misgiving that I voted against Dr. P. But the majority which defeated him was twenty ; and I did not influence a single vote, as I could not make up my own mind till nearly the moment of voting. As to viewing his line in the matter with suspicion, or anything but respect, it is of course impossible. But there may be occasions when persons ' in office ' find themselves obliged to take a course in which their adherents cannot, and perhaps should not, follow them. I must avow that I conscientiously object to endowing Jowett in any way, direct or indirect. He does a great deal of work ; true. But (1) his friends, *e.g.* Conington, complain that his work is philosophy, and not philology, nor is he the best man for the Greek Chair. As a Greek scholar he is notoriously inferior to Riddell or Jones. And (2) his philosophy is in reality throughout suggestive of his theology ; his whole influence in Oxford is thrown into the scale of negative and destructive thought. . . . Because we refuse him a triumph, we are not bound to proceed at once to his impeachment ? There is surely, in practice, a middle course. . . . You must forgive the great freedom with which I put before you what is said or what more or less occurs to myself. But be assured that nothing will interfere with the affection and gratitude which I feel and owe towards the Doctor."

This vigorous bit of defence was entirely mistaken, as events soon proved. A little more foresight and a clearer knowledge of the power which is at the disposal of an able and pertinacious opponent who prosecutes his cause in the simple name of abstract justice, although it be to the exclusion of all other balancing considerations, would have saved many of the heart-burnings that followed. For, had the younger High Churchmen supported Pusey at that moment, nothing would ever have been heard of the prosecution of Professor Jowett for heresy.

On his return to Oxford he renewed his intimacy also

with Benson, the Vicar of Cowley. He was constantly at his house in what is now called Old Cowley, on the hill near Littlemore, where Benson lived with his mother. The iron church, in what has since been called Cowley St. John, was then being built. On May 14, 1859, Liddon writes in his diary—

"Dined in the middle of the day with Benson and his mother. In evening tea with Benson. Wasted the evening sadly. Said Compline with Benson amid the rafters of the now rising iron church in the St. Clement's corner of Cowley parish."

Now, also, he first became intimate with Bishop Hamilton, of Salisbury, an acquaintance which influenced his life as deeply as his relation to Keble and Pusey. In his memoir of the Bishop[1] he draws a lifelike picture of the Bishop's character ; but even the earlier allusions in his diary show the type of Churchmanship which the Bishop represented and endeavoured to produce in others. At his first visit to the Palace at Salisbury, Liddon records two conversations.

"*August* 10, 1859.—In afternoon walked with the Bishop to Old Sarum. He spoke very earnestly of the importance of the Daily Office. Recommended it to his clergy on all occasions. Thought the danger of formalism just as applicable to Family Prayer. Thought that the recognition of the obligation [to recite the Daily Office] would more than anything else lead to unsecularise the clergy. What an unspeakable blessing it is, he said, that the Church should have laid such a law upon us !

"*August* 14.—The Bishop spoke to me on the question of using Roman devotions. They are much richer than our own, but he thought that they prevented our fully accepting our position. He said that he never could go abroad ; he felt the pain of separation so very keenly. The best hope of ultimate union lay in making the best of actual blessings."

At the conclusion of this visit the Bishop expressed a hope that Liddon would stay with him whenever he desired to do so ; and from that date, until the Bishop's death, ten years later, prolonged visits to Salisbury were one of the greatest pleasures of his life, and they naturally became

[1] "Walter Kerr Hamilton, Bishop of Salisbury: A Sketch," by H. P. Liddon : 1869.

more frequent after the Bishop made him one of his Chaplains in February, 1863.

A year or two of such varied and wearying work as was gathering round him convinced Liddon that some change must be made.   Twice he considered whether he should accept Christ Church livings that were offered to him, but only to decline them.   But when Mr. Hubbard asked him, through Bishop Wilberforce, to be the first Vicar of St. Alban's, Holborn, he felt it necessary that he should come to some decision about his life.   He consulted both Keble and Pusey.

From the Rev. J. Keble.

"August 4, 1861.

"This is a puzzling case.   The solution, μάλιστα κάτ᾽ εὔχην, would be what you thought about Mackonochie.   Could it not be managed? On the whole, what with Commentary and what with some other things, I think I should say ' No,' even to Hubbard.   There would probably be less difficulty in filling your niche there, than where you now are."

From Dr. Pusey.

"Pentire, August 5, 1861.

"I have no doubt that your vocation lies in Oxford, and that this positive vocation outweighs opportunities for removal.   Parish work thoroughly fritters away time.   The heart—Oxford—is too weak already.   But apart from this, I think that intellectual development is your line.   Our great want in this day is to find people who will give themselves time to think, and to know what matured and holy minds have thought before them.   I am astonished, with all my experience of human weakness, how very little of tolerably matured judgment there is ; how people are out at sea or crotchety where there should be no doubt.   We want a dam against all this wild speculation on Holy Scripture and the Faith ; and your calling is to do what lies in one man with most of life, please God, before him.   It is amazing what with God's help may be done by one concentrated energy.   The *Westminster Review* speaks of one who, not without effect, gave thirty years of life to oppose Voltaire.   Mr. Hubbard would sympathise with you if you tell him that you think your calling to be, or that your calling is thought to be, to concentrate yourself in resisting Rationalism.   . . 'The harvest is plenteous : the labourers few.'   But as one cannot throw one's self into everything, one must make one's choice. An opportunity to go elsewhere, even to an important post, is not a call. I have felt for above twenty years that very few bishoprics are so influential as a position in Oxford. —— is laying himself out for influence with young men for evil ; we want, not tutors who live in a round of dining out, but men using energy, like his, for good. Yours is a mind which will write effectively. God will give you much ; and He has given you a hard head which will push against those hard-heads-for-evil. . . . I should be glad to set you free. We do want missions in London terribly. I should be glad to see a hundred missions there ; but although you would be a good missionary there, you have a call of yet more moment. You may form missionaries, please God, but you yourself must be at our Oxford Propaganda. God give you strength and grace and blessing for His work ! "

These letters decided him to refuse Mr. Hubbard's offer, and to recommend his old fellow-curate at Wantage, Mr. Mackonochie, in his place. A serious attack of illness in the summer of 1862 made him resign his work at St. Edmund Hall; in November he refused the Wardenship of Radley College, and in the following month he went into rooms in Christ Church, to which his Studentship gave him a claim, with a presentiment that it was his last move. In the event he retained those rooms till his death, twenty-eight years later.

CORRESPONDENCE, 1860–1863.

To the Rev. J. Keble.

"Wantage, March 31, 1860.

"There is a volume of ' Essays and Reviews,' published by J. W. Parker, which has just appeared, and which seems to go further in the race of Rationalism than anything which I have yet seen. Between Jowett's and Wilson's essays, the Gospel history simply evaporates ; as Jowett considers the three first Gospels to be merely three forms of one tradition, but ' not three independent witnesses ' to our Lord's sayings and acts (an exaggerated development of Bishop Marsh ?), and Wilson sees in St. John an element of legendary and ideal embellishment, which contrasts disadvantageously with the predominant moral element of the ' Synoptic ' Gospels. Certainly nothing nowadays seems to 'make a sensation' excepting only the Catholic teaching, as if the principle of rationalism had been generally admitted and it was merely a question of degrees. This book has already sold *largely* in Oxford."

To the Rev. J. Keble.

"The Palace, Sarum, Easter Tuesday, 1860.

" . . . I have ventured to bring the 'Essays' under this Bishop's notice. What he will do, I don't know. He insists much upon the necessity of large consideration for others, as a condition of holding things at all together. Of course, it becomes a question of limits."

To the Rev. W. Bright.

"July 16, 1861.

" . . . I have made the acquaintance of the Bishop of Quimper, who introduced me to Father Felix. This last is a most striking person—realising what one imagines the Jesuits to have been during the first half-century of their existence—uniting complete devotedness of purpose with the highest measure of intellectual culture. Of course, he paraded some of the stock arguments against the English position ; but this done, his conversation was very improving, and I wish one could have had more of it. He spoke very rapturously of Newman, and with a certain qualified respect of Dr. Pusey, which it was pleasant to hear.

"Philip Pusey is in Paris ; I dined with him on Sunday. He is alone, working at the St. Cyril in the Library. Next week he goes to the Escurial. Considering his great bodily deficiencies, I am astonished at his self-possession and *savoir faire* amongst foreigners."

To the Bishop of Salisbury.

"Oxford, Ascension Day, 1862.

"My knowledge of the Bishop of Natal's book (of which I do not possess a copy) is too cursory and superficial to enable me to offer any suggestion that could be of service to your Lordship.

"Its only *original* error, so far as I remember, was the notion that heaven will be a state of probation, and *may* end. In this he is loyal to the necessities of his argument at the cost of a larger inroad upon the Christian Creed than is generally made by kindred thinkers. The Universalist theory of salvation, with its corollary, the Denial of an Eternal Doom, *seems* absolutely to empty his own labours as a missionary to the heathen of their meaning and value—if, indeed, it does not represent them as mischievous."

To the Bishop of Salisbury.

"Oxford, November 19, 1862.

" . . . Of all troubles, that book of Bishop Colenso's seems the saddest just now. It is exactly adapted to the modes of thought current among laymen who have no very clear and definite faith ; and will strike them as a straightforward and sensible view of the matter, or at best they will say that it is a mistake to apply mathematics to poetry. What strikes me most on a hasty reading of the book, is its impatience of any hypothesis for dealing with apparent difficulties which is not somehow, if not immediately, derived from the text. Obviously, no ancient historical document, to be interpreted at all, can dispense with something of the kind, not merely for the removal of seeming difficulties, but that, as far as may be, the whole series and aspect of events, of which the document itself only gives a section, may be restored to completeness and life in the mind of a later age."

To the Same.

"Christ Church, December 11, 1862.

"Thank you much for what you are so good as to say about Bishop Colenso's matter. There could be no doubt about the convictions and feelings of the English bench of Bishops as to such a case. But, in the absence of information, the Bishops might naturally be unwilling to act upon a mere supposition that the book is unsettling people in other directions than the Rationalistic one.

"Independently, however, of its direct result of promoting thorough-going disbelief of the truth and contents of Scripture, that book is the best move for the Church of Rome since Newman's secession—or, at least, since the Gorham case. Since I last wrote to your Lordship, I have seen enough of its effect upon the minds of *several* thoughtful undergraduates to be painfully convinced of this. An intellectual assailant may make Bishop Colenso's notions of Biblical Criticism look very ridiculous ; but this does not vindicate the character of the English Church as a witness to the Apostolic deposit of Creed and Scripture."

F

CHAPTER IV.

VARIED WORK—LIDDON AND STANLEY—FIRST VOLUME
OF "UNIVERSITY SERMONS"—GROWING INFLUENCE
—BAMPTON LECTURES.

1863-1867.

THE events of the last Chapter will have recalled the fact
that in the early Sixties Oxford was still in the throes of
that great struggle for religious truth which ensued after the
direct work of the Tractarian Movement in the University
had been suppressed. That Movement was, in the minds
of its chief promoters, a great effort to prepare to withstand
the incoming tide of Rationalistic thought—"Theological
Liberalism," as it was called—which was already sweeping
over Germany in the first quarter of the century, and, before
the Tracts began in 1833, was beginning to show itself in
England. The popular view of Tractarianism as a mere
opposition to Evangelicalism is due to misunderstanding.
It was really, as it was in the history of Liddon's own
mind, the necessary complement of Evangelicalism and not
its opponent. The Tractarians felt that the real defence
against "Liberalism" was to be found in reasserting and
insisting upon the whole area of the Catholic Faith ; this,
they felt, would give a basis for a reasoned resistance to
Rationalism which the narrow popular Evangelicalism
could never supply. But the Evangelicals of Oxford had
misunderstood the attempt, treated it as necessarily Roman,
and as hostile to their conception of the Christian Faith;
and in 1841, when argument failed, they threw in their lot
with the "Liberals," and used the antiquated forms of the
University to crush it.

"If you crush Tractarianism," it had been said during the struggle, "you must fight 'Germanism.'" And in 1863 the Church in Oxford was fighting for the maintenance of the central positions of the Creed, not only against the teaching of those who directly denied the Faith, but also against any attempts to conciliate such opponents by surrendering any part of the Creed. Such attempts were commonly associated with the names and the teaching of Professor Jowett and Dr. (afterwards Dean) Stanley.

Into this struggle Liddon now threw all his powers. His freedom from office of any kind left him at this moment abundant time for study, preaching, and interviews ; and his intimacy with Pusey and Bishop Wilberforce, and his social relations with a very large number of the junior and senior graduates of the University, gave him exceptional opportunities for this work. But it was of necessity a work without a history, although mentally and physically exacting, and of very great value to individuals and to the Church. Now and again great calls for some special effort would bring him into prominence, but the eight years that followed his leaving St. Edmund Hall do not admit of a lengthy record.

When he returned to Oxford for the Lent Term of 1863, he found his new rooms in Christ Church in a state of wild confusion, and, therefore, gladly accepted Dr. Pusey's offer of a home in his house for a while. He lived with him for nearly three months, and happily and gratefully helped his great friend in every possible way. For himself he had no definite and detailed plan of life, except to do whatever came to his hand. As he said about this time to Bright, "As life goes on, it seems to teach the lesson of thinking little of private plans and hopes, and much of God's general providences." At first his only regular work was his Sunday evening lecture at St. Edmund Hall, and a course of Lent sermons on the Passion at All Saints, Margaret Street, London ; but his life soon became as full as ever it had been. Kitchin appointed him Pro-proctor ; Bishop Wilberforce used him to work up theological points for his own purposes, and to preach mission sermons in his diocese; and Bishop Hamilton was constantly making exacting demands on him as his Chaplain. One fortnight of this time, as described in his diary, gives a good idea of the amount of work which he was attempting.

"*February* 21.—Newbury Lent Mission. Left Oxford 7.55. At Reading met Woodford and Archdeacon Randall. . . . Reached Newbury Rectory —. Gave an opening address to the communicants in the schoolroom at 6.30. It lasted for three quarters of an hour. The people were very attentive; but I did not feel that I was doing any good.

"*February* 22.—Evening I preached at parish church to a very large congregation, probably two thousand people, on the Manifestation of Christ—the principle of conversion in the instance of St. Paul.

"*February* 23.—Gave the Communion address on Thanksgiving after Holy Communion. At eleven preached at St. John's on the study of Holy Scripture.

"*February* 24.—Preached in parish church to two thousand people on 'the Manifestation of Christ, the deliverance from the snares of the world' (St. Matthew).

"*February* 25.—Went to London.

"*February* 26.—Preached at eleven o'clock service at All Saints' on 'A Human Sufferer.' My second Passion lecture.

"*March* 1.—Preached concluding mission sermon (at Newbury). The church filled by an overflowing congregation. I never felt less equal to such work.

"*March* 5.—Preached with much difficulty and great dissatisfaction to myself [at All Saints'] on the Divinity of our Lord as Victim of Calvary. Returned to Oxford feeling very unwell.

"*March* 6.—Very unwell during morning. Evening preached at St. Giles' on the Sin against the Holy Ghost, feeling the difficulty of the subject very keenly. Borrowed much from Dr. Pusey's sermon on the subject. Felt that my preparation was incomplete, and that I kept my eye too much upon the paper. There was also a want of unction. I did not feel frequently what I was saying. 'Pardon me my sin, O my merciful God.'

"*March* 8.—At evening my lecture at St. Edmund Hall fairly attended, but felt great difficulty in giving it, and much dissatisfaction at it when given."

This kind of life was very exhausting in itself, and it was also very different from what Pusey had hoped for him. He wished him to be a student, and, above all, to work at the Bible Commentary which he had so greatly at heart. In this Liddon had now undertaken to write on the Book of Leviticus, laying aside for the time the Pastoral Epistles ; but day after day passed and nothing was done. Pusey first spoke, and then pressed, and then spoke very seriously ; at last, on June 2, 1864, Liddon notes in his diary—

"Called on Dr. P., who was very sharp about my having done nothing with the Commentary. 'You preach sermons an hour long at St. Paul's, and nobody hears you, and you are knocked up for a fortnight afterwards. You have done nothing.' He contrasted my idleness with Kay's promise to finish Genesis within the year. 'Kay,' he said, 'is not two years older than you. When I was your age, I had finished my tract on Baptism, and my Arabic Catalogue.'"

But although he was greatly distressed at such a rebuke, he was clear that a large portion of his work lay on the practical side of the Church's life, and that he must not devote himself exclusively to Oxford and its interests and studies. Pusey did not change his mind, and Liddon continued his own line of work. Immediately after the scene just described, he had a short holiday on the Continent, and then spent three weeks with the Bishop of Salisbury on his Visitation tour, and ten days with him at Penmaenmawr, full of work and preaching, and entering with hearty interest into the many sides of Church life which the society of the Bishop brought to his notice. Shortly after this, the Bishop offered him the prebendal stall of Major Pars Altaris in the Cathedral of Salisbury.

To the Bishop of Salisbury.

"September 10, 1864.

"Your offer of a prebendal stall in Salisbury Cathedral is singularly welcome to me on its own account, and yet more welcome as a signal proof of your Lordship's undeserved confidence and kindness. I accept it very gratefully ; I am sorry that I cannot at once accept it unconditionally. But some time since the Dean and Chapter of Christ Church passed a bye-law, which declares that any Student who accepts 'preferment' from any other patron than Christ Church does by so doing forfeit his Studentship. As I fear that I could not afford to give up my Studentship, I have written to the Dean of Christ Church to ask whether, by accepting 'preferment' which did not imply income, I should bring myself under the terms of the rule in question. On hearing from the Dean, I will at once write to your Lordship. Meanwhile, if among the many clergy of your diocese, who must naturally have occurred to you as having claims to such an honour, any names should present themselves with greater force than was the case before your writing to me, I would earnestly beg you, under all circumstances, to consider that letter as so much waste-paper, and to believe that I value most what I retain in any case—the kindness which makes the offer, and which is the true measure of its worth."

He found that his fears were unfounded, and that he could continue to hold his Studentship if he accepted the Bishop's offer ; he was, therefore, installed at Salisbury on September 24, 1864.

The following Christmas vacation, as well as many others, he spent at the house of his friend, Mr. Mire-house, at Brownslade, in Pembrokeshire. Miss Mirehouse gives the following account of his life there :—

"Dr. Liddon used to spend many weeks with us in Wales, and in our daily walks or drives his intense love of Nature was always being brought out. The piece of moss under his feet, the wild flower in the hedge, ever gave him a subject for some beautiful simile, or some lesson to be learnt from it. He loved the sea in all its aspects, and those who knew his nervousness over some things, would have wondered to see him dressed up in a pea-jacket, and with a 'sou-wester' tied well down over head and ears, crawling in a heavy gale of wind, on hands and knees, to the very edge of a high headland, and, drenched with foam, lie there (for no one could stand) and watch the Atlantic waves rolling in and dashing over the iron-bound coast. The roar of wind and waves prevented all speech, but the look of awe upon his face spoke more of his thoughts than any words could have done. The real delight and joy he felt was, I think, in the realisation of the might and power of the Creator. Each aspect of Nature—the thunder or the smile of the ocean, the zoophyte in the pool, the shells on the seashore—afforded him endless subjects for dwelling on the love and greatness of God.

"His special delight was to say his Offices amongst the rocks. As he stood bareheaded in their depths, the caves would re-echo with the Glorias as he shouted them out, and he would chant Psalm after Psalm of praise, as if nothing could sufficiently satisfy the exuberance of his thankful heart.

"How well we remember his delight one day in the winter of 1864, when we took him into a little ruined chapel, halfway down the cliff, where Dr. Pusey had once been! After poking about in every nook and corner with his usual keen interest, and standing in the little cell of the hermit, he knelt down before the stone altar and spent many minutes in prayer. Then came a train of thought as to the life of the old saint who had inhabited the chapel, and, with his usual eloquence and earnestness, he poured out all he was imagining of the life of devotion he had spent there, and of the prayers he had offered for the sick who visited him, and for those in peril on the sea. The thought of the hermit seemed to have affected him to such a degree, that he never ceased loudly chanting Hymns and verses of Psalms all along the road home. It was quite immaterial to him who heard him, or whom we met, though I fear his companions were not so indifferent."

When Liddon first came back to live in Christ Church in 1863, Dr. Stanley was one of the Canons, and held the Regius Professorship of Ecclesiastical History. There was much to attract these two men to one another, in spite of the great difference in age and position, and the far more serious difference in theological thought. In his diary Liddon frequently alludes to discussions and walks with him, as well as to his repugnance to his opinions. At the close of 1863, when Stanley was giving up his Professorship at Oxford to be Dean of Westminster, not a few people hoped that Liddon would succeed him. Stanley himself wrote to him to say that, with the exception of one person whose appointment he believed on general grounds would be the best of all, he had shared those hopes.

"I have often thought that in Oxford at this present time a place is open for a High Churchman, such as yourself, to exercise a wholesome influence such as none other could command."

After expressing his disappointment at Pusey's position, he added—

"I will not altogether abandon my hope that in the coming years you may be led to see this opening as clearly as it presents itself to me."

Early in the new year, Stanley was endeavouring to arrange a course of sermons at the Abbey which would include preachers of every shade of opinion within the English Church, not excepting those whose names were prominently identified with the "Essays and Reviews." Only a short time before, two of the clergy who contributed to that volume had been acquitted by the Judicial Committee of the Privy Council of the charge of teaching anything contrary to their Ordination Vows—a decision which had caused profound dissatisfaction to High Churchmen and Evangelicals alike. In order to show their disapprobation of the book, Pusey and Keble declined to go out of their way and to be associated with any of its writers in the published lists of preachers which Dean Stanley was preparing ; but they both thought that Liddon might accept the invitation, as he had already been a preacher at the Abbey in the time of Dean Trench. But Liddon believed that such an act might appear to compromise the truths which the "Essays and Reviews" had assailed. He immediately declined.

To the Dean of Westminster.

"Christ Church, March 8, 1864.

". . . I trust you will not deem me wanting, either in respect or gratitude to yourself, or in duty to the Church, if I beg you to allow me to decline your invitation. The recent Judgment of the Judicial Committee of the Privy Council has thrown not a few minds among us into the greatest perplexity. It is my duty to do nothing knowingly, which in any degree with any one mind will increase this (in my judgment) very natural distress.

"There is a current report that you will ask Professor Jowett, Mr. Maurice, and other clergymen of the same school to preach at the Abbey. You have an unquestioned right to do so, and the generosity which prompts you to ask me, who have never concealed my dissent from Latitudinarian principles, would, *à fortiori*, lead you to ask men of undeniable eminence, and with whose convictions you so much more nearly agree. Therefore, I do not take the liberty of inquiring whether the reports be true. I assume it to be so.

"But every clergyman, however humble his position, has a certain number of persons who look up to him, and whose case he is bound to keep in mind, not less in his public acts than in his public utterances. If, at the present serious juncture, I should voluntarily range myself side by side with men who notoriously rejoice at the recent disastrous Judgment, such conduct on my part would be understood by not a few people to mean that, after all, I believed the questions at issue to be of little real importance—mere questions of words which ought not to divide educated and large-hearted men. The result would, or, at any rate, too probably might, be, in some cases, indifference ;—in others, the Church of Rome.

" If, of course, my own conscience was perfectly clear as to the duty of public acts of fellowship with men like Mr. Maurice, etc., it would be right to disregard consequences. But, on the contrary, I cannot but recognise the fact that on the most sacred questions we are hopelessly divided—on questions which touch nothing less than the revealed Character and Attributes of Almighty God. A legal (rather than a moral) bond retains us within the same Communion ; or, rather, God's providence does so—I hope and pray— with a view to future unity of conviction, however improbable that may seem at present. But, meanwhile, I shrink from being a party to presenting these sharp contrasts (as some men would say) between different opinions,—as I am bound to say between truth and error, —before the people of London at a time when so much is at stake. I am not insensible to the privilege you offer me of preaching in the first of English cathedrals to the first of English congregations. But you would be the last man in the world to recognise ambition as a legitimate motive in these matters, and I must trust to your kindly interpretation of what I have said as to what seem to me to be the real merits of the question. To the people of London at large, and to yourself, it cannot make a shade of difference whether I preach or not. Some one else will do much better in my place. To me it seems to be a question between truthfulness and insincerity of purpose."

In his answer Stanley complained of the attitude of the leaders of the High Church party in now openly allying with the Evangelicals against the " Essays and Reviews," whilst they refused to preach under the same roof with "a man so holy and self-devoted as Frederick Maurice ; " and he complained also of the latest vote of High Churchmen in the painfully protracted controversy about the stipend of the Professor of Greek.

Liddon replies—

TO THE DEAN OF WESTMINSTER.

" Christ Church, March 10, 1864.

" I could not but fear that my letter would cause you pain. So far as I know my own heart, I meant nothing personal—nothing that (as I thought) was not due to conscience and principle. That I expressed myself unskilfully is only too likely. That you do not consider my letter a reason for suspending our intercourse is a fresh proof of your generosity for which I cannot but thank you. It is only by his books and by his letters in the newspapers that I know anything of F. D. Maurice. What you say about his holiness and devotedness is only what others have said before.

"That he is so good a man I rejoice to believe with all my heart. It is an earnest of his return to the Faith of the Church. That so good a man should be mistaken is a very perplexing mystery of the moral world. But he is not its only illustration. No doubt he is a rebuke to most of us who hold truths which he denies. Tyre and Sidon have always a lesson for Chorazin and Bethsaida.

"But *mere* moral goodness is not a sufficient basis for engaging in a public profession to teach the people a common Faith. You must draw the line somewhere ; and the question is one of degree. No one doubts Channing's goodness, yet Channing taught Socinianism in terms. One of the many miseries of the recent Judgment is undoubtedly *this*—that it must lead to an increase of sectarian feeling and action among the clergy. When, through the long-deplored deficiencies of administration in her public law, the Church is no longer protected against the most serious forms of error, individuals cannot but feel that their moral responsibility to God and man for appearing publicly to countenance such error is almost indefinitely increased. Thus opinion tends more and more to supersede law. This is deplorable ; but in spiritual matters especially, law should emanate from sources which command the respect of conscience. How different are the principles enunciated in the Statute of Appeals from the facts of the actual Judicial Committee of Privy Council !

"But here you will not agree. I, too, deplore the vote of the day before yesterday ; but I am not surprised. As the *Times* pointed out, the recent Judgment is the real culprit ; and while I lament the mistake which so ignored or misconstrued the clause of the Statute, as to refuse Professor Jowett the endowment, and to acquiesce (one knows not for how long) in a false and painful position, I cannot lament the truly Christian feeling of distress, and something more, which the Judgment has elicited from men of the widest knowledge and the greatest holiness of life, *e.g.* Mr. Keble.

"You speak, my dear Mr. Dean, of a period of transition. 'Transition' to what ! One current of thought flows towards Mr. John Stuart Mill and Positivism beyond ; another towards Baur and the school of Tübingen, and the desolate waste beyond that. . . . The Girondins of Revolution have their day ; but they make way for its Jacobins. . . .

"All might have been saved if Newman had remained with us, or if (pardon my boldness) some one like yourself had taken up his work, and had endeavoured to recover the hearts of the English people to the principle of authority—a recovery to issue in God's good time, and with due respect to the gains achieved by the Reformation, in a reconciliation of the Churches of Christendom. As it is, the prospect is dreary ; one can only trust to Him Who rides above the storm. But the co-operation of High and Low Churchmen in defence of truths which they hold in common is surely a feature of the present crisis for which to be thankful. That the *Record* should be the vehicle or symbol of this reconciliation may be unwelcome, but it is hardly so serious as your allusion implies. Mr. Maurice writes to a paper so flagrantly disloyal to Christian truth as the *Spectator.* I do not suppose that he would endorse its editorial irreligion ; he merely illustrates in one way, as Dr. Pusey in another, the exigencies of a position.

"You say, my dear Mr. Dean, that we refuse to preach in the same church with yourself. You will, I trust, forgive me for saying that Churchmen have hoped—hoped and prayed, hoped against hope —that one from whom so much might be expected, as yourself, would one day be with them. Even now we do not acquiesce in the miserable conviction that you have cast in your lot with men, like Colenso and others, who are labouring to destroy and blot out the Faith of Jesus Christ from the hearts of the English people. We still believe that your generosity, rather than your judgment, links you even to Mr. Maurice and Mr. Jowett. We are quite sure that your love of truth, your sense of moral beauty, and in an eminent degree your historical tastes and wide sympathies, link you to us, who cherish the Movement of 1833–50, as to no other men in the English Church. You will, I trust, forgive the extreme freedom with which I have answered a letter, to which silence might have been the most respectful answer, if it had not been open to misunderstanding."

Stanley's reply set forth more clearly his meaning when he expressed his hope with regard to Liddon's work at Oxford.

From the Dean of Westminster.

"Deanery, Westminster, July 18, 1864.

"Your letter expresses your own views with as much force and as much kindness as the case admits.

"It is useless to argue the matter further. I will only say that my view of the position, which might have been adopted by High Churchmen like yourself, was founded on the unquestionable facts of one, like Origen in the early Church, like Döllinger in the Roman Catholic Church, and like many whom I will not name, but who must be well known to you in our own.

"And I am no less confirmed in the strength of my own position by the reflection that the course now adopted by the joint action of

Dr. Pusey and the *Record* would have, if successful, repelled from the Church such men as Arnold and Robertson, and denied the name of Christian to the best and holiest persons that I have known on earth.

"Pray accept my assurance that I should consider it false to myself and to the Church of England were I [to] allow these differences to interrupt social intercourse or ecclesiastical friendship."

In the following month Stanley took the opportunity of Liddon's preaching at St. Paul's to invite him to dinner at Westminster. Liddon describes both the dinner and the sermon in a letter to Keble.

To the Rev. J. Keble.

"40, Eaton Square, S.W., April 18, 1864.

". . . On Saturday I dined with Dean Stanley, partly to meet my brother, although I was not much up to going out. Only it seemed well to keep clear of 'personalities' as far as possible, and his invitation was so urgent as to leave little choice. The Bishop of London and Mrs. Tait were there ; also a great *posse* of Liberals, the two Lushingtons, FitzJames Stephen, Mr. Burdon, Mr. Forster, Mr. E. Colebrook, Fremantle, and others whom I know nothing about. I ought not to forget Hugh Stowell, who contributed 'variety' to the entertainment. Already Dean Stanley is surprisingly up in the whole history of the Abbey and precincts, and *this* part of the evening was delightful. *Inter alia*, Dean S. made a very vigorous panegyric on Cardinal Wiseman, considered as a popular lecturer, which obviously distressed Hugh Stowell not a little.

"I got through St. Paul's (D.G.). Garibaldi did not come, but the congregation was immense. There seemed to be literally no standing room down to the west end of the nave. It was like talking out into infinite space.

"I am not vigorous to-day, but taking care of myself."

Stanley renewed his invitation to preach in the next year ; but Liddon again declined, "after a great struggle." When, however, he found that Bishop Wilberforce and Mr. Carter, of Clewer, had accepted, he was for a moment in doubt. He adds in his diary—

"Perhaps I was wrong in refusing after all. Mr. Carter may have reasons connected with the House of Mercy of which I am ignorant. And the Bishop felt no difficulty about it last year. However, a man can only act for the best, and leave the result to God."

The following year Stanley invited him again. Liddon alludes to the correspondence that followed in the last letter that he ever wrote to Mr. Keble.

To the Rev. J. Keble.

"March 19 [1866].

". . . I have just had another correspondence with Dean Stanley, who renewed the offer about preaching in the Abbey, and insisted on going into the whole question. He is so very amiable and so perfectly indifferent to all questions of doctrinal truth whatever at the same time, that it is very, very difficult to deal with him."

Stanley wrote in reply to say that he would not again trouble him with a request to preach in the Abbey.

In October, 1865, Liddon published his first volume of Sermons. It consisted chiefly of Sermons which he had preached before the University, and, because of their apologetic character, the volume was entitled, "Some Words for God." At the suggestion of his friends, this title was dropped in the second edition, and it was simply called "Sermons preached before the University of Oxford." They were dedicated to the most intimate and most like-minded of all his contemporaries, "William Bright, Senior Fellow and Tutor of University College, Oxford, in affectionate acknowledgment of the many blessings which are inseparably connected with his friendship and example."

The Sermons bear all the marks of a time of great strain and anxiety, having been preached in the height of the great conflict for the Faith which was, to all Churchmen, the most prominent feature of Oxford life in the third quarter of last century. The very titles of the Sermons show the intensity of the struggle. Liddon does not argue so much for any specially Christian doctrine, as to establish the reasonableness of believing in any true sense in a Personal God, in a personal immortality, and in human liberty and responsibility. Conversations with undergraduates in the perfect freedom of his unofficial position had taught him that these were the difficulties which were really troubling them and keeping them back from the fulness of Christian faith and practice.

The style and method in these early sermons is interestingly compared with the preaching of Wilberforce, Newman, and Pusey, by a reviewer in the *Guardian*—

"A series of striking lessons developed out of a single expression—sometimes a slightly quaint expression, as in the sermon (a most original one) on the Lessons of the Holy Manger—seems to exemplify Mr. Liddon's favourite type of sermon. But in several of the discourses of the present volume the line of connection is of a more argumentative kind. Mr. Liddon has combined in them, as in the sermon on 'the Law of Progress,' or in that on the 'Freedom of the Spirit,' a chain of powerful reasoning, with a style almost always ornate, yet never overloaded with ornament, while his evident earnestness breathes life into his argument and addresses the heart as much as the intellect. One might guess that he had listened to the Bishop of Oxford. And he has obviously studied modern French models—no contemptible school of eloquence. And in one sermon, that on the Divine Victim, we fancy we recognise a familiarity with a sermon, never to be forgotten, of John Henry Newman.

"Yet his style and turn of thought are his own ; not the wondrously simple yet profound analysis of reasoning and pathos both, such as issued from the parish pulpit of St. Mary's thirty years ago ; not the accumulated pile of profound devotional theology that Dr. Pusey is wont to build up in language of which the one merit lies in the profundity of its pregnant meaning ; not even the slightly manneristic torrent of eloquence with which Bishop Wilberforce clothes an argument or an exhortation, yet of the same school with it ; a style which a little lacks both simplicity and variety, which is rather apt to treat all topics in a like ornate tone both of language and of sentiment, but which in Mr. Liddon's hands has a wonderful power of eliciting profound and striking meanings out of the most simple truths, and of presenting an able argument in a form to arrest both heart and imagination."

Liddon had acknowledged in the preface his many debts to various authors for thoughts and lines of argument; but he was truly distressed at an article signed "C. K. P." in the *Theological Review* for October, 1867, which not only estimated his personal influence at Oxford so highly that it seemed to him ridiculous, but also charged him with unacknowledged plagiarism from the

" Spiritual Exercises " of Ignatius. He was easily able to satisfy his reviewer on this latter point.

To the Rev. C. Kegan Paul.

" Christ Church, October 31, 1867.

" . . . Before your remarks led me to look closely into the matter, I had no idea that my sermons had anything in common with the 'Spiritual Exercises' beyond a general pursuit of the same line of thought as that which is followed in the opening Meditations. And I had no recollection whatever of my indebtedness to Manrèse.

" The simple account of the matter is that the first sermon in my book was composed from MS. notes compiled or jotted down at various times for the purpose of extempore preaching, and unaccompanied, I regret to say, in almost all cases, by any reference to the sources from which the several notes had been taken. Somewhere between 1852 and 1854, when I was curate at Wantage, I must have made the extracts from Manrèse which, by-the-by (although that does not matter, as doubtless the book is the same), I never saw except in a French form. I cannot profess to remember in detail the process of composition in the case of a sermon which I wrote in 1863. But I do not doubt that I believed myself to be copying or enlarging notes of my own, of which the book before me was mainly full. The sermon was printed in 1865, and except when I had to correct the printer's copy, I have not looked at it until now. And I do not doubt that the same account applies to the other sermon which you notice, preached in 1860—Christ's Welcome to the Penitent. It was preached extempore, and written out afterwards.

" I do not think that I ever set up for being original in my life, or have been thought so by those who know me, and I am as far as possible from being disappointed at being taken at my true measure. But I am quite sure that you would not seem to have attributed to me deliberate concealment of an obligation, based upon a calculation that I was not likely to be found out, if you had known the facts of the case. Indeed, I would quite as readily have acknowledged my obligations to Manrèse as to Père Félix."

With regard to Liddon's influence at Oxford, his reviewer had written—

" In the reaction which is undoubtedly taking place against Liberal opinions among the younger students at Oxford, Mr. Liddon stands out by the common consent of all as the man who has had the greatest sway. He exercises a personal open influence such as has not been known at Oxford since the days when the Heads of Houses were alarmed because the undergraduates flocked in troops to attend Mr. Newman's lectures at St. Mary's. Times have changed, for it was then gravely considered how best might be checked this dangerous teaching ; now the hall of a College which is not Mr. Liddon's own is placed at his disposal, that he may receive in it a Sunday evening Bible-class drawn from any or all Colleges, though unauthorised and nominally private. . . . What Newman was to the men of his time in his University, that is Mr. Liddon to those of the present.

"Nor do we wonder that he has gained such a position. We will not presume to repeat anything of what may be floating in the way of general discourse, about the charm of Mr. Liddon's private life, his easiness of access by those that seek his counsel ; but as a preacher he rules over the minds of his hearers as is given perhaps to one man only in each generation. 'I came,' said one of the wisest men in England, by no means of Mr. Liddon's school, as he left the Church after a special sermon by that gentleman—'I came to hear the finest preacher in England, and I am not disappointed.' 'He raised his hearers,' said another, equally well qualified to judge, 'from earth to heaven, and kept them there for more than an hour.' Like almost all sermons, save those of Bishop Taylor, Newman, and Robertson, much of this charm has evaporated with the voice and manner of the preacher ; but even as we read them very critically, and disagreeing with the whole form of thought, as well as the entire dogmatic theology they represent, we admit that the opposite side to our own is put most forcibly, that the writer does not inveigh, as do so many others, against that of which he is ignorant, but that, as a man of much culture and deep and varied learning, he has looked the problems of our modern life in the face, and deliberately adopted the Catholic resolution of them." [1]

In reply to a protest from Liddon against what he regarded as a most inaccurate and misleading description, the writer added some interesting details of the evidence on which it was based—

From the Rev. C. Kegan Paul.

"Bailie, Wimborne, November 2, 1867.

". . . I should be sorry to misrepresent your influence in Oxford, and it is natural you should think it less than I take it to be. But I have not gone on the report of one or two alone ; I have been several times in Oxford lately, and from undergraduates and dons I hear the same story. You are looked on as practically the great influence in the reaction against Liberalism which is so marked just now in Oxford.

[1] *Theological Review*, vol. xix. pp. 589, 590.

This I hear from Liberals and High Churchmen alike, and leading men on the Liberal side consider you their most dangerous opponent. I only mention this to show that I have not, as I think, exaggerated your influence.

"And I for one am very grateful to the influence you have had and have over more than one very dear to me who, honestly taking the side of Christianity to which you belong, has found help and guidance from you. . . .

"P.S.—You may be gratified to know, what I had no right to state publicly, that the two men who spoke as I have quoted of your sermon were Deans Milman and Stanley. It is the former, not the latter, that I have qualified as one of the wisest men in England."

On this point, for perhaps the first time in his life, he had failed to find any sympathy from Bright, to whom also he had complained that language like that of his reviewer exposed him to certain ridicule.

FROM THE REV. W. BRIGHT.

"University College, October 16, 1867.

". . . Don't talk about men laughing at or resenting what C. K. P. said. The fact is, that you are not the best judge as to the precise extent of your 'influence.' As to the Doctor, of course he *cannot* bring himself to bear directly on any large number of Oxford men. You are the best judge on the point of real interest for this particular occasion, *i.e.* that you never do, did, or could, seek influence for its own sake. And, indeed, any one who imputed this to you would be worthy of being 'laughed at.' I should say less than you have written about the main currents of Oxford thought flowing still in an unCatholic direction. Why should we encourage our foes?"

In March, 1865, Bright suggested to him that he should stand for the Bampton Lectureship in 1866. Pusey was against it on the ground of the Commentary, which he thought should be Liddon's first work; but after much hesitation Liddon decided, on March 18, to send in his name as a candidate. His application was late, for the electors had already had one meeting; and at the election, on May 16, seven Heads of Houses voted for Rev. A. W. Haddon and seven for Liddon, and the Vice-Chancellor, Dr. Lightfoot, of Exeter College, gave his casting vote for the former. Early, however, in November, Haddon resigned

G

from ill-health, and Liddon was unanimously elected in his place.

To the Bishop of Salisbury.

"November 8, 1865.

". . . It will interest you to hear that, Haddon, who was elected Bampton Lecturer in the spring, having been obliged to resign from ill-health, the electors have appointed me to take his place. To a certain extent this places me in a difficulty, as I have nothing but the vaguest idea of my subject, and, of course, have not written one line.

" But one must trust in God and set to work."

Nearly every day has some note of work done or not done for his Lectures. At Oxford, Brownslade, and Brislington, and again at Oxford for the Lent Term, he is either pained with the tone of the books he has to read, or with the mass of the work still before him.

"*November* 14.—Read some of Strauss's new 'Life of Jesus,' and felt wretched. His cold infidelity chills one's soul to the core.

"*November* 17.—Wrote the beginning of my first Bampton, but unsatisfactorily.

"*November* 22.—Out of heart about my Bampton.

"*November* 23.—Wrote some part of the first Bampton.

"*November* 28.—In the morning wrote a good piece of my first Bampton.

"*November* 29.—Wrote some Bampton lecture. Rewriting Bampton Lecture No. 1. More fertile to-day than heretofore. *Deo gratias.*

"*December* 8.—Making scarcely any way with my Bampton. Shall have to rearrange all I have yet written.

"*December* 9.—No work done to-day on the L. matter. What can I do?

"*December* 11.—Wrote some B. L., which I shall have to rewrite.

"*December* 16.—Wrote B. L. No. 2 in the morning, but not much, to my satisfaction.

"*December* 19.—In the evening read a great deal of 'Ecce Homo.' It is, I feel sure, Dr. Temple's. The passage on Education in the chapter headed 'The Law of Edification,' and the theory again and again put forward of law as ceasing with education's earlier stages, instead of being obeyed afterwards on higher principles, are unmistakable traces of his thought. The man, too, is a scholar ; he lives in the atmosphere of the Classics, and uses them with that perfect freedom which indicates familiarity.

"*December* 21.—Made a little way with the B. L. No. 3. Shall have, I see, to rewrite some of the others. They want heart and enthusiasm.

"*December* 22.— . . . Wish that I could see my way to finishing my Bampton lectures. They will be a very feeble production.

"*December* 27.—Making slow way with my Bampton lectures. Do not like anything I have yet written. Would that I could do better!

"*January* 1, 1866.—*Deus misereatur.* Up at 6.30 and walked by moonlight into Bristol, where I communicated at 8 at St. Raphael's Church. Wrote a little Bampton lecture, but nothing really satisfactory.

"*January* 8.—Tried to begin another Bampton lecture, but could make no headway.

"*January* 9.—Attempt to make way with Bampton lecture. O Dne Jhu, help me.

"*January* 11.—Wretched about B.L. I can make no real way whatever. Am trying to manage No. 2, but make no progress with it.

"*January* 18.—Letter from Burgon [Vicar of St. Mary's, Oxford], warning me not to make the Bamptons too long.

"*January* 21.—Wrote some B.L. Thought much about St. Paul on the Doctrine of the Saviour's Godhead.

"*January* 22.—Wrote a good deal of B.L. on St. Paul.

"*January* 23.—Think that I must alter my B.L.s yet again to manage them well.

"*January* 26.—In very low spirits about my lectures. I cannot make way with them or arrange them satisfactorily. O Lord, help me, though most unworthy.

"*February* 3.—Lunched with the V.C. Read the Will of the Rev. J. Bampton.

"*February* 4.—The first [Sunday evening] lecture this Term on the Epistle to the Romans. Felt that it was a feeble lecture. But it was magnificently attended, scarcely less than two hundred men. The hall of Queen's quite full.

"*February* 10.—Finished a lecture in a kind of way. But it will not do. I am wretched about them. They will be poor and thin beyond all words. *Deus in adjutorium meum intende!* or else make me see that a failure will be to Thy glory.

"*February* 12.—Began over again my first sermon.

"*February* 27.—Made a little way with Bampton Lecture No. 2. Quite alarmed about next Sunday.

"*March* 1.—I fear that my first Bampton lecture is much too long. What can I do?

"*March* 3.—A very uncomfortable letter from Burgon, warning me to be brief in my Bampton lecture.

"*March* 4.—Preached my first Bampton lecture—one hour and a quarter, reading very rapidly. The church was very greatly crowded.

"*March* 11.—Preached my second Bampton lecture—one hour and twenty minutes. On the testimony of the Old Testament to the doctrine of our Lord's Divinity.

"*March* 12.—The Doctor told me that Palmer had said that my

Bampton yesterday was rhetorical, but that the logical element in it was feeble. He spoke strongly—from what motive I do not know.

"*June* 3.—Preached my last Bampton lecture at St. Mary's. It lasted one hour and forty-one minutes. I omitted a large portion in the middle of it."

He had chosen as the subject of his Lectures, "The Divinity of our Lord and Saviour Jesus Christ." His plan was to examine the Messianic predictions of the Old Testament, and the historical and doctrinal statements of the New, and thus to show that the assertion of the Nicene Creed with regard to the Person of Christ was the only consistent interpretation of the language of Scripture taken as a whole. The Miraculous Birth, the Words and Works of our Lord, the witness of His consciousness as described in the Gospels, the teaching of St. John and St. Paul and St. Peter, all converge to this one great conclusion, and that conclusion must have the most important results on the thoughts and lives of those who admit it. Throughout, the Lectures assume a belief in God and in the trustworthiness of Scripture ; and they are, therefore, addressed to those who, while they accepted these fundamental doctrines, either denied the Divinity of Christ, or, under the influence of the general unsettlement on matters of Faith, hesitated to recognise the cogency of the arguments for the Incarnation or the practical consequence which must follow from its acceptance. He hoped that by this means he might draw Churchmen together, and also rally round the Church the disunited bodies of Nonconformists in defence of the great central citadel of the Church's creed. These hopes find expression in a letter to Dr. Jeune, who had but recently passed from being the Head of an Oxford College to take charge of the see of Peterborough.

To the Bishop of Peterborough.

"Brislington, Bristol, December 30, 1867.

" I must lose no time in expressing to your Lordship my very sincere gratitude for the kind terms of general approval in which you notice my Lectures. Your own long, and still recent, residence at Oxford gives an additional practical value to an opinion, for which, as coming from one of the rulers of our Church, I must in any case have been deeply grateful. The book has, in truth, caused me a great deal of anxiety ; it is no light matter to make mistakes in dealing with such a subject. And, partly in consequence of the haste with which the Lectures were thrown into shape, partly for other and, I fear, less accidental reasons, the volume contains, as I know full well, a very large measure of shortcomings. Your indulgent estimate of it as a whole will, however, strengthen my hope that, whatever be its literary or critical demerits, it may be accepted as a help towards promoting among our countrymen in our day and generation the rightful honour of our Blessed Saviour.

"If I know my own heart, that is my one earnest desire in connection with it.

"The Sacramental passages in the book, of which your Lordship is unable entirely to approve, were, as you will believe, inserted with no controversial animus. They grew naturally out of my everyday thoughts on these subjects, and your kind words lead me to hope that others who may be unable to accept them will not allow a difference as to the means of our receiving the Grace of Christ to obscure the blessing of entire agreement as to His Person and Redemptive Work.

"Some years ago, at Oxford, you said to me that, ' with infidelity around us, Christians ought to understand each other.' And since then, although public attention has been given to other matters, this reason for union has not become weaker. The questions raised year by year appear to me to be more and more fundamental—to strike at almost all Theistic as well as Christian truth."

The enormous congregations which gathered Sunday by Sunday to listen to him, and the very wide circulation of the Lectures when printed, are proofs that they were neither inopportune nor ineffectual. To attempt on such a scale, in a popular form, to refute the negative criticism of Renan, Baur, and Strauss was a tremendous task, and the success of the work resulted from many other qualities besides width of knowledge, clearness of argument, and brilliancy of diction. Beyond everything else the Lectures found an echo everywhere, because of the transparent sincerity and passionate earnestness of the preacher, and his indomitable certainty in the ultimate triumph of his own convictions.

During the summer of 1866, he was chiefly at Brislington, trying to prepare them for the Press. Keble's death, which occurred at the end of March, the mass of

correspondence in connection with the foundation of Keble
College, the death of an uncle, and his own election to the
Hebdomadal Council in October, all helped to delay the
work, in addition to his ordinary engagements and the special
anxieties of several secessions to Rome. He had delivered
the Lectures from a manuscript that was far from complete,
and he had practically to rewrite everything. Each portion
as it was printed was sent to Bright for his revision.

To the Rev. W. Bright.

" Brislington, Bristol, September 8, 1866.

" I reply to your kind letter by sending you so much of the Lectures
as have reached the sheet form. You see that they look unnaturally
long, because, acting on a very strong opinion of Fraser's [of Oriel], I
have thrown *all* the notes into the shortest possible form at the
bottom of the page, and mean only to have one or two excursuses at
the end.

" I should be very grateful to you for the freest possible criticism,
as I am deeply sensible of the presence of all kinds of shortcomings in
the Lectures, and of the probability that there is a great deal more to
which I am not alive. One can, however, only, I suppose, modify
honestly up to a certain point, *i.e.* actual error.

" I have looked over, I believe, the Scripture references, and those
to philology, but none, or almost none, of the Fathers as yet ; and the
notes I made in the spring were so hurried that there must, I fear, be
many inaccuracies.

" Also, would you tell me when my meaning is not obvious ?   I am
conscious of often writing very confusedly.

" I cannot say how much I prize your kind interest and assistance.

[*Private.*]

" During this week I have had to be at Salisbury, and met
Gladstone there. I had much talk with him about ' Ecce Homo,' and
the Test question in Oxford. He seems fully alive to the grievous
faults of ' E. H. ;' but rests his admiration for it on a belief that its
constructive value altogether outweighs these, and that it supplies a
species of evidence to our Lord's Person which is peculiarly adapted
to the wants of the present day. . . .

" As to Oxford, I confess I fear Gladstone's Doctrine of the
Inevitable (so to term it), although he was very kind and generous in
his admissions. I pressed him hard with the fact that the question
lies not between Church and Nonconformists, but between Christians
and non-Christians. He did not like this ; but it was, I hope,

sufficiently urged. He admitted at one time, that while the Nonconformists might be conciliated, the theological ultra-Liberals never
could. I confess that the conversation left one with a heavy heart as
to our future—in Oxford. He thought that scepticism would have a
great career in England, and spoke with deep sorrow of it; but he
said, ' There is one bright spot in the horizon. Erastianism is certainly
doomed, and Erastianism is the parent and the protector of scepticism.'
So much for Stanley, Bishop Tait, and the *Pall Mall*.

" My thoughts have been much drawn to the dear Medd by seeing
that he has been courteously attacked in the Bishop of Llandaff's
Charge on the score of his admirable essay. Also, to a certain extent,
in an execrable article in *Fraser* for this month . . . wherein it is
suggested that the best way to destroy Catholic belief, etc., by the
root, would be to prevent Imposition of Hands at the Consecration of
Bishops, leaving all the rest of the Prayer-book intact.

" The article is worth reading; it hits some exaggerations in
recent language, as I think; but its hatred is clearly directed against
all that is to a real Christian precious and sacred."

At the end of 1866, the Regius Professorship of Ecclesiastical History was vacant by the death of Dr. Shirley.
Liddon and Bright had, each of them, great hopes that the
other would be elected, and neither of them had any wish
for it himself. Writing to a friend at that time, Liddon
says—

" As far as I know myself, I do not wish for preferment, or for the
responsibility of either accepting or declining it. It does not increase
any man's moral power ; and it may very easily diminish it. Anyhow,
it is a guarantee given to the British State ; and it more or less
cramps perfect freedom of speech and action. I have everything I
can possibly want as it is, and am thankful to be, and to be left, where
and as I am."

Bright had endeavoured to secure the appointment of
Liddon, but Liddon had anticipated him.

" We have been," writes Bright, in a long letter, setting forth his
own unfitness for the work, " at cross purposes. That is, I wrote to
Lygon and to the Bishop, entreating that they would consider whether
anything could be done towards bringing *you* before the Government
for the Chair of Ecclesiastical History. And you—you traitor ! Lygon
coolly writes back that *before* my first letter came, he had resolved to
mention *me* to Lord Derby, and ' he lost no time in doing so.' When
my letter came, it seems that one came from you suggesting that I
should be put forward. Then, when I wrote a letter stating (with

scientific precision and fulness) the urgent reasons, as I think them, for your being put forward, and asked leave to place the letter in the Bishop's hands, the subtle prelate smiled a humorous and mysterious smile, and said, 'Liddon has anticipated you; he has been with me, suggesting another person,' etc."

Liddon would not listen to any of his arguments.

To the Rev. W. Bright.

"Brislington, Bristol, St. John's Eve, 1866.

". . . I hope and trust, dear Bright, that if the E. H. Chair is offered to you, you will accept it at once and without hesitation. You must remember that you owe this to the Church. [A. S.] Farrar would be much better than some who have been mentioned, but I would rather see Mansel there than any other resident who is likely to be thought of after yourself. He would build the walls of Jerusalem with big blocks of metaphysic, 'considered historically,' and I fear that some of our friends, however unintentionally, 'aid and abet Gashmu.'

". . . I have not seen the *Pall Mall Gazette* of late. But you hit the deepest point of difference between it and Christians. I remember an observation of Lecky's in his 'History of Rationalism,' that the sense of sin was the secret of the strength both of the Evangelical and Tractarian Movements. This sense, of course, he viewed as a superstition, and wished to see weakened. *Verb. sap.*"

At that moment the Chair of Ecclesiastical History was given to the Rev. H. L. Mansel; two years later, Mr. Disraeli offered him the Deanery of St. Paul's, and, to Liddon's surprise and joy, made Bright Professor in his stead.

To the Bishop of Salisbury.

"November 7, 1868.

"Bright's appointment has caused me great joy, and, indeed, the Doctor and every one here is of one mind about it. Certainly Mr. Disraeli could not have done better. No Liberal can deny that Bright knows more of his subject than any other six people in Oxford, and his devotion and loyalty to Church truth are as eminent as his knowledge. On the whole, we must, I think, admit that Mr. Disraeli has given away his Church patronage better than any Government for a long while since, and with a more single eye to the Church's strength and progress."

It was not until May 31, 1867, that he sent the last of his Bampton Lectures to the press. They were published in October, and the first edition of 2500 was at once exhausted. He had been at issue with the publisher about the price of the first edition, and now Lord Beauchamp generously offered to guarantee him against any possible loss if he could succeed in making the second edition yet cheaper. After some trouble, he arranged with Messrs. Rivington that, without cutting down the Lectures, the book should be reduced in size and sold at five shillings a volume. Up to the year 1880, 25,000 copies had been sold in this manner ; after that year, a ninth edition was issued after a most careful revision of every page. In view of two Unitarian criticisms of the Lectures, he went through each paragraph, sparing no pains to reply to every argument that called for an answer. The volume in this corrected form continued to sell at the annual rate of about 800 copies until the year of his death. His very last piece of literary work was the Preface to the fourteenth edition, dated St. Peter's Day, 1890 ; in this he replies to Dr. Martineau's work on the " Seat of Authority in Religion," so far as it touches upon this subject of the Lectures. The proofs of this Preface were revised during the long days of pain and discomfort of his last illness, and were sent to the publishers only on August 9, just a month before his death.

CORRESPONDENCE, 1863–1867.

To a Friend who had joined the Church of Rome.

" Christ Church, December 9, 1863.

" The notice of your reception into the Roman Catholic Church met my eye. It seemed useless to write. You, I know, would have understood my feelings of sincere sorrow. I thank you for writing now, at a time when your head and heart must be sufficiently full.

" I fear from your letters that you suppose me likely—one day—to join the Church of Rome. This, believe me, is an entire mistake. It is better that we should understand each other. By God's grace I am thankful to live, and earnestly hope to die, where He has placed me, in the belief that it is His Will that I should do so.

"You speak of the 'Voice of the Holy Ghost in past years' to me. I do not wish to say anything disrespectful of your subjective impressions, but you cannot communicate them by mere description. *If* the Roman claims are what you hold them to be, your language may be a natural though not a necessary consequence. But to one who thinks that he has sufficient reasons for a different conviction all such language must read like a *petitio principii*, or, what I am sure you did not mean it to be—rhetoric.

"In our conversations at Starcross—which I probably remember much less accurately than you—it is not likely that I had time or power to state to you all that I believed, and why. Religious conviction is a thing of gradual and complex growth, and does not admit of being exhibited, except rudely and in outline, within the limits of such a short interview, at least by an unskilful person like me. I have and had no right to be surprised that I did not succeed in persuading you to remain in the English Church. But it would be wearisome to you, and I fear now useless, to enter at length upon the many reasons, negative and positive, which must prevent me from following you, or from regarding your act as other than a serious error.

"Certainly the modern theory of development—as practically illustrated by the recent addition of the doctrine of the Immaculate Conception to the Roman Catholic creed—seems to me of itself fatal to the Roman claims. I do not know what your authority may be for referring to the language of the Commonitorium, and your reference is not, as I think, equal to the exigencies of the facts of the case. No symbolical document, I believe, teaches development, although divines, who like Dr. Newman are thoroughly far-sighted and honest, can see that nothing else is equal to accounting for the actual area of the Roman Catholic creed. No doubt such a principle would account for a great deal more. This is the hypothesis of a continuous Revelation (which Bellarmine disclaims in terms almost identical with those in which it is put forward by Dr. Manning), and, alas! there is also the theory of Baur."

To the Bishop of Salisbury.

"March 17, 1864.

"During the last fortnight I have been trying to organise an Essay Club among the abler undergraduates (some of them Jowett's own pupils) whom I happen to know. There are already two such clubs in existence, which are a great means of propagating sheer unbelief, *e.g.* one Paper which obtained great notoriety at the beginning of this

Term was directed against the immortality of the soul. It was written by a junior Fellow of a College. I hope that we have got together a sufficient body of clever men to make our Club intellectually respectable, and it will open next Term with an introductory essay on the relations of Theology to Philosophy, which will define the line to be taken subsequently on questions which bear on Revelation."

To the Rev. J. Keble.

"40, Eaton Square, April 22, 1864.

"The breakfast at Mr. Gladstone's came off yesterday morning, though I am too unpractised a conversationalist to have made much use of the opportunity.

"During breakfast, at which Lord Lyttelton and some ladies were present, the conversation was necessarily restricted to general topics.

"After breakfast Mr. Gladstone took me aside, and I pressed as hard as I could civilly about a New Court of Appeal.

"1. He admitted in the very fullest manner the *demoralising* character of things as they are, viz. a body of Formularies the general sense of which is recognised, yet which is subscribed by men who notoriously deny that sense, in virtue of judicial constructions imposed by a court of lawyers. He thought the Gorham Case more damaging than the 'Essays and Reviews'—viewed in this light.

"2. He was very explicit in saying that the Essays and Reviews school struck the faith of the people in its heart, viz. the Bible, and that Mr. Wilson's scheme of 'restoration' was inconsistent with any ultimate hold on Christianity. It had all the appearance of correcting the Christian Faith by the light of a modern speculation. He did not, however, see such difficulties in the supposition that the soul might be destroyed. That would satisfy the language about an 'eternal destruction,' etc. He did not know that there was any real reason for believing in the indestructibility of spirit ; he himself did believe it, but the reasons for the belief were not apparent. I pleaded that it was a truth of Natural Religion—part and parcel of the immortality and personality of the soul. He doubted this. . . . I must write to him again about this, when I can put something into order."

To the Same.

"Christ Church, Whit Sunday, 1864.

". . . I send you Goldwin Smith's book, wherein observe (1) his fanatical horror of dogma, (2) his equal dislike (almost recalling Toland, Tindal, etc.) of the clergy as an order. He expresses a moderate phase of the modern Oxford spirit. I told you of the Essay

Club at which last Term the immortality of the soul was denied outright as a vulgar notion (by one of our younger imitators of Fichte). And I fear that 'nice pleasant fellows who believe in nothing at all' is a true definition of not a few of the cleverer men who are turned out hence into the London world. . . .

"Dr. Newman's 'Apologia' is the greatest treat I have had for a very long time indeed. There are some odd bits of mysticism, and some few hints already which make one's heart ache, but the whole is beautiful beyond words. I shall be thankful if he does not make the fifth and sixth Numbers occasion for a propagandist move. It would be hard to avoid it.

"That you are going to preach at Cuddesdon delights me. Though I shall not be there, and now know only a small part of those who assemble on these occasions, I love the place heartily, and hope that your presence will give it a push (which it is said to want) in the right direction. But you will like the Principal, Mr. King."

To Mrs. Hamilton.

"Lugano, July 3, 1864.

"St. Moritz is a bathing-place in the Upper Engadine, about 6000 feet above the level of the sea. The waters are in great repute, and the air, which probably is of more real consequence, is very bracing.

"The whole of the Upper Engadine is Reformed, and the Protestant Services are conducted in the Romansch language—a curious mixture of the Latin and the old Rhætian dialect. But a great many of the peasantry are Catholic, and a Friar comes over the Julier Pass every Sunday to preach and celebrate in the open air. Each Sunday there was a great gathering of the poor people, and Father Hilarius, as he was called, preached sermons of great simplicity and force to them, from which there was indeed much to learn. We visited the mountain lions of the neighbourhood ; among them the Bernina Pass and the Rosegg Glacier were, perhaps, the most remarkable. I have often tried to make out whether one learns more of God from mountain scenery or from the sea. I suppose that in reality He is equally to be studied everywhere in nature, but it has seemed this year as if one meets Him in the 'strength of the hills' as nowhere else. Their stillness, their height, their abysses, their robe of perpetual white, their numberless beauties and dangers, unexplored by the most daring climbers, their very material so unlike the formations of lowland districts, their mysterious beauty changing with the hours of the day, yet at bottom the same,—all remind one of Him."

On Roman Difficulties.

" Sherborne, Dorset, August 22, 1864.

" . . . What you say about the Roman unity is just what one feels—at least, what I feel—whenever I return from abroad. But, on the other hand, (1) such external unity was not primitive ; even now those portions of the Greek and Syrian Churches which communicate with the Roman See retain their own rites. (2) The strictly Latin unity is purchased by the suppression of even legitimate opinion. Newman may not write on ' Faith and Reason.' Passaglia must either hold a particular *political* doctrine or leave Rome. (3) It does not bear examination, or I should rather say it is obliged to hold everything it has ever sanctioned, even indirectly, with equal and indiscriminating tenacity. Thus, for instance, I confess to you that I never pass the Festival of the Assumption (August 15) without being thankful that I am not a Roman Catholic. For here you have an instance of a presumed fact, resting on no historical basis whatever, yet itself made the basis of a devotional expression which rivals Easter Day itself (in the Breviary) in its rank and form, and is, supposing it to be justifiable, exceedingly beautiful. I cannot doubt that, *e.g.*, Newman, in his secret soul, must wish that the Church was rid of this difficulty—a vast devotion resting confessedly on the basis of legend. To me it would be a source of perpetual irritation and distress ; since it would confuse the region of absolute Truth in my mind with the realm of fancy, and make me doubt, at times, whether, after all, my belief was anything better than a sublime and antique poetry. . . . You will think me a great Protestant ; but I am merely saying that I do not think that our own great sores and sorrows are unbalanced by any difficulties elsewhere. Nor does there seem to me any hardship in the double obligation on the one hand of receiving Catholic doctrine, and on the other of remaining loyally where we are. For the question of remaining is one not of taste but of duty. There are many features in the Roman Catholic Church which are much more in harmony with my mind and soul than the corresponding features of our own Church. But the question for us is, not what do we like best, as to this or that, but what is God's Will ? If the Church of England is an organ and channel of our Lord's Life, if she retains the framework of Belief and Hierarchy through which He acts, then it is not for us to ask whether or no she is weak, or diseased, or inadequate to our ideal, or inferior in this and that respect to the Church elsewhere.

" Indeed, it would be wonderful if the schisms of the Tenth and Sixteenth Centuries had been followed by no weakness in the Body of our Lord ; only, if we are to measure Rome by her own standards, we must in honesty admit that she too has lost as much, if not more than we, since she has been drifting forward under the pressure of a doctrinal Development, which union with the East and ourselves would have checked, towards a point, at which her appeal to Antiquity becomes nugatory; and her attitude in presence of the trenchant scepticism of the day is most embarrassing, and fraught with danger to Christianity itself.

"Of course, the 'Apologia' is a wonderful drama; and I love Newman more than ever for his generosity and tenderness towards our friends. But, intellectually, he is the advocate and preacher of a dilemma, ' Rome or nothing '—which I don't believe [is] warranted by the facts of history, but which, if it were so warranted, would, I am well assured, drive more men of our time into sheer unbelief than we can contemplate without a shudder."

" Christ Church, November 7, 1864.

". . . I have read Mr. Allies's ' See of St. Peter,' of which I possess an Italian version, which was given me in Rome in 1852. On comparing it with ' The Church of England cleared from the Charge of Schism,' second edition, I cannot doubt that it was written under a strong sense of the necessity of saying something ; but no independent judge would say that it is a *reply* to his former work. Mr. Allies left the English Church on account of the Gorham Case ; but the Gorham Decision did not alter the real history of the Roman supremacy. How completely the ' See of St. Peter ' failed to answer ' The Church of England cleared from,' etc., was pointed out at the time in the *Christian Remembrancer*, in an article attributed to Mr. R. W. Church, of Oriel College.

" Indeed, we English are not more free of the Roman chair than was the Church of Africa in St. Augustine's day. It had been founded from Italy. Yet it legislated for itself ; and its Bishops were not confirmed from Rome. Look at the case of Apiarius. The Pope of that day did not venture to rest his authority upon the inherent rights of his see, but on a [supposed] warrant of a General Council. St. Augustine simply asked for the Canon, which was not forthcoming. [See the letters of the African Bishops to Boniface and Celestine in Mansi.]

" No one denies the primacy of the West—a primacy, that is, of order—to the Roman Chair. St. Augustine's language, which you quote, must be interpreted by his conduct, and by his language elsewhere. St. Jerome, though living in the East, was himself a Western ; his words amount, at most, to a passionate assertion of the relative peace of the Western patriarchate in his day when contrasted with the distracted East. It is no disrespect to say that he wrote at times very impulsively; his language about Bishops has been part of the stock-in-trade of Presbyterian controversialists since the days of Calvin ; and in defending Virginity against Jovinian, he uses language about marriage which Roman Catholic writers would not defend. In saying this, I am doing little more than translating words of Dr.

Döllinger, which I happened to light upon two or three days ago, and the truth of which I have verified.

"2. When you say that the Immaculate Conception was always held, I am *obliged* to demur. Even if it had been (as, indeed, cannot be proved) always held as an opinion, that fact would not prove it now to be an article of the Catholic Faith. But if St. Thomas says of the B. V. that 'she was immaculate at the time of her birth, but not at that of her conception,' he, in effect, yields the whole point at issue. If the genuineness of the Acts of St. Andrew be admitted, the word 'immaculate' does not prove the 'immaculate *conception*' any more than the expression 'pure virgin' in the Collect for Christmas Day proves it.

"Your quotation from Luther is entirely new to me. His language can only have weight with those who would listen to him when he is writing, say, on the doctrine of Justification, or on the authority of the Epistle of St. James.

"3. I do, indeed, sorrow over your great personal embarrassments. I do not forget you in my prayers—such as these are. Dr. Newman has said that he had an overpowering sense of our Lord's Presence in the Blessed Sacrament, even up to the time of his leaving the English Church. It may help you to recover faith in that Presence, if you reflect on the grace and sanctity which at this moment it yields to so many thoughtful yet believing souls in the English Church. After all, there are times when we must throw ourselves on the authority of others. To receive the Blessed Body of our Lord as if It were merely bread, and as if It suggested nothing beyond an act of spiritual communion, must be very damaging to the spiritual life—to say nothing of the dishonour to our Lord, however little any such be intended, and I am very sure that your intention is to give Him His due. Yet could you not make an act of faith, or pray earnestly for faith, before Communion, with a good hope that He would reveal Himself, at our altars, as clearly to your soul as He does to the souls of numbers of His servants?

"The 'circumstances' which hinder you from leaving us are, and have been all along, a part of His loving Providence, and you do justice to them in allowing yourself to reconsider the convictions which, as you say, date from 1851. It has been said that the one mind of the *highest* order which we have lost is Dr. Newman. And his 'Apologia' proves his conversion to have resulted from the idiosyncrasy of his genius, rather than from obedience to any law, or laws, which can have weight with the many. He himself says enough of the learning and sanctity of Mr. Keble and Dr. Pusey; and *they have no doubts.*

"But I owe you a third apology for thus insisting on what is nearest to my heart; and, although you will regret the having formed an acquaintance with so importunate a correspondent, you will not deny me the pleasure of hoping against hope for your peace and sanctification in the English Church, and of praying our Divine Lord that my hope may yet be realised."

To the Bishop of Salisbury.

"September 7, 1864.

"While you are listening to the successor of St. Paulinus in the nave of your Cathedral, I, *lentus in umbra*, am writing to beg you if you can make any time to read Dr. Pusey's 'Daniel,' which is at length out. If he has not sent it to your Lordship, as he will probably have done, I shall bring my copy at the Ordination. Although I heard several of the Lectures read in the Divinity School, and had gone over the substance of part of them with the Doctor in conversation, I am fairly astonished at the richness and beauty of the published book. One owes this work to Dr. R. Williams, in the same sense as that in which the 'Apologia' is due to Mr. Kingsley. While the notes and purely philological disquisitions must recommend the book to scholars, there are passages of vivid descriptive beauty which every one must understand, and which pour a flood of light upon the prophet's mind, *e.g.* the character of Daniel in Lecture 1 is in Dr. Pusey's happiest and most characteristic style. Nowhere else does he seem to me to unite intellectual strength to lofty spirituality of aim and tone so wonderfully as in this book. It is a real gift of God to the Church."

To the Rev. W. Bright.

"December 23, 1864.

" I don't quite agree with you, dear friend, as to T. T. Carter's letter. I do not understand him to be enthusiastic for ultra-Radicalism, though such an enthusiasm would be more respectable, *selon moi*, as having more of a principle in it than enthusiasm for Whiggery. But he thinks that the Church must have her own politics, and vote for faithful men on either side of the House—*e.g.* he would, I am sure, vote for Lygon with great pleasure ; so should I. But Lygon is not merely a Conservative, and one could not vote for him simply as such. If you look at such specimens of the party as Sir John Pakington, and Mr. Walpole, or ———, or ———, etc., in Oxford, you can't see that you gain much for the Church by identifying yourself with the mere Conservative principle.[1] To men of this temper the Church is merely a part of the Constitution ; and although their traditional tone towards her is more respectful—perhaps I should say less insulting— than that of the Whigs, they have no notion of her Divinity, or of

[1] In sending this letter Dr. Bright remarks, " I must have been rather left to myself if I indicated to Liddon a reliance on the Churchmanship of all Conservative politicians as such ! "

any practical measure which implicitly asserts it. Gladstone expresses an extreme recoil from the disposition to sacrifice spiritual to material interests—to sink the Church in the Establishment. But you won't agree with me, and we are too near Christians to get upon a political difference, or rather a difference as to how best to ensure the same end under difficult circumstances.

" The Doctor's reply to ' Anglicanus' [correspondence in the *Times* between Dr. Pusey and Dean Stanley] seems very full, although he does not touch upon ' Anglicanus's ' glorification of the Nicene Creed (at the expense of the Athanasian) in the teeth of the Articles which put the three Creeds on one level. But every letter of A.'s opens some fresh side of attack, and there is danger of losing sight of the point at issue, whilst pursuing him into the recesses of his wanton inaccuracies."

To the Bishop of Salisbury.

" February 22, 1865.

" I thank you with all my heart for your fatherly kindness in saying that there are passages in my sermon[1] which you would have wished away. Such a criticism is much more welcome and more helpful than the general approval, which no one knows better than I to be undeserved ; and if when I see you I may ask you to say which passages you mean (though I think I can guess), I shall be very grateful. . . . For some of the secular allusions and phraseology St. Chrysostom is responsible. It is curious to see how much of Constantinopolitan life there is in his Homilies ; but, of course, it may be carried too far, and I am peculiarly likely to overstep the line of prudence and true feeling in the matter.

" I had a presentiment that you were ill at the end of last week."

To the Same.

" Pau, Monday in Holy Week, 1865.

" Father Capel is an active, tolerably well-informed, and very gentlemanly man, and does all he can for the ' English Mission.' He came here to luncheon yesterday. After luncheon I had an argument with him of two hours and a half ; it was impossible to allow some of his statements to pass unchallenged. The argument ended as such arguments generally do, in leaving both of us much where we were at starting, and illustrating Madame Neckar's *mot* about arguments in general. But it has done this incidental good : that Father Capel

---

[1] Apparently the sermon preached at St. Paul's on January 22, 1865, and printed by request It is reprinted in " Sermons on Special Occasions," No. IV.

H

has written to me this morning, inviting me to discuss the doctrine of the Church *ab ovo usque;* and I have replied by saying that I have read Passaglia's book on the subject, that I do not suppose that Father Capel can add to Passaglia's arguments, and that I do not think them convincing ; that, on the contrary, I rejoice to live and die in the Church of England.

" I heard Père Félix at Notre Dame. His subject was the Positive Philosophy. His audience almost entirely composed of men—seats being reserved for great literary and political notorieties. His method was wonderfully clear ; his style trenchant and incisive ; his manner apparently too vehement and passionate for a philosophical discussion. His sarcasm was unsparing, and two or three times the suppressed murmur of applause threatened to become a shout of approbation. He reserved the religious and spiritual touches for his wind-up. They were very effective and beautiful. At Bordeaux I heard Père Combalot, a celebrated preacher of a different type. The Cathedral was crowded from end to end, and the preliminary scramble for chairs seemed to me to illustrate the superiority of forms, at any rate where there is a chance of a crowded congregation. Happily, I did not break my leg. Père Combalot was full of anecdotes and epigrams ; he preached for an hour and twenty minutes with an abundance of illustration and resource which was most marvellous.

" He must be at least sixty or sixty-five years of age, his white hair falling down his back in curls ; yet his language and manner were full of fire and eagerness. Of course, I lost some of the touches which evidently excited keen interest in the immense congregation at the foot of the pulpit ; but his denunciation of the Imperial Government for suppressing the Societies of St. Vincent de Paul some time ago, and his picture of the ungodliness of Paris, ' the focus of crime and revolution,' were wonderful passages—plain and bold enough in all conscience. The *Miserere*, which was chanted by the assembled thousands before the sermon, and the *O Salutaris* and other hymns which accompanied the Benediction of the Blessed Sacrament afterwards, were exquisitely beautiful.

" In such a congregation, at such a time, one seemed to realise the too often separated truths, of the solitary life of the soul on the one hand, and of the shelter which Christians find in the majestic and world-wide empire of the Church on the other, with wonderful vividness."

To the Bishop of Salisbury.

" July 22, 1865.

" Of the extent and results of that signal disaster [the rejection of Mr. Gladstone at Oxford] one cannot yet form any tolerably fair estimate ; but, speaking of one consequence which lies in my own line,

I cannot doubt that it will have a baneful influence upon the reviving Church feeling among the undergraduates. Gladstone was a living answer to the often urged objection that practically high intelligence and Church principles were irreconcilable. The majority of the Oxford constituency will now be understood to have decided that the objection is a sound one, to have pronounced—that ' if you wish to be a good Churchman, you must be like Mr. G. Hardy.'

" The pathos of the speech at Manchester makes one love and respect Mr. Gladstone more than ever ; and if I were to trust my feelings I could go in for a very advanced Liberalism in political matters. That the Carlton Club and the *Record* newspaper should oppose Gladstone, was natural and right ; they acted after their kind. That our friends should have enabled them to carry out their wishes is one of the saddest episodes in the history of the Church Movement."

To the Same.

" November 7, 1865.

" What a wonderful Rectorial address was that of Gladstone's ! He seemed to me to overrate the Greek ingredient, so to call it, in modern European life ; we Westerns are much more Romans than Greeks in our whole world of thought and action. His argument obliged him to be hard upon the earlier Apologists for their estimate of the Greek civilisation and culture ; but the Apologists had a great deal to say for their position. Still, what a grasp of a subject lying altogether apart from the field of his daily work and interests did the Address exhibit ! How vivid were its salient points, *e.g.* his discussion of the ' theological use, so to call it, of Apollo ' ! how profoundly religious the resulting moral of the whole !

" Some days in bed are far from an unmixed evil. When one can think or read at all, they yield the passive advantages, at any rate, of a Retreat. One gets a new moral spring, which is a constant need, at least so I find it, at Oxford."

CHAPTER V.

TOUR IN RUSSIA—DEATH OF KEBLE—HEADSHIP OF KEBLE COLLEGE—DEATH OF BISHOP HAMILTON AND CAPTAIN LIDDON—THE CANONRY AT ST. PAUL'S —THE IRELAND PROFESSORSHIP OF EXEGESIS.

1867–1870.

As soon as Liddon had sent his Bampton Lectures to the press, he started for a two months' tour in Russia, with the Rev. C. L. Dodgson, one of his fellow-Students at Christ Church (better known, perhaps, as "Lewis Caroll"). This was only one of many foreign tours; but it has special interest of its own, and the extracts from his diary illustrate well his keen delight in travelling. They stopped at Brussels, in the hope of getting some letters of introduction from Prince Orloff, whom Liddon had recently met in Oxford. But the Prince was away, and they could only arrange to have letters sent to them at St. Petersburg. On their way, they stopped a night at Cologne, and in his diary Liddon writes—

"*July* 15.—Dodgson was overcome by the beauty of Cologne Cathedral. I found him leaning against the rails of the Choir, and sobbing like a child. When the verger came to show us over the chapels, he got out of the way. He said that he could not bear the harsh voice of the man in the presence of so much beauty.

"*July* 17. *Berlin.*—(After two picture galleries in the morning.) At five started on a walk in the *Under den Linden* to the Brandenburg Gate, and round by St. Peter's Church. An evening Service was going on in it. A sermon on the devotion due to Jesus Christ of the whole man; followed by an extempore prayer to 'Herr Jesus Christ,' during which the people all sat, and the Blessing, begun with uplifted hands, and ended with the sign of the Cross. The earnestness and devotion of the young man were very admirable.

"*July* 18.—Spent three hours in the picture gallery of the Musée. I was much delighted with the Italian school, which I had time to study at leisure, specially with the Ghirlandajo's.

"*July* 20. *Saturday.*—After breakfast went with Dodgson to the Jews' Synagogue. The music was equal to some of the very best I have ever heard in Christian churches. It was easy to detect the germ of the Gregorian tunes. The ceremonial at the unveiling and replacing of the Torah was very impressive.

"*July* 22. *Dantzic.*—Went to see the Cathedral, and spent three hours within it, and one on the top of the spire. It is exactly like the grand Nuremberg churches, in its rigid preservation of all the pre-Reformation ornaments. A large number of altars and triptychs behind them are untouched. So is a magnificent 'Christ' over the entrance to the chancel, and a 'Sacrament House.' Murray does no sort of justice to this magnificent cathedral."

At Königsberg he fell ill, and Dodgson compelled him to see a local doctor, who, he says, is "like a very intelligent Chinese." He reached St. Petersburg after a thirty hours' railway journey in the company of a Scotch merchant, "who has great sympathy with Rationalism."

"Our Scotch friend woke us early, and insisted upon talking about Jowett and matters of that kind. He had great sympathy with Jowett's school. I don't doubt that he was a Free Kirk man. . . ."

St. Petersburg struck him greatly.

"The number of the churches and the quaint Eastern character of the inhabitants is unlike anything I ever saw in my life. I had no idea of such a sight in coming here.

"*July* 28. *Sunday.*—Went to St. Isaac's Cathedral. The High Celebration of the Liturgy was proceeding. In front of the holy gates there was a long carpet, upon which most of the ceremonies took place, the people crowding in on either side. The Archbishop was present in a magnificent crown. He blessed the people repeatedly, and they kissed his hands very fervently as he left the church. The devotion of all classes is wonderful. After church a long argument with Dodgson. . . . To-day I feel that for the first time in my life I stand face to face with the Eastern Church. To the outward eye she is at least as imposing as the Roman. To call her a petrifaction here in Russia would be a simple folly. That, on the other hand, she reinforces Rome in the cultus of the B. V. M. and other matters is too plain to be disputed."

To the Rev. W. Bright.

"Hotel de Russie, St. Petersburg, July 29, 1867.

". . . I wish you could have been with me yesterday morning at the Great Celebration in St. Isaac's Cathedral. Of course, the ritual was elaborately complex—bewildering—indeed, to an English mind. But there was an aroma of the fourth century about the whole which was quite marvellous. The vast Church was crowded with people of all classes, from the lowest to, I imagine, the very highest. The Archbishop was present—assisting on a throne in the middle of the church looking toward the holy gates. The choristers wore bright gold-coloured dresses, shaped like dalmatics ; the celebrant and deacons were, of course, very gorgeous.

"There was a short sermon in modern Russian, which, I believe, is very different from the old Church Slavonic ; but, of course, I know nothing of either. A number of very young children communicated ; and troops of infants in arms were brought by their mothers and soldier-fathers to kiss the Icons which were on the Iconostasis, and indeed all about the Cathedral. The devotion of many of the people was exuberant, passionate. They threw themselves flat upon the pavement where there was room ; they kept their heads *close* to the stones for minutes together ; they crossed themselves with a kind of business-like energy, which would be equal to some mechanical labour, such as working at a pump.

"I got between three cabmen, as I imagine them to have been, who were doing this ; and the practical result was—in a crowd—very appreciable. But one would not have had them stop for anything. The entire absence of seats in the churches, the extraordinary glitter of the screens and Icons, and the invisibility of the ministering clergy during large parts of their ministrations, make the appearance of the Eastern Services very unlike anything in the West.

"I cannot understand anybody coming here and saying that the Eastern Church is a petrifaction. Right or wrong, it is a vast, energetic, and most powerful body, with an evident hold upon the heart of the largest of European empires ; indeed, a force within the limits of Russia to which I believe there is no moral parallel in the West.

"This may *seem* a rash conclusion after so short a visit ; I shall retract if necessary. But the churches yesterday surprised and impressed me very greatly, and would account for a rash generalisation of this sort, if it be rash."

Whilst waiting for their introductions, they pushed on through Moscow to Nijni Novgorod.

"Here we reach," he writes, "the easternmost point of our tour.

. . . I am delighted to have been at Nijni Novgorod. It is a peep at the East, the only one I have ever had in my life. For the first time, too, I came upon the traces of the false prophet, but in a country where the Cross, not the Crescent, is in the hearts of the people."

On returning to Moscow he found his long-looked-for introductions.

To the Bishop of Salisbury.

"Moscow, August 14, 1867.

"I have delayed writing to you till I could write about more interesting matters than the ordinary materials of a tour, and since we have been here there has been no lack of this higher interest. Prince Orloff had given me an introduction to Leonide, one of the Suffragan Bishops (there are two) of Moscow, and his kindness has been excessive. He was for some years an officer in the Russian Army; he then became a monk, and has been thus raised to the Episcopate, which is in the East, as your Lordship knows, entirely reinforced from the ranks of the regular clergy.

"Bishop Leonide is a person of great intellectual activity; he takes the keenest interest, for instance, in English politics, and was much concerned to know all that he could about Mr. Gladstone. He had read Renan, Strauss, etc., with great attention, and was very anxious to know how we, in England, dealt with the difficulties which were raised by the German theologians. He 'thought that moral weakness of some sort was generally at the bottom of it. People had reasons for not wishing to believe.' Bishop Leonide is most cordial in his dispositions towards the English Church. He has no doubt, I think, at all about the validity of our Orders, and he rejoices to make the most of all points of *rapprochement.*

"He very earnestly advised me, for instance, to get the English Church Catechism translated into Russ, with notes, in order to point out its fundamental agreement with the orthodox doctrine. And the English Ordinal in like manner. He 'would endeavour to circulate these documents among his clergy, so that we might be better understood.' He entirely admitted our claim to approach the Eastern Churches on a distinct ground from that of the Lutherans and the Protestant communities in general. He gently hinted that our loyalty to our rule of primitive antiquity was not as complete either in theory or, still more, in practice, as might be wished; 'but,' he said, 'I consider the great progress which unbelief is making in Europe is God's voice calling Christians to unite under the banner of Christ, and, that they may do this, to ascertain what the true teaching of the Church of God really is.' He said, 'We are looking with great interest to the proceedings of the Synod of Anglican Bishops which has been summoned by the Archbishop of Canterbury. Something ought to be done to clear the Church of England from the appearance of complicity with that unhappy Dr. Colenso. You appear to me to let him go on as a Bishop just as much as before.'

"I explained that Dr. Colenso had been deposed and excommunicated by the Synod of Cape Town, and that he was only maintained in his present position by the civil authority, which in the colonies, as in England, was very much in the hands of the enemies of the Church of Christ. I think that I succeeded in partially convincing him. 'But, at least,' he said, 'it is due to the souls of the people in Natal that an orthodox Bishop should be consecrated at once.' I told him that this was in immediate contemplation, and that nothing but some technical difficulties had delayed it. He thought that 'the Church of England, if true to herself, ought at the approaching Episcopal Synod to sanction and ratify the acts of the Metropolitan of Cape Town.'

"On Monday, Bishop Leonide allowed me to accompany him to Troitska, about forty miles from Moscow. There I had an interview with Philaret, the Metropolitan. He is in a country retreat near the great monastery. The house is of the humblest description, and very plainly furnished. He received us in a room which had no carpet on the floor, and no papering on the walls, but a *prie-dieu* and several Icons and religious pictures.

"There was also a large print of Canterbury Cathedral, which contrasted strangely (and very pleasantly) with its Oriental surroundings. The Metropolitan spoke Russian, and Bishop Leonide kindly interpreted my remarks ; the interview lasted an hour and a half.

"We discussed the 'defects' (as the Metropolitan considered them) of the English Communion Service, *several* of which (as I insisted) are common to it, with the Roman and other forms of the Petrine Liturgy, which the East had recognised before the Separation. This is especially the case with that on which he laid most stress, viz. the absence of a formal Invocation of the Holy Ghost upon the Sacramental Elements. . . .

"The Metropolitan entered warmly into English Church matters, and into the circumstances of Roman Catholicism in England. He thought the principle of Development was fatal to the old Church principle of an unvarying tradition of the Faith of the Apostles ; he 'could not understand Newman's accepting it, or acknowledging anything so baseless in ecclesiastical history as the Pope's claim of Supremacy.' . . .

"He was deeply grieved at the welcome which had been given to the Sultan of Turkey in France and England, but especially in England. 'To us Eastern Christians,' he said, 'it seems a national repudiation of the Name and Authority of Jesus Christ, when you thus welcome the head of a religion which is His great enemy and which persecutes His servants.' Of course, I urged that the Christianity of England was one thing and its Government another ; that the latter was not, as in Russia, controlled, except in rare cases, by Christian principles; and that the welcome of the Sultan was dictated by considerations of State policy, with which Religion had absolutely no concern whatever. I assured him that many English Christians longed to see the time when Sancta Sophia at Constantinople would be again in the hands of the Œcumenical Patriarch. . . .

"He wished to know whether the University of Oxford was still Christian, or whether it had been deprived of its religious character ; and this led me into a long explanation of the attitude of the anti-religious Liberals.

"Next Saturday (August 17) is the Metropolitan's Jubilee, *i.e.* the fiftieth anniversary of his consecration as Bishop. As Bishop Leonide has promised to take us again inside the Iconostasis, at the celebration of the Liturgy, we are going to be there, please God. Sixteen Russian Bishops and a great phalanx of clergy will be present in the Cathedral of the Assumption at Troitska. I ventured to say to the Metropolitan that I was perfectly certain that if your Lordship (and the Bishop of Oxford) had known of the occasion, you 'would have desired me to present to His Eminence your earnest and respectful congratulations.' The Metropolitan was pleased to reply most cordially, saying that he greatly prized the sympathy of the English Church and her rulers. Bishop Leonide translated his words thus—

"' Dites aux Evêques d'Oxford et de Salisbury que j'accepte avec la plus vive reconnaissance les expressions et dispositions fraternelles dont vous m'assurez—je les accepte avec réverence, avec amour.'

"I presented a letter from the Bishop of Oxford, which, however, the Metropolitan did not read until after I had left him ; probably he could only make it out with great difficulty and with a dictionary, or it would be translated to him by the Rector of the Spiritual Academy at Troitska. . . .

"I would, however, venture to ask your Lordship to write a short formal letter of congratulation to the Metropolitan on the occasion of the Jubilee. It will arrive a little late, but Bishop Leonide told me that such expressions of sympathy would be greatly valued by the Metropolitan and the Russian Episcopate. I have written a similar petition to the Bishop of Oxford, and have further asked him to beg the Archbishop of Canterbury to write to the Russian Metropolitan.

"We have seen a great deal of the Russian Church for passing travellers, and have received a great deal of kindness both from clergy and laity. The two features which have most impressed me are the size and number of the monasteries, and the immense hold of the Church on the people. Of course, the outward forms of Russian religion are even more unlike English ways than those of Roman Catholic countries. But the sense of God's presence—of the supernatural—seems to me to penetrate Russian life more completely than that of any of the Western nations which I have seen, except perhaps the Tyrolese and Styrians.

" The crowded churches and the almost ubiquitous representation of religious truths and ideas by shrines and Icons are beyond anything I have seen in the West. I dare say there is a dark side—indeed, Bishop Leonide hinted as much—in the lack of moral correspondence to religious obligation and the like, but at any rate in Russia Religion has fair play.

" The New Testament in Russ, published at the Synodal Press for about threepence or twopence halfpenny, has the widest circulation. The Old Testament is also published, but is, I believe, less read. The singing in the churches is most beautiful. No organ or other instrumental accompaniment is allowed ; and the human voice seems to be capable of melodies which I at least have never heard in any Western cathedrals. The Liturgy generally used is that of St. Chrysostom, translated into the old Slavonic ; on ten days in the year St. Basil's Liturgy is used. I go with a Greek copy, and follow pretty closely. . . .

" The English Chaplain here, Mr. Penney, is a very good Churchman, and does what he can to cultivate friendly relations with the Russian clergy. I preached at the English chapel last Sunday. One feels that here it is giving the Sacraments to our own people, and not doing spiritual mischief to others—which is, I fear, more than can always be said."

As August 17 was to be observed as the jubilee of Archbishop Philaret, they stayed to see the ceremonies of that day, and spent the interval in a visit to the Convent of the New Jerusalem.

" *August* 15.—Up at six, and left by the eight-o'clock train on the St. Petersburg line for Kriakovo. Thence down to the village of Eriniyo, where we saw a Russian College inside as well as out. Dodgson drew it ; but in this way we lost three-quarters of an hour, and only arrived at Virschchusk at two. Dodgson found one of the monks, F. Nicolas, who could speak French, and he was accompanied by F. Benedict. We saw the Church of the Holy Sepulchre thoroughly ; it is an ' exact ' copy of that at Jerusalem. The dome over the Sepulchre is the most striking feature. Nicon, who built it, is buried there ; and his boots, hat, saws, and other relics were shown to us in the sanctuary. After our dinner we had tea in F. Benedict's cell with two very pleasant ladies, one of whom is directress of the gymnasium at Moscow. We saw the Imperial apartments in the convent, St. Jerome's Cave, the Well of Sychar, the Chapel of the Pool of Bethesda, and the ' skit ' or hermitage, in which Nicon lived while superintending the building of the New Jerusalem monastery. Here was his room and his bed of straw and pillow.

" *August* 17.—Jubilee of Philaret at Troitska. To-day has been a day of disappointments. The weather was very fine, and we started in good spirits. But we did not see Bishop Leonide at the station. On reaching Troitska, we went to the Church of the Assumption, where the Liturgy was being celebrated by the Archbishop of Jaroslaf, assisted by eight other Bishops, one of whom was Philaret, and another Bishop Anthony. We got inside the Iconostasis ; but after some time were turned out. Dodgson made his way round to the other side of the church, and so into the very sanctuary itself ; but I was drifted about in the nave, and saw and heard little or nothing, except the choir. The robes of the Bishops in the distance seemed very gorgeous ; and the final blessing was most touching. Bishop Leonide, it appeared, was celebrating in the other church. After this there was a long delay, during which Dodgson made several efforts to get hold of the Bishop, but to no purpose. We dined at the inn, drove to Belaisne, and saw the monastery there, with its singular church representing the Iconostasis on the top of a natural hill ; then returned and went up the tower of the Troitska Monastery, from which we enjoyed a truly magnificent view, the town of the Troitska, so to call it, being on every side bounded by the forest. Dodgson bought some toys, and at seven we left for Moscow. It is pleasant to have been present on such an occasion ; but the violence of the mob in church made devotion impossible, and I cannot but feel that we have wasted both our time and money in staying here for the Jubilee !

"*August* 18.—Went to the Cathedral of the Assumption, in the hope of meeting Bishop Leonide. A Russian gentleman very kindly took us behind the Iconostasis ; and I was present at a most beautiful and enjoyable Service, which began at about ten and ended at twenty minutes past twelve. Bishop Leonide celebrated ; he was assisted by another Bishop, four Priests, and a great number of Deacons. The Archbishop communicated himself and all the other clergy standing, although there had been a profound prostration when the Consecration was completed. Bishop Leonide's face was beautifully illuminated by moral beauty during the Celebration. [In the evening] we walked in the Kremlin by moonlight. The night was one of extreme beauty, and has left me with an impression of the mysterious charm of that central group of churches and palaces which I shall not forget. To-day the atmosphere has been throughout the dry clearness of Italy : anything like it is rarely visible in England."

He sent an account of the latter part of his stay to Bright before he left Moscow.

TO THE REV. W. BRIGHT.

"Hotel Dusaux, Moscow, August 18, 1867.

". . . Since writing to you we have been to Nijni Novgorod, the Troitska monastery, and the New Jerusalem monastery. Nijni was

' of the earth,' curious to a degree as a great meeting-point of Europe and Asia—a Tartar mosque, from which I heard the Muezzin proclaimed, finding a place among its sixty Greek churches. I should have rejoiced much in going down the Volga into the Caspian Sea, and so home somehow across the Caucasus ; but it could not be, for various reasons. We were taken to Troitska last Monday by Bishop Leonide, one of the Suffragans of Moscow, to whom I had an introduction from Prince Orloff. Bishop Leonide has been exceedingly kind to us in many ways. On Monday, as I said, he took us to Troitska, and to the skit, or hermitage, to see the Metropolitan Philaret. The skit is a wooden cottage in a forest, with a chapel attached. Hard by there is a monastery of penitents, where there are some subterranean solitaries. The caves in which they lived were truly marvellous : they all converged in an underground Church, in which, however, there were some richly jewelled Icons. Philaret was kindness itself, and allowed me to talk with him, through Bishop Leonide, an hour and a half. He was very anxious to know all that he could about English Church matters, particularly what we thought of the Immaculate Conception dogma. . . .

"Philaret has about £7000 a year, all of which he gives away except about £200. His life is evidently modelled on a sterner and grander type than we are familiar with—one which would, perhaps, be impossible in England, but which secures to the Church here an unbounded influence over the people.

"Except perhaps in the Tyrol, I have seen nothing like it in the West. After the celebration of the Liturgy, for instance, this morning, in the Cathedral of the Assumption, Bishop Leonide was nearly crushed by the rush of people seeking to get his blessing ; and this is *always* the case.

"When he took us to Troitska, and we appeared on the Moscow platform, there was a general rush of porters, stokers, cab-drivers, and persons in better circumstances too, to kiss his hand—just such a scene as might be produced in England if Mr. Peabody were to shed shillings and sixpences at Didcot Junction. These people have a profound belief in the blessings which Christ gives in His Church ; although, of course, there are features in their expressions of this faith which seem very strange to us. The frequent use of the sign of the Cross, and the devotions to the Icons, and to particular Icons, exceeds anything of that kind which I have seen in the West ; but the genuine sense of God's presence implied in the universal, or almost universal, practice of praying when starting on a journey, or when passing a Church or a Bishop, or even when bathing, before jumping into the water, is very remarkable.

"Among the higher classes there is, I fear, from what Bishop Leonide said, just now a growing taste for Renan and books of that sort ; but there are a great many deeply religious laymen in the highest ranks of Russian society—more, I should think, in proportion to the whole class than among ourselves; certainly more than in France and Germany. . . .

"I wish you could see St. Chrysostom's Liturgy celebrated here; it is a most beautiful rite. Of course, I don't understand the old Sclavonic; but the Greek Constantinopolitan Use, although differing in a few details, is practically a sufficient guide. The practical difference with the Western Rituals as to the nature of the act of Consecration strikes one much in practice; the Greeks treat it as altogether incomplete until after the Invocation of the Holy Ghost. . . ."

Church questions at home were now seen in a different perspective. Writing to one in perplexity about Roman questions and Anglican difficulties, he says—

To ———

"Hotel de Saxe, Dresden, September 1, 1867.

". . . Bishop Leonide's words, 'The West appears to us to be becoming more and more of a spiritual wilderness,' are really not so 'extreme' a judgment as they sound, when one contrasts Dresden, half Lutheran, half Roman, with St. Petersburg and Moscow. . . . However, these things must be left to the Bon Dieu; one can no more touch the vast issues they involve than the courses of the stars.

"You say that you feel out of heart at the prospect of Reunion, etc., etc. Of course there are plenty of things to make one despond, according to any human principle of calculation. But the distinctive peculiarity of the kingdom of Jesus Christ is that it brings *super*human agencies to bear, and is therefore constantly defeating the most reasonable anticipations of human reason. The report of the Ritual Commission is now the furthest horizon in view. Whatever that Report may be, there are eternal and undying principles at stake, which cannot be either destroyed or advanced by any earthly power. We shall be guided to see what they involve or do not involve; but, meanwhile, God is very well able to take care of Himself, and is not likely to allow the Low Church party to arrange how much of His Truth shall be suppressed or discoloured. So 'hope thou in the Lord, and keep His way.'

"One is tempted to think too much of persons and parties in the immediate foreground, and to forget the Great Agent, Who, as St. Augustine says, 'can afford to wait, because He is Eternal.' . . . Besides which, we must remember that although controversy is very painful and offensive to those who are already, by God's mercy, in possession of truth, it is a necessary instrument for conveying truth to others, and they are sometimes learning the lesson which is to save

them, while they are still holding the raiment of the stoners of St.
Stephen, and doing what they can to oppose and oppress the teachers
of the Truth."

When he returned to England, he found much work
to be done with reference to the foundation of Keble
College. While in the midst of his Bampton Lectures, in
March, 1866, he heard that Keble, whose health had been
failing for some time, had become seriously ill; and almost
immediately afterwards he received news of his death on
Maundy Thursday. Since his early Oxford days, the name
of Keble had been to Liddon one of the most revered of
names; since 1854, when he first came to know him well,
Keble had been the wise guide as well as one of the
greatest examples for him in life. Outside his strong
family ties, no life, except Pusey's, had had so profound an
influence on him; and apart from personal questions, Liddon
felt that the whole Church of England owed a great debt
to the patience, strength, courage, and high example of the
author of the "Christian Year." As soon as the news of
his death came, Liddon determined to do his utmost to
perpetuate his memory worthily in Oxford.

"*April* 5, 1866.—A letter from Mr. Gladstone, proposing immediate
measures about a memorial to Mr. Keble. At 3.10 left the Waterloo
Road Station, with Upton Richards, and Sir Frederick and Lady
Rogers, for Hursley. There at five. Found Mr. Richard Champer-
nowne there with his boys. As the evening advanced others arrived.
(1) Sir George Prevost, (2) Mr. Tom Keble and two boys, (3) Le Geyt.
At 8.15 we went out on the Southampton Road to meet the hearse
coming from the Chandlers Ford Station. It left Bournemouth at
four, and came *viâ* Christ Church, Ringwood, Bishopstoke. It was a
beautiful and starlight night; and the silent movement along the road
in front of the hearse filled me with wonderful thoughts. Dr. Pusey
arrived last of all from Ampfield, where he had left the Bishop of
Brechin. He wishes the College at Oxford to be the memorial: and
to be called Keble College. I trust that this will be so. Before going
to bed we (Dr. Pusey, I, and Tom Keble) went into the study where
the body is laid out, with a cross of white primroses stretching the
entire length of the coffin and a cross and candles at the end. We
remained there in prayer for an hour.

"*April* 6.—Up at 6.30, after sleeping in a room with Mr. Thomas
Keble's boys. The body was taken to the parish church and placed
in the chancel before the early Celebration. The Celebration by

Mr. Richards at 8 a.m. Afterwards I found Dr. Pusey in his bedroom (Miss Keble's old room, close to the dressing-room) quite overcome and unable to speak. With great difficulty could I persuade him to take any food. We went up to the park and saw the Bishop of Salisbury ; and the plan of a College at Oxford, which I had started the night before at Hursley Vicarage, was agreed upon. It is to be called Keble College. Matins at 11.30, followed by the actual Burial Service. The Doctor again nearly broke down when the coffin was lowered into the grave. After the funeral a fuller meeting of ten persons at Sir W. Heathcote's, at which a series of resolutions was drawn up."

Liddon became one of the secretaries of the fund for Keble College, and worked as hard at collecting funds for it as his other engagements would allow. But beyond this Pusey hoped with all his heart that, when the College was started, Liddon would be its first Head, and would pilot it through the troubles of its early days, and give it the impress of his mind. The day after the last Bampton had been delivered, Liddon notes in his diary—

"*June* 4, 1866.—Dr. Pusey said to me to-day, 'You will be startled ; but I hope that you will be the first Head of the new College.' I protested. In the evening I wrote to Lord Beauchamp, telling him why I thought it impossible : (1) on account of the share I had had in getting up the idea of a College ; (2) on account of my not being a First Class man ; (3) on account of the Cuddesdon row when I was 'blown upon.'"

The offer was repeatedly renewed by all who were most interested in the Memorial—

"The Bishop of Oxford pressed me very hard to accept Keble College, and he combated my objections in detail. But he did not persuade me—or anything like it ! Lord R. Cavendish and Mr. Shaw Stewart very eager about the Keble College. What shall I do ? *Deus in adjutorium.*"

In June, 1868, it was important that the matter of the Headship should soon be decided. On June 3 Pusey wrote to ask whether, " apart from his supposed disqualifications, he considered his present work of more importance than the Headship of the College ; " and to Pusey's intense disappointment Liddon sent a reply which was meant to be a final rejection of the offer. But a meeting of the Trustees of the Memorial, on the 18th, empowered the Archbishop of Canterbury formally to offer the post to him ; and on the 20th he received a letter from the Archbishop and two others from Bishop Wilberforce and Lord Beauchamp, urging him to accept it. After two days' consideration he wrote to the Archbishop to decline the offer, and expressed his reasons at length to Lord Beauchamp.

To Lord Beauchamp.

"Brislington, June 22, 1868.

"I scarcely know how to say to you what I must say, without appearing insensible to all the kindness and generosity of your letter. But after giving two full days to a careful and anxious consideration of the Archbishop's letter, I have felt it to be my duty to write to his Grace this morning declining the Headship of Keble College.

"You will remember that when Dr. Pusey first broached the subject a year ago, I wrote to you, begging you to use your influence with him to persuade him to think of some one else. Since then he has from time to time hinted at the subject more or less plainly, and in a way which made one feel that I might have to face the present question, and that it was a duty to consider it. I can truly say that for months I have brooded over it with no little anxiety, but I have never really had any opinion but one as to my real unfitness for a position of the kind. The effect of the Archbishop's letter is not to disturb the intrinsic grounds upon which, as I think, that opinion rests, but to oppose to it an overwhelming weight of authority. It may be said that I ought to close my eyes and obey, and during the last two days I have been considering whether or not this is indeed the path of duty.

"It appears to me clear that to constitute a real call from God there is required not merely the outward voice of authority but the inward ratifying verdict of the conscience. In the present case this last is altogether wanting, or rather, in place of it, there is a distinct and energetic conviction that my actual powers, and still more the experience of my past life, ought to make it morally impossible for me to entertain the question.

"I do not, I assure you, undervalue all that is involved in your assurances respecting the appointment of a bursar, and the restriction of the direct educational duties of the President to Divinity Lectures. But these concessions to my sense of unfitness are dictated, I cannot but feel, by your friendship for myself rather than by your judgment of what is best for the interests of the College. Even if, as is probable, a bursar would under any circumstances be necessary, he must be controlled actively and vigilantly by the President, unless the College is to get into financial embarrassments, or the real administration of the place is to pass into the hands of the bursar. And looking to the probable material that any President could command in the way of tutors, I do not think that he could, consistently with the interests of the College, confine himself to Divinity Lectures. As Medd said to me some time ago, ' He must be head tutor, and the ablest of the tutors too.'

" In any case, if the College is to realise the expectations which are formed about it, the President must be a person to whom on intellectual, as well as on moral grounds, respect will be paid by tutors of first-class ability. For, as I need not say to you, the real battle-ground in modern Oxford is not so much theology, as mental philosophy. So long as Mill, Bain, and Herbert Spencer hold their present position of predominance in the Honour work of the Literæ Humaniores school, and in examinations for the best Fellowships, all serious Theology is fatally undermined, because the first and highest Theistic truths are denied either point-blank, or by necessary implication. If Keble College is really to grapple with the gigantic evils of modern Oxford, it must be by creating an intellectual, as well as a moral enthusiasm, which shall secure it a good place in the Class-List, without exacting the loss of faith as the price of success. Deeply convinced as I am of the necessity of this work, I also know, well enough, that I am not the man to do it, and indeed that no President of the College could hope really to succeed in it, who was not himself prepared to assert his intellectual control over the subjects which are most essential to high academical success.

" These considerations may convince you that it is desirable to get a man of very different intellectual calibre from myself, and I should add, if possible, a younger, or anyhow a more vigorous one, whose past life does not reinforce any presentiments of failure with the reason of experience. But I shall not easily forget all your kindness in the matter, or cease to regret that my love and honour for Mr. Keble's name must, beyond everything else, prevent my obeying the wishes of so many persons in high authority who are so eager to honour it."

But he could not escape so easily. He was urged again by all his friends to change his mind.

" *June* 27.—Sat some time with the Bishop of Oxford, who is very anxious that I should take Keble College. Wrote to the Bishop of Salisbury, asking him to decide the Keble College question for me authoritatively. Left for Windsor at 5 p.m. Did not get out at Slough, supposing I had been put into a Windsor carriage, and was carried on to Taplow. Had to drive thence to Windsor through Burnham. Mr. and Mrs. Gladstone staying in the house [Deanery]. Mr. Gladstone thought Lord Salisbury's a very fine speech [on the Irish Church

Suspensory Bill the night before], although there were some violent arguments in it.

"*June* 28.—Went with the Dean to Matins in the Private Chapel at 10 o'clock. At 12 to Litany, which the Dean of Windsor said, and then I read the Communion Service and preached the sermon on 1 St. Pet. v. 5 : ' Humility '—extempore. The Duke of Edinburgh sat next to the Queen. Duckworth said that the Queen was pleased."

He had been specially anxious about this sermon, and had asked Bishop Wilberforce's advice whether he should on this occasion preach a written sermon instead of preaching without notes, as was his general habit at this time of his life. The Bishop told him that he should certainly preach just as he always preached. And so he preached on Humility, as being based on a sense of living in the presence of Him Who is the Ideal of Perfect Human Virtue, and on a realisation of our indebtedness to the Love of God. He pointed out that it was in no way inconsistent with the necessary assertion of Truth, with the duties of exalted station, or the demands of a busy life.

This was the only occasion that he preached before the Queen, and many absurd stories have been told about what he said. The only letter at this time referring to his Windsor visit was to the Bishop of Salisbury.

To the Bishop of Salisbury.

"10, St. Andrew's Place, June 30, 1868.

"The Windsor episode was made very pleasant by Mr. and Mrs. Gladstone's being at the Deanery, where I stayed. Mr. Gladstone always reminds me of dear Mr. Keble's words, 'If he could only spend his Saturdays and Sundays with the country clergy in succession, there would be no doubt of his being returned for Oxford.' He was very full of the Suspensory Bill.

"What an extraordinary speech was the Bishop of Oxford's last night ! His fertility and resource are astonishing. But I could have wished that one or two things had been left out ; and the demonstration of the doctrinal identity between St. Patrick and the present Archbishop of Armagh is not quite conclusive. The Archbishop's Protestantism interferes with the argument too energetically."

The Bishop of Salisbury refused to have any discussion

with him at that moment about the Headship of Keble College; but he corresponded with Pusey about it, and advised Liddon to take his holiday before finally deciding. In August Liddon seemed for a moment shaken by the weight of authority against him; but he never really wavered in his decision. Even as late as April, 1869, when Liddon was urging Edward Talbot's qualifications for the post, Pusey again pressed it on him. Liddon only replied—

To Dr. Pusey.

"April 16, 1869.

"As to myself, I deeply feel and thank you for all your kindness. You see all your friends—and me beyond others, I fear—in the light of your love and generosity. But, as you know, my own conviction of my unfitness for such a post has, from the first, been clear and strong. Had it been otherwise, I must long ago have yielded to so much pressure. As it is, I cannot help feeling in all sincerity that, whomever you may appoint, you will appoint a better Principal than I could be."

In the latter part of 1868 and the greater part of the following year, Liddon was very little in Oxford. As has already been said, after Dr. Pusey and Mr. Keble, Bishop Hamilton had the greatest influence on his life; and now the Bishop's work was over, and the shadows of a long illness were closing round him, and Liddon spent at his side all the time that he could spare. Their conversation was naturally about the anxieties of the Church, and especially about Mr. Disraeli's nomination of Dr. Tait to the See of Canterbury and of Dr. Jackson to the See of London.

To Mrs. Ambrose.

"Palace, Salisbury, Christmas Eve, 1868.

". . . The Bishop does not, I think, improve. He gets sleep by means of opiates, but he is very restless and ill during the day.

"You see that the Judicial Committee has decided against Mackonochie on all the counts, and he is to pay the expenses in both Courts. . . . It really seems as if everything were going against the Catholic party in the Church of England. Between these miserable appointments [to Canterbury and London], and these miserable decisions of a Court whose very existence is, religiously speaking, a crying outrage, we are very hard pressed. I feel sure that all sorts of troubles are ahead; both the Puritans and the Rationalists are more bitter and menacing than ever, and, what is worse, our own people are very far from wise. God will help us, I think, if He means the English Church to go on witnessing for Him at all—to any purpose. But I confess to having fewer hopes of the future than for many years past."

At the beginning of January the Bishop went to London for medical advice, and remained there in a critical state for six months. Liddon was with him as much as possible. He used to go to Oxford from Saturday till Tuesday for his Sunday evening Lectures and the meetings of the Hebdomadal Council; but he put off all other engagements as far as possible, including a course of sermons which the Bishop of London had asked him to preach at St. James's, Piccadilly. This prolonged stay in London brought him into a closer relation with the London view of Church matters, and into contact with Bishop Hamilton's constant visitors, including Mr. Gladstone, Lord Carnarvon, and Sir Robert Phillimore, and also with many other intimate friends of his later years.

To Mrs. Ambrose.

" 10, St. Andrew's Place, Regent's Park, March 16, 1869.

". . . The Bishop is at much the same level as when I last wrote to you. He may go on as he is for a very long time. Dr. Gull now again speaks of months. He constantly alludes to his death in all sorts of ways. Yesterday he saw Sir Robert Phillimore, and the day before Edward Denison, who has just got into Parliament, in the Liberal interest, for Newark, and to whom the Bishop gave some very sound advice.

"Dr. Pusey was here for two days in last week—to see people. I was delighted to find out that he and others are thinking now quite seriously of somebody else for Keble College. So I *hope* I am out of that wood, or near the mouth of it.

"If Coleridge's Bill becomes law, as I suppose it will, I shall, I think, leave Oxford, and attach myself to one of the High Church churches here in London as a fellow-worker. But this is at present only an idea, although one to which my mind more and more inclines. My long absence from Oxford this spring would of itself lead naturally to my losing my seat in the Council at the Michaelmas election, and that is a chief tie which binds me to the place. When all has been handed over to the infidel party, it will be the best course for Churchmen, as it seems to me, to let things get as bad as they possibly can, by withdrawing to other fields of work, of which, as God knows, there are plenty. I am more grieved than I can say to see that Mr. Gladstone supports the Bill this year. If the real object had been to admit Dissenters to Fellowships, that might have been secured by giving up a certain number of the Colleges to them, without destroying the religious character of the whole. . . . The only great difficulty about leaving Oxford will be the Doctor ; his sanguine temperament refuses to look at the full bearings of an adverse case.

"The cold here has been very great during the last two or three days, and the green things which had begun to grow look terribly pinched, like Christians after a ' Judgment' of the Privy Council. By-the-by, I have got into a certain sort of hot water for a Sermon about that P. C. at Oxford the other day, which accordingly I must print."

On July 29, the Bishop was moved to Salisbury at his own wish, as it was clear that the end was very near. Liddon was spending a few days at Clifton, where his father was lying very ill ; but the news from Salisbury was so serious that he decided he had better go there at once.

"*July* 31.—Found him in the drawing-room, on the south side, lying under Bishop Burgess's picture. He was much moved at seeing me, but could say nothing. Could not bear to be talked to. Is greatly changed since Wednesday week. In the evening I prayed with him, and on my saying that he would feel the truth of our Lord's promise, ' When thou passest through the waters I will be with thee,' he pressed my hand and nodded assent. In the morning he had told Mrs. Hamilton that he was quite ready to go. He is not to-day suffering any pain. *Deo gratias*.

"*August* 1.—At twenty minutes after midnight Mirehouse called me, and I found the Bishop breathing with increased difficulty. Prayed with him at intervals. ' O Saviour of the world, Who by Thy cross,' etc., and the Passion prayer from the Litany. Breathed short ejaculatory prayers to our Lord into his ear. Said the *De Profundis*, and a commendatory prayer as he was dying."

The next day he returned to Clifton, to be near his

father, who had rallied, and was ready to talk eagerly of his old life in the Navy.

"*August* 2.— . . . My dearest father's conversation was quite delightful. He described the violence of Captain Burdett of the *Maidstone;* the history of his imprisonment at Cumana, in South America ; his kindly treatment by the Spaniards ; his escape, after breaking his parole advisedly and being locked up ; the capture of a schooner and their voyage to Jamaica ; his escape by twenty-four hours of being sent by the *Heureux*, which foundered, to Halifax ; his capture of the *Dolphin* privateer in the Rappahannock, whose Captain's sword he still possesses."

He went back to Salisbury for the Bishop's funeral, and preached the funeral sermon in the Cathedral on August 8. After the funeral he remained there to write a short life of the Bishop, the revision of which occupied much spare time at many places. In acknowledging a copy of the sermon, Bright added some expressions of deep regret at some verses on the Bishop's death which had been attributed to Liddon.

To Dr. Bright.

"Clifton, August 24, 1869.

". . . I quite agree in your feeling about funeral sermons. But I had no choice ; anything less would have been open to misconstruction. Besides which, I always fear the mistake of interpreting large popular moral instincts by one's own fastidiousness. The people expect eulogy when it is due, as they expect many other things when they are due, and to disappoint them is to create a positively false impression.

"This being the case, one is obliged to forego the 'luxury of silence' in order to redress the balance, and avoid misunderstandings which damage those who entertain them. Certainly, in such a case as Mr. Keble's, a funeral sermon would have been an impertinence. I was asked to preach one at Hursley on the Sunday after his funeral, and declined. But when the Dean of Salisbury asked me to say what I thought of Bishop Hamilton's character, I felt that, in presence of a vast array of hostile criticism and prejudice, I had no moral choice in the matter ; although, as you will perhaps have observed, I relieved myself of as much responsibility as I could by making the dear Bishop speak for himself.

"As to the verses, they are *not* mine. In the *Salisbury Journal* of August 7, where they first occur, the order of the initials is H. L. P. This may naturally have been taken for a transposition of *my* initials ; but they are, I believe, those of Mr. Prior, an excellent layman, who lives in the Close at Salisbury. Although I have never heard this, I have no doubt of his being the author. As for me, you, dear friend, might have reflected that so prosaic a person could never have written anything at all up to their mark of excellence. It is, I think, fifteen years since I ever tried my hand at any versification ; I won't say— poetry.

"We have the shadow of a great sorrow here, I think, resting on us. My father's condition has become so much more critical, that for the present I have abandoned all thoughts of going abroad. On Sunday we thought he was sinking away ; but there is a considerable rally to-day. However, we are told not to think of his pulling through the coming winter ; and this makes all the remaining time very precious—more, indeed, than one can say or think.

" I have not seen the *Church Review*, but conjecture that the verses must be those which I have before me in the *Salisbury Journal*."

He had returned to Clifton before writing this letter, and was waiting at his father's bedside for the rapidly approaching end.

"*August* 25.—He told me in the morning, ' I know very well that I cannot be here for long ; I pray God that the passage may be as little painful as possible.' On my asking him, he said, ' I wish to ask you before you go away to administer the Holy Communion to me. I did receive it down at Taunton.'

"*August* 28.—At 7 a.m. I administered the Holy Communion to my dear father. He followed the Service throughout most attentively, saying, ' Amen, amen,' at the close of it. He told me that it had given him the ' greatest gratification.'

"*August* 30.—At 11, my father had terrible pain. . . . ' Death itself,' he said, ' could not be worse than what I have gone through.' . . . I told him to put his trust in our Lord, and be sure that He would help him. ' I have had,' he said, ' an assurance of that.' After my reading the *De Profundis*, he said out clearly for himself, ' Lord, have mercy, Christ, have mercy, Lord, have mercy.' Then several times the word, ' Pardon, pardon, pardon.' His breathing became more rapid towards midnight—then a sudden slowness of breath ; the last was drawn at one minute to 1 a.m., August 31, by my watch. *Requiescat in pace.* What a solemn August this has been, beginning on the 1st with the death of my dearest Father in Christ, and ending on the 31st in that of my dear father in the bonds of nature ! May I have grace not wholly to miss the lesson ! "

FROM DR. PUSEY.

"September 4, 1869.

" I only had your letter to-day, having been detained on the road. *Requiem æternam dona ei, Domine.* I will remember him at the altar to-morrow. It is a different world when there is no father on earth to look up to, and to have only to look to those who look up. God comfort you all."

In varied ways Liddon had been so much before the public that it was taken for granted that he would soon receive some ecclesiastical preferment from the Crown. Two days after Bishop Hamilton died, the *Daily News* deprecated his appointment to the See of Salisbury, almost as if it was taken for granted. Early in September the Bishop of Exeter, Dr. Philpotts, resigned; and when Liddon was staying for a short holiday at Penzance, he found a West-country paper announcing that the appointment had been offered to him, and a reporter waiting upon him to know if it was true. "I was thankful to say 'No,'" he adds in the diary. On November 5 he received a letter from Sir R. Phillimore, begging him not to decline the Canonry at St. Paul's, which Canon Dale was expected to vacate, in case it should be offered to him.

Liddon had been spending his Christmas vacation first in Pembrokeshire and then at Bristol, trying to prepare his deferred course of Lent Lectures at St. James's, Piccadilly, when, on February 6, he received a letter from Mr. Gladstone, asking him if he would be willing to accept a Canonry at St. Paul's, in case he should make an arrangement which would involve a vacancy there.

He went at once to Oxford to consult Pusey and Bright.

" *February* 6.—Dined with Dr. Pusey; he was not at first adverse, but gradually he became so, on the ground that I should be taken away from Oxford, and ought to remain to work the Theological School and prevent its getting into the hands of the Rationalists. He became very pathetic and emphatic.'

In the end he wrote to Mr. Gladstone, saying that the conflicting claims were so perplexing to his advisers and to himself, that he should be heartily satisfied with any decision that Mr. Gladstone should reach.

But it was not settled so easily. At that moment the Ireland Professorship of Exegesis at Oxford fell vacant by the unexpected resignation of Dr. Scott, the Master of Balliol. Pusey set his heart upon Liddon's being appointed in his place ; and it was taken for granted by many who differed very widely from Pusey that Liddon would be elected. He was clearly marked out for it by the position he already held in the University. But if he was made Canon of St. Paul's, would he be qualified for, or, if elected, be able to undertake the Professorship ? Pusey hoped he would hold both (as the emolument of the Professorship was very small), if only he did not disqualify himself by severing his connection with Oxford before the Election. In reply to a most earnest appeal, Liddon wrote—

To Dr. Pusey.

"Brislington, February 8, 1870.

". . . As to the future, I gladly undertake not to leave my residence at Christ Church until I am either turned out by the Censors or obliged to enter upon daily duties elsewhere. The latter obligation may be beyond my control.

"I had not heard of the Master of Balliol's resignation. If St. Paul's comes to nothing, I cannot for the moment promise to be a candidate for the Exegetical Chair, for the very reason that it involves a candidature. The chief recommendation of St. Paul's, as of all that I have hitherto had to do in life, is that, if it comes to me at all, it comes without any effort on my own part to get it. This was a point on which Mr. Keble used to lay much stress ; and I think you would do so in the abstract, and where all your personal tenderness was not embarked on one side of the question. (In the case of the Bampton Lectures, I was rejected when I sent in my scheme in April, 1865 ; then Haddon, who had been elected, fell ill, and the Heads asked me to fill the gap at a pinch as well as I could.) For the Exegetical Chair there would be many candidates, and much self-advertising would be necessary in order to succeed."

But he felt so keenly the pain of disappointing his

revered friend in his age and loneliness, that in his distress he wrote again the same day, authorising him, if he thought the interests of the Church required him to stay in Oxford, to write in his name at once to the Prime Minister and decline the Canonry. Pusey was deeply touched. "Thank you," he wrote, "for all your loving confidence in me. God bless it to you." But he declined to interfere with a decision. "When a decision is made with a Prime Minister, it looks like shilly-shally to change it." And Liddon's appointment to the Canonry was announced in the *Times* of February 16.

Congratulations, of course, poured in from all sides. One only need be quoted ; it strangely links the past of two lives with a future of which neither of them then dreamt.

FROM THE REV. R. W. CHURCH.

"Whatley Rectory, February 11, 1870.

"The days are a long way off when we used to meet at the Observatory. But though I feel that I am almost taking a liberty in writing to you about anything happening to you now, I hope the remembrance of those old times will excuse me for venturing to say how exceedingly glad I am that you are beginning, in place and outward function, to be something answering to what in reality you have so long been among us. You do not need congratulations. But I cannot help remembering how Johnson used to feel about you ; and I cannot help imagining what he would have said now. I hope you may long be able to do us the services of which your heart is full, and of which we have had the first-fruits."

Liddon replied—

TO THE REV. R. W. CHURCH.

"Christ Church, February 12, 1870.

"I do not know how to thank you, as I should like to thank you, for all the kindness of your letter. It alludes to much that I at least have never forgotten and can never forget—and which brightened my earliest years in Oxford. Dear Johnson's kindness was the great sunshine of my undergraduate life ; and your part in it was only less than his. In the retrospect those years seem to me like the threshold of an ideal world, which, in the event, I have too nearly lost sight of. In some ways, however, I hope—and am sure—that they have been a permanent blessing, although, of course, much less than they might have been."

In the Lent of 1870 Liddon fulfilled the promise which he had made to the Bishop of London in the preceding year, by delivering a course of Sermons on Sunday afternoons at St. James's, Piccadilly. It was the last course he ever undertook outside St. Paul's. The Bishop wished his Sermons to deal with the special form of religious difficulties which were at that time current in educated society ; and their appropriateness for this purpose was abundantly shown by the attendance of men in crowds Sunday after Sunday to listen to closely reasoned Lectures three times the length of ordinary Sermons. The subjects were the fundamental truths of Religion, God, the Soul, Sin, Prayer, and a Mediator. The Sermons were published as soon as he could manage to find time to prepare them for the press, under the title, "Some Elements of Religion."

Meanwhile, Pusey was continuing to use every effort to secure his appointment to the vacant Professorship. But Liddon absolutely refused to be one of many candidates for the Chair ; he thought such a candidature would be unseemly self-intrusion ; nor would he on any account canvass any of the electors. So Pusey had to plead with him in these terms—

From Dr. Pusey.

"Christ Church, March 24, 1870.

"Now, may I say to the Vice-Chancellor, 'Liddon has the greatest (or if you will, an insurmountable) objection to offer himself as a candidate. The Canonry of St. Paul's came to him without any thought of his own. But if the Professorship came to him equally without any instrumentality of his own, it would be equally a call from God, and he would account it a duty to accept it'? Now, I have not said one word to advocate your being so appointed. Professor H. Smith expressed the spontaneous feeling of all sides, 'It will be Liddon, and we shall be well satisfied with it.' Of course, he might have preferred an advanced Liberal, but he thought it a good appointment in the interests of solid knowledge and power.

"I have not the slightest doubt that if I were to say, 'Liddon, if elected, would think it his duty to accept it,' you would be elected unanimously. Now, do let me say thus much. I will promise not to say one word more or in any way to bias any elector. It is an easy promise, for there is no need. Whether or no to retain the Canonry is easily settled. People take it for granted that the two are compatible. If not, in the interest of Oxford and the Church through Oxford, I should say, 'Let St. Paul's go, and trust in God's providence.'"

Liddon still protested. His diary is strangely a blank for all the early part of 1870. But on June 11 he writes in it—

"At 4 p.m. I was elected by the Heads of Houses Professor of Exegesis. Saw Bright and the V.C. A letter from the Dr. in the highest glee."

He received the degree of Hon. D.C.L. at the Encænia on June 22, and was made B.D. and D.D. by decree of Convocation on November 22.

Thus, in eight years of active unofficial work Liddon had come to be recognised as one of the leaders of thought in Oxford, and as one of the most attractive and powerful defenders of the Faith and preachers of Righteousness in the English Church. Now, he unexpectedly found himself placed, against his will, in two great offices, each of them happily matching his high gifts, and each by itself sufficient for a man's whole strength.

CORRESPONDENCE, 1868–1870.

On our Lord's Human Knowledge.

"January 11, 1868.

"Your difficulty appears to me to assume that a limitation of knowledge and a liability to error necessarily go together—that because our Lord admits His 'ignorance' of the date of the Day of Judgment, He is ignorant also of the authorship and claims of the Pentateuch, about which He does not profess ignorance, but, on the contrary, makes distinct assertions.

"Now, I should have thought that the reverse was the more natural inference.   If a human teacher tells me that he is ignorant of A, but goes on to talk confidently about B, I am led to trust his profession of knowledge in the case of B all the more readily from his admission of ignorance in the case of A.

"You will, I fear, think me superstitious, or foolish, but I should not 'allow' our Lord's ignorance of other languages, besides Syro-Chaldaic, in the absence of proof that He was so ignorant of them. The natural assumption is that He knew them, unless His ignorance had been revealed.   So about losing His way in going from village to village.   We have only one distinctly recorded instance of limitation of His knowledge, and we have, as it seems to me, absolutely no ground for inferring ignorance in any other case, certainly not in cases when it is clear that He spoke as believing Himself to know.

"What I have said about our Lord's moral perceptions being at fault, refers, of course, not to the denial of the Mosaic authorship of the Pentateuch, but to the positive Rationalistic theory about Deuteronomy, viz. that while professing to be Mosaic, it was really composed for a particular purpose in the reign of Josiah.

"It seems to me, if this was the case, our Lord was not only ignorant of a fact of archæology, but that He was unable to detect the moral obliquity which must enter into the structure and thoughts of a forged document.

"But however this may be, it seems important to observe that it is not merely the 'authorship' of the Pentateuch which our Lord's quotations assume, and which is disputed by modern Rationalism.   It is whether the Pentateuch contains legends instead of history.   Our Lord, for instance, refers to the Noachian deluge, to Lot's wife, and—to take another case—to Jonah's being in the fish.   It is admitted that He refers to these things as literal matters of fact.   Modern Rationalism says that they are legends.   If we accept this conclusion, I do not see how we can trust our Lord when He says, in St. Matt. xxv., that He will come to judge the world.   Why should He not have been mistaken here, too ; first, in attributing to the prophecy of Daniel the force of a description which was to be literally fulfilled, and, secondly, in claiming Himself to fulfil it ?

"In short, I do not believe that it is possible to draw a line between Christ's ' doctrine concerning His Father and Himself,' and the other parts of His teaching.   To suppose that our Lord is really ignorant of any one subject upon which He teaches us as One Who believes Himself to know, appears to me to admit a solvent which must speedily break up all belief in His authority and teaching whatever."

To ———

On the Unity of the Church.

"Salisbury, Easter Monday, 1868.

"The answer to Père Hyacinthe's argument, in my mind, is as follows :—

"1. It is true that our Lord meant His Body to be visibly One. St. Paul speaks of One Body as well as of One Spirit.

"2. He also meant it to be perfectly holy, without spot or blemish, and Catholic—that is, literally the religion of the whole human race. These last two points I need not prove to you ; they are admitted.

"3. Can any one Christian body—the Church of Rome any more than the Church of England, or the orthodox Eastern Church—pretend to full possession of the 'note' of Sanctity? There are saints in her, no doubt. But the net contains more bad fish than good ; the sanctity is attributed to an abstraction, not to the concrete mass of men and women who receive the Sacraments of the Roman Church. In like manner—Is the Church of Rome, as yet, Catholic, or anything like it, in the sense of the promises? Why! all Christians taken together do not form a third of the human race ; and unbelievers are telling us every day that the promised conquest of the world is an utter failure. And on this point, how do we reply to them, whether at Rome or in Oxford? We say that the ideal range and the ultimate fulfilment of these promises is one thing ; the historical travail of the Church, another. Centuries are nothing to God. The Church is Catholic enough to make us sure that she will one day be literally more so ; holy enough, to satisfy us that Christ is in the midst of her. These 'notes' will be completed one day, and meanwhile we wait, in patience.

"4. Why is it not to be thus with the 'note' of Unity? You say that Unity is a visible, matter-of-fact thing which we do or do not see. Yes ; but the promise, 'All nations shall fall down before Him ; all people shall do Him service,' is a matter-of-fact promise which has or has not been kept. You say, that Unity was to be an evidence of Christianity patent to the eyes of heathens. Yes, but a holy charity was also to be such an evidence : 'By this shall all men know that ye are My disciples, that ye have charity one towards another.' In point of fact, the note of Unity, like the other notes of Sanctity and world-embracing Universality, has been only partially realised in history. As yet, between the promise and its fulfilment, there is a gap. Suppose that you give up the English Church to the tender mercies of Père Hyacinthe. What do you say to the orthodox East? I presume —— would term it 'Photianism,' making a depreciatory term do the work of an argument. But read Mr. Ffoulkes's second volume on the Divisions of Christendom—I do not say for its opinions, but for its facts. Unless history be utterly untrustworthy, it is *certain* that in the controversy which led to the Separation of the Tenth Century, Rome was wrong, and that the process by which the *Filioque* was introduced into the Creed was a flat defiance of the Œcumenical Council of Ephesus. Under these circumstances, who is the real schismatic? Certainly the Russian Bishops have no doubt on that point. They too say that the Church ought to be visibly one ; but then they speak of their own exclusive possession of that unity with a calm certainty which, to say the least, is quite on a par with the Roman tone. They deplore the sin and the danger of the one Patriarch who continues in wilful separation from the Four, and who only separated from the Four because they would not allow him to establish an autocracy in the Church which Christ had willed to be ruled by a band of brothers, whose co-operation should be secured not by a piece of governmental mechanism, but by supernatural charity. As Mr. Keble said two years before his death, ' If the Church is never one, other than visibly, *then* it is a question whether the one Church does not exist only in the East.' . . . You may say that you have no sympathies with the stiffness, etc., of the Easterns. But the question is not one of taste, but of rigid historic fact ; and if the Romans appeal to history—they are not quite prudent —but to history they must go. And the history of the Church forces on any fair mind the conviction that neither the East nor Rome *can be* external to the kingdom of the Saviour. But this implies that visible Unity may be suspended—whether for a day or for ten centuries, it matters not—and that on either side of the dividing line there is to be found the Presence of Christ. In other words, the note of Unity is, historically speaking, modified, if you like, obscured ; just as are the notes of Sanctity and Universality. Wherever there are the Sacraments, and the Succession, and the Œcumenical Faith, there is Christ ; there, too, is the capacity for reunion of other portions of the Body which retain these things. Unity in potentiality, as distinct from Unity always visible in fact, is our Lord's own historical interpretation of His promise hitherto ; that it will always be so, is not what we should expect, but a point beyond the present discussion.

" This, then, to my mind, covers the case of the English Church. If the East did not run out like a jetty, breaking up the advancing wave of the Roman argument, our position, I admit, would be a much less defensible one. As it is, I could only acquiesce in the *à priori* considerations pressed by Père Hyacinthe, on grounds which would incline me to look to Constantinople rather than to Rome for relief. It is just as certain that the Supremacy is an up-growth of the Western Church, having no real justification in antiquity, and modelled upon the secular type of the imperial authority rather than anything else, as that the Prince of Wales is the son of Queen Victoria. This being so, such an earthly element has necessarily produced disintegration, as from time to time it has put forward claims to be divine. So it was in the East under Photius ; so it was in Northern Europe in the sixteenth century. The Supremacy was the real author of the ruins introduced by the Reformation, as it had been of the heartburnings of the East. In England those ruins were large enough, but they left the vital framework of the Church intact. Probably Père Hyacinthe knows as much about the rights and wrongs of the question of English Orders as I know about the working of the Roman Congregations. He takes what he hears and reads for granted ; to him the question is external, speculative, and of secondary importance ; to us it is vital and of the first importance. When he says that English Church-men are out of communion with the Pope by their own fault, it is, of course, true that in a free country no man belongs to the English or any other Church except on the ground that he deliberately wills to do so. But it is not the fault of England that she is out of the pale of Rome ; it is the fault of Rome insisting upon uncatholic terms of com-munion. The divorce question of Henry and the rabid Calvinism of Edward's advisers had been ended by the reconciliation under Mary. With Elizabeth the wound was reopened ; and the excommunication of England by Pius V. was simply due to the self-asserting spirit of the Supremacy, resolved, at all costs, to maintain an autocratic authority in the West. Had the English yielded on that one point, all else would have been conceded.

" The real question, then, is : What is the evidence for the Roman doctrine of *the Supremacy* (not the Primacy in order) of the Pope? This would take a book to answer ; and you know that we have often talked it over. But this is the real point on which the question of conduct hinges, and not any *à priori* theory of unity. If the Romans are right about the Supremacy, all follows ; if wrong, then either Constantinople is the centre of the Catholic world, or the Unity of the Church is dynamic, and there is room within its pale for the English Episcopate, as well as for the Bishops who communicate with the Pope. . . ."

To Lord Carnarvon.

On the Relation between the State and the Church.

" Palace, Salisbury, June 13, 1868.

" . . . I have long felt that the old theoretical arguments for Establishment, to the effect that the State, as a corporate person, must have a conscience, and therefore a religion, was fatally ruined by William III.'s proceedings in Scotland. Since the establishment of Presbyterianism in that country, Great Britain has had two con-sciences on the subject of religious Truth, which is, I fear, equivalent to having none. If Ireland had been treated on the principles which obtained in the case of Scotland, Roman Catholicism would have been established in Ireland. To say that Scottish Presbyterianism and Anglican Episcopacy are only two varieties of Protestantism, which the country accepts in some generic shape, is, of course, to beg a large theological question, besides ignoring the fact that the history of the Church of England and of Presbyterianism is such as to imply that the differences are serious.

"However, many theoretical anomalies go on among us until some practical reason for putting an end to them arises. And, speaking in the abstract, one would much rather have the State, for its own sake, recognise Religion in an illogical kind of way, than not at all. But people say generally, as you say, that the Disestablishment of the Irish Church is now inevitable, and the question is how to do the best for her under the circumstances. My own line would be to accept Disestablishment for Ireland, and to endeavour by doing so to secure two advantages, or so much of them as possible. (*a*) First, the preservation of the Endowments, or of as much of them as could be saved. Disendowment may mean the transfer of what has been dedicated to God from one religious body to another. It may mean the secularisation of religious property, and it is, I fear, likely to mean this in the case of Ireland. Such Disendowment involves, to my mind, a far more serious blow to the interests of Religion and to the due honour of God among us than any Disestablishment. There are, of course, precedents for it, as in the case of the monastic property at the Reformation ; but the cases are as far as possible from being analogous. The Irish Church *might* thrive on the voluntary system ; but to turn a Church out into the cold, after centuries of opulence, is to expose it to a trial which no young Church, however poor and unprovided for, should have to undergo.

"(*b*) The other advantage that might be secured by accepting Disestablishment is, to my mind, more important. I mean freedom of spiritual action, and in particular freedom from the doctrinal jurisdiction of the Judicial Committee of the Privy Council. The constitution of that Court, aggravated by the decisions which it has actually given, is assuredly the weakest point in the armour of the Church of England at the present day ; but if, as we are told, some such assertion as State control is the inevitable correlative of a wealthy Establishment, there can be no reason for maintaining it, when the advantages of Establishment, or most of them, have been surrendered.

"As to English clerical opinion, it is clear that for the present the Irish Church debate has enlisted the sympathies of the great mass of the clergy on behalf of the present Government. Even the leading Liberal clergy, such as the Bishop of London and the Dean of Westminster, are, in this matter, at issue with their friends in the House of Commons, although, as the papers show, they do not carry all their followers with them. High Churchmen are less unanimous than Low Churchmen, but the great majority of the High Church clergy is opposed to Mr. Gladstone's proposals, as involving Disendowment, rather than as involving Disestablishment. The motive

K

of this, I need not say, is not greed of property, but the fear of profaning that which has been dedicated to the service of God. But if this feeling could be consulted by provident and tender legislation, a large section, at least, of the High Church clergy would soon acquiesce in the Disestablishment of the Irish Church.

"If the tide runs strongly the other way at present, as the Bishop of Oxford's speech at St. James's Hall, and his recent address to his Rural Deans sufficiently show, this is due, no doubt, in part to the excitement of a party struggle, and is not a fair criterion of the average level of clerical opinion some months hence.

"In England, I believe, we have most to dread, not Disestablishment, but a careful protection both of our social position and of our property, *combined with* a systematic endeavour to destroy all firm hold upon doctrine, under the plea of making the Church national. This really points to a gradual secularisation of all the revenues of the Church.

"The fate of the Irish Church, disestablished and impoverished, would be a very welcome alternative to the destiny, which, if some active minds among us could have their way, is in store for ourselves.

"Forgive the dogmatic mood of my letter, and, I fear, its incoherence. I have been writing amid interruptions, and with a wish to be brief."

To the Rev. W. R. Churton.

Presbyters at Ordinations.

"Christ Church, November 2, 1868.

"To the first of your two questions, viz. why the canonical number of presbyters assisting at an Ordination was fixed at five, I cannot give any answer. Indeed, I was not aware of the fact, although that does not at all disprove it.

"But the second, and graver, question admits, I should suppose, of a clear answer. When you ask, 'How far the assistance of presbyters is necessary,' I understand you to mean, necessary to the validity of the rite, and not merely necessary to legal compliance with an ancient and imposing tradition of Western Christendom. And the answer would be, to my mind, 'Not at all.'

"1. The great fact which establishes this, is the present and immemorial custom of the Eastern Churches, in which the Bishop alone lays hands upon the presbyters. The Apostolical Canons represent the presbyters as 'standing by,' but they limit Ordination to the Bishop. This is the Eastern practice now. Nobody disputes the validity of Eastern Ordinations. Nobody denies that in matters of this kind the East is a better representative of primitive practice than the West.

"2. The Western practice is, I suppose, due to the Fourth Council of Carthage [Canon 3]. The rest of the West followed Africa in the matter—the East never did so. It is, of course, observable (1) that this Council, however weighty, is not Œcumenical, and (2) that, as Bingham observes, the Canon expressly reserves the Benediction or Ordination prayer to the Bishop only.

"Morinus discusses this Canon in a passage with which you are no doubt familiar. ['De Sacris Ordinationibus,' Pars III. Exerc. vii. cap. 2, p. 108.] He admits that the greater part of modern authors consider the assistance of the presbyters to be only a matter of ceremonial propriety. He himself leans to an opposite opinion. But he seems to think more highly of the authority of the one Western Council than is really justifiable, and to lose sight of the fact that ancient and contemporary Ordinations of undisputed validity were invalid, if his doctrine, or rather his prepossession, be sound. Elsewhere, he himself argues against the *necessity* of the *traditio instrumentorum* on this very ground ; and the assistance of presbyters is also, though not to the same degree, wanting in the *quod semper* and the *quod ubique* sanction.

"Estius says plainly that 'impositio manuum quæ fit ordinando ab aliis presbyteris non est sacramentum, neque pars ejus, sed nuda ceremonia' (L. 4, d. 25, s. 2, p. 44). The ceremonia had, I suppose, a moral signification—the solemn reception into the great brotherhood of pastors—as distinct from the transmission of a specific grace, which the Bishop only could transmit.

"Two things are clear in antiquity : (1) that in the East always, and upon occasion (as in the case of Novatus) in the West, Ordination by a Bishop alone was held valid ; (2) that Ordination by presbyters alone was held invalid. This certainly seems to imply that the presbyters who assisted did not, in the judgment of the Church, contribute anything essential to the grace of Orders.

"You will have consulted Bingham, 'Antiquities,' II. 3, § 5. His quotation from St. Jerome is very much to the point. And Mr. Mackenzie Walcott's 'History of the English Ordinal,' pp. 205–229, seems to contain almost everything that can be said on the subject.

"Professor Selwyn's inference in favour of Presbyterian Ordinations would be justifiable only if he could show, not merely that the co-operation of presbyters is necessary to a valid Ordination, but that the presence of a Bishop might be dispensed with."

To the Rev. W. Bright.

On the Religious Aspect of the University Reform Bill.

"South Place, Clifton, December 28, 1868.

"Thank you for allowing me to read Rogers's interesting letter. Whether one agrees with him or not, he is so reasonable, and so really a religious man, that to think him over is always instructive.

"As to the large political background of his letter, I say nothing. He knows a great deal of such matters ; and I very little. But as regards the specific proposal for which Dr. Pusey and I, in different senses, are responsible, it strikes me that our friend does not do it his wonted justice. He asks whether 'it is not manifestly a confession that religious Truth needs a special protection for its existence.' That phrase has always seemed to me to involve a fallacy. Speaking absolutely, we know that religious Truth can take good care of itself, or rather that, in history, in the long run, God will take very good care of it, because it is His Truth. But in the concrete and particular case of young men living together, tempted to every sort of moral mischief, and eager to get rid in their worst moments of the sanctions and control of Religion, it is no disparagement to religious Truth to say that it does need protection. Rogers himself admits this principle, in the case of his own children ; he does not invite advanced Liberals to his house, who suggest that there is no Being in existence Who hears prayer, and 'the like ; so that, after all, the difference between me and Rogers on this is merely one of degree. To treat Oxford undergraduates as in all respects men, appears to me the greatest possible mistake.

"Nor do I think that the redistribution of property in Oxford between the Church and the sects need be a temporary arrangement, *i.e.* if the Church, as would be wise, gave up what was really their share on population principles to the separated bodies. Rogers's contrary opinion seems to assume that, in the years to come, the Church will continue to lose her hold on the people. Unless she does so, no further redistribution in the sense he presumes will be needed. But why should she do so? In spite of all our evils, facts at present tell the other way ; and unless—which God forbid—the Puritan and Rationalistic parties should acquire a permanent preponderance in the Church's councils, there is no reason for so dreary an anticipation.

"Nor can I agree with Rogers's sanguine hopes respecting the state of things which he wishes to introduce. I know too that the irreligious Liberals do not agree with him. They look to Sir J. Coleridge's Bill as to a measure which will 'drive the Church into the background in Oxford,' by suppressing many of its agencies for reaching souls. They too are the rank-and-file of Sir J. Coleridge's supporters. I cannot think of any other prominent advocate of the measure among our residents whom I should rank with Rogers as a loyal Churchman, while it would be easy to name only too many who hate all earnest Christianity whatever with their whole hearts.

"It seems to me that they, and not our friend, are right in their anticipations. *They* do not look to a continuance of Chapel Services or Divinity Lectures. Rogers says that the Privy Council and the Visitor would 'protect' Services against a majority of Dissenters or infidels. But why? Surely 'there is no frivolity' in these matters ; and the 'hardships' of the infidel or Dissenting majority of the Fellows who are compelled to maintain an 'odious superstition' in the Chapel, would admit of a great deal of eloquent denunciation on its behalf.

"My own entire conviction is that the only alternative, practical as well as logical, and practical because logical, to the denominational system, is a thoroughly *secular* system, which shall get rid of all acknowledgment of God, for the simple reason that to acknowledge Him in any way whatever will provoke endless disagreements among persons who differ *fundamentally*, and each of whom has an equal claim to consideration. I cannot bear to be throwing cold water upon what a thoughtful and earnest friend of the Church says at a crisis of such gravity as the present. But if the Liberals succeed, two sets of people, and two only, will profit in the long run—the earnestly irreligious Liberals and the Roman Catholic Church.

"With the reasons for this opinion I will not trouble you now, but Rogers evidently has a confidence in the religious strength of Protestant Dissent which I cannot affect to share ; it will go down like mown grass before the keen Rationalistic scepticism in the air of a University. The Roman Church will come on her own terms or not at all ; the former, if I mistake not, and that sooner than some of us anticipate.

"If, unhappily, Coleridge does pass his unhappy measure through Parliament, I cannot help feeling that one will be able to do better work for God somewhere else than in a place which will have done its best to get rid of Him. The question is not one of the Thirty-Nine Articles ; the terms of subscription might be altered. It is not one mainly between the Church and Dissent. We who live in Oxford know the hollow fallacy of that representation. It is whether the sons of Christian parents are for all time-to come to be made over to infidel teachers of history and philosophy, with an undisputed legal right to teach them infidelity. We must not, we *dare* not, lose sight of this— the real point before us."

To ———

"Brislington, near Bristol, January 23, 1869.

"The best line to take with such a young man would be, I should suppose, 1. To advise him to give up discussion, especially with those who know as little or less than himself of these subjects, and to give as much time as he can to earnest study and prayer for guidance into the Truth ; and to advise him to master thoroughly Butler's 'Analogy,' and Luthardt's 'Fundamental Truths of the Christian Religion.' He is a Lutheran writer (his book has been well translated, I believe, by Miss S. Taylor). These books will supply him with topics and materials for dealing with matters beyond him. . . .

"2. The question about God's Goodness and His Omnipotence resolves itself simply into the difficulty which underlies all others, of the *origin of evil*. Physical evil is a consequence of moral evil. Moral evil is a result of the abuse of God's generosity by a creature whom He has endowed with free will—that is, with the power of rejecting Him, the Sovereign Good. If it be said that God must have foreseen this, it can only be replied that in the Judgment of Infinite Wisdom, more good was to be done by making men and angels free —with sin and Redemption in prospect—than by creating a mechanical universe in which sin only could not exist, because there was no moral freedom. This is St. Augustine's answer to the difficulty.

"3. All prayers, such as 'For Rain,' and for all other goods temporal and spiritual, are accompanied with a provision—expressed or understood—'If it be Thy Will.' We *may* pray thus according to our lights ; God answers or not as He sees best for us.

"4. Eternal punishment *is* certainly taught by our Lord Himself, as in St. Mark ix. It is the correlative to Eternal joy. To deny an endless penalty for sin is to deny an endless blessedness in heaven. The same word in Scripture warrants each ; the supposed moral difficulties in the one can only arise from an imperfect idea of the nature of moral evil.

"5. We believe the Bible for a variety of reasons : partly external, partly internal. We cannot separate the Bible from the Church which recognised and has preserved it. The Divine Book and the Divine Society are the two factors of the one Revelation—each checking the other. By way of a beginning on this subject, and with a view to seeing the critical aspects of the matter stated with great accuracy and fairness, I would advise a careful study of Canon Westcott's 'Canon of the New Testament,' as also of his 'The Bible and the Church.'

"Of course, Truth is one, and I should despair of producing any serious effect by answering a few isolated questions. But the great thing to impress on your friend is that his difficulties are not at all new ones, and that they have been honestly faced and answered by many Christians who have afterwards lived and died in the unquestioning service of our Lord. A little knowledge of scepticism is much more dangerous than a great deal ; as Bacon says of something else, ' *Pleniores haustus ad religionem reducunt.*' "

CHAPTER VI.

ST. PAUL'S IN 1870—OBERAMMERGAU—FRANCO-PRUSSIAN
WAR—THE CHOIR AT ST. PAUL'S—THE PURCHAS
JUDGMENT—APPOINTMENT OF DEAN CHURCH.

1870–1875.

ST. PAUL'S CATHEDRAL in 1870 must not be identified,
except in external structure, with what the words mean to
an English Churchman at the present day. In those days
Londoners were very cold-hearted about it, and not without good reason. "I wonder," said the Bishop of London,
Dr. Blomfield, to Bishop Wilberforce one day as they drove
together up Ludgate Hill—"I wonder what that great
building has ever done for the cause of Jesus Christ." As
Liddon was arguing with Pusey about the offer of the
Canonry, he pointed out the state of St. Paul's, and the
imperative demand for drastic reformation. "Yes," said
Pusey, "it is, in fact, an Augean stable." Those may seem
strong words certainly; but they expressed what was
felt by good Churchmen about many of our Cathedrals of
that time. There was a great work which Cathedrals, and
Cathedrals only, could do; but there was also first a great
work to be done in them.

As a place of worship, the condition of St. Paul's in
1870 has been well described[1] by one who has had much
to do with making it what it now is.

"Hitherto it had been a magnificent architectural monument,
waiting, in dignified renown, for the discovery of its activities. Its
main bulk lay practically idle, except for special occasions, such as

[1] "Life and Letters of Dean Church," pp. 208, 209 (Paper by the
Rev. H. S. Holland, Canon of St. Paul's).

the Festival of the Charity Children, or on great public functions, such as the burial of a hero. At all other times, over the length and breadth of its large area, cold, naked, and unoccupied, mooning sightseers roamed at large. Its Daily Services had always been hidden away in the Choir, behind the thick organ screen against which Wren had so vehemently protested. There, in seclusion, a tiny body of cultivated musicians sang to a sprinkled remnant of worshippers. Everything was done on the smallest scale, and much was mean and slovenly to the last degree. The attendance of the Chapter and of the Cathedral staff was reduced to a minimum. There was little attempt at discipline or at dignity in the conduct of the Daily Services. An eloquent preacher could, of course, make a difference at St. Paul's, as well as elsewhere, and no one would wish to forget the stir caused by the beauty and the nobility of sermons like Henry Melville's. For him the small space of the Choir, which alone could be used, would be thronged. But any such momentary stir came and went with the preacher. It had no relation to the Cathedral as such ; it had no bearing upon its corporate worship, nor did it affect its ordinary existence, except for the one afternoon Service on Sundays, when this or that preacher was in residence. For the rest of the week, the Cathedral droned on as usual."

Nothing short of a most radical change was demanded in the "ingrained habits" of the place : immemorial conditions which made advance impossible had to be altered, and vested interests stopped the way on every side ; destructive traditions and solid blocks of resistent sloth, "strong in their charters and inherited abuses," had to be removed.

Liddon had learnt from Bishop Hamilton a high ideal of what a Cathedral should be. In the August before his appointment to St. Paul's, he had sketched it out with a loving hand and longing heart, while recording the Bishop's work as Precentor of Salisbury Cathedral ;[1] and now he had been given a very large share in the grandest opportunity of realising his ideal. In 1870 the work had already begun. Canon Gregory, who had been appointed by Mr. Disraeli two years before, had, with Dean Mansel, effected not a few reforms. When Liddon joined him

[1] "Walter Kerr Hamilton," by H. P. Liddon, pp. 22–32. It is sketched again with special reference to St. Paul's in a stirring sermon called "St. Paul's and London," printed at the time by request of Dean Mansel, and republished at the end of his volume of "Christmastide Sermons."

such reform was still necessarily slow ; the older Canons did not move as readily as the younger ; but yet something could be done and was done. Just a hint of what was happening occurs now and again in Liddon's diary. In the first year, his months of residence were May, September, and January ; these were afterwards altered to April, August, and December, to suit his new Professorial engagements at Oxford—a change which has given the Church the great collection of his Easter, Advent, and Christmas Sermons.

Gregory had asked Liddon to provide a good Form of Service for his installation as Canon, for nothing could have been worse than his own installation in 1868.

" The gas was turned out, the congregation dismissed after Evensong ; and then the Residentiary (Archdeacon Hale), by the light of what looked like a farthing dip, said one or two Prayers and put me into my seat, and all was over."

Liddon was able to suggest a better Form.

"*April* 27.—At the afternoon Service I was installed as Canon in St. Paul's Cathedral, according to the Sarum Use. All the Canons and the Dean were present.

"*May* 1.—Preached my first Sermon in the afternoon as Canon— on the Gospel for the Festival. The service very well attended."

This and the other Sermons in his May residence were preached in the Choir, as described by Canon Scott Holland in the extract already quoted.

On May 15 he spoke to the choir after his Sermon on their behaviour in the Cathedral. A little later he notes—

"*July* 12.—A long talk with Gregory. . . . He said that Archdeacon Hale had written a warning letter to Dean Mansel about apprehended changes at St. Paul's."

The next day he started for a holiday on the Continent. The Franco-Prussian War had all but begun. He went to Brussels and got through from Luxembourg to Metz by the very last train that passed the frontier, and was in the midst of preparations for war and movements of troops, and saw sad scenes which he never could forget. He went to Oberammergau, and then to Munich, where he called on Dr. Döllinger. "Delighted with his conversation: so fresh, although he is seventy; so sincere and simple as to remind me of Mr. Keble."

To THE REV. H. N. OXENHAM.

"Baierischer Hof, Munich, July 29, 1870.

"I owe you so much for the pleasure I have had in seeing Dr. Döllinger, that I must write you a few words of grateful acknowledgment before leaving Munich. We came here on Friday in last week, but left almost immediately for Oberammergau, where we were just in time to see the last representation for this year. The war has put an end to the Passion Play for the present, as several of the most important characters have been called out, and sent to the frontier. This was considered a good joke by the railway officials at Immenstadt, where we first heard of it, and they expressed themselves not quite reverently: 'Der Christus selbst ist schon eingerufen, auch mit Pilatus.'

"The Play quite exceeded my expectations; there was nothing throughout the whole that was not edifying, and the dramatic power, reverence, absence of self-consciousness—in fact, downright reality of the whole thing—were quite wonderful.

"On Tuesday we returned to Munich, and on Wednesday I sat some hour and a half with Dr. Döllinger. Yesterday I dined with him, and had the pleasure of meeting (with Plummer, who is reading here) Sir Rowland Blennerhasset. To-day I am going to walk with Dr. Döllinger at 6. To-morrow, I am sorry to say, we leave Munich for Innsbruck.

"A large amount of our conversation, of course, turned on the Council and the Definition; and he speaks with the most entire unreserve. He says that the great danger now is lest the Bishops of the minority, being separated from each other, and exposed to the powerful influences which can be brought to bear on them, should gradually acquiesce. Nothing would be worse for the cause of the Church in Germany than the spectacle of such submission to a purely external and not really competent authority (he dwelt much on the *schema de concilio*, as completely destroying the freedom, and so the authority, of the Council), with a notorious absence of any internal assent. The Archbishop of Munich is very anxious. He told Dr. Döllinger that the deputation which went to the Pope, begging him to spare the Church, nearly carried its point. The Bishop of Mainz had thrown himself on the ground at the feet of the Pope, with passionate earnestness. No decided answer was given, but the next day Archbishop Manning and the Bishop of Ratisbonn went to the Pope and told him that if he yielded to the prayer of the petitioners he would be for ever disgraced in history; he would be 'a second Honorius' (no great discredit, by-the-by, this, if Archbishop Manning is right about Honorius). The consequence was the Definition in its present trenchant form : the *sine consensu ecclesiæ* was inserted at the instance of the Spanish Bishops. . . ."

Meanwhile the war had begun in earnest ; his sympathies were entirely with France.

To Miss Mirehouse.

"Milan, August 7, 1870.

"Yes ! My sympathies *are* certainly with France. Bismarck is a much nearer reproduction of the *bad side* of Napoleon I. than Napoleon III. is. He is, as the Germans call him, 'a man of blood and iron.' His dealings with Hanover, Frankfort, and Denmark were injustices of the grossest kind, and apart from the Spanish question, France has, I think, *ample* grounds for her quarrel with Prussia in the evasion of the Articles of the Treaty of Prague. Our English prejudices are too strong to allow us to look at things as they are ; and probably, as regards the Treaty project, Napoleon's hands are not perfectly clean, though they are certainly not so dirty as Count Bismarck's. . . . However, I am thankful not to be the arbiter of Europe or to have to sit in judgment on these people."

On his return home, in a letter to Mr. C. T. Redington, a Roman Catholic friend in Ireland, he comments at length on the journey and the war.

To C. T. Redington, Esq.

"Christ Church, November 8, 1870.

" . . . I saw a great deal of Dr. Döllinger at Munich. He more than realised all my expectations ; it was a very great privilege, I felt, to know him. He was much depressed about the Council ; but maintained that its Œcumenicity was really what he challenged, partly on the ground of the absence of real freedom in debate, and partly on the score of the substitution of the principle of 'parliamentary majorities' for that of literal or moral unanimity, in taking votes on questions of Dogma. He did not despair of the ultimate issue ; but thought that there would be much troubl before it was reached. Since my return, he has sent Lord Acton's remarkable 'Sendschreiben' to the German Bishop, which I see has been reviewed, not quite as I could have wished, in the *Times*.

" Certainly the events of this autumn have been momentous and tragic beyond any that have occurred in our lifetime ; we are too near them as yet to do any justice to their magnitude. English opinion does not do justice to France, partly, I suppose, on the ground of our old historical antagonism, and partly because the blustering tone and immense mistakes of the successive French leaders have blinded people here to the original claims, as I hold, and the moral interest of their side of the question. Certainly the Republic threatens to become, by turns, ridiculous and pernicious ; but the real France is independent of its Government, and ought to be treated more respectfully than it is. And the unscrupulous *pro ratione voluntas* of Bismarck is a real danger for Europe, not the less real because he has the good sense to avoid giving unnecessary alarm.

" The Church debates in Dublin are regarded by good Churchmen here with simple despair for the future of the Irish Church. If the Prayer-book *is* altered in any vital particulars, it will lead to a separation ; and such alteration seems, alas ! to be quite possible. I do not believe in ' a Protestant Episcopal Church strengthened by Methodism.' Such a position is essentially transitional; the Episcopate, and what remains of the Sacramental System would be out of place, and would gradually have to give way to the demands of the purely subjective and Puritan theory. However, this, as all else, is in Wise and Loving Hands; and in the separations and recombinations of the future He probably has designs for the renewed strength and unity of His kingdom which we cannot at present penetrate."

In September he went to London for his second month of residence at St. Paul's, and all the difficult work of trying to reform its abuses and make it useful to the Church. "You must be patient," he said in reply to a too eager friend, who was congratulating him on his Canonry, "an elephant may be taught to dance, but the process is not a quick one." On the first Sunday of this month his Sermon was preached in the Choir, as had always been the custom ; before the next Sunday he announced to the Chapter his intention of preaching in future under the Dome, which had hitherto only been used for the special Sunday evening Services in winter. Some of his fellow-Canons tried to dissuade him ; they said that they would never do it themselves, and that no one would come to listen to him ; but he went his own way, and they did not remain behind.

"*September* 11.—In afternoon went into the Dome pulpit, and preached on the Gospel for the day. Spoke to the choristers about their behaviour in the Choir.

"*December* 16.—Slept in my new house in Amen Court for the first time in my life. *Benedicat Deus.*"

There are many notes and letters describing the steps by which minor details of the Services were improved. The choir was a constant source of trouble. The two following letters of a later date show how great the difficulties were:—

TO THE REV. R. GREGORY.

" 3, Amen Court, August 25, 1873.

". . . I have had a large part of the choir into the vestry this morning, and have talked to them at length about behaviour in church. Specially on these points : (1) standing about and talking in their surplices, before Service ; (2) talking to each other when going to the Choir ; (3) sitting during the Prayers ; (4) talking and sending notes to each other during Service, on matters *not* connected with the Service ; (5) irreverence at Holy Communion, just before and after receiving. On this point I went at length into the intentions of the Chapter in insisting on having communicants ; we wanted *religious* men first ; then, if we could get them, accomplished musicians.

" They took what I said well, I hope ; anyhow, I could not *but* say it. Every time I reside, the hollowness and mockery of our Service strikes me more and more ; it *must* be unspeakably offensive to Almighty God, and I *know* how much it does to produce in the minds of half-believers and unbelievers a conviction that our whole work is based on hypocrisy and insincerity. Of course, people of that kind do not distinguish.

" I wish that *we* Canons could enter into a compact (1) not to talk on secular subjects in the vestry before Service, and (2) to avoid all lounging and looking about while we are in the Choir. Do you not think I might mention this, without offence, at a Chapter ? We cannot *hope* to get our subordinates to be reverent if we do not take pains to be reverent ourselves ; they are quick to observe in us what they do not dare to mention. Speaking for myself this morning, I freely acknowledged to them the imperfections and shortcomings of my own service ; I am sure we shall only win them by downright sincerity of this description with ourselves."

To Dr. Bright.

"Christ Church, May 9, 1878.

" When I first came to St. Paul's, I think that all, or nearly all, our boys lived with their parents, or with friends—generally, too, in the suburbs of London. They came to the Cathedral in time for the 10 o'clock service, and spent the interval between it and the 4 o'clock service at 1, Amen Court (which was then occupied by Mr. Coward), partly in school, partly at dinner, and partly at play. At 5 p.m. they went home.

" London, of course, affords exceptional opportunities for getting into mischief and evil of every description, and our poor boys made the most of them, on their way to and from the Cathedral. Of these evils, the general practice of singing in music-halls was one of the least. The parents were often not well off, and the boys were highly paid for such work, which, of course, led to a great deal beyond. . . .

" Nothing but a very strong feeling that the evils to which these boys were exposed were a direct consequence of their employment in the service of the Church would have led the Chapter to face the great expenses which were necessary to remedy it. The *site* and buildings of the new Choir House cost us a sum which still cripples us ; and we could not have done what we have done, had not the Ecclesiastical Commissioners behaved very generously. We laid our plans and the reasons which made them necessary before the Commissioners, who recognised the strength of the case without any sort of difficulty. Our new house is built to hold forty choristers, the number to which we hope to raise the choir in the course of a few years.

" In answer to your question—so far as my memory serves me— our first move was to take all the boys who lived in lodgings, and some others, into 1, Amen Court, which then passed under the care of Barff. Only two or three still went home. The change coincided in point of time with a considerable increase in the number of the choir ; and in the case of all new boys we made living in our house a *sine quâ non*, whether their parents were living in London or not. As we did what we could to improve the education given in the school, and provided the boys, at our own expense, with a very comfortable home, the parents were glad enough to assent to our terms. We have found it necessary to make another change. The boys *were*, almost all of them, the sons of tradesmen—we have been driven to admit only the sons of gentlemen, chiefly of poor clergymen. Not merely the cockney pronunciation in church, but weightier reasons made this restriction necessary ; although in *the abstract* I regretted the change, as partly cutting off the Cathedral from the sympathies of the people. But the event has justified our decision. Having once made up our minds as to what had to be done, we got rid of our old boys as quickly as we could, without doing an injustice. As it is, if a boy's parents lived next door, the boy would have to live in the choir house, and would only see his parents when the Master of the choristers allowed him to do so.

" You will, I think, find that *all* the choristers ought to live together, if real good is to be done, or rather, if real evil is to be kept at bay. Oxford, of course, is not London ; but I know something also of Salisbury—and am sure that more precaution is necessary than we may think. . . . And, in dealing with parents *we* have found it necessary to state our own terms, whether they agreed or not. This plan sometimes forfeits a good voice, but in the end it is of the greatest advantage to the choir—as *now* admission is considered a very great privilege, and no parent would think of interference with our rules.

" Judging from our experience, I should venture to press this point on your attention. Living at home is no real protection against the evils to which a chorister's work, alas ! exposes him, in a manner and degree unknown to other boys. It is a dreadful comment on our Christian civilisation that this should be the case, but it is foolish to blink facts. If a boy lives under the care of a clergyman, who is alive to all their mischiefs, and who possesses his confidence, there need be no real risk whatever.

" In time we hope to make some systematic provision for the future of our choristers at St. Paul's—for passing on as many of them as may be to Holy Orders, and for providing careers for others. But the difficulties of doing this are very great indeed, and for the present our hands are full of other and pressing matters. However, one boy who came to St. Paul's under the old system, and then passed into Barff's hands, has just gone to India, where he will be ordained as a Missionary, and with every promise of doing good work.

" I am so thankful that you are stirring in this matter, which lies as near as anything can to the very heart of Christian work."

From the time that he went to St. Paul's in 1870, Liddon began to take part in Ecclesiastical questions of the day far more than before. In the great work of defending the Faith he had taken a leading place for several years ; but now his position in London forced him into prominence, not only in questions which he felt to be vital, but also in such subordinate matters as controversies about points of Ritual which were at that moment being exaggerated by heated party spirit into a prominence out of all proportion to their intrinsic importance.

The anxiety and strain in the Church of England in the year 1871 were intense. On one side there were efforts in the highest quarters to remove the Athanasian Creed from the Services of the Church ; on another, there was great fear of the growth of a form of Church Service which admitted no rule except the will of the Incumbent of the parish ; on another, the Church Association was pursuing a vigorous policy of prosecution for details of ritual, which, if it were successful, would only have the result of making the position of High Churchmen untenable within the limits of the Church of England. This last trouble reached one of its critical points just at this moment. The importance of the struggle did not lie so much in the point of ritual round which it raged, but in those far greater questions of Ecclesiastical Courts, and of policy and of doctrine which emerge in the correspondence that follows.

On February 23, 1871, the decision of the Judicial Committee of the Privy Council was pronounced in the Purchas case. The only point in the Judgment which could have any bearing on the Services of St. Paul's Cathedral was the decision that the Eastward Position in celebrating the Holy Eucharist was illegal. But the whole Judgment was, to Liddon's mind, equally unsatisfactory, and he wrote at once to Mr. Gladstone about it.

To the Right Hon. W. E. Gladstone.

"Christ Church, February 28, 1871.

". . . So far as I have any means of influencing others, I shall do what I can to allay the exasperation which this Judgment has aroused.

"The real difficulty about counselling obedience lies in the constitution of the Court. If, as Mr. Keble used to express it, the Court 'could be brought anyhow into or under the Fifth Commandment,' there would be, at least for me, no ground for hesitation, whatever ceremonials it might enjoin or forbid. But, as it is, we are thrown back upon considerations of expediency ; and they are in truth, in this present case, most seriously perplexing. Great as are the social and moral mischiefs of ostentatious disobedience to the Civil Law on the part of the clergy, and serious as the penalties attending such disobedience will probably be, there is, on the other hand, the question of the effect of obedience upon entire congregations, both in London and elsewhere.

"It is, I fear, morally impossible for not a few of the clergy to obey such a Judgment as this, regard being had to the temper of their flocks ; and they would rather risk the deprivation which the continued activities of the Church Association may very probably entail, than face the certain consequences of revolutionising their Services in obedience to a jurisdiction which they cannot defend. A partial obedience would irritate one party without satisfying the other.

"I can only hope that delay and abstinence, if it can be secured to any considerable extent, from fierce language in print or speech, may point the way to some practical compromise as an escape from our difficulties."

The Judgment was not to be left a dead letter. On March 1 the Church Association held its annual meeting, jubilant at the triumph it had secured over Mr. Purchas, and insisting on the necessity of rigidly applying the Decision against all clergy who broke it. "Wherever there is a clear infraction of this authoritative Decision," said the chairman, amidst loud and repeated cheers, "let the Bishop have no peace until he interposes." Other speakers were equally vehement ; and there was every prospect of widespread persecution at the hands of this Association. On the other hand, Liddon and Gregory had already decided that the Association should not be left to choose its own battle-grounds ; they thought that it would be for the peace of the Church if they themselves should be the first to be prosecuted. They therefore acted as their own delators to the Bishop of London on the day after the meeting of the Church Association.

TO THE BISHOP OF LONDON.

"London, March 2, 1871.

" . . . We, the undersigned, being Canons of your Cathedral Church of St. Paul in London, beg to state very respectfully to your Lordship that we have heretofore been accustomed to stand in front of the Holy Table during the Service for the administration of the Lord's Supper, at and after the Nicene Creed. We have carefully considered the recent Judgment of the Judicial Committee of the Privy Council in its relation to our obligations, and to the general law of the Church ;

L

and we are unable to recognise in that Judgment any sufficient reason for departure from our existing practice.

"Your Lordship will allow us, in making this declaration as in duty bound, to assure you of our respect for your person and office.

"ROBERT GREGORY.
"H. P. LIDDON."

The Bishop immediately replied.

FROM THE BISHOP OF LONDON.

"London House, S.W., March 3, 1871.

". . . I am not about to defend the Judgment; nor the constitution of the Final Court of Appeal. Let it be admitted, if you please, for the present, that the former is a mistake, and the latter unwisely framed. But I would ask you seriously to consider what judgment would be passed on any two persons of character and position in Church or State who should deliberately declare their intention of disobeying a decision of the Queen's Bench, or the Court of Chancery, or of the Committee of Council itself in an appeal from a Civil Court, on the ground that *they* could not in *their own* judgment reconcile it with their obligations to the common law of the land. Would it not be said that they were violating the first principles of civil society and good government, and by their example encouraging anarchy?

"For where is the difference? By our Canons and Statutes the Crown is over all persons, in all causes ecclesiastical as well as temporal, supreme. In all causes, then, ecclesiastical as well as civil, the final appeal must be to the Crown. The legal advisers of the Crown, in determining such appeals, have from time to time varied. At present the Queen is advised by the Judicial Committee of the Privy Council. It may be a bad tribunal for the purpose. I do not say it is; but if it is, let all legitimate means be used for altering it. But, as the law stands, it is the Queen's adviser; and on its advice *she* decides; and till she decides its advice is *nil*. And if so, let me ask, with all deference, but in all earnestness, Can deliberate disobedience to such a decision be reconciled with 1 Pet. ii. 13; Rom. xiii. 1, 2? Unless, indeed, the position of the Minister, at one side of the Holy Table instead of another, were a distinct ordinance of God—which will hardly be maintained.

"I must add one word more. I need not tell you that the present is an anxious crisis for our Church. On the wisdom, forbearance, and moderation of leading men of all parties depends, under God, the future. Men's passions are roused. Inflammable matter is all around us. Such action as you contemplate, deliberately pursued by men of your position and character, may fire the train and shatter the unity of our Church. Will life be long enough for the regret which such a result must cause?"

The reply to this letter was sent by Canon Gregory.

CANON GREGORY TO THE BISHOP OF LONDON.

"March 3, 1871.

"I am favoured with your letter; and as you have been so good as to speak very freely to me, I feel sure that you will allow me to reply without any reserve.

"You dread anarchy; I cannot but feel that the Church has been suffering from it for some time, nor will anarchy cease while a Judicial tribunal assumes the power of legislation. The Civil Courts to which your Lordship refers keep within their province, and only administer the laws which Parliament makes. The Court of Final Appeal both judges and legislates; it legislates under the semblance of Judicial decision; and it is the sense of this which revolts consciences and creates anarchy in the Church.

"If the authority of the court were beyond controversy, it would risk that authority by such procedures. But its authority over consciences is the very question at issue. You quote St. Peter and St. Paul (1 Pet. ii. 13; Rom. xiii. 1, 2). Their language has been quoted in the interest of Charles I. against Hampden; of Charles II. and James II. against the political Opposition; of Louis XIV. against the Huguenots. It is unnecessary to remind your Lordship that the Apostles are referring to obedience in *things civil*, and that even in civil matters these texts could not be pressed, as they were pressed under the House of Stuart, without condemning English constitutional liberty. Your Lordship would not have quoted them in the interests of unqualified obedience to high prerogative generally, *e.g.* to the Court of High Commission. And that, if referred to the things of God, such texts have their limits is clear (1) from our Lord's own limitation of the rights of Cæsar in the Gospel by the rights of God; and (2) from the idea of the Royal Supremacy accepted at the Reformation, as specifically *exercising itself through spiritual Courts*. Mr. Gladstone has abundantly shown that this condition of the Royal Supremacy was a part of the constitution of Church and State as established in the sixteenth century.

"Our obedience to the Sovereign is sworn, in ecclesiastical as in civil matters, to her authority as exercised *constitutionally*, and not to a personal autocratic authority. The objection to the Judicial Committee, when it claims authority over conscience in virtue of the oath of the Royal Supremacy, is that it is not a constitutional organ, or instrument of that Supremacy.

"But the authority of such a Court would in all probability be respected, if it were not strained, as it is, in the present case; the Court confesses that it is dealing with a difficult question, which the law of the Church has not decided. It decides, upon the whole, in favour of a particular side of the Holy Table, as probably intended to be the position of the celebrant. In doing this, it really legislates for the future of the Church; it assumes the functions of a Synod; it decrees deprivation eventually against all who shall disobey its new decree. A lay Court (proper) would say that in all penal causes, when there is a doubt, the decision must be for the acquittal of the defendant; the Court of Final Appeal inflicts heavy punishments for disobedience to conclusions which, to an independent critical judgment, appear open to the largest question.

"I have promised canonical obedience; and when the obedience demanded is contrary to the Canons, and in my firm belief in opposition to the written law of the Church, I am obliged to consider the whole question. Your Lordship would not claim for any earthly tribunal a literally unlimited obedience under all circumstances. To do so would be to imply the infallibility of such a tribunal.

"I am well aware that Cæsar bears the sword; and that he can make his power, however exerted, felt. It is well that it is so. It deepens the sense of responsibility; and I only advert to this side of the subject to show that I have thought it well over.

"Your Lordship deems it impossible that any one can regard it as an ordinance of God, to stand, while celebrating the Holy Communion, on this side rather than on that. If nothing more were really at stake, it would be difficult to explain the violence which so simple an observance as that recently proscribed is regarded by the Puritan party. But if it be that the position of the Celebrant is a matter of itself indifferent, it is not a matter indifferent whose order we obey in adopting or discarding it.

"Moreover, in the eyes of thousands of young men recently won from the kingdom of Satan to Christ, this, and similar observances, are looked upon as matters of deep moment. These men are half-educated, ill-informed, narrow, dependent largely upon the imagination in the life of faith, but zealous, earnest, and advancing to higher things. The Church of England had made very little way with men of this class until quite recently. The 'offence' this Judgment will cause to them God only knows. The many it will wound, and cause to doubt and eventually drive from Him, He only knows. I am obliged to think of them. Their souls are very precious—more precious than the Establishment. Nor can I forget the many young men who, if this Judgment is really enforced, will most certainly abandon their present intention of taking Orders in the Church of England.

"I would humbly ask your Lordship whether it be yet too late to avert from the Church the manifold and great miseries which this decision will entail, by praying Her Majesty in Council not to confirm it.

"I am writing with a deep sense of my responsibility. If I am right, may God strengthen me. If I am wrong, may He convert me. Whatever is before me, may I seek only His glory!

"P.S.—I have Dr. Liddon's authority for saying that he 'concurs' in this reply to your Lordship's letter."

The Bishop then proposed the interview which Liddon describes in the following letter :—

TO DR. BRIGHT.

"3, Amen Court, Wednesday night, March 22, 1871.

"We have had our interview. The Bishop evidently expected concession, and talked of how much depended on our decision. We argued the matter at length, and I hope put most of its bearings before him. He was very patient when I told him that the Judgment was unjust somewhat emphatically. In fine we said that, for various reasons which we stated, we *could* not submit ; that we hoped he would take proceedings against us, before doing so against any of the parochial clergy, who might be less able to defend themselves ; and that, as we both adhered to the same practice, we wished our names to go into one indictment. We had evidently anticipated a threat. The Bishop 'had thought that it would be his duty to deal with us first ;' it 'would give him the greatest pain.'

"Gregory and I, however, think that he will not try; however, we must prepare for eventualities."

In the next month Liddon published a vigorous letter to Sir John Coleridge, in which he stated at length the grounds for his attitude, and pleaded for the adoption of a policy widely differing from that of "the rude controversialists of the Church Association." He concludes—

"There is enough, God knows, in the England of to-day to make every man who thinks at all anxious about the future, and every religious man anxious for religious union. The social chasm which threatens to open beneath our feet and pour out a burning torrent of revolutionary lava calls for all the self-denying charity which a united Church can yield, while there is yet time, to heal the wounds and strengthen the hands of a diseased and divided society. The moral sores of that society are not skin deep ; and infidelity never threatened, not Christianity merely, but Theism of any intelligible description, more seriously than it does now. It is piteous indeed that we should be wrangling over such questions as are raised by this Judgment in presence of these absorbing anxieties ; but wounds are not healed by ignoring them, and I see no path of safety except in frank and mutual toleration and respect. High Churchmen, I trust, will never be guilty of endeavouring to force the Evangelical clergy into surplices, which would disturb good men or offend their congregations, or into copes, which would make their wearers grotesque. On the other hand, it is not yet too late for the higher minds of the Evangelical party to determine that they will discourage all attempts to enforce an oppressive Judgment, a Judgment which, whether it be reheard and reversed or not, you have shown to involve a miscarriage of justice." [1]

In May, however, the Bishop circulated a Letter to the clergy of his diocese, in which he expressed his opinion that he was bound to act on the recent Judgment, and that he desired that its rulings should be obeyed in the diocese. Liddon and Gregory replied in a published Letter to the Bishop ; they respectfully canvassed his arguments and repeated the decision which they had already announced to him. They added—

"It is, of course, no light thing for inferiors to determine in a particular case that it is a duty to ignore even the most trivial or indefinable decision of any in authority ; but we are unable, after patient consideration, to escape the unwelcome conviction that in the one point in which the recent Judgment touches on practice in your Cathedral Church—that of Consecrating before the Holy Table—we cannot obey the recent Judgment without, at least indirectly and under existing circumstances, casting a slight upon a portion of the Revelation of Christ."

They were still waiting for the result when Liddon went abroad for a holiday.

To Miss Mirehouse.

"Hotel Windsor, Paris, July 3, 1871.

"No, nothing, so far as I know, has as yet come of the pamphlet. [*Private.*] There was a very stormy meeting of the Bishops about it at Lambeth. The Bishop of London asked his brethren, 'What was to be done? He could not let the matter rest.' Some were for dealing with us at once ; you can imagine who. Winchester (who told me all about it) was for doing nothing. The *Record* is very eager for a prosecution ; and the lawyer of the Church Association proposed 'a friendly suit,' in which, if we were beaten, the penalties might be declined. I refused, because the unwillingness of a Civil Court to imprison us for six months is part of the strength of our appeal, and if I was shut up it would give me time for a great deal that I have no

[1] "The Purchas Judgment : a Letter of Acknowledgment to the Right Hon. Sir J. Coleridge " (London, Rivington, 1871), pp. 47, 48.

chance of doing now, besides answering all applications about preaching for a long time to come. . . .

" I have had a long and kindly letter from Sir J. T. Coleridge ;
and the Bishop of London has said nothing. He is, I expect, greatly
vexed, as Gregory and I defeated the proposal to provide him with
a cope in St. Paul's, and he had to bring one.[1] The Dean of Windsor
tells me that the Low Church people are much alarmed, and will not
press matters. I am not sure about that ; but I am happily able to
leave the whole matter in other Hands, as I am clear about the path
of duty. I wish I could say this of some other things—specially at
Oxford.

" The ruins of Paris are terrible ; few things, more tragic, or more
beautiful in the whole history of the Church, have happened than
those martyrdoms at La Roquette and in the Rue Haxo. Archbishop
Darboy has crowned a noble life with a death of glory. There have
been few such men in such a position in this age."

On June 28 the Bishop replied to their published Letter,
and announced his intention of prosecuting them under
the Clergy Discipline Act if they broke the law as they
had announced, and if he was " duly called upon by the
authorities of the Cathedral to which we belong to take
cognisance of the offence." Certainly this decision of the
Privy Council was not obeyed at St. Paul's, nor were
Liddon and Gregory prosecuted. It can only be supposed
that the authorities of the Cathedral did not think it
necessary to call upon the Bishop ; and as time went on,
changes in the Cathedral staff made such an appeal still
more improbable.

Early in 1871 Canon Melville died. He and Liddon
had hardly known one another until the latter was made
a member of the Chapter of St. Paul's ; and in their
common work there were many points on which they
could not have agreed, especially those which had been
so prominently asserted by Liddon and Gregory. In his
last sickness Liddon was by his bedside to minister to
him, and Melville said afterwards of his junior colleague,

---

[1] The Privy Council had at the
same time declared that a Bishop
should wear a cope in his own Cathedral Church. Liddon and Gregory
opposed the proposal to provide one
for him, as such an action would have
appeared to recognise the authority
of the Privy Council.

"I have liked and admired many men, but I never *loved* any man as I do Liddon." When he passed away, Liddon and Gregory did their utmost to secure the appointment of the Rev. R. W. Church as their fellow-worker. Happily they were for that moment unsuccessful, and Mr. Gladstone appointed to the Canonry Professor Lightfoot, who, with characteristic energy, used all his great abilities in cordial co-operation with the main idea of their work. At the end of July, the Deanery of St. Paul's fell vacant through the sudden death of Dean Mansel ; and Liddon endeavoured to secure that this far more important post should be offered to his old friend ; and this time he had better success.

"*August* 19.—Church arrived. He had declined the Deanery ; but I think I prevailed on him to pause. We both returned to Mr. Gladstone, . . . after lunching there, we parted in the Strand, he promising to do justice to our side of it."

With the greatest reluctance he at last decided as Liddon desired.

"'Years after,' writes Canon Scott Holland,[1] 'the Dean had been engaged in an attempt to induce Liddon to consider the question of a Bishopric, and I remember well the amused smile with which he told me how, as he listened to Liddon's fervid arguments against any such offer being made him, he could not help recalling the way in which that very same fervour had disposed of the very same arguments when he himself had used them to Liddon as his reason for declining the Deanery.'"

The new Dean came up to stay with Liddon "to survey St. Paul's," and wrote to a friend of the work that he found before him.[2]

"It is clear that what I am to come in for is a very tough, practical business ; and that I am not to be as other Deans have been. It is to set St. Paul's in order, as the great English Cathedral, before the eyes of the country. I mean this is what Gladstone has in view, and what Liddon, Gregory, and partially Lightfoot expect of their Dean."

The parts which the several members of the Chapter

---

[1] "Life of Dean Church," p. 206.
[2] *Ibid.*, p. 280.

took in the great revival at the Cathedral are difficult to distinguish. They acted in such thorough harmony that the work was the work of the Chapter as a whole. Yet, of course, they were variously qualified for their complex task, and Canon Scott Holland thus draws some distinctions in their united actions. After sketching the admirable financial reform which Canon Gregory had already begun, and without which little else could have been accomplished, he says—

" . . . The personal factor by which the claim of St. Paul's to become once more a wide spiritual home for London could make itself heard and felt over the hearts of large multitudes, was to be found in the preaching of Dr. Liddon. That voice reached far and wide. It fixed the attention of the whole city on what was going forward in its midst. It kindled the imagination, so that the big world outside was prepared for great things. It compelled men to treat seriously what was done. No one could suppose that the changes in the Services and Ritual at St. Paul's were superficial, or formal, or of small account, so long as that voice rang on, like a trumpet, telling of righteousness and temperance and judgment, preaching ever and always, with personal passion of belief, Jesus Christ and Him crucified. It is impossible to exaggerate the value of Liddon's presence for these twenty years at St. Paul's, in the way of making acceptable and justifiable to reasonable men the type of worship which was to be asserted under the leadership which now made it practicable. And it was of unspeakable importance, therefore, that Liddon should have been what he was to the new Dean. Not only were they in absolute accord on the practical aims which they were bent on making good, but Liddon placed also at the Dean's service an enthusiastic veneration for one who was, for him, the ideal of that perfected and chastened Christian character which Tractarianism, in its highest mood, had fostered. Chivalrous loyalty belonged to the innermost fibre of Liddon's nature, and all of it was freely offered to him whom he was delighted to accept as his chief. There was nothing which he would not submit to the Dean's verdict. His delicate sensitiveness would be ever on the *qui vive* to interpret and to ratify the Dean's judgment. There was no one in England, except Dr. Pusey himself, to whose authority he could more joyfully and entirely surrender himself.

" Gregory and Liddon, then, were already in action, and all their activity was at the immediate disposal of their new Head. To them had just been added Lightfoot, with his unrivalled reputation as a critical scholar, his glowing ardour of speech, his robust sense of equity, his delightful geniality. There could never be any difficulty in securing his co-operation in anything that made for the effective utilisation of the great Church; and the united force of such a body carried along with it the kindly courtesy of Bishop Claughton, who had just been appointed to the Archdeacon's stall. Thus the Dean found himself in the rare position of heading a Chapter which was prepared to act with practical unanimity. It was not, as is so usual in Cathedral bodies, an odd assortment of stray bodies, a collection of contradictory specimens, each of which had been specially selected in order to neutralise the others. It was a corporate body that was animated by a single purpose, and possessed of sufficient coherence to prosecute this purpose with some consistency and continuity of will. It was ready and able to act together in its integrity, so that it might create a regularity in the life and the worship associated with the Cathedral, such as would survive the monthly succession of Canons in residence. These might come and go, but the tone, the atmosphere, the type, of which each, during office, was the responsible guardian, would abide unchanged now that the sequence of liturgical actions and ordered Services, carefully considered and fixed by a united Chapter, could be laid out on authoritative lines and secured against the whims and freaks of individualism. It was to this unity of purpose and mind that Dr. Liddon continually attributed all that the Chapter succeeded in achieving at St. Paul's; and this unity, as he was never tired of asserting, became a practical fact through the incomparable authority that resided in the character of the Dean. . . . Within the Chapter, as without in his relations to the Church at large, he stood as a judicial conscience, up to the standard of which all must be brought. If it was a matter of liturgical order or devotional rule, Liddon would be set to frame a scheme; if it was a bit of financial or administrative business, Gregory would make his proposal. But, always, there was a judgment to face which would be anticipated by each as they worked at this task. Every plan must be such as would satisfy the sensitive and delicate estimate of right or wrong which was so pre-eminently characteristic of the Dean."[1]

But as the months went on, the strain of endeavouring to fulfil the duties of a Canonry of St. Paul's, as he understood them, and of his Oxford Professorship, became so severe, that nothing except his affection for Dr. Pusey prevented him from devoting himself exclusively to London work. As 1871 was drawing to a close, and the Lent Lectures at St. James's, Piccadilly, were still unprinted, Dr. Bright was urging him to hurry on their publication for the sake of the many readers who were needing them, and as being a part of an invaluable work which he was

[1] "Life of Dean Church," pp. 216–221.

doing for undergraduates at Oxford. He argued warmly against the claims of Oxford being crowded out by the insatiable demands of St. Paul's. Liddon replied—

To Dr. Bright.

"3, Amen Court, December 13, 1871.

". . . *If* I had not taken the week-night Lectures I could not have attempted the editing of the 'Evidences' [Lectures at St. James's]. For literary work of that kind I, at least, require an amount of undistracted thought which I *never* get here—with eleven posts a day, and endless interviews with all sorts of people. I have, indeed, made up my mind, some time since, not to think of publishing the book, at least while I hold my Canonry and Professorship together. To do it properly is, for me at least, impossible. And I think that much more harm than good is done by careless publications on these subjects in these days.

"But I *could* not have declined the week-day Lectures. Cathedrals are on their trials—this one most of all—as to whether they can do anything to justify their existence—anything to redeem them from the utter and shameful uselessness of past years. I might, of course, give up my Canonry ; but you do not say that I ought to do that. If I hold it, I must do what I can with it. The Doctor's theory of it, as a mere endowment to an Oxford Chair, appears to me—well, I won't say what.

"None of us, I think, can put ourselves really in the position of another, and look at obligations in the order in which they present themselves to another conscience without some faults in the perspective. You speak, I observe, dear friend, of an 'obligation' to publish the St. James's Lectures. What 'obligation'? Of course, I shall pay Rivington for the expense I have already put him to. But there the matter ends. The preaching them at all was a voluntary effort ; the intended publication a questionable act of concession to some of my listeners. But I never made any conditions whatever as to time ; I declined to do so. . . . Clearly this cannot compete in my conscience with work which properly belongs to my position here, and which another man would do if I did not ; or with the work (all too miserably neglected) of my Oxford Professorship, for which I now find it strictly impossible to *read* or *write*, as the position demands in such days as these.

"Forgive this explanation ; but—I bitterly regret the moment of weakness in which I allowed myself to accept a Chair for which I would not stand. As you know, there is only one consideration which prevents my resigning it. But, it is useless to discuss that. . . ."

CHAPTER VII.

THE ATHANASIAN CREED CONTROVERSY—DEATH OF
BISHOP WILBERFORCE — PUBLIC WORSHIP REGU-
LATION ACT—LIMITS OF RITUAL—BONN REUNION
CONFERENCES.

1872–1875.

DURING this period the controversy about the Athanasian
Creed was at its height. In September, 1870, in an
Appendix to the fourth Report of the Ritual Commission,
Dr. Tait, the Archbishop of Canterbury, had openly declared his desire that the use of the Creed in public
worship should be discontinued ; and soon after he endeavoured, though unsuccessfully, to obtain legislative
sanction for his wishes, by means of a clause which he
wished to add to the Bill which authorised the new
Lectionary.

In June, 1871, the Upper House of the Convocation of
Canterbury resolved itself into a committee to consider the
question ; and forthwith the newspapers were full of letters
on the subject, including many from Pusey and Liddon, in
which they declared their uncompromising hostility to any
such proposal.

In consequence of these letters, Bishop Wilberforce
wrote in October to Liddon, on behalf of the Archbishop,
enclosing a statement of objections which had been made
to the Creed, and asking for Liddon's replies to them.
For himself, he said that the only question was whether
the Church would lose more by " grieving you and Pusey
and Bright . . . than by saving this as a Creed." For
himself he wished it to be placed in the same position as

the Articles. Liddon replied in a long letter, and also had an interview with the Bishop before writing the following formal letter :—

To the Bishop of Winchester.

"3, Amen Court, E.C., October 19 (early), 1871.

" . . . I enclose the Paper you sent me, and together with it another Paper of my own, in which I notice the writer's objections to the continued use of the Athanasian Creed, only too briefly but *seriatim.*

" I am bound to add that, great as is my love and respect for the handwriting, the Paper has made no sort of impression on me as to the grave question at issue.

"Retranslation is, considering our experience of such processes, a sufficiently deplorable prospect. But it need not be fatal. The promoters may, or may not, wish to play a popular liberal game. But when they have a Latin document to *translate*, they can only diverge from fact within certain limits. They will not wish to have the world making fun of their scholarship.

" To disuse the Creed or to mutilate it, will be to take up a totally new position with respect to fundamental truth in the face of Christendom. I cannot undertake to accept such a position. I accepted office in the English Church, upon a totally different understanding ; and the more I think the matter over before God, the more difficult I find it to escape from my convictions of the extreme gravity of the issue raised.

" Practically all will have been lost, if the Creed is placed among the Articles, as entirely, I cannot but think, as if it is first retranslated, and then ignominiously expelled from the Prayer-book.

" If your Lordship would but say that, so long as you are a Bishop of the English Church, the position as well as the substance of the Creed *must* be left untouched—we should be safe.

"To give way in this matter is to give a fearful impetus to the demoralisation, so to term it, among our best people, arising from an increasing conviction that high authorities are prepared to make an unpopular stand *nowhere ;* almost no stand whatever, except against Rome, and what is supposed to lead to her ; that we are on an inclined plane, leading swiftly and certainly towards a Socinianism tempered by indifference.

" I feel the depressing force of this conviction in my inmost heart at times, more painfully than I can say, and it takes all vigour out of one.

" Surrender in this case opens the floodgates. It establishes, in an instance of capital importance, the principle of Prayer-book revision. It will constitute an *à fortiori* argument, for revising the

Baptismal, Ordination, and Visitation of the Sick Services in the sense of the anti-Sacramental Puritans. This done, it will authorise the elimination of all direct adoration of Christ, our Eternal God, in order to satisfy the Socinian School in our midst.

"Our only course, as a matter of human prudence no less than of duty to our God, is *obstare principiis.*

"For myself, I see no future when the first step on the road to spiritual ruin shall have been fairly taken by the English Church."

The series of objections to the Creed which he had been asked to consider were as follows :—

"1. Is not properly a Creed. It is hardly or never called a ' Symbolum ' in any authority earlier than the twelfth century ; but *Fides Athanasii, expositio Catholicæ fidei—Fides—Quicunque vult, etc.*

"2. It was not used in the ' Offices of the Church,' probably anywhere, till the time of Charlemagne. In the Roman obedience, generally about 930 A.D.

"3. It is notoriously of Western origin, whatever date be assigned to it, has no authority of a Council, has not been *generally* received in the East ; indeed, is viewed there with suspicion, from an unpronounced notion that it is at variance with the Nicene Creed.

"4. Is now used by the Roman Church at Prime on Sundays. But Prime is essentially an office for the clergy ; at least it has become so. In practice, the people never use it.

"5. Its use as a popular Creed is very doubtful. I do not think this Creed is *the* stumbling-block to Nonconformists, as some think. But I think, to our own people it is a difficulty : first, from its form, which is that of a theological treatise ; second, from the Anathemas which would never be mended by any new translation. The original Nicene Creed had Anathemas appended, but so as to be easily separated. The Church has separated them, and used that Creed without the Anathemas.

"6. The use, therefore, of the Athanasian Creed as we have it, has no universal nor even venerable authority on its side. It will be argued, that to disuse it is to throw down a bulwark. I doubt, myself, whether it gives us any strength."

His replies were as short as possible.

" *Objection* 1.—The Athanasian Creed not properly a Creed.

" *Answer.*—Article VIII. calls it a Creed. So do the Greek and Roman Churches. It was called *Fides* before it was called Symbolum. Fides, *i.e.*, in the objective sense, of something to be believed. Between this sense and that of Symbolum, the practical difference is *nil*. It was treated as a Creed to all intents and purposes before it was called Symbolum.

" The question is verbal and untheological ; even if we term it a hymn or a psalm, the *real* question has to be asked: Is it true, or does it contain propositions which are demonstrably false ? If it ought thoroughly to be received and believed, the name to be attached to it may be left for discussion. If not, it ought to be got rid of altogether. No hymn containing false propositions ought to be tolerated because it is a hymn and not a Creed.

" *Objection* 2.—It was not used in Church offices until the time of Charlemagne.

" *Answer.*—This rests upon precarious, because upon negative evidence, and cannot be accepted as satisfactory. The position of the Creed in the ninth and tenth centuries points necessarily to a much earlier acceptance and use.

" Let me say, in passing, that Mr. Ffoulkes's account of its date and origin seems eminently unsatisfying. But it is adopted—naturally— by Dean Stanley, as against Waterland.

" *Objection* 3.—(*a*) The Athanasian Creed notoriously of Western origin.

" *Answer.*—' Notoriously' is too strong a word, whatever the pro- babilities of, *e.g.*, Mr. Brewer's argument. But if it be, what follows ? The Nicene Creed is notoriously of Eastern *origin*. This does not interfere with its Œcumenicity.

" (*b*) ' Athanasian Creed has no authority of a Council.'

" *Answer.*—It is in the same case as the Apostles' Creed. Both depend on the tacit approval (expressing itself in the usage) of the whole Church—a sufficient guarantee for Œcumenicity, St. Augustine would say against the Donatists.

" (*c*) ' Has not been generally received in the East."

" *Answer.*—This requires proof.

" (*d*) ' Is viewed in the East with *suspicion* from an ingrained notion that it is at variance with the Nicene Creed.'

" *Answer.*—Russian Bishops have told me that their only objection to it is that which they feel against the Western version of the Nicene Creed, viz. on the score of the *Filioque*. They are much too good theologians to assent to the modern sciolist theory that there is any real contradiction between Catholic doctrines of subordination and coequality of the Eternal Son—as if these terms were used ' *Secun- dum idem.'*

" *Objection* 4.—' Is used by the Roman Church only in the clerical offices.'

Answer.—This is equally true of the *Benedictus, Jubilate, Bene- dicite;* almost equally true of the *Te Deum.* The object of the Reformers was to restore to the laity language which had become clerical *in practice.* The present Roman use is therefore not in point ; *or* the objection ought to carry us a great deal further than the Athanasian Creed.

" *Objection* 5.—' The Creed objectionable not to the Nonconformists but to our own people,' (*a*) from its form, which is that of a theological treatise.

" *Answer.*—'Theological treatise' not quite accurate. The Creed enunciates ; it does not treat nor discuss. I doubt the fine literary perception which would object fiercely to the Creed only on account of its form.

" (*b*) From the Anathemas, which would never be mended by any new translation.

" *Answer.*—No doubt the real crime of the Creed in Latitudinarian eyes is, that it is an authoritative disclaimer of the theory that, whether a man holds doctrinal truth or error, it will not really matter in the eternal world. No mending of the translation will suffice to reconcile the strictly irreconcilable phases of opinion, the 'liberal' and the believing or Catholic, on this vital question. The differences in question reach the very basis of thought and faith.

" To a sincere believer in the revealed Nature of God the Blessed Trinity, and in the Incarnation of the Eternal Son, the Anathemas are speculatively as certain as the other propositions of the Creed, while practically they have no higher value than any other portion of it. Certainly, the Nicene Anathemas were detached from the Nicæno-Constantinopolitan Creed. But (1) they are related to that Creed differently from those in the Athanasian Creed to it. They are merely an appendix ; the Athanasian Anathemas are, as Dean Stanley has observed, part of its very substance and structure, placed at its beginning, middle, and end.

" (2) The English Church can point to no authority, which would warrant *her* acting separately from the rest of Christendom, to deal with the Athanasian Creed, as the Universal Church dealt with the Nicæno-Constantinopolitan, even if the structure of the document admitted of this.

" *Objection* 6.—The Athanasian Creed has no universal or venerable authority to plead for its use.

" *Answer.*—What does the writer mean by 'universal'? What by 'venerable'? And how will he adjust his new definition of these words to the actual history of the reception of the Apostles' Creed in the Church? He ' doubts whether the disuse of the Creed will forfeit any strength.'

" It will do *this :* It will convince a large number of minds that, if only a sufficient amount of negative and unbelieving pressure can be brought to bear, there is no Truth, however central and hitherto undisputed, which the Church of England is prepared to proclaim before God and man as strictly necessary to eternal salvation.

" The disuse of the Anathemas will be held to imply that the Arian, the Sabellian, the Nestorian, will, however deliberate their heresy, however great their opportunities of escaping from it, do just as well in the world to come as the faithful children of the Church to whom her Creed is a serious reality. I do not think that Dean

Stanley would deny this, or would phrase very differently his own idea of the advantage to be gained by doing away with the Creed."

At Dr. Pusey's urgent request, however, Liddon joined with the other Oxford Professors of Theology in proposing, at the Archbishop's desire, a form of explanatory rubric which would state what the Warning Clauses of the Creed mean; and it seemed for the moment that this course would be finally adopted, and that there would not be any attack on the established use of the Creed. But the *Times* of December 23 contained a letter from "Anglicanus" which removed all hope of any such speedy settlement of the question. Liddon, therefore, wrote on the same day to the Archbishop.

To the Archbishop of Canterbury.

"3, Amen Court, St. Paul's, December 23, 1871.

"As I gather from a letter signed 'Anglicanus' in to-day's *Times* that the attacks recently made on the Athanasian Creed are likely to be renewed at no distant date, it is not, I trust, obtrusive or other than right in me to state formally to your Grace, that if this most precious Creed is either mutilated by the excision of the (so-termed) Damnatory Clauses, or degraded, by an alteration of the rubric which precedes it, from its present position in the Book of Common Prayer, I shall feel bound in conscience to resign my preferments, and to retire from the ministry of the Church of England.

"If I should unhappily be driven to this, by the action of the English Bishops, it will become a duty, perhaps, to justify my step at some length, and to point out the wound and insult to *fundamental* Truth, which, as I conceive, would be inflicted by either of the courses referred to.

"For the present it is enough to say that, having subscribed the statement that this Creed, in its integrity, 'ought thoroughly to be received and believed,' since 'it may be proved by most certain warrant of Holy Scripture,' I cannot possibly acquiesce in any measure the most avowed object of which is to deny the proposition thus affirmed in the Eighth Article of our Church."

The Archbishop replied [1] that such a threat ought not to be thrown out in the midst of calm discussion, and when

---

[1] The letter is given in full in "Life of Archbishop Tait," vol. ii. p. 138.

the question was about to be submitted to the Councils of the Church. He could only believe, he added, that by "mutilation" and "degradation" Liddon meant none of the "reverent and reasonable" modes that had recently been suggested. Liddon seized the opportunity to make his meaning more clear, and also to state his reasons for the step which he had taken.

To the Archbishop of Canterbury.

"3, Amen Court, December 28, 1871.

"I must express my regret that, through any want of clearness, I failed to convey my exact meaning to your Grace.

"By the 'mutilation' of the Creed, I meant the omission of any one of its existing clauses. By the 'degradation' of the Creed from its present place in our Prayer-book, I meant, (1) the rendering its use only permissive; or (2) a reduction of the number of days on which it is now appointed to be used; or (3) still more, its removal from the Public Service of the Church, and relegation to a place among the Thirty-Nine Articles. And I ventured to intimate to your Grace, that, in the event of any of these changes being adopted, I shall feel bound in conscience to retire from the ministry of the Church of England, and to give my reasons for doing so.

"On the other hand, I did not, and do not, retract my signature affixed to the Report presented to your Grace through the Bishop of Gloucester and Bristol, on the subject of the Athanasian Creed. I should not have signed that Report, unless I had meant to adhere to it. When your Grace remarks that it is 'the opinion of some' that the explanatory rubric proposed by the Oxford Professors 'has virtually the effect of cancelling' the (so-termed) Damnatory Clauses, I do not for a moment suppose that your Grace endorses any such opinion. When those persons who hold it think well to support it by argument, I make no doubt that the Oxford Professors, who certainly did not contemplate any such 'effect' as a possible result of their proposal, will be happy to discuss the question. The effect of the explanatory rubric proposed by the Oxford Professors, is to place our responsibility for believing the dogmatic truths affirmed by the Creed on precisely the same footing as our responsibility for obeying in detail the precepts of God's moral law. In both cases knowledge is essential to responsibility, and in the same sense. The rubric does not traverse the solemn fact, that a man who, in God's sight, has sufficient opportunities for arriving at Revealed Truths, as defined in the Creed, and who deliberately embraces the heresies which the Creed rejects, thereby loses his part in Eternal Life.

"Your Grace thinks that I intended to hold out a 'threat.' I meant simply to inform your Grace of a resolution, at which I have arrived after much serious thought. Ever since the publication of the Fourth Report of the Ritual Commissioners, it has been evident that a large party in the Church of England is resolved to get rid of the Athanasian Creed, if possible. Of this, the substance of the Report, as well as the letters and pamphlet of the Dean of Westminster, afford ample evidence. When the main current of letter-writing and declamation flows all one way, your Grace might not unreasonably come to think that legislation in the sense of Dean Stanley, or the Bishop of St. David's, would meet with general acceptance, if not with universal welcome. At a meeting of Rural Deans in your diocese some time since, your Grace was reported to have dwelt upon the general consent in favour of doing something ; you did not, I believe, specify any particular measure. It seems then a duty in those who, like myself, have strong and clear convictions on the subject to lay them before your Grace—not as 'threats,' but as materials which may contribute to the survey of facts upon which your final decision may be based. I am not for a moment supposing that my convictions on the subject will seriously affect that decision, but when the names of Dissenting ministers who would enter the ministry of the Church, if the Church would consent to repudiate a Creed, which, as she asserts, 'ought thoroughly to be received and believed,' are ostentatiously proclaimed in the newspapers, it seems right to say that there are at least some of her clergy who will cease to serve her, when the understanding into which they entered at their Ordination has been violated in a point of such vital importance.

"My assent to the proposal of the Oxford Professors did not imply any admission of the necessity or expediency of legislation with respect to this Creed. The recommendations of the Professors, your Grace will remember, are hypothetical ; they are submitted to your Grace *in case* the Bishops think it right to move in the matter. The prior question whether any such movement was advisable was not before us ; and we accordingly did not discuss it. We were, however, though probably for reasons sufficiently various, quite of one mind as to the inexpediency of raising so delicate and irritating a question in the existing circumstances of our Church. Of course, I admit the extent of opposition to the Creed among a large body of the laity, and a section of the clergy, to which your Grace refers. So far, however, as my observation goes, I should not have ascribed such opposition to the 'most orthodox and attached members' of the Church ; the most prominent opponents being very accomplished persons, who would regard the imputation of 'orthodoxy' as a compliment of a very doubtful character. I have no doubt that they are perfectly sincere in their dislike of the Warning Clauses, and, in some cases, of the general theology of the Creed ; but it is difficult, at least for me, to reconcile the language which they employ on the subject with perfectly honest subscription to the Eighth Article of our Church. I have no wish to press this against them, but I do not think that 'uneasiness' of this description ought to be made a ground of legislation in one direction, while uneasiness of another kind, often sufficiently regrettable, is invariably denounced by the rulers of our Church as disloyal and dishonest.

"If I have written with undue freedom to your Grace, I must ask your pardon. I trust I am not unmindful of your position in the Church of Christ, or your personal kindness to myself. But if I write at all on subjects of such importance, it must be with perfect sincerity; and unless I altogether mistake your Grace's character, you will see in my outspokenness, the best proof I can offer of my respect."

As the Cambridge Theological Professors did not take the same view of the question as those of Oxford, the Archbishop thought that an interview with Professor Lightfoot, Liddon's fellow-Canon at St. Paul's, might be of use, and requested the Professor to call on him to discuss the proposed changes. Little was gained by the interview, the result of which Liddon reported to the Archbishop.

TO THE ARCHBISHOP OF CANTERBURY.

"3, Amen Court, January 2, 1872.

"Professor Lightfoot has been here to-day, and we have had the conversation which your Grace desired. Nothing, of course, could exceed his kindness and patience, and, if the object of our meeting had only been attained, I, at least, should look back to it with unmixed and thankful satisfaction. But I fear I must add that it leaves matters where it found them.

"Our differences were not as to facts, but as to principles. Whether the Provincial Synod can rightly tamper with the text of a document of Catholic authority, is a question of *Church* principle. Whether a body of Churchmen, who have solemnly affirmed, each at very sacred moments, that a Creed 'ought thoroughly to be received and believed,' can deal with the Creed on the avowed understanding that certain parts of it, at the least, need not or ought not to be believed at all, is a question of moral principle. To me it seems clearer than ever that it is the truth or falsehood of the Eighth Article which is in dispute. If it is false, we must change our definitions as to fundamentals. If it is true, the unpopularity of Truth can be no reason with a Christian against proclaiming it.

"Professor Lightfoot's own view of the formation of the Athanasian Creed was of course very interesting to me, so far as he developed it.

I rejoiced to find that he does not endorse Mr. Ffoulkes's recent theories about Paulinus of Aquileia. He admitted, too, that very formidable objections, of a kindred kind to those which Dean Stanley and his allies put forward against the Athanasian Creed, might be pressed with equal justice against the Apostles' Creed, or parts of it ; and that they will be so pressed, if the justice of the present assault is practically admitted, does not admit of a doubt. Indeed, the destructive energy of the unbelieving School will not stop with the Creeds, as your Grace's knowledge of the existing condition of controversy with respect to the books of Holy Scripture would assure you.

"For myself, I fear I must say very respectfully, but firmly, that I adhere entirely to the terms of my first letter to your Grace."

Liddon was far more deeply roused by this question than by the Purchas Decision, or by the fears of any Privy Council Judgment on the doctrine of the Holy Eucharist in the prosecution of Mr. Bennett.

To Dr. Bright.

"Brislington, January 11, 1872.

". . . As to the Bennett case, of course we *are* on the edge of a precipice. But I feel that one must go on as usual, just as those people do who read Dr. Cumming about the Seals, etc. If the crash is to come, it will ; and the more ties it snaps and confusion it causes, the better for the sinews and material of the Kingdom of Order, which, as we must hope and pray, will in God's own way come somehow out of the supervening chaos. To say the truth, I feel now habitually, that so many *vital* matters are pending, that I leave things more happily in God's Hands than I did some time ago, and do not, I hope, much mind, if only what is best for His Cause takes place, as far as we are concerned—or rather, as far as our responsibility goes.

"I am much pressed by medical people not to go back to Oxford next Term, at least. But how can I not? It is dreadfully embarrassing, and one can only wait *de die in diem*."

To the Same.

"Brislington, Bristol, January 26, 1872.

". . . Dr. Ogle came down here to see me, and was so decided about my not returning to Oxford, that I felt I had no choice. However, I almost doubt now whether I could not have managed. Certainly I *am* better than at the beginning of the month ; quite a different person, as far as feeling goes. Among 'second causes,' if the expression is still philosophically correct, cod-liver oil holds a prominent place, which accordingly I consume in great quantities. By way of *really* resting, I am refreshing my old memories of the Waverley Novels. How I wish people read them more nowadays than, I fear, they do ! As narrative, each seems to me *perfect*, like a mosaic— you cannot leave a bit out without spoiling the whole. And morally they are far more invigorating than anything modern that I ever came across of the same kind. Ecclesiastically, Sir Walter ploughed, and Newman followed him with the seed-bag. . . . They make me envy you your knowledge of Scotland, which I have only visited twice —the last visit nineteen years ago.

" . . . Of course, I have no feeling for the Articles as in themselves worth a desperate struggle. I wish that we were without them, if we had anything to put in their place, and prevent the upgrowth of extraordinary heresies. But, as it is, they at once protect and impede us. . . ."

But in regard to the Athanasian Creed, he felt there was an urgent call for frequent and energetic remonstrances, on the ground that no proposal to alter the use of any of the Creed ought for a moment to be entertained ; if carried into effect, it would, he maintained, alter the status of the English Church radically.

To Dr. Pusey.

" Brislington, February 4, 1872.

" . . . We cannot disguise from ourselves that it is no Civil Court but the Bishops, the guardians of the Faith, who are attacking the Catholic Creed in the Upper House of Convocation. The moral effect of the removal of the Warning Clauses will be a proclamation of indifference to the Doctrine of the Blessed Trinity, and the Divine Incarnation ; a proclamation that the man who, with his eyes open, adopts the blasphemies of Sabellius and Arius, will be just as well off as a Catholic believer in the Eternal World. This is what poor Stanley means, and he *rules* at Lambeth. Depend upon it, if the Creed is mutilated or disused, he will know how to push his advantage—and with irresistible effect. Probably if Convocation were to decide *against the Creed* we might be saved, by the disinclination of Parliament to meddle with Theology. But what a salvation ! To be saved from our own Bishops by the vote of an unbelieving Legislature ! "

It was no mere threat of retirement which he had addressed to the Archbishop ; he fully meant what he said, and he was careful that his sister, who had always lived with him at 3, Amen Court, should so understand it, for she would be specially inconvenienced by his carrying it into effect.

To Mrs. Ambrose.

" Brislington, February 12, 1872.

". . . I fear sometimes that you may not have quite realised what my own language on this subject involves. I must *act* on what I have said to the Archbishop of Canterbury, and, more recently, to Lord Lyttelton. If the Creed is mutilated or degraded, I retire from the ministry of the Church, which, by such an act, will in my judgment so fatally impair its claim to Catholic authority. Provincial Churches are beneath the Catholic Creeds, not above them—to be judged by them, but utterly incapable of judging them without condemning themselves. I do not wish, then, to retract my language if I could ; but I could not now do it, if I would, without something like dishonour. But I fear, as I said, that you may not have realised that this literally means nothing less than the *probability* (for it is more than a *possibility* now) of your being again without a home at Midsummer. It is necessary to look this right in the face. When it comes to this, we shall be able to talk details over ; but it is only important to be prepared in thought and feeling, as well as in other ways.

" It will be a great sorrow to me to have offered *you* a home which turns out, after all, to be like the floating island in ' Gulliver ; ' but one thought that the Creeds, at least, were safe in the Church of England.

" Drs. Pusey and Bright evidently think that the matter will be pushed to extremities. At least, so I gather from a letter of the former's received this morning.

" I suppose that if Convocation decides upon degrading or mutilating the Creed, the Act of Parliament will scarcely pass before June or July. Perhaps we should know at Midsummer, or soon after—I mean with a view to giving our servants warning and other things that will have to be looked to about the house. Of course, I can *date* my resignation when I like, *i.e.* within a few weeks of the settlement of the matter."

Thus he had burnt his ships, and left himself no possibility of compromise ; he even began to form plans for his life after resignation.

" I too," he writes to Pusey on February 16, " cannot become a Roman, because I entirely disbelieve the Pope's Infallibility and other things too. And, like you, I have seriously thought of the Old Catholic Movement. If, *e.g.*, I am stranded at Midsummer (things will not, I suppose, come to a head before that date), I shall go to Munich, I think, and do any work for Döllinger that I can, and get such knowledge as may be useful for us hereafter in England."

Because of ill health he had been obliged to obtain leave to be absent from his Oxford work for the Lent Term, and he spent most of his time with his sister at Brislington, resting. His diary is very rarely written, unless some special event called him to London and had to be recorded.

" *February* 27.—Thanksgiving Day [for the recovery of the Prince of Wales]. Held a breakfast party at seven. Mr. Foster, John and Mr. G. A. Spottiswoode, as wand-bearers, were present. We all got into church at 9.30. I spent about two and a half hours in making people take off their hats, and in otherwise trying to find them seats and to keep order. . . . Went at 12.30 with Bishop of London, the Dean and Chapter, down to the west door of St. Paul's, and met the Royal procession. The *Te Deum* was grand. The Archbishop's sermon cold, thin, passionless, but well-intended."

About the same time, in commenting on the action of the Archbishop of Paris with reference to Père Gratry, he writes to one of his intimate friends—

" The Archbishop of Paris seems to go on much like another Archbishop with whom you and I have more to do—*mutatis mutandis.* There is something in the position, I suppose, which damages people— all except a very few. But it is painful and odd that one should associate Bishops so generally with qualities which the ideal of their office does not make room for. Dr. Newman tells us that most of them were much the same in the Arian times. No doubt they were, if, as I suppose, something in the position makes its holders timid and imperious at once, quite oddly."

At the end of his April residence he resumed work at Oxford in a more hopeful mood. He thought that the Decision of the Lower House of Convocation had settled the question about the Creed according to his wishes.

" *April* 26.—My first Lecture. Very largely attended. More than a hundred men. End of discussion of the Athanasian Creed. A great majority for Lord A. Compton's motion [in the Lower House of Convocation]."

He was over-sanguine about the result of that vote in Convocation, for the whole matter was reopened in the Upper House of Convocation in the following July by Bishop Wilberforce. Before doing so he consulted Liddon about his plan for dealing with the position of the Creed in the Prayer-book. Liddon replied—

To the Bishop of Winchester.

"Hatfield, July 1, 1872.

". . . Your proposal that the Bishops should have a legal power of dispensing in writing, upon application from an incumbent, with the use of the Athanasian Creed as enjoined in the Prayer-book, does not appear to me, upon further consideration, to involve the abandonment of principle. Such a power is part of the *jus liturgicum* anciently believed to be inherent in the Episcopate, although suspended by the Papal usurpations abroad, and, by later legislation, among ourselves. This power never extended, as your Lordship knows, to the *matter* and form of the Sacraments, or to the main features of the Eucharistic Office, but it would certainly have enclosed a right to deal with the contents of such a Service as our ' Morning Prayer.'

"As far as this goes, the Bishops might, in their collective capacity, have advised the omission of the Creed in such a Service ; only they could not, as I believe, do so under the existing circumstances of our Church without being guilty of an act of conspicuous *unfaithfulness to Revealed Truth.*

" If all that is conceded be that it shall be within the power of a Bishop to give a permission to disuse the Creed in particular parishes, upon application from the incumbent, and not otherwise, the witness of our Church would still be substantially intact ; nothing would be done beyond recognising the toleration of partial disuse which prevails already. What would happen in such places as Westminster Abbey, or most of the College Chapels in Oxford, I do not know ; nor can we be sure that some Bishops would not use this power against the Faith. But we should have been spared these changes in the Prayer-book which just now would compromise us so fatally before Christendom, and which would impair the inheritance of Faith which we hold in trust for those who will come after us."

In the hope that such a solution, which he would not find intolerable, would be adopted, he went off for a holiday in Ireland, which he describes in the two following letters :—

To Dr. Bright.

"Kilcornan, Oranmore, July 12, 1872.

". . . Your letter of the 10th finds me here—in the west of Ireland. I was anxious to get out of London for a short time before my August work, and here I am altogether out of the way.

"On Monday, I met Newman at dinner,[1] and for the first time in my life. It was like coming into contact with the *fons et origo*—at least of most of the great moral forces which we have known much about—in a concrete form. He, of course, was simple, and very interesting and studiously uncontroversial, without avoiding subjects that might have furnished matter for controversy. He had the Doctor's manner of significant silences, as well as some other characteristics ; he held his hands just as dear Mr. Keble used to—out on his knees, and close together, while talking, as if one or the other might run away. He was evidently up to everything that is going on among ourselves— no one more so—*e.g.* keen as to the real age and value of this Utrecht Psalter."

To Mrs. Ambrose.

"Kilcornan, Oranmore, July 16, 1872.

". . . By this time, as you would suppose, I have quite reached the tame-tom-cat stage of my visit, and feel as if I had formed regular habits with regard to this place, and should go on indefinitely as I am. Nevertheless, it will come to an end—probably on Friday, when I shall go to Limerick. . . .

"It is so odd seeing nothing but Roman Catholic laity. For no priest ever comes to the house by any chance, unless he be an Englishman. Redington evidently views his parish priest here as a 'machine which can produce the Sacraments properly,' as somebody once said. When English Roman Catholic priests stay in the house, there is daily Mass in the chapel—not otherwise. . . . The Protestant element in this part of the country is too insignificant to excite much attention ; and, so far as I can make out, there is no trace of animosity. But the R.C. gentry are all of one mind about preventing their own clergy from getting political power at elections, as Redington, *e.g.*, is at war, in a respectful sort of way, with the Archbishop of Tuam. On Saturday we went to the —— : he a Roman Catholic Irishman, she an Englishwoman and a convert of some twenty years' standing—a relative of Mrs. Hawkins, of Oriel. Yesterday, into Galway, where I

---

[1] His diary records it : "*July* 8. —In the evening dined at the Deanery to meet Dr. Newman. His manner was quite that of Mr. Keble, in its simplicity and intensity. He was much amused with the Metaphysical Society, and said that they ought not to be eating any dinners."

saw a Captain O'Hara, a leading Orange Protestant, but a very gentlemanly pleasant man, and the Lynchs, *passim*, who have always been Roman Catholics.

"There was one Service at an 'Anglican' Church a mile and a half from here, on Sunday, at 12 o'clock. I thought it better to go, that I might not be mistaken ; so I set off while all the rest went to Mass at one of the three Chapels just outside the park. This evidently disconcerted the Irish peasants, who, I think, supposed me previously to be a Roman, but could not make out so equivocal a proceeding. On the same ground, to avoid being mistaken, I have *not* attended prayers in the chapel here. As there is no chaplain, Redington would say what prayers are said ; and he could not, if he would, ask me to say them. On the other hand, I could not accept this arrangement without compromising my position ; so I don't go to the morning and evening prayers. *En revanche*, I say Grace for everybody at dinner, which is odd when every single person at table is a Roman Catholic.

"The Service was characteristic. The clergyman said the Litany *standing*—looking due west—and in the way of fervid declamation. He paused for a long time at anything that struck him, and thumped the cushion on the reading-desk. So the Nicene Creed, and throughout. There was no Celebration. The Sermon was the climax. The language, of course, as Irish as you can imagine ; but I am now quite accustomed to that. But the arguments, so by courtesy to term them, were more Irish still—Irish in their delightful puzzle-headedness and ingenuity, so much more clever and so much more absurd than would be possible to the average British intellect. There was another and better vein ; but on this it was difficult to fix attention. On coming home I found that Redington had had an Irish-American priest preaching at his chapel, who had discoursed fervidly on the glories of Ireland, and had assured the party from the hall that he meant to go back to America as soon as he could, immediately after Service.

"The country hereabouts is not pretty, except that the sea is almost always in view, and the park, of course, which is very extensive, has a beauty of its own. Galway is full of antiquarian interests ; and there are numbers of ruined chapels and monasteries all about the country which are full of interest of antiquarian and other kinds. I am surprised at the carelessness of the Irish about their graveyards. Yesterday at Clare—Galway Abbey, a beautiful Franciscan church ruined by Cromwell—I counted eighty skulls and innumerable other bones exposed to the air. It appears that they turn one body out of a grave to put another in without scruple—like hermit crabs. Redington deplores this and other things of the same kind ; but he says that Irish clergy, as a rule, are without right feeling on these subjects—ages of persecution have left them content with the barest necessaries of Church life.

"But since I have been here I have heard of almost nothing but

Mr. Justice Keogh—' Mr. K'o,' as the Irish call him. How he fished every day during the trial at Galway, and for salmon ; how he took off his judge's wig to declaim more effectively in court ; how he got up early to 'refresh' himself ; how the R.C. Bishop of Galway winked at him in court ; how full of genius he is, and, at the same time, how perfectly unscrupulous—this and more to the same effect."

The Athanasian Creed controversy dragged on until at last in December a Committee of the two Houses of Convocation decided that the Creed was not to be altered, but that there should be a Synodical Declaration as regards the meaning of the Warning Clauses in it. To press this advantage to the utmost, it was arranged to hold a Public Meeting in St. James's Hall on January 31, 1873, before Convocation assembled again. Liddon had been adverse to such a gathering ; he thought it difficult for persons who hold the Truth to deal with such a subject in a manner which "would be, on the one hand, accurate and reverent, and on the other, rhetorically effective. We must move," he adds, "as if among china, and this is not the best way of producing a popular impression that shall move and arrest the world." Yet he consented to speak at the Meeting. Very rarely did he appear at public gatherings of the kind. He always dreaded them for his friends when they went to them, and far more for himself when he was obliged, as in this case, to appear on the platform. When Liddon rose to speak on this occasion he was received with a tumult of applause ; the whole of the vast assemblage of men, which filled the floor to the galleries of St. James's Hall, rising to their feet, and cheering him again and again. He wrote about the Meeting to Pusey and to a friend some days after.

To Dr. Pusey.

"February 10, 1873.

" I have not heard directly what the Primate thinks of the Meeting, but Dr. Stanley and his friends say that now it will be impossible to deal with the Creed for another generation. . . . Lord Salisbury said to me at the end of the Meeting, ' Certainly it seems to me now that this has been a good move ; but I shall be better able to judge of its real effect, when I see what opposition or counter-protest it may call forth, two months hence."

To Miss Mirehouse.

"Christ Church, February 12, 1873.

". . . The A[thanasian] C[reed] Meeting *was*, I think, a success ; it has evidently impressed some of the more hostile newspapers. Lord Salisbury was sarcastic, which made the Mother Record angry, about 'the clergy being honourable as well as pious.' The delightful thing was to witness the enthusiasm of 3000 men in one room on behalf of the Catholic Faith. They certainly did shout ; and at the Doctor's name there was a perfect ovation. His illness has been a terrible anxiety. Of course, it was a foreshadowing of what must come.

"I get some very fierce anonymous letters about the Athanasian Creed, which would amuse you, if they were not so sad as to what they imply on the part of the writers. The last tells me that I am a Pharisee, and should have helped to crucify our Lord. It is very odd that people should think, much more write, such things ; but the *passion* of unbelief is a very serious thing while it lasts.

"I am glad that the good Archbishop of Dublin is taking a holiday ; he needs one. Nothing can exceed the difficulty, if not the misery, of his position. A sensitive, high-minded scholar and Churchman, like Daniel in the lions' den—only that the Irish lay delegates do not seem to possess very lionlike attributes. May God strengthen him and carry him through ! "

But the success of the great Meeting was not counter-acted, as Lord Salisbury had feared, and in the Meetings of Convocation in the May following the alternative of an explanatory note to the Creed was adopted, and the Creed was allowed to retain its place in its unmutilated form. The extent to which this decision was due to the action of Pusey and Liddon, was regretfully admitted by the Arch-bishop of Canterbury, who, in his Primary Charge as Arch-bishop, attributed the failure of his efforts to the statements of "certain eminent men whom we greatly respect, that, if certain courses were not taken, they should feel it their duty to retire into lay communion with the Church of England."

Less than six months after this, on July 19, 1873, Bishop Wilberforce was thrown from his horse and killed. In him Liddon lost one of the most revered friends of his

life. Since he left Cuddesdon, in 1859, he had, of course,
not seen so much of the Bishop as before; but there was
no coldness or estrangement between them, though on
many points they had widely differed. As will have been
seen, up to the end the Bishop had readily consulted him
on the anxious questions of the day, and Liddon had always
appealed to him instinctively in full confidence and with
unabated affection, whenever he wished to have the convictions and intentions of himself and his friends forcibly
represented to the Meetings of English Bishops.

He was abroad when the Bishop died, and wrote at
once as soon as the news reached him.

To Mrs. Ambrose.

"Le Mans, July 24, 1873.

". . . I can truly say that since my father's death, I have had no
such personal sorrow. The Bishop of Winchester deserved and had
my sincere affection, and I have always resented, as you know, the
vulgar and false notions of the young men about town, as to his
insincerity and the like. He did not always do or say what I could
have wished; but if he erred, his heart, I am quite sure, was in its
right place. May he rest in peace and light, beneath the Throne of
our Gracious Lord, Who knows what we all of us are, at the best, and
Who alone can make us worthy of Himself.

"I shall not hasten my return to England—I can do nothing more
for the dearest Bishop *there*, than *here;* and I am glad to be *quite*
alone, and out of the way of gossip and the English language."

Two years later, on November 2, 1875, he preached a
Sermon, in the presence of the Archbishop of Canterbury
and several Bishops, at the reopening of the Church at
Graffham, in Sussex, where Bishop Wilberforce had once
been Vicar. The Sermon, which was a sketch and defence of
the Bishop's character, was printed "by desire." As soon
as it appeared, Liddon found himself obliged to defend the
Bishop in public and private controversy because of his
refusal to admit that the versatility of his great friend
involved any moral inconsistency. Among others, Dean
Stanley, with whom on many points Liddon was in frequent

and most friendly correspondence, sent him several extracts from statements made by Bishop Wilberforce at various times, which seemed somewhat difficult to harmonise. Liddon replied—

To the Dean of Westminster.

"3, Amen Court, December 4, 1875.

". . . I am not in possession of the knowledge which would enable me to explain these different statements of the Bishop harmoniously ; but surely that does not show that they are irreconcilable with each other. The Bishop was very distrustful of himself, very impressionable, and constantly liable to sudden changes of opinion on points as to which he thought he had made up his mind. This may have been an intellectual infirmity ; and it was certainly, at times, a source of practical inconvenience. But it is strictly compatible with general integrity of purpose, and my 'eulogy' only amounts, after all, to a denial of the proposition that the Bishop was grossly dishonest.

"I was thrown into the closest contact with the Bishop for five years. We were so far from agreeing about matters which I deem of great importance, that, in the end, I had to leave Cuddesdon College. It was the only great disappointment of my life. I am therefore under no temptation to indulge in insincere eulogy about him, or to close my eyes to the faults of his character.

"But I had and have entire belief in his sincerity of purpose— that sort of robust belief which intimate contact with a man only can warrant, and which is not at all disturbed by two or three apparent inconsistencies, the explanation of which is not forthcoming. Mr. —— thinks of him as of Balaam and Demas ; but then, I have no means of knowing that Mr. —— knew anything about him at all, except what he might glean from a newspaper. As for me, had he been twice as eloquent and diligent as he really was, nothing would have induced me to say a word in his praise, had I believed him to be insincere."

On the same subject he wrote also to his old Christ Church tutor :—

To the Rev. G. Marshall.

"Christ Church, Oxford, November 28, 1875.

". . . Of course, in what I said, I did not attempt anything so formidable as a complete estimate of Bishop Wilberforce's character ; I only insisted on one side of it, which might be usefully dwelt on by those who have survived him, and which *is* the key, as I think, to its most striking ingredients. That he disappointed, precisely because he was so great, I quite agree; but, after all, this is only to say what must be said within varying limits of all human excellence. And I was under no particular temptation to over-estimate him—rather the reverse. Much of our intercourse was calculated to bring out the less favourable sides of his character; but I have always believed in his sincerity of purpose—although at times his sympathies gave the law to his understanding more than I at least could have wished. But he is, in some quarters—and not least in Oxford—so cruelly and so absurdly depreciated, that when Reginald Wilberforce asked me to preach that Sermon I could not say No, though I made the attempt very reluctantly. And the Archbishop of Canterbury wished me to print it; but there are sentences in it which made me think it better *not* to put his Grace's name on the title-page. . . . I may, of course, be mistaken, but I tried to say what I believed to be true about him, and not without some reserves which truth also seemed to require."

The General Election in February, 1874, resulted in the complete defeat of Mr. Gladstone's Government, and Liddon feared greatly for the probable results to the Church of the Conservative tenure of office under the rule of Mr. Disraeli. Liddon was not himself naturally a politician, but his confidence in the good intentions of Mr. Gladstone was only excelled by his complete distrust of the policy of his successor. He expresses his fears in a letter to his eldest sister.

To Mrs. Poole King.

"Christ Church, February 14, 1874.

". . . What a reversal of hopes and fears it all has been! I sometimes wish that I *could* sufficiently get rid of my thorough-going disbelief in Dizzy's principles to rejoice with him in so unique and extraordinary triumph. But I cannot. That the affairs of this country should be handed over to *him* appears to me a misfortune of great magnitude. However, we have now got to the end of the reaction, and in a few months the tide will turn, and Englishmen will begin to think that they have been unjust towards their greatest statesman. My main fear is as to the effect of all this upon the temper of the Liberal party—upon Gladstone himself—and upon the inevitable future. So unaccountable and in some respects irrational a recurrence to Toryism is certain to lead to a counter-movement. How far will the pendulum go when it next swings strongly in the Liberal direction ? *That* is really the serious question, and I see that already destructive Radicals of Mr. Morley's school are rejoicing at the turn things have taken as delivering us from Gladstone—his 'half-measures' and 'his theological prejudices.'

" However, no more."

His worst fears were soon confirmed in the legislation which the new Government at once proposed, in order to suppress Ritualism. In the Ritualistic controversy which was then raging with an acrimony which it is now difficult to understand, there could be no doubt about Liddon's sympathies. Not only did he delight in the beauty and dignity of liturgical worship, but his sense of history and of justice, and his knowledge of the Prayer-book, pointed to the same side. Already he had put himself forward for prosecution to shield others ; and he was always ready to use the influence of his name and position to protect any hard-working clergyman who had given up everything to serve the cause of his Master, and was being maligned and persecuted on the ground of an ambiguous rubric, and at the hands of men who habitually neglected the clearest directions of the Prayer-book. He was one at heart with the persecuted, and did all he could to help and to steady them. But he felt, of course, the absolute necessity for loyal self-restraint within the limits of the legitimate inter-pretation of the Prayer-book, and refused to countenance any disloyal ritual or any forms of devotion inconsistent with the teaching of the English Church.

Early in March some articles in the *Times* forecasted the coming " Public Worship Regulation Bill." Liddon immediately consulted Lord Salisbury as to the fact, and Sir Robert Phillimore as to the measures that should be taken to stop the Bill. Lord Salisbury assured him that the Arch-bishop's mind was set upon carrying some such Bill, and that the Bishops as a body concurred ; for himself he greatly deplored it, but he dwelt long and anxiously on the difficulty created by the advanced Ritualists, and on the importance of getting them to moderate their way of

N

going on. Sir Robert Phillimore urged an immediate attack upon the proposal before it was even presented to Parliament.

"I also," Liddon added, in a letter to the Dean of St. Paul's, "called on Mr. Gladstone, who talked very freely on the subject, and said that it was always of late a painful question in his mind whether 'the Church of England would not sink through clinging to the gold which she carried.' This *à propos* of the churchwarden rate-paying element in the Diocesan Councils, with a view to a 'national' basis. He spoke with great warmth of the proposed work of those Councils, too ; but 'Why don't you go to the Government?' I did not tell him that I had seen Lord Salisbury, or I might have been pressed, and could not say what I know with perfect fairness to Lord S. But how great and how loveable Mr. G. is, in what the papers call his 'fall'!"

In consequence of these consultations, Liddon wrote at once to the President of the English Church Union, to stir up immediate opposition to the Bill, and to try to place a check on any excess of ritual which could be used as an argument on its behalf.

To the Hon. C. L. Wood.

"Christ Church, March 14, 1874.

". . . It may occur to you that we had better wait until the Bill is drafted, and can be then criticised in detail and on its merits. But it is, on the other hand, easier to destoy such a creature in the embryonic stage than after birth. Its emergence into print, as a serious legislative proposal, endorsed (unless I am misinformed) by the active or passive concurrence of the entire Episcopate, would of itself be a scandal to our Church of the gravest kind. We saw in the history of the Athanasian Creed controversy that the present Primate, while capable of very audacious attacks upon the Faith and Discipline of the Church of England, does not venture to encounter a formidable opposition, or, indeed, to do anything that would risk the shell of the Establishment. Perhaps, therefore, if a sufficient number of persons can be convinced that matters are serious, we may escape this threatening mischief.

"We have, of course, friends in the present Cabinet. I don't forget the Orange fanaticism of the Lord Chancellor, and, to make a descent, of Lord Sandon. But there are others, as you know, who will help us if they can, although we shall miss Mr. Gladstone at the helm. The Archbishop would not have ventured on such an enterprise during the late Government's time.

"How I wish, too, that we could do anything to persuade our friends to avoid much which they do and say—much which is in no way necessary—which keeps up constant irritation, and involves them in the suspicion of secret disloyalty to the English Church ! Could a meeting of any kind be arranged by Mackonochie, R. West, and others with a view to minimising points of offence, and so removing the excuse (so far as it might be done lawfully) for such legislation as that in question ? "

On the same day he and Pusey sent a long communication to the Rev. A. H. Mackonochie, the Vicar of St. Alban's, Holborn, to the same effect as the closing paragraph of the preceding letter. The text of it is given in full in the " Life of A. H. Mackonochie," pp. 222-226 ; its main proposal is contained in the following passage :—

" Must it not be acknowledged, in view of the exaggerated ceremonial and ill-considered language which are sometimes to be found among (so-called) ' Ritualists,' that there are grave reasons for anxiety on this head (*i.e.* whether we ever act or speak in a way calculated to cause needless offence)? We at least cannot help thinking so, and we are therefore writing to ask you to use your great influence with many of our brethren, in favour of a course which appears to us to be recommended alike by charity for souls, and by loyalty to the common Truth.

"Would it not be possible to take some early opportunity of considering how much of recent additions to customary ritual could be abandoned without doing harm ? We will not attempt to go into details. But surely matters of taste or feeling, not necessarily, or of long habit, associated with the enforcement or maintenance of doctrine, yet calculated to alarm the prejudiced and uninstructed, ought, on St. Paul's principle, to be at least reconsidered."

Pusey in this matter had more hope than Liddon that the storm would pass over. But Liddon regarded Archbishop Tait, then and always, as the champion of a policy which he thought disastrous for the Church, and in this Public Worship Regulation Bill he found the clearest proof of his suspicions.

But when the passing of the Measure became certain, he began to see much less cause to fear its results.

To the Hon. C. L. Wood.

"Kilcornan, Co. Galway, July 21, 1874.

". . . I suppose, from what I have learnt since coming here, that the Bill will become law. The question is whether it will be at once put in force on any considerable scale. I am inclined to hope not. Numbers of people have been supporting the Bill in order to prove to their middle-class Protestant constituents that they wish to be doing something ; and before the exact value of what they have done can be appreciated in the light of experience, a new combination of colours, we may hope, will be presented by the political kaleido-scope. I have written to Mr. (or rather to Mrs.) Gladstone to thank *him* for so generous a speech ; and I should be curious to know what our chivalrous friend at Madresfield [Lord Beauchamp] is thinking of *his* political chief. I never believed in Mr. Disraeli, and am not disappointed to find that he is prepared to throw anything or anybody to the sharks in order to catch the *popularis aura.* . . . I wish we could have a Church party in Parliament which would make purely political issues of secondary importance to religious ones.

" Of course, there is no reason for despondency. No Legislature can really destroy a religious conviction, except by exterminating its holders. It is historically too late to do that, and we shall live to see the drowned Egyptians on the seashore even yet."

As will have been seen by the letter to Mr. Mackonochie, the defence of some of the more extreme men among the Ritualists was not easy. And in his endeavour to shield them, Liddon sometimes found himself in difficulties. At the end of this year, a leading article and many letters in the *Times* from writers whose position was certified by the prominence and type of their anonymous charges, were directed against Ritualism ; and at last one letter appeared from Monsignor Capel, charging the Ritualists in general and Liddon by name, with disseminating doctrines peculiar to the Roman Church, and causing a continuous supply of converts to Rome. This charge of teaching Roman doctrine Liddon immediately denied emphatically, not only for him-self, but also for all his friends, and so he fell into a trap. For his correspondent at once produced in support of his statement a collection of passages from recent publications ; and although Liddon was able to defend all the passages for which he was himself even remotely responsible, he was bound to admit that some of the quotations from other Anglican writers transgressed the limits of loyalty to the Formularies of the English Church. But in regard to the conversions to Rome, he attributed them not to any such doctrinal slips of some of the Ritualists, but

"to the restless, faithless, fatal policy which at one moment would rid us of our Creed, at another would ignore our Orders, at a third would invite a Parliament consisting of men of any or no religious belief to regulate our Worship of Almighty God." [1]

As regards Monsignor Capel's whole position, he pertinently says—

"I cannot make out why it is that, if they (the Ritualists) are really, although unintentionally, doing the work of the Church of Rome, her most prominent champion in this country should be so anxious to draw attention to them." [2]

Yet Capel's letters were hailed with delight by the Church Association, and circulated throughout the country in their monthly publications.

The tone of this correspondence caused Liddon to welcome the far more just estimate that Newman took of the position of the Ritualists.

To Dr. Newman.

"3, Amen Court, St. Paul's, E.C., January 15, 1875.

". . . Like the rest of the world, I have, of course, been reading your reply to Mr. Gladstone ['The Vatican Decrees'], and I only venture to write to you about it, that I may assure you of my grateful sense of the extreme consideration and generosity which, as I conceive, marks the passage (p. 75) in which you allude to the 'Ritualists.' You might, with perfect truth, have said some hard things about them, because they say and do that which it is hard to defend on the score of consistency in several particulars.

"But at a time when they are down, and the general public is thinking that nothing is too bad to say about them, and Roman Catholic controversialists can make capital out of Puritan feeling, if they like to do so, I for one am keenly alive both to what you have said and to what you have left unsaid. Not that I should have

[1] *Times*, December 24, 1874.   [2] *Ibid.*, January 18, 1875.

expected anything else from you, if you alluded to them or to our affairs at all; but this does not make me less grateful. There is, of course, much in your letter, as to which I cannot follow you; but I never think of this without regret, or of yourself without deep gratitude and affection."

But the *Times* correspondence had also this further result: it made Liddon continue his efforts to restrain illegalities of ceremonial and doctrine, even with men over whom he had little direct influence.

To ——

"3, Amen Court, E.C., January 15, 1875.

". . . I must ask your very indulgent consideration for what I am going to say. You may have seen a recent correspondence which, certainly without my wishing it, I had to manage with Monsignor Capel in the *Times*, and which I did manage unskilfully enough.

"But it has forced on me very strongly the conviction that our whole position is really imperilled by anything which seems beyond the warrant of our Formularies, and I have been trying to think what I could do to prevent our being open to the assaults of the Romano-Puritan leagues. I have been looking, *inter alia*, at your book, and I am bold enough to beg you to withdraw it quietly. I don't see how we can defend it with our Subscription to the Articles. If this costs you money, as I fear it will, I will do my utmost to meet such expenses if you will kindly allow me. I feel that I am making a serious demand upon your kindness, but I shall trust, in any case, not to be misunderstood."

To the Same.

[Undated.]

" I wish that something could be done to get —— *not* to celebrate without administering to two persons. He might easily arrange always to have two communicants. Not to do this is to give a fatal advantage to the Puritanical party, because there is absolutely not a shadow of a doubt as to the law of the Church of England on the subject. *Do see* if something cannot be done. The real weakness of our position is that people will not see the differences between defending principles and flourishing red rags before wild bulls—rags, I mean, which are not flags of any known principles."

It was in connection with this and another correspondence with Monsignor Capel that Dean Stanley, in writing to Liddon, added a request that he would fill an unexpected vacancy in the list of preachers at the Abbey.

"I write this," the Dean added, "not unmindful of former difficulties. But, to tell the truth, I had, irrespective of this emergency, thought of taking some occasion of renewing my request, and I therefore venture to hope that you will perhaps lend a willing ear."

Liddon's engagements compelled him to decline at that moment; but he expressed a hope that he might be able to take a place in the next list of Abbey preachers, and it was arranged that he should preach on June 18, 1876. The Dean was anxious to make his guest in every way at home, and even offered to make a special rule that Canons of St. Paul's Cathedral should always preach in the Abbey in surplices, so that Liddon might avoid wearing a black gown. The Sermon was on the Gospel for the day, the Parable of Dives and Lazarus,—insisting on the sufficiency of our present opportunities for holding the Faith and leading a good life.

As soon as his residence was over in August, 1874, he went off to the Bonn Reunion Conference, to which Dr. Döllinger had invited him. At it there were present representatives of the Church from Russia, England, and the United States, to discuss with the Old Catholic body the possibility of the restoration of communion between the East and some parts of Western Christendom, on the basis of the doctrine of the Church before the separation between East and West. It was a project which Liddon gladly welcomed, and for the completion of which he spared no labour.

"*September* 14. *Bonn.*—Up at 6. Saw a deacon ordained by Bishop Reinkens in the University chapel. The Bishop was in pontificals, and the Roman Ordinal was used throughout. At 9 we assembled in the musick salle of the University. Professor Reusch made a short introductory speech, and Dr. Döllinger followed. At 11 we had a meeting in the hotel as to the line to be taken by the English. The Bishop was very firm and moderate. . . . At 3 reassembled. A long debate on the *Filioque*, in which I took part, opposing the excision. At 6 the Russian committee sat. The Russian delegates objected strongly to our resolution of the morning, and a long and animated discussion between them and Professor Knoodt and Bishop Reinkens ensued.

"*September* 15.—At 7 went to the ordination of the Alt-Katholik priest who was made a deacon yesterday. The ceremony was most interesting. At 9, after a preliminary discussion, resumed debate in the musick salle. The question of the Double Procession was finally settled by a formula to the effect that it was desirable that the whole Church should consider the question of the *Filioque* being in the Creed. We then traversed some very delicate ground, and I was defeated in an endeavour to avoid condemning the Immaculate Conception *as an opinion*. A lively discussion on Prayer for the Dead. The Greeks could not receive the statement about Invocation of Saints. The Dean of Chester has behaved very generously throughout. The Bishop of Pittsburg was angry with me for taking the line I did with respect to the Immaculate Conception.[1]

"*September* 16.—Conference at 8 of Howson and Bishop of Pittsburg with myself in Dr. Döllinger's rooms. After much difficulty we agreed to a formula about the Eucharistic Sacrifice, which will, I hope, do. The Bishop [Reinkens], Dr. Döllinger, and four Professors came to dine with me to-day at the hotel. There was much German 'hoch'-ing after dinner. I sat between Janyschew and Bishop Reinkens. Closing meeting of the Conference at 3. It was a discussion of the St. Petersburg Sendschreiben, point by point. There was a considerable difficulty about Baptism, but the Greeks were more yielding than yesterday. A walk in the evening with Bishop Reinkens."

To THE HON. C. L. WOOD.

"Salisbury, September 26, 1874.

". . . The Bonn Conference may, I hope, have done some good in the way of showing that, with a little forbearance, there is a real possibility of 'doing something' in that direction. What was done does not go very far ; at least I think not. But some of the difficulties which might have been foreseen were surmounted much more easily than we had any right to expect. Of course, Dr. Döllinger's commanding learning kept possible criticism and opposition at bay, and I am bound to add that I was agreeably surprised by the moderation and fairness of Dean Howson. Still, there were some miscarriages, as you will have seen from the skeleton Report of our proceedings which has appeared in the newspapers, and unless we had had private meetings, etc., there would have been more. . . ."

[1] He was severely attacked for this in the *Times* of September 30, and he explained his meaning in a letter, October 2, which is printed at the end of this chapter (see p. 195).

The gathering at the Conference of representatives from so many parts of Christendom appealed to Liddon's imagination, and roused great hopes of the possible work of the Old Catholics, and of the value of such a meeting. In the following year, he published a translation of the authorised Report of the discussions, and expressed his hopes in the Preface.

" The Old Catholic body," he said, " seem to hold out to the English Church an opportunity which has been denied to it for three hundred years. Catholic, yet not Papal ; Episcopal, with no shadow of doubt or prejudice resting on the validity of its Orders ; friendly with the Orthodox, but yet free from the stiffness and one-sidedness of an isolated tradition ; sympathising with all that is thorough and honest in the critical methods of Protestant Germany, yet holding on firmly and strenuously to the Faith of Antiquity—this body of priests and theologians and simple believers addresses to the English Church a language too long unheard, in the Name of our common Lord and Master." [1]

He regarded the first Conference as only a fragment ; but saw great value in the Report because of Döllinger's hopeful statements about the relations of the Eastern Church with the West, and his acceptance of the validity of Anglican Orders.

In the following August there was a second Conference at Bonn. It was gathered, not by special invitations, as in 1874, but by a general notice, and was, therefore, more numerously but not so satisfactorily attended. Liddon had not intended to be present, as he was in residence at St. Paul's ; but Gregory insisted on his going, and undertook the duties at the Cathedral in his stead. His diary and letters give an account of his own share in the proceedings.

" *August* 11. *Bonn.*—Soon after our arrival we went to Döllinger's. A very large English contingent was present, including Bishop Sandford, and, to my discomfiture, Lord Plunket and Master Brooke. Sandford wondered at my presence. Thought I was at St. Paul's, in residence."

[1] " Reunion Conference at Bonn, 1874," Preface, p. xxv.

To the Right Hon. W. E. Gladstone.

"Bonn, August 12, 1875, 11 p.m.

". . . The first day of our Conference is over. The proceedings in the morning (9–1) were entirely in German, as between the Old Catholics and the Easterns. They were opened by a speech of an hour and a half in length from Dr. Döllinger. In the earlier parts of it he traced, from the writings of Aquinas downwards, the growth of the influences which culminated in the Vatican Council. In the latter, he addressed himself to the dogmatic issues connected with the *Filioque*—the main obstacle to a good understanding with the East. He and the other Germans are less disposed to surrender than was the case last year. They insist that such Greek Fathers as St. Cyril of Alexandria and Epiphanius quite cover the Western belief, which is 'something more than a verbal matter;' and that the Greeks cannot condemn us without condemning their own great names.

"The rest of the morning was passed in the Russian criticisms on a paper of 'Bases for an Understanding,' which had been drawn up by the Germans. The Easterns were, I thought, still very stiff; they would not, *e.g.*, allow *any* difference of meaning between *procedere* and ἐκπορεύεσθαι. I fear that no explanation that we can make will induce them to consent to our retaining the *Filioque* in the Creed.

"In the afternoon the results of this discussion were submitted to the English and Americans, in English. Nothing very definite was arrived at; but to-morrow morning a series of propositions, gathered from Athanasius, Cyril, and other Greeks of authority, will be submitted to the Greeks. If accepted, they would amply cover the Western doctrine. But I fear that they will be 'explained'—as such theses are.

"The Easterns are very strong here—some twenty in all. Two Roumanian Bishops and two Archimandrites sent to represent him by the Patriarch of Constantinople, and with a great reputation as Patristic scholars, are among them. All the Russians, I *think*, of last year are present, with some additions.

"Of our own Church, the Bishop of Gibraltar, Dean Howson, Mr. Meyrick, Mr. Hogg, MacColl, Mr. May are the most prominent names. Two members of the Irish Synod have turned up, in the persons of Master Brooke and Lord Plunket. The Americans have no Bishop [here] this year. Dr. Nevin and Dr. Langdon are here, and the two houses of the Convention have sent their secretaries, Dr. Potter and Dr. Perry. The general invitation appears to me to be less successful than private invitations to persons believed to be competent and interested in the subject.

"I was careful to give your message. Your letter was read this afternoon, but MacColl stated that it was not intended for immediate publication in the newspapers."

[*Diary.*] "*August* 13.—The morning discussion was on the Patristic theses submitted to the Greeks by Dr. Döllinger. They objected to them (1) on the ground of the immediate and remote control; (2) as paraphrasing the original rather than translating it; (3) as giving too much weight to the Fathers. In the afternoon my proposition was discussed. Dr. Nevin attacked me for making the retention of the *Filioque* subject to the decision of an Œcumenical Council. Howson objected to my definition of an ʻ Œcumenical Council,ʼ because it included the Romans and excluded the non-Episcopal Protestant bodies. Bishop Sandford made a speech, *à la* Tait, on the mistake of discussing old-world questions of dogma. Master Brooke asked me to prove the Double Procession from Scripture, etc. In the evening a long talk with Lord Plunket about the Irish Church and its doings. He was very conciliatory, but not very satisfactory.

"*August* 14.—Committee meeting at Dr. Döllinger's at 8–1. Present : Archbishop of Tenos, two Archimandrites, Professor Ossinin, and Janyschew. They had three propositions, the second of which would make all further proceedings impossible ; it condemned the doctrine that the Holy Ghost had his ὕπαρξις through the Son. They were half afraid of Cyril of Alexandria on this question, and they wanted John of Damascus. We finally agreed to ʻthe Fathers of the Undivided Church.ʼ At the afternoon sitting Dean Howson read a retractation of his assent to the thesis about the Eucharist last year. Dr. Overbeck, I observed, made the greatest use of this. It will, I fear, be fatal to our making any way whatever with the Greeks.

"*August* 15.—Went to Dr. Döllinger's to work at theses at 7.30. At 9 attended the Old Catholic service. Bishop Reinkens celebrated with great dignity and reverence. Professor Knoodt preached. The Mass, low, was accompanied by hymns in the Rhineland style. After this, went back to the committee, and helped to draw up six propositions from the works of St. John of Damascus, with Dr. Döllinger and Professor Langen. . . . After dinner, stated to the English what had been done, and returned to the committee, where five Orientals met four Germans and three Anglicans. The Orientals would not accept the third proposition of the morning's scheme, the keystone of the arch of the whole. Left Bonn at 8.30 for Cologne.

"*August* 17, *Tuesday. London.*—Saw MacColl, who tells me that on Monday all was happily settled. The Greeks accepted the third article. Sandford seems to have made a very good conciliatory speech in conclusion. Dr. Overbeck was greatly discouraged."

To C. T. Redington, Esq.

"Christ Church, October 26, 1875.

" . . . The Bonn Conference was very interesting in many respects. The Orientals were there in great force—Russians, Roumanians,

Constantinopolitans, Athenians. They could only understand each other through the medium of German, and had a great many private meetings before deciding on their line towards the Westerns. We English Church people were as poorly represented as it is possible to imagine ; it was a great mercy of God's that more mistakes were not made. The Old Catholics appeared to me to be more averse to innovation than in 1874, although no doubt a great many people have tacked themselves on to Döllinger, and claim the sanction of his name, who would rejoice in a complete Ecclesiastical Revolution ; but they will not improbably be disappointed. What 'Old Catholicism' lacks as a popular force, it seems to recover as a principle, resting on a solid basis, and illustrated by great sincerity and learning on the part of its exponents. . . . If it should be a mediating influence, as seems not impossible, between the sections of divided Christendom, it may yet, in God's Providence, achieve a truly noble work. But here again prophecy is imprudent, and duty and prayer seem the safest rule.

"If I were, *per impossibile*, an Irish Roman Catholic Bishop, I think I should do as they in the matter of education. As you know, I cannot but think that they threw away an opportunity which will not repeat itself, when they rejected the Irish Education Bill. But for the Church of Christ everywhere, the struggle against a secular system of education is *vital ;* and secular education is all that the State will, in future, uphold in Ireland.

"When you come to England you will, I hope, come and see me. There is so much to talk about—and life is so short."

The Report of the Conference again appeared in English, with a Preface from Liddon. He had been attacked, as soon as he came home, by the *Times* and the *Tablet*, and also by Dr. Pusey. Pusey thought that the *Filioque* clause was in danger ; the others attacked from the practical side. Liddon tried in his Preface to answer both criticisms without damaging the cause of reunion abroad by increasing disunion at home. He felt sure that the hostility of Pusey to the Resolutions of the Conference would greatly weaken the credit of the Conference in England.

To Dr. Bright.

"Brislington, January 16, 1876.

"I don't at all go as you do, manfully into texts, but keep to the region of generalities, in which, as we know, *dolus latet*. But I wanted to avoid the appearance of controverting the Doctor, and yet to save the results of the Conference from the effect of his letters. He has, indeed, dear man, without meaning it, placed me in a very difficult position, as Beresford Hope, etc., have been trying to make me write something on the other side in the *Times.* I am sure that anything is better than parading our differences. The Doctor has not much power of putting the Eastern case *vividly* before his imagination, or he would not, I venture to think, have written of the Easterns, or of the Western plan for conciliating them, as he has. He surrenders himself with absolute unreserve to that solemn side of truth which is undoubtedly affirmed by the Filioque, and he is intolerant of anything that limits it."

A few days later his diary shows the sides taken by his many friends in Oxford.

" *January* 28.—Dined with Dr. Pusey, who was full of his letters to the *Times* about the Bonn Conference. I hope that I partly softened him as to the mind of the Greeks and as to there being no risk of getting rid of the *Filioque.*

" *January* 29.—Walked out with Ffoulkes, who argued against the *Filioque* the whole way up to Foxcombe and back, as ' destructive of Church authority so long as it remains in the Creed.'

" *February* 4.—Walked out with Master of Balliol. Talked chiefly about the Old Catholic Movement. He did not think that it would come to very much. He wished to know *how* I thought the Bible could be made useful to people nowadays ? I could only say by their believing and reading it. The point of the question was, I suppose, that they did not believe it.

" *February* 18.—Dr. Pusey told me that if the English Church gave up the *Filioque*, he must either shut his eyes and go to Rome, or trust that God would save him out of any Church at all. He could have no part in it."

Pusey's objections to any kind of surrender on the Theological question were insuperable. He remonstrated in private letters, and wrote so strongly to the *Times*, that Liddon dreaded lest his arguments should diminish the great authority which was attached to his name. Discussion proved that the conclusions which the Easterns had accepted at the Bonn Conference were not free from ambiguity, and that Pusey had understood them in a way which their framers had not intended ; therefore, Pusey published a lengthy letter to Liddon entitled "On the Clause ' And the Son,' " in which he suggested several amendments to the Re-solutions of the Bonn Conference, and above all counselled delay. But for other reasons no third Conference was ever possible. In 1876 Döllinger himself decided against one.

To Dr. Döllinger.

"Christ Church, Oxford, June 23, 1876.

". . . Mr. Meyrick has sent me your letter to him, in which you announce the resolution not to hold a Reunion Conference at Bonn this year. We regret this very much indeed, but I can quite understand that, under present circumstances, no other decision was possible. Dr. Overbeck has evidently succeeded in alarming the Orientals ; and, indeed, by his English pamphlet, 'The Bonn Conferences and the *Fitioque* Question :' London, Trübner, 1876,' he has done his best to make those few Englishmen who read him hostile or indifferent to our efforts after peace. I hope that God may spare your life for many years, and that before 1877 it may be possible to convince the Orientals that the subject-matter of the Seventh Council is really disciplinary, and, therefore, not to be classed with the dogmatic decisions of the previous Six Councils.

"When, in your letter, you put Dr. Pusey into the same category with Dr. Overbeck, you *unconsciously* do the former an injustice. Dr. Pusey entirely sympathises with our object ; but, for the present, he hesitates about some of the language we have employed in order to attain it. Dr. Overbeck, unless I mistake him, does *not* sympathise with our object ; and he quarrels with our language because he is afraid that it may succeed in uniting those whom he wishes to keep separate. . . ."

Two years later, Döllinger suggested another Conference, but English feeling on the Eastern Question was running so very high that Liddon advised him not to attempt it. It does not appear to have been mentioned again. Thus all the great hopes of 1874 and 1875 were for the time frustrated. But surely, like every other earnest attempt at the reunion of the Catholic Church, the Bonn Conferences have left to the Church at least the witness to a great duty, which they tried to fulfil ; and the example of a faith —disappointed, indeed, for the moment, but quenchless—in the Reunion which is yet to be achieved in God's time by other methods.

CORRESPONDENCE, 1872–1876.

On teaching Confession in the Church of England.

"3, Amen Court, April 7, 1872.

" The Prayer-book teaches distinctly (1) that a priest has the power of pronouncing Absolutions which are ratified in heaven. This can only be evaded by an unhistorical and non-natural interpretation of the plain words of the Ordinal, and ' Visitation of the Sick' Service. If preaching forgiveness in Christ's ' Name ' was all that had been meant, a very different form of words would not merely have answered the purpose of the Church, but would have answered it much better.

" 2. That Confession to a priest is advisable (*a*) when persons ' cannot quiet their own consciences,' and (*b*) under any circumstances in illness ' the sick person is to be moved to make a special confession of his sins, if he feel his conscience to be troubled with any weighty matter.'

" In insisting upon these words, you keep within the letter of the law. You are strictly in your right in saying that the Church of England leaves the healthy laity at liberty to come to Confession, and that she leaves you free to receive confessions, and to tell people that you are free to do so, by the law of the Church.

" 3. When you tell the Bishop that it is *best* for the penitent to come to Confession, you go a step beyond this. I agree with you, of course. It is the common sense of faith ; it is a fair *inference* from the premises with which the Church supplies you in her Ordinal and elsewhere. Still, it is an inference.

" The actual *letter* of the Formularies does not cover it.

" If men preach (1) the reality of Absolution through the application of the Blood of Jesus Christ to the soul ; (2) the liberty of coming to Confession granted by the Church of England ; (3) the nature of sin, which can never leave an instructed and sensitive conscience at peace until there is an assurance of forgiveness ;—it is all we want. The teaching is within the lines of the Church Formularies ; we need say nothing about its being *best* to come. People will ask to come, just as they will for medicine when they are sick and in pain. And this is better than the Roman system, which by enforcing Confession mechanically often makes it sacrilegious.

" The advocates of ecclesiastical liberty ought to be the last men in the world to endeavour to tie your hands ; and, although such a position is very far indeed from that which a Churchman would desire, it is, as it seems to me, the best for your patron, and for the many poor people who, if deprived of your ministrations, can find no honest Church teaching in the neighbourhood, and will be too probably lost to our Communion.

On the Unauthorised Publication of Sermons.

"3, Amen Court, April 25, 1872.

". . . I fear I must decline to correct the proof of my Sermons, or to authorise their publication.

"I know that I cannot help what is done by another publisher ; my only resource is, to say that I am in no way responsible for the details of language which is printed as my own.

"People write to me and ask what I mean by particular expressions which I have never used, and which convey ideas more or less erroneous. I can only reply that I cannot help being paraphrased by reporters and correctors for the press, and that I am not responsible for what I would do anything to prevent.

"The publication of a Sermon is, on a clergyman's part, an act of much responsibility. He may preach many Sermons which he does not wish to publish ; not because he has not, to the best of his power, said what he believes to be true, but because he has been unable, from pressure of other work, to exhibit his thought as perfectly as he would wish on matters of such supreme importance.

"This, at least, is often the case with me, and I cannot, by correcting proofs which are sent me, acquiesce in the surrender of a part of my own inalienable responsibility."

To a Lady.

On Differences within the English Church.

"Killarney, July 23, 1872.

". . . 1. There are undoubtedly very wide differences in the English Church. Upon these I observe : (1) that some differences are to be found now among the teachers of all Churches—the Roman included.

"At this moment there are many open questions among Roman Catholics. Whether Inspiration is 'mechanical' and literal, or only 'dynamical,' is one. Until two years ago, whether the Popes are, or are not, infallible, was another. The list might be added to considerably.

"(2) That there were great differences within the Catholic Communion in primitive times. To suppose that the number of open questions in the Church of St. Augustine's day was not larger than the number of open questions in the Roman Church of our day would be to make a great mistake.

"(3) That, admitting the differences observable between English clergymen to be excessive, and such as would not have been tolerated in the early Church, what does this prove ? That the English Church is diseased ? Yes—*that* no wise and honest Churchman would deny, as he must assert the same thing, though for different reasons, of the Church of Rome. But—that the English Church is dead! No— unless the presence of error in a Church forfeits its life. What does the Apostle mean by saying, 'For this cause shall there be heresies *among you,* that they which are approved may be made manifest among you'? He does not say heresies 'external to the Church, with which you never come into contact.'

"In particular, I do not know how the subjective doctrine of the Eucharist Presence can be denounced as 'heresy' in the sense in which we should apply that term to Arianism, for instance. The Undivided Church never defined the objective doctrine Œcumenically. The Lateran Definition is long after the Division of East and West. Of course, the general consent of ancient teachings and the statements of great Fathers leave us in no doubt as to what the Faith of the ancient Church really was. It was not Transubstantiation, or they would not have spoken of the 'Elements' after Consecration in the way they do. It was not 'Subjectivism ;' but in the absence of early Catholic language to the same effect one would shrink from terming the subjective theory a formal heresy, however much it may be, as it is, at issue with the general mind of 'Antiquity.'

"2. As to the Separation of the sixteenth century : it would never have taken place if the Pope had been content with the position of 'Western Patriarch.' It was because he claimed Supremacy towards the whole Catholic Church that the Reformation became possible. Too often it happens that in rejecting error we impair the claims of Truth ; the Pope's position as Western Patriarch *has* been, doubtless, lost sight of. But, who is responsible before God ? Clearly those who claimed to wield a jurisdiction which He had never given them, and which provoked a perfectly legitimate resistance. Everything really turns in the last resort upon *this*—whether or not the Papal Supremacy was a thing of Divine institution or of human growth. Believing, with all my soul, that the latter answer is *certain*, I can understand and bear all that has followed its rejection, however much I may deplore a great deal of it.

"3. Let me beg you to consider (1) that, if the Catholic Church must be at all times visibly 'one,' unvarying in its teaching in all *times* as well as in all *places*, the Eastern Church has a much better claim to be considered the Catholic Church than the Roman. It contains four Patriarchs as against one. It has not denied the Immaculate Conception for centuries—through the voice of a great Order like the Dominicans—and then taught it as of Faith. It did not separate from the West, but *vice versâ.*

"(2) That in adopting a new religious system, you make yourself responsible for anything that is evil in it in a totally distinct sense from that in which you are responsible for those of the system in which God, by His Providence, has placed you, and which you can only leave by an act of your own will. In other words, you are much

O

less responsible for what the English Bishops may, or may not, say and do than you will be for the recent Vatican Definition, and the like. For you will have made the latter your own by an emphatic act."

On relaxing the Rule of Fasting when in Ill Health.

"Christ Church, March 6, 1873.

". . . I think that, in view of the enclosed [medical] opinion (supposing the writer not to have a notorious *animus* against Church ways), it would *not* be right to go without meat on Fridays. Eat something cold, if you like, and as few delicacies as you can. But *vox medici, vox Dei*, in these matters. We have no *right* to impair health in order even to subdue the flesh to the spirit. Of course, prayer that there might be no loss on such a score would be obviously prudent. I always think, at such a time, that the use of an old-fashioned book like Challoner's 'Meditations'—of which Mr. Keble was so fond—is very invigorating. One only remembers that he is a Roman Catholic about once in six weeks."

On protesting against a Public Ball in Lent.

"3, Amen Court, January 20, 1874.

". . . I do not see my way to taking the initiative in the protest which you propose.

"1. To begin with, my doing so would probably have the effect of detaching the sympathies of a great many persons who would regret the ball in Lent as much as I do.

"They would say, in the phrase of the day, that the agitation was of a party character.

"2. But, besides this, I doubt the wisdom of the protest. We must recognise the fact that a large proportion of the English people, and especially those in high places, are strictly indifferent to the rules of the Church, if not actively hostile to her. . . . Our protest would be represented as an attempt to force our own ideas of religious duties upon other people; and would probably only lead to another attempt, on a large scale, in the same direction at no very distant time.

"I should, therefore, agree substantially with what I see has been said by my colleague here as to the best course to take. In these days, if people in leading positions are to be prevented from acting against Religion, it must be by the silent action of social discouragement, which will grow with an increasing hold on the principles of our Church as taught in the Prayer-book.

"Lent has been on the whole better observed of late years than formerly, because it is known that there are people who will not take any part in festivities during that season. We may trust that in time this *better* feeling will reach the highest quarters; and meanwhile I think we had better not assume that the Church is in a position to command that respect for her rules at the hands of the State, or of public bodies, which would have been natural enough in the days of George III."

On placing " the Stations of the Cross " in a Church.

"3, Amen Court, August 8, 1874.

" . . . First of all, let me say that I quite agree with you in thinking that, in the abstract, and apart from particular circumstances, Stations of the Cross are very instructive and edifying—as teaching people to think of our Lord's Sufferings in detail, and with much more reality than they generally do.

"But no one would say that they are necessary ; and we are therefore at liberty to consider their expediency, *under present circumstances.*

"Here, too, I entirely agree with you. The times are not favourable to introducing novelties of any kind ; the air is charged with electricity, and the lightning may be attracted at any moment. These Stations, too, are rarely considered on their merits ; they are associated in the popular mind with Rome, and it is taken for granted that resemblance to Rome is the real object of their being introduced. This is irrational enough ; but theological passion is not rational, although it is sometimes very powerful. Surely, if we wish to keep things together, to disinterestedly work for the future, and not to invite collision, which must precipitate a catastrophe, the right course is to consider whether anything can be given up, *without prejudice to the Faith,* in order to conciliate prejudices against it ; and the last thing we should do is to exasperate feeling, which is already sufficiently heated.

" Certainly I should not refer the matter to the Bishop, if it could be helped. He would only be alarmed, and would, perhaps, form opinions of dear ——— which would do him an injustice. He could only rule the matter, under present circumstances, in one way. The best way would be to ask ——— to let them remain—for some other Church, or until times are changed for the better. ——— would not be, perhaps, in the way of feeling how really serious the crisis through which we are passing is. The tone of the House of Commons is very ominous of evil. Our wisdom surely is to avoid giving prominence to exasperating topics ; and to do quiet work more earnestly and thoroughly, if it may be, than ever.

" We shall win in the end, if we are unselfish enough to check all provoking language and action just now."

To the Editor of the *Times*.

" Brislington, September 30, 1874.

" Sir,—You observe, with reference to the Amendment which I moved at Bonn to the Declaration on the subject of the Immaculate Conception, that ' Dr. Liddon was not concerned that the Conference should give any expression to what it deemed to be the Truth upon this subject.' It would have been more accurate to say that I wished the Conference to express only such Truth as appeared to me to be necessary for its purpose. What the Conference had at heart was to deny that the Pope is endowed with an Infallibility enabling him to make substantial additions to the received Faith of the Church. When, in the year 1854, the Pope undertook to raise the Immaculate Conception from the rank of a permitted but controverted opinion to that of an Article of the Catholic Faith, he did by implication, and very emphatically, assert his Infallibility; so that the Vatican Council only stated in terms a doctrine about the Pope's endowments which had been already tacitly admitted in practice. It was natural that the Old Catholics should be anxious to repudiate not merely the Conciliar definition of Papal Infallibility, but also the act whereby, sixteen years before the Council, the Pope had practically claimed to be infallible when defining doctrine *ex cathedrâ*. For this purpose it was enough to state that the Conference rejected the Immaculate Conception as a dogma of Faith, since this statement repudiated alike the Bull of 1854 and the Conciliar definition of 1870.

"To go further than this, and dogmatically define the falsehood of the Immaculate Conception as a speculative Theological opinion, was, as it appeared to me, to employ Ultramontane weapons against Ultramontanism. There was no adequate reason, as I thought, for our thus undertaking to pronounce in favour of the old Dominican controversialists against their Franciscan opponents; and I was the better able to say this because, unlike at least one member of the Conference, I certainly do not believe the Franciscan opinion in question to be speculatively true. If, indeed, the Conference had wished consistently to condemn all the Theological propositions which its members generally disowned, there would have been more reason for this particular condemnation, but in that case we should have spent our time, not on questions which mainly divide the great Churches of Christendom, but on the propositions of the Syllabus, and on many other mistaken assertions nearer home. We were, as it seemed to me, logically bound to go a great deal further if we went thus far; and yet, had we done so, should we have helped forward our common object? Surely, sir, men and Churches are united, not by the mutual recognition of the frontiers of errors, but by practically embracing positive and substantial Truth; and this principle was, as I am glad to remember, in the main acted upon during the Conference.

"However, as I subsequently learned from Bishop Reinkens, the German theologians had reasons over and above those which were given by Dr. Döllinger for insisting on their original statement; and, anyhow, I am glad to think that your criticism on this head does not touch the action of the majority of the Conference, but only that of myself and some English and German friends.

"As to the results achieved by the Conference, an Englishman would perhaps naturally be less sanguine than your able American correspondent. It was impossible not to feel again and again that when we had surmounted the preliminaries of discussion we must find ourselves on the edge of a theological chasm ; and indeed nothing but the genius and temper of our President could have enabled us to manage as we did. Still, these difficulties could not have been unforeseen by any one who accepted Dr. Döllinger's invitation, and in theological matters the moral and personal incrustations of a controversy often present more formidable obstacles to a good understanding than any differences of a purely intellectual character. I rejoice to think that much was done towards clearing the ground of irrelevant matter and reducing the questions before us to a shape which makes a future understanding at least possible.

"In some cases we certainly went much further than this, and if the terms in which we expressed agreement were inclusive, or, as our critics would say, ambiguous, this objection has been urged before of Anglican and even of Tridentine Definitions, and is perhaps not always so damaging as its assertors suppose. There is no necessary want of real straightforwardness in laying stress upon points of agreement rather than upon points of difference, although undoubtedly the ingenuous ferocity of some of our English controversy would have been out of place at Bonn. As it was, if we escaped some obvious dangers, the result was due, humanly speaking, in the first place, to the commanding qualities and authority of our chairman, but also, and especially as regards the English contingent—it is a duty and a pleasure to say so—to the true moderation, forbearance, and justice of the Dean of Chester.

"For the rest, peacemaking is proverbially thankless work, and those who have a hand in it know, or ought to know, their inevitable position. But whatever the probabilities of immediate failure they work for a distant future, and they remember humbly but thankfully Who has promised a blessing on the peacemakers."

On Eternal Punishment.

"3, Amen Court, November 30, 1874.

". . . A letter is not of much use in these cases ; it cannot be cross-questioned, and perhaps it makes more difficulties than it removes. But I must say a few words.

"Certainly I believe that the 'usual interpretation' of those passages of Scripture which speak of 'Eternal' Punishment is the true one. Mr. Maurice's treatment of that word, as descriptive of a quality having no relation to time, always struck me as more ingenious than true. And, as you know, the doctrine does not depend only upon passages in which the word occurs—*e.g.* the closing verses of St. Mark ix. and some very awful verses in the Apocalypse do not contain it [the word 'eternal'].

"Nor can I think that your proposals for getting over the difficulties which you feel about the doctrine will really hold water.

"As to the first, we cannot think that God frightens us with threatenings which He really does not mean to carry out, without doing Himself obvious dishonour.

"As to the second, although we may rightly shrink from saying that any given individual is certainly so unfaithful to light and grace as to incur the eternal loss of God, we do know that many are so. God knows who they are.

"It is impossible—for me at least—to doubt that this awful doctrine is a part of Divine Revelation. But does it really present a difficulty different in kind from that of the greatest of all difficulties—the origin of the existence of evil?

"How many of us have, perhaps, dared sometimes to think, 'If I were an almighty and perfectly good being, I never would have allowed evil to exist at all'!

"We quench that thought by reflecting that the All-Wise sees further than we do, and even that He permits us to see enough to warrant something more than the suspicion that our *primâ facie* view of the universe, and His relation to it, is wrong. What, then, is eternal evil but an extension of this our original difficulty? As the existence of evil—physical and moral—is ultimately referable to the perverseness of the free will of a created being (God respecting the freedom which He has given, even when it is turned against Himself), so eternal evil—which is its own eternal punishment—is merely the continuous development of this unchecked freedom of a will alienated from God. Of this Satan is the most fearful illustration; but your difficulty would remain in full force if all lost human beings were destined to some sort of restoration, so long as the first of fallen angels was still to be restored. We can only say that in giving the great gift of moral freedom, God gave it to immortal beings, with all its awful liabilities, as well as with its inconceivable capacities for good.

"We can only get beyond this by saying that, in view of His own Attributes, He ought to have stinted His gifts. . . . And if we shrink from this, the alternative is to suppose that, in another life, we shall see the whole *rationale* of evil—in its origin and its consequences—with other eyes; and shall understand why He Who allowed it to mar His work so early, in the end has curbed and punished without annihilating it.

"The reason will probably be that there are necessary consequences of the gift of free will, and that free will was too great a thing to be withdrawn only because it was attended by those stern liabilities.

"Do not lose heart. All men who think at all find difficulties in some parts of Revelation. How *could* it be otherwise, considering what our minds are, and Who it is that reveals Himself to us?"

To a Lady.

On Intellectual Difficulties.

"3, Amen Court, E.C., April 10, 1875.

"Your first difficulty about other possibly inhabited worlds depends on an hypothesis which cannot possibly be verified. Surely until we think that a difficulty rests on a *solid* basis we should treat it just like a superstition.

"It is quite impossible for us to know whether other worlds are or are not inhabited, and whether if inhabited they contain creatures which are capable of moral probation, and so, conceivably, of failure, and so needing reconciliation. Faber's hypothesis will do as well as any other in a sphere where ignorance is a necessity.

"I cannot see how Sir E. Bulwer Lytton, Lamartine, or other 'educated people,' who may prefer a 'philanthropic Christian' to Christianity, are arguments against Christianity. The Church had more educated opponents in the first centuries than she has now. Deism if *serious, i.e.* if involving real belief in a Personal, Moral God, is weighted with as many difficulties as Christianity, as Butler has shown. People do not like to think themselves atheists, so they project a shadowy Deism, which on examination turns out to be a thinly disguised denial of the existence of any real God.

"As to educated unbelievers, you have to consider (1) whether they have moral reasons for wishing Christianity to be untrue ; and (2) whether *they* have really studied *this* subject, instead of bringing a series of generalisations to bear upon it which they have gathered elsewhere, and which for various reasons are more or less inapplicable. The great mass of Christians *are* uneducated, because they bear a proportion to the great mass of human beings, and the mass of human beings are uneducated. A philosophy might be the monopoly of an educated class ; a Religion, to deserve its name, belongs to humanity.

"As to 'putting a padlock on the mind,' I do not at all agree with you. I do not know any part of Truth—however axiomatic—(except pure mathematics) to which some objections may not be raised ; and there are always minds which dwell on the objections rather than on the facts. The difficulties about believing in any Moral Governor of the universe appear to me to be on the whole greater than any which can be urged in detail against any part of the Christian Creed ; yet they are over-ruled—as you, I think, would admit—by overwhelming considerations.

"Certainly the evidence for Christianity is *moral,* not mathematical. Those who expect the latter must be disappointed. But moral evidence is sufficient ; and if faith is, as the New Testament represents it, a criterion of man's moral state, mathematical evidence which should *compel* rational assent would be out of place.

"Of course, I think that *thorough* research into the question is a very good thing ; but I dread playing with such matters. If you are not prepared for the former, the wise alternative surely is to take it for granted that Christians are right, and ask God to give you faith; the act of faith itself is a gift from Heaven. And if you ask God reverently, He will give it to you, as He has given it to thousands.

"Pray observe that I do not deprecate inquiry ; but then I hope that inquiry will end in bringing you to a point at which, for every satisfactory reason, you must ask God to help you.

"As to motives—try to be simple and downright ; and do not think too much of them. S. T. Coleridge has said some very sensible things about this.

"And as to the Holy Communion—I should not advise you to receive it, if you have still serious doubts as to the Godhead of Our Lord, or His Will and Power to save you in time and eternity. Wait until you have recovered your sight.

"You would find 'Modern Doubt and Christian Belief,' and Luthardt's 'Apologetic Lectures on Fundamental Truths,' useful to you, I think."

On the Meaning of " Quod Semper."

"3, Amen Court, August 21, 1875.

"Your difficulty seems to be in the meaning of 'Semper' in the Vincentian Canon. Vincentius certainly used it in the sense of 'from the first' rather than of 'all along.' Thus in the matter of the Eucharist the question would be, what is that common element of positive Truth which has been taught from the Apostles downwards. If later language on the subject impaired this truth, either by positive additions or by negations such language would have to give way— after being considered. Probably a real Œcumenical Council dealing with the Eucharist would fall back upon Church language prior to the Reformation—prior too to the Berengarian controversy, and the Lateran definition.

"Neither the Reformed nor the 'Transubstantiationist' ought to complain of an appeal to their own principle of teaching what had been held 'from the first.'

"'Quod Semper' is Vincentius's epigrammatic way of expressing that appeal to what had been held in bygone times which we find so often in the early Councils.

"It does not exclude the fact that later language—or decisions— may have to be abandoned. Thus *e.g.* at Nicæa, the Fathers had no doubt that they were stating, although in new language which the times required, a pure Apostolical tradition, yet they set aside the Antiochene decision as to the use of the Homoousion.

"You are not quite accurate when you say that if the Council said there was a Real Presence in the Holy Sacrament, Hooker and his followers must be ignored. His mode of stating it might be modified, or set aside—but he certainly conceived himself to hold it in a certain manner.

"And you forget, I think, that the ' Quod semper, quod ubique, etc.,' principle was not invented by the Anglican divines—they only took up what was already a commonplace, in Theology. Bossuet or Bellarmine would have had no doubt about the value of the Canon or its applicability to the existing doctrines of the Church of Rome. But modern investigations have rendered this position untenable ; and men of great learning and genius, like Moehler and Dr. Newman, have practically admitted it to be so, by falling back on the new principle of Development, which may lead to many other conclusions than Rome —as modern unbelief has not been slow to discover. I will not say that the Church of England corresponds in all ways to the Vincentian principle ; but I believe that she does so much more nearly than the Roman Church.

"That principle is in substance an appeal to Antiquity. And no one, it seems to me, who knows what Antiquity really taught can imagine that the recent decrees about the Pope's Infallibility, or the Immaculate Conception of the Blessed Virgin were any part of its Creed."

To the Rev. A. H. Ward.

On attending the Services of Churches abroad.

"Brislington, January 17, 1876.

"I. In my opinion there is no possible doubt about our right to attend the Mass abroad. I have myself never scrupled to act on this conviction, nor do I see any reason for changing it.

"In advising others I have been accustomed to treat the question as one of spiritual expediency. Where people are (1) quite unacquainted with the Service, and see in it only a vast assortment of music and ceremonial, or (2) when they are disposed to become Roman Catholics and likely to be open to æsthetic as distinct from intellectual attractions, I have always discouraged it. This I may add was Mr. Keble's plan, and Bishop Hamilton's.

"In cases where I have 'sanctioned' it (to use that expression), I have begged people not to join in such things as the Litany of Loretto (which is sometimes said at Benediction, immediately afterwards), but to occupy themselves with the *Te Deum,* or some Psalms or Prayers with which they are familiar, in our Prayer-book.

"Upon the principles which make attendance at the Services of the Church a duty in England, the real difficulty is to justify the English Church Services abroad. They can only be justified, I suppose, as temporary expedients—bandages to serve while a limb is broken—but not as having any of the authority and claim which comes from jurisdiction.

"The Bishops of London and Gibraltar regulate all sorts of Services on the Continent—a proceeding which may be inevitable so long as the Roman Church imposes terms of communion which we could not accept, but which is surely irregular, and only to be justified on the ground that 'a broken leg cannot be dealt with as if it were a sound one.'

"P.S.—Perhaps I ought to add, that to *communicate* in a Roman Catholic Church abroad, without saying that one is an Anglican, does not seem to me justifiable. The administering priest would refuse the Holy Sacrament if he knew the real state of the case, and though his reasons for doing this may be, in our judgment, insufficient, to claim it without explanation is a sort of *ruse,* which, in so sacred a matter especially, must surely imperil or rather forfeit any grace we might hope to obtain."

On Difficulties in the Way of taking Holy Orders.

"Christ Church, February 8, 1876.

"1. It would not, I apprehend, be a sufficient warrant for saying, 'I trust so,' in the Ordination Service, if a man *only* meant that by being ordained he could do more good as an educator.

"But probably this reason encloses another which *would* justify the answer. You think that you would be more useful as an educator, if you were ordained, *because* you thus would be the minister of God's Revelation of truth and mercy in His Blessed Son—a Revelation with which it is of the last importance that every human being should become acquainted, and the preciousness of which you yourself feel in your inmost heart, and therefore desire to communicate to others under your charge, as the best means of doing them good.

"This would be a very sufficient reason for saying, 'I trust so.' And is not this really what you do mean?

"2. 'Unfeigned belief' in 'all the Canonical Scriptures' is not, I think, compatible with the opinion that the account of the Creation is *only* allegorical : though it may be interpreted allegorically, and considered as an account of the origin of the present physical state of things, it may and must be understood with the explanations with which you are probably familiar—and which Dr. McCaul, for example, has stated concisely and well in his reply to Bishop Colenso. On the other hand, although the Mosaic authorship of the Pentateuch, as a whole (to the exclusion, I mean, of theories with which we are familiar about Deuteronomy), *seems* to be involved in the claim of these books to be 'Scripture' in the sense of the Ordinal, a man may, and, indeed, should recognise the hand of Ezra in some late additions. As to 'numerous errors in several books of the Bible,' I am obliged to ask— errors of what kind ?

"3. The Articles were intended to be construed liberally, and they always have been so construed, especially those Articles on Nature and Grace which embody one side of the mind of St. Augustine. But I do not think that you need be embarrassed by the title of Art. xiii. The 'works' of the unjustified man to which it refers are those acts to which neither the Grace of Christ, nor the Inspiration of the Spirit have contributed anything—such as the good works of the heathen done from the traditions of their race, and force of circumstances, and from fear of the public opinion of those around them. But heathen lives contain acts done by the grace of Christ—as when a heathen acts from a high sense of duty, or is capable of true benevolence, or, like Cornelius, makes the very utmost of the natural opportunities which have been given him. The prevenient grace of Christ—the Light that lighteth every man that cometh into the world—is the real principle of all this in heathen lives ; and it must not be confused, even with their 'splendida vitia'—acts of generosity, purity, and the like, performed from a motive of 'self-respect,' *i.e.* perhaps of pride. Then in Art. xviii.—it is sufficient to believe—what it seems to me a Christian *must* believe—that of those who die apart from Christ, we know nothing positively as to their destiny hereafter. We cannot say that 'thousands are saved,' because, *inter alia*, that would destroy the reason for the Incarnation and Passion of the Son of God, through Whom alone is salvation warranted to any human being. How far His mediatorial work may, in its effects, radiate beyond the frontiers of His kingdom, is a matter of which we know really nothing one way or the other. But much *hope* in this direction is compatible with honest assent in the Article.

"As to the nature of Inspiration, nothing has been defined authoritatively, and there is, therefore, large room for difference of opinion. Certainly I should say that the Inspiration of Scripture differs *in kind* from that of Socrates ; but I am not at all prepared to say that a man who holds it to differ only in degree would be a dishonest minister of the Church of England, since she has said nothing at all upon the subject, at least *directly*. If you do not know it, you would find Archdeacon Lee's book on 'Inspiration' exceedingly useful and instructive.

"You are, I think, quite wrong about the word αἰώνιος, as applied to the future state of the lost, because, among other reasons, our Lord's expressions in St. Mark ix. fix its true sense upon the highest authority. But I do not understand you to say that you have made up your mind upon this vast and intricate question.

"You will see that I have written with perfect frankness and I fear sometimes in appearance abruptly, because briefly. If I might add a word, it would be, 'Do not trifle with real scruples of conscience' (I am sure you would not do this) ; but also 'do not be hasty to conclude that all scruples necessarily represent the logic of facts.' If instead of forcing yourself quickly and prematurely to a decision, you make the points which embarrass you matters of study and prayer for some time, you will find, I think, that much which is at present distorted will gradually assume in your mind its true outline and proportion. Do not abandon the hope of taking Orders, if you can possibly help it. It is much better to look difficulties in the face before Ordination than— for the first time—after it ; and you will be stronger and clearer in your clerical life and teaching for having done so. If you come up to Oxford we may, perhaps, revert to the subject. Meanwhile, believe that I shall remember you as best I can."

CHAPTER VIII.

THE EASTERN QUESTION, 1876—TRAVELS IN SERVIA —THE RITUALISTIC CONTROVERSY—CHANGES AT ST. PAUL'S CATHEDRAL — THOUGHTS ABOUT THE POLITICAL SITUATION.

1876–1878.

IN the summer of 1876, the news of the insurrection in Servia and of the atrocities committed by Turkish troops in Bulgaria, directed the attention of all Englishmen to the East of Europe, and to the general character of Turkish government. Of some of the alleged atrocities there was no possibility of doubt ; the questions beyond were whether the Turkish Government was responsible for them, and if so, why the foreign policy of our country should be committed to the support of a Power which was thus outraging the most elementary sentiments of humanity ? Liddon at once took up the question with characteristic courage and thoroughness ; he joined with those who held the Turkish Government to be morally responsible ; as an Englishman and as a Christian he raised his voice against any kind of alliance which would make England an accomplice in the brutal excesses of a non-Christian Power.

Very rarely during the twenty years that he preached at St. Paul's did he deal at any length with current political questions. But at this moment he could not be silent ; in his eyes, the political side of the question was merged in far greater moral and religious considerations. In a sermon on August 13 he explained the reasons which compelled him as a Christian teacher to break his self-imposed rule of silence on the political questions of the day.

"As a rule," he said, "it is undoubtedly better for us, the ministers of Christ, to avoid reference to topics connected with the public action of the country—to refrain from any language which may, however undesignedly, make the task of those to whom are committed the responsibilities of government, more difficult than it is. But there are times when silence is impossible without manifest disloyalty to the cause of Christ. . . . Such a time surely is upon us now, when we as a nation are slowly awaking to a true estimate of recent events in Eastern Europe, and of our involuntary share in them.

"Day by day we English are learning that this year of grace 1876 has been signalised by a public tragedy, which, I firmly believe, is without a parallel in modern times. . . . People now scarcely mutter the word 'exaggeration.' They know that when all that must be deducted has been deducted on this score, the remainder of solid unassailable fact is unspeakably horrible. . . . Not merely armed men, but young women and girls and babes, counted by hundreds, counted by thousands, subjected to the most refined cruelties, subjected to the last indignities, have been the victims of the Turk. . . .

"It might fairly be pleaded for the Power which has perpetrated these acts that it knows not the Name of Christ, and that its proceedings are not to be judged by the standard of a European and Christian civilisation. Be it so; but that which makes the voice falter as we say it, is that, through whatever misunderstanding, the Government which is immediately responsible for acts like these has turned for sympathy, for encouragement, not to any of the historical houses of despotism or oppression, not to any other European Power, but alas! to England—to free, humane, Christian England. The Turk has, not altogether without reason, believed himself, amid these scenes of cruelty, to be leaning on our country's arm, to be sure of her smile, or, at least, of her acquiescence!"

The political crisis was closely connected also with the hopes of reunion with the Eastern Church. At Bonn he had worked heartily with that end; now the heart-rending sorrows of the Christian dependencies of Turkey gave occasion for a real expression of sympathy. So at the end of August he determined to go himself to Eastern Europe, and assure our fellow-Christians there of the sympathy felt for them in England.

To C. T. Redington, Esq.

"3, Amen Court, August 29, 1876.

". . . On Saturday I hope to start for Vienna, and then go on, if I can, to Belgrade. There will be no time to do more, but I should be glad to assure leading Servians of the change which has happily come over English sympathies, within the last month, since the hideous atrocities of the Turks in Bulgaria have been known.

"This change is, indeed, striking, and, as I am informed in trustworthy quarters, has already frightened the Government. The Bulgarians, I hope, will not have died in vain, if the British fleet remains where it is—*not* to support the barbarous Government of the Sultan, but to threaten Constantinople—in the event of any repetition of brutalities which are scarcely less disgraceful to England than to Turkey.

"No, I do not despair of the cause of the Eastern Christians.

"These Christian races of the Balkan are the predestined heirs of the future. The Turk is gradually but surely sinking beneath the weight of his own nameless corruptions, which would prove fatal to the finest race. . . . How one burns at the thought of all that these Christians have suffered since the dark day when Mahmoud II. took Constantinople! It has been one long story of unspeakable wrong. England, too, has done wrong in her time—not least in Ireland—but we can afford to confess it, and to try to do better. But the Turk is *semper idem*, the same varnished savage that he was four centuries ago. How I should delight to see St. Sophia once more in Christian hands! It is not wholly impossible, although Lords Beaconsfield and Derby won't help it forward."

In addition to his Letters to the *Guardian* in September and October, his private letters and his diary describe in full this interesting tour.

To Sir Robert Phillimore.

"Munich, September 9, 1876.

"I am fulfilling your parting charge by writing you a line from this place, which we leave for Vienna on Monday morning. Dr. Döllinger is here, and I have spent the greater part of the last two days with him. He is well, and in fairly good spirits, although less hopeful than I could have wished about the great cause of Christian union. The Greeks—or rather the Russians—have been worked upon by Dr. Overbeck, and are less disposed to be reasonable—at least in some particulars—than was the case a year ago. They insist, in some of the letters which I have been reading, more peremptorily upon the excision of the *Filioque* from the Nicene Creed, and they require (I believe in consequence of a decision of the Holy Synod at St. Petersburg) *our* acceptance of the Seventh Council (Second of Nicæa). This involves, as you know, a burning question. We should never hear the last about the Homily against Peril of Idolatry.

"Dr. Döllinger thinks that he sees his way through the difficulty by insisting that the subject-matter of the Seventh Council, unlike that of the preceding Six, belongs not to dogma, but to variable discipline. The use of Images is certainly variable, since they were never used at all before the fourth century. If the Greeks would admit this, and, as a consequence, would not insist upon our practical deference, *as a Church*, to the Canons of this Council (its ' Acts ' contain a good deal of forged matter), then we, on the other hand, ought to admit the Council in general terms, and leave the practice of the Eastern Churches undisturbed. Unless Churches are prepared to admit great latitude in everything that is not a matter of faith or morals, or essential to the organic structure of the Church, no proposals for Christian union are other than a waste of time.

"Döllinger is full of the Eastern Question, and thinks that he sees his way to a provisional proposal which might avert a general war, and secure justice and civil privileges to the Christian populations of European Turkey. He thinks that an International Commission, on which the Great Powers should all be represented, should sit in permanence at Constantinople until the Government of Turkey should be managed on European principles. The duties of such a Commission would be to administer European law (as distinct from that of the Koran) in European Turkey, while paying a modified allegiance to the Sultan. In this way the integrity of Turkey would be preserved, and the Christians protected. Bosnia, probably on account of the peculiar characteristics of its population, would have to be annexed to Austria. The question of this annexation already has created a fierce party war between the Hungarian party and that headed by the Archduke Albert.

"Döllinger discussed the great difficulty of getting the Great Powers to consent to an arrangement of this kind ; but he thought them not insurmountable. How wonderful and edifying it is to see the *Times* of Thursday prostrating itself at the feet of Mr. Gladstone, and snubbing Lord Beaconsfield in an editorial note ! This conversion of England from Palmerstonian Turkism to Christian sympathies is like a dream of childhood—too good to be thought of as true, and too exhilarating to allow one to think about anything else. Döllinger is greatly struck by it ; such a phenomenon is probably impossible in any Continental country. As for the Turks, whether British or Oriental, they *must* be aghast at so weird a change of political fortune. I see something of this in the German papers."

[*Diary.*] "*September* 12. *Vienna.*—Drove to the British Embassy. Sir A. Buchanan not at home ; but Mr. Gladstone's pamphlet, which he had sent me, was forwarded by Mr. Edwards, the first secretary of the Embassy. Then to the Russian Embassy, where we left our cards on Madame de Novikoff ; and then to the French Embassy, where we used Mr. George Williams's introduction. The Danish Minister was at the time with the French Ambassador, and we had a long conversation with both. They were greatly interested at the agitation in England ; expressed surprise at nothing having been known of the atrocities before. The Danish Minister said that the Servians had been furnished with arms from Berlin, which, oddly enough, had reached Servia by way of Constantinople. He was a very humorous person, whom I should like to have seen more of.

"*September* 13.—In the afternoon we went down by the Southern Railway to dine with the English Ambassador, Sir A. Buchanan. [He] is a fine specimen of the old English gentleman. Like all the diplomats here, he is moderately Turkish. The Turks, he says, had no troops at their disposal but the Circassians and Bashi Bazouks. They are really gentle, civilised people in their way—would not kill a bird or hurt an animal for the world. They had acted under the influence of terror. Sir Andrew thought the Servian War a piece of unjustifiable ambition, got up by the governing classes."

To the Right Hon. W. E. Gladstone.

"Agram, Croatia, September 16, 1876.

" I have purposely delayed thanking you for your great kindness in sending me a copy of your pamphlet on the Bulgarian horrors, until I had read it through more than once, and also until I had observed, as well as I could, what the newspapers in this part of the world say about it. They judge it, of course, from their own point of view, and this is generally Turkish. Of the leading articles which appear daily in Vienna, two-thirds, Dr. Döllinger tells me, are written by Jews ; while the *Neue Freie Presse*, a very well-written paper, with 30,000 subscribers and a large independent circulation, has been bought this year by the Turkish Government. Still, the most hostile of these papers, so far as I have observed, are respectful ; and their anxiety to make the most of a recent speech of Lord Derby's shows how greatly they fear a fundamental change in the Eastern policy of England.

" If I may at all measure the feelings of our English people by my own, your pamphlet will have earned more general and admiring gratitude than anything you have ever written before. It is a great moral relief to know that justice and humanity have had the benefit of such advocacy, and that, as a people, we are no longer likely to be very seriously misunderstood.

"We found Dr. Döllinger full of the Eastern Question, and ready with a plan of his own, which he talked about at length, and which he thought not unlike Lord Stratford's. . . .

"At Vienna we profited much by your kindness in giving us introductions to Sir Andrew Buchanan. Sir Andrew has furnished us with letters to the consuls at Pesth and Belgrade, and we dined and spent a very pleasant evening with him at Baden, where he has

P

a country house, about eighteen miles from Vienna. He was much interested—more interested, I think, than altogether satisfied—by the recent movement of opinion in England, as it would, I suppose, make short work with some of the traditions of diplomacy. But diplomacy at Vienna—so far as we had experience of it—was generally inclined to Turkey. The French Ambassador, the Count de Vogüé—a man full of knowledge about Eastern Christendom—was, as I understood him, on the whole, of this mind. The Russian ghost has not yet been laid, at any rate, in the embassies.

"We are here on our way to see Bishop Strossmayer, who lives at Diakovar in Sclavonia. Dr. Döllinger gave us an introduction, and the Bishop has written to ask us to visit him. He seems, just now, to be the most popular man in Croatia and Sclavonia, and, I imagine, is proportionately unpopular among the Magyars in Hungary. The Archbishop, whose suffragan he is, lives here in Agram; but *he* is apparently quite overshadowed by Strossmayer, whose picture is in all the shops, and whose name, I observe, is given to some of the new streets and terraces. These South Austrian prelates must be the wealthiest in Christendom.

"Here, within view of the hills of Bosnia, the Primate of Croatia has an income of more than 1,000,000 gulden—more than £80,000. Bishop Strossmayer himself has 600,000 gulden a year, which they say he spends entirely on public objects. He has endowed the University here, added to the picture gallery, and built churches and schools right and left. He has recently sent £3000 to the Servians, and is even more influential as a politician than as an ecclesiastic. He combines the character of Bishop Wilberforce with that of a great popular leader, and, as the Count de Vogüé said, 'has all the threads of the present Eastern Question perfectly in his hands.' Of the Primate, they say that he is 'furchtlich reich, aber er gibt nichts.'

"After visiting Diakovar, we hope to go on down the Save to Belgrade, thus passing under the nose of the Turkish fortresses, and then we turn homewards, spending a day, at any rate, in Munich, to see Dr. Döllinger."

[*Diary.*] "*September* 18. *Sissek.*—Up at 4.30. The steamboat for Semlin left the Quai at 6. It was at first cold and raw, but the day improved. We were fortunate in making the acquaintance of the Roman Catholic priest of——, in the diocese of Diakovar—Mr. Odzic. He complained of the English policy as the true cause of the miseries of the Christians in Turkey during the last year; he even believed that the English Government had supplied the Turks with money to enable them to put down the insurrection. We passed two chief scenes of the insurrection, and by the bank were a series of Turkish military stations. In front of each of them sat a group of Turks, grave and imperturbable; and close to each [*sic*] of these stations, surrounded by a palisade, was an impaled man, and other poles on which insurgents had been impaled. Mr. Odzic said that some of them lived for four days, some only for twelve hours. 'And the men who do these things,' he said, 'are our neighbours. England wills it.'

"*September* 20. *Belgrade.*—Went with Mr. Christitch to Service at the Greek cathedral. It is the Nativity of the Blessed Virgin in the Greek Calendar. The Metropolitan Archbishop celebrated, assisted by a choir from Moscow, and the voice-accompaniment was beautiful indeed. A sermon on those who have fallen in the war was preached by the Archpriest Popovich, who read from a manuscript. Prince Milan, the 'grossmutter' of the Prince, and his wife's two sisters, were present. After this we had an interview with the Metropolitan, conversation being chiefly on the possibilities of the reunion of Christendom, and on the new temper of the English people in regard to Eastern affairs. Thence we went over the Turkish and Jewish quarters of Belgrade—in the first, two mosques ; in the second, two synagogues. The attendant of the mosque accompanied us up the minaret, but would not look out with us from it.

"*September* 21.—To see Mr. Restich, the Prime Minister. He looked anxious and weary, but struck me as a man who was doing very difficult work with great seriousness and simplicity of purpose. Dined at 12 with the Metropolitan Michael. The Ministers of Public Worship and Finance were there, with Mr. Christitch, and the secretary of the Russian Embassy. Our conversation was almost entirely on the Eastern Question. The Metropolitan asked anxiously about Bishop Colenso, but I hope we satisfied him.

"*September* 23. — Drove in a wicker-work trap of the rudest description, without springs, from Vukovar to Diakovar. The poor boy who drove us took us a short cut, across roads indescribably bad, and the consequences were we were much bruised before we got to Diakovar. Stopped at New Mikanovics (?). The spires of the new Cathedral were visible long before we reached the town. The porter had some little difficulty in making out what we wanted ; but the butler soon found that we were all right, and took us to our rooms. After dressing, we spent the rest of the evening in the Bishop's company. He talked a stream of vivacious French for more than an hour, almost entirely on the Eastern Question. The points he insisted on were the impossibility of reforming Turkish rules and administration, the general character of the Servian War, the desirableness of uniting Bosnia to Servia and Herzegovina to Montenegro. We had a *maigre* supper, at which an artist and I were the only persons present. The servants who waited wore livery.

"*September* 24. *Bishop's Palace, Diakovar, Croatia.* — At 8 o'clock the Bishop said Mass in his private chapel attended by his two chaplains. At 9 High Mass in the old Cathedral, built after the Turkish occupation on the site of a mosque ; a sermon in Sclavonic, to which we listened from a window in the private chapel. Then the Bishop took us all over the new church which is rising just beyond—a work which is truly worthy of the Middle Ages for its beauty and magnificence.   It is in Italian Gothic, and is being decorated by two artists named Seitz, father and son, pupils of Cornelius and Overbeck respectively.   There are no subjects except Scriptural ones.   At 1 we dined ; twenty-four people sat down, most of them persons engaged in work in the Cathedral, one Franciscan monk from Bosnia, an Austrian general, etc.   After dinner the Bishop acted as cicerone over his Gallery, which is really very beautiful.   It is all to be given to the National Croatian Collection at Agram.   During a walk in the late afternoon he talked about the Council ; he had told the Pope that nothing would be gained by the Definition—that it was only an outward law, etc.   He believed that the *élite* of characters everywhere were on their way to understand each other, and that the union of Christendom would come in God's own time.

"*September* 25.—The Bishop sent us in his carriage to Esseg, three hours' drive away.   He took leave of us in the most affectionate manner, and promised to come to London, if he could, next year."

To the Right Hon. W. E. Gladstone.

"Budapest, September 26, 1876.

". . . MacColl will have told you about our two days' visit to Bishop Strossmayer at Diakovar.   Certainly he is one of the most remarkable men I ever met in my life—a true king of men, combining the great ecclesiastic with the great leader of the people and statesman.   He desired me to express to you his sense of the 'almost incalculable value of your pamphlet at this crisis.'   'Catholic Bishop as I am,' he said, ' I should like to go to England, if only to kiss the hand that wrote it.'

"Bishop Strossmayer, whose jurisdiction extends over the Roman Catholics in Servia and Bosnia, is very strongly of opinion that the best arrangement, with a view to the happiness of the people, will be to unite Bosnia with Servia, and Herzegovina with Montenegro.   He fears that Austro-Hungary will oppose this, from its anti-Sclavonic prejudices and selfish fears ; and that Russia will oppose it, from its dread of seeing any strong independent Christian state south of the Danube and Save.   He hopes and trusts that England will see that *this* arrangement will be for the good of the people immediately concerned ; as it certainly will do more than anything else to create a barrier against Russian ambition, and to endear England to the South Sclavonic populations.

" I begged him to state to you in detail the reasons which determine his opinion, and he is going to write to you in a few days.   My object in writing is to account for his letter ; you will at once recognise its importance.   No other educated man in Europe, probably, could speak on the subject with such a personal knowledge of all its bearings.

" His conversation was interesting in every way ; not least in what he said about the Vatican Council and its results. He is more sanguine about the future than I should have expected. He firmly believes in a future union of all true Christians ; the presentiment of this, which he finds in the hearts of all really religious and thoughtful men in all the quarters of Christendom, will not be falsified by the recent proceedings at Rome.

" He is heart and soul with Servia. 'Never,' he says, 'in all history was there a war undertaken from nobler motives, or more likely to win a blessing for those who are sacrificing so much in prosecuting it.' "

On his return to England, he tells the impressions which the tour had left on his mind to one of his friends.

To C. T. REDINGTON, ESQ.

" Highclere Castle, Newbury, October 11, 1876.

" I have returned even more of an anti-Turk than I went out, and am sorry to see public feeling in England misled by one or two 'will-o'-the-wisps' into a partially renewed approval of the Turk and his ways. The Russian bugbear has certainly helped the *Pall Mall* and the bondholders. But what can be more natural than this rush of Russian volunteers to help their Christian brethren in Servia ? . . . Never was there a more righteous cause than this. . . . After all our experience in the past, it would be folly to trust the Turks. The Russian Ambassador said the day before yesterday that his master would be delighted if English troops would share the occupation of Bulgaria, in equal or greater numbers than Russian. Russia, I am persuaded, does not want war, and (you will perhaps not easily believe it) is not anxious for more territory. She has enough on her hands as it is.

" The assistance to Servia is the result of deeply moved religious and humane sympathy. . . . I admit that the Turkestan doings (I have only seen the extracts from Mr. Schuyler in the *Allgemeine Zeitung*) were very bad. But there is this difference between Russian proceedings in Central Asia (or our own in India after the Mutiny) and those of the Turks : the latter do not simply exterminate : they accompany the process by (1) torture in all its refinements, and (2) the indulgence of impurity in all its worst forms. In these respects, the proceedings of the Turks are unmatched by any races that own the Name of Jesus Christ ; and although the *Pall Mall*, etc., may not see much in the distinction, it is, from the point of view of Christian morality, a very great one indeed. Of course, I am not defending Russian tyranny in Turkestan or elsewhere ; yet, on the whole, M. Vambéry's book on Bokhara is enough to convince any one that the Russians have put an end to horrors which beggar description."

In his next month of residence at St. Paul's he notes—

"*December* 3.—A large number of people came to St. Paul's this afternoon expecting a political sermon. I disappointed them.

"*December* 8.—National Conference (on the Eastern Question) at St. James's Hall. I spoke 4 p.m. Was cut short at the end of twenty minutes by Lord Shaftesbury (in the chair). Mr. Gladstone's was a magnificent speech, Mr. G. O. Trevelyan's the most polished."

The various phases of the Ritualistic question and of the troubles in Eastern Europe fill his letters at this time. He fears every day that England will go to war to help Turkey against Russia, or that Mr. Tooth, who has just been pronounced contumacious by Lord Penzance, the Judge in the Court established by the Public Worship Regulation Act, will be imprisoned.

To Dr. Bright.

"Longleat, Warminster, January 19, 1877.

". . . I have been staying here during the last three days with Mr. Gladstone and E. A. Freeman, and we have talked incessantly about the Eastern Question. For the present the Turk appears to be having it all his own way. The atrocities have *never* ceased ; and no doubt Midhat and Co. will think that the time has come for paying the Christians out on the score of all the trouble which they have given.

"Lord Penzance is clearly determined to drive the iron into the soul of the Ritualists. His calling himself an Ecclesiastical Judge in the same sense as Sir R. Phillimore was, is simply an afterthought and a somewhat barefaced fiction. He is what he is, not by free delegacy from the Archbishop, but under the provisions of an Act of Parliament. The Archbishops used to appoint of themselves ; *now* they must have the consent of the Crown ! They were restricted in their choice to a Clergyman or an Ecclesiastical Lawyer ; *now* they must have a layman and a common-law lawyer who knows nothing of Ecclesiastical Law. Of old the Archbishop could, if he would, sit *with* or *instead of* his judge in his own provincial Court ; *now* he can do neither, because the judge represents not himself only but also the Crown.

"I cannot help feeling that the P.W.R.A. has lodged a barb in the Church of England, which will not be extracted (if it can be extracted) without pain, and which, if left in where it is, will have worse results. Parliament is well convinced that the English clergy care for nothing so much as 'the Establishment,' and that, therefore, they will submit to anything rather than imperil their relation to the State. May we not live to see that this impression is unfounded?

" The *Guardian*, as usual, goes in for pure and (so to put it) *brutal* Erastianism.

" I have been reading some manuscript letters of Ken's which are preserved here. How *purely hateful* is the idea presented by the ' State' which could expel Ken and patronise Burnet and Tillotson ! "

On May 12, 1877, the Judicial Committee of the Privy Council pronounced Judgment in the Ridsdale case, and among other points declared the use of the Eucharistic Vestments to be illegal. The Decision and the ground on which it was based caused great distress to a large number of English Churchmen.

To Miss Mirehouse.

" Christ Church, June 2, 1877.

" . . . As to the Ritualists, first of all, they cannot be put to death, however desirable that consummation might appear. That being so, they have to be reckoned with. . . . There are victories which are fatal to the conqueror ; and the Ridsdale Decision is likely to be one of them. . . . It does not appeal to a supernatural warrant, and yet it asks us to believe that the Second Year of Edward VI. means the Seventh Year of Elizabeth !

" For myself I cannot think that in the long run this violent contempt for history and language will really succeed, even though it is indulged in in the interests of the popular Puritanism. The more cultivated and honest Liberals here, while they express their satisfaction with the results of the Judgment, ' do not see *how* it can have been arrived at.' . . . I hope and believe that the day will come when it will be valued at its true estimate ; when the Privy Council will be ranked with the Star Chamber.

" Meanwhile, the case of the Church of England does *not* depend on the intentions of Mr. X. (I shall be sorry if he makes the mistake of resigning), or on the depressed looks of dear Mr. Z. It is broader and deeper than that."

To Professor Burrows.

" Christ Church, June 3, 1877.

" When you asked me about the ' Ritualists ' to-day I fear that I may have expressed myself with more warmth than I could wish. But what I desired to say was *this*.

" When you have (1) a Court like the Judicial Committee of the Privy Council, the religious authority of which has been consistently challenged by the best men in the Church of England (Mr. Keble denied that it could anyhow be brought under the head of the Fifth Commandment), and (2) a Decision like that about the Vestments which, as Dr. Pusey has said, and many of those who least agree with him admit, is based on a non-natural interpretation of the Prayer-book, you cannot proceed to enforce such a Decision of such a Court as 'law,' without grave risks. What these risks are, in the present circumstances of the Church of England, you must know as well as I do. No doubt the subscribers to the ' Church Association' expect an outward and visible return for their money, but they will be indulged, if at all, at the cost of the Church Establishment, and of much which is of more value to religious men than the State Establishment of any Church."

It has already been seen that Liddon's position in the troubles about Ritualism was not a little difficult. On the general principle he was entirely in agreement with those who were being attacked, and on that ground openly supported them. But he was far from agreeing with all the actions of those whose main position he was ready to defend. The two following letters about the controversy on the book called " The Priest in Absolution," and on the difficulties of a Clergyman with his Bishop, will illustrate his position.

To ———

" 3, Amen Court, August 27, 1877.

" . . . If distressed consciences cannot get relief in the English Church, they will go to Rome to get it. The old Puritanical device of Justification by excited feelings no longer serves with serious people as a substitute for sincere investigation into the real condition of conscience, and this, in numberless cases, means Confession. Parliament can disestablish the Church of England, but it can no more interfere with Confession than with the sun and moon.

" If it attempts to tamper with the doctrines of the Prayer-book, the result will be a disruption—and at no distant time the disestablishment and disendowment of the body which tried to save its revenues at the cost of its doctrines and its historical honour."

To ———

" 3, Amen Court, E.C., December 10, 1877.

" I have read the Bishop's letter as you desire. Perhaps I had better say nothing about it, as, although it suggests a great many obvious remarks, I shall too probably, if I begin, say something for which I shall be sorry hereafter.

"The question is, What ought you to do? I am a very bad adviser in these matters, as you know, but I will try to put myself in your position, with my own convictions, and to write accordingly.

"You have three great obligations to keep in view, while making up your mind.

"1. There is your obligation to obey the Bishop. There can, I suppose, be no doubt that the *jus liturgicum* which was believed by the ancient Church to reside in the Bishop, had a very wide range indeed, including almost everything that was not a matter of Œcumenical decision, or that did not touch the Creeds or the form and matter of the Sacraments. And if a Bishop abused this power, that was a question for his own conscience before God, but—at any rate, within limits—it did not relieve the clergy from their duty of obeying him.

"2. There is your obligation to the law of the Church of England, of which the Ornaments Rubric is a part. And I assume that you do not consider this obligation to be modified, *in foro conscientiæ*, by the decision of a *numerical* majority of judges in a civil Court of Appeal. This obligation, I may remark, binds the Bishop too, however he may interpret it.

"If, *e.g.*, he accepts the Ridsdale Judgment as a substantial modification of his duty to obey the Rubric, it is difficult to see how he conceives himself morally at liberty not to use the old Episcopal dress himself. For the appeal to the Advertisements upon which that Judgment proceeds, certainly leaves the Bishops who are unaffected by the Advertisements, face to face with the original sense of the Ornaments Rubric as regards themselves. And nobody doubts what that sense is. However, as I have said, this is an affair for the Bishop's conscience.

"3. There is your obligation to your flock. You have to consider what will distress, upset, scatter it : and in what degree. This is an element in the question which you only can estimate, but it is one to which your Ordination vow binds you as much as to anything else.

"In view of these obligations, I should, if I were in your place, endeavour to combine the *maximum* of concession, which I could conscientiously make to the Bishop's demand, with the *minimum* of spiritual loss and disaster to my flock.

"Of the points which he specifies in his letter, some, at any rate, are not prescribed by the law of the Church of England. There can be no doubt of a Bishop's '*Ecclesiastical* right' to enjoin or forbid things of this kind, and I should, if I could, give them up at his desire. 'If I could,' because it is conceivable that concession, beyond certain limits, would be so ruinous in its effect upon the souls for whom I had to answer, that for their sakes I might consider disobedience to him the lesser moral evil of the two. There are times when an army is saved by a subaltern's disobedience to his commanding officer. The subaltern is on the spot, knows his men, sees the danger ahead, and is really responsible for acting with this nearer and fuller knowledge. You see, I don't think the theory of unconditional resistance to a Bishop in these matters is *morally* justifiable. But the duty of obedience to him is clearly modified by other obligations—above all, by the obligation not to offend 'Christ's little ones' committed to your charge, to their eternal loss.

"You have to bear in mind that the Bishop has you in his power ; he might withdraw your licence, without any reference to the Courts. If you make no concession to his Episcopal authority, he will be morally, as well as legally, in a strong position against you. If you concede what your conscience will permit—I mean, your conscience as governed partly by your sense of obligation to the law of the Church of England, and partly by your duties towards the souls of your flock —you will occupy a strong position, in declining to give way on *all* points, *e.g.* about the Vestments. You might, I think, appeal to any Bishop with very great moral force, not to oblige you to break up a congregation of souls to whom you have ministered for I know not how many years, in deference to a legal misinterpretation of the old law of the Church, which is condemned by the emphatic dissent of such lawyers as the Lord Chief Baron and the Dean of the Arches. Whatever you write, write as for publication; and in view of the implacable Puritanism which the Bishop is possibly obeying in thus applying to you, and which will give no quarter to any mistakes that you may make. I fear that this will not help you much, but I write simply as I think I should try to feel and to act, if I were in your place. May God help us all to that difficult grace of acting as for Him under trying circumstances like these, and of so doing justice to the respective claims of apparently conflicting obligations."

The gradual but very great changes at St. Paul's Cathedral were of necessity attracting attention. An article in the *Guardian* of March, 1878, incidentally describes the work in which the Dean and Chapter were so successfully engaged.

"How great that work is can only be appreciated by those who remember what the Cathedral was a score of years ago, when you paid twopence at the door to enter a vast and dreary area abandoned to dust and damp and uselessness. All that has long ago been altered. No one now feels the chill of an unused building as he enters unquestioned the long aisles abundantly fitted up for Worship. Even the vast Crypt, formerly a mere lumber-hole, is being gradually cleared out, and a portion of it is already used for some of the many Services which, in the various demands made and accepted on the Metropolitan Cathedral, are occasionally jostling one another ; and if the renovation of the whole fabric is still delayed, it is rather from a wholesome desire to wait for the final award of deliberate taste and judgment in so important a matter, than from a lack of enterprise or despair of funds. Meanwhile, that which is really the life of the Church goes on with unremitting, and indeed ever-increasing vigour. . . . The nation and the City both look to it as the conspicuous embodiment of their visible Worship, the bond of their united religious action, the heart which sends the pulse of Religion bounding actively through a thousand different channels. It has borne a striking witness to the power which may flow from a great ecclesiastical Institution rightly planned and diligently and wisely worked in the midst of a teeming and busy population."

One of Liddon's many stories about the Cathedral may find a place in this connection.

" Did I ever tell you how the attendance of non-communicants at the midday Eucharist at St. Paul's first began? When I first came there, the vergers used to go to people who were remaining after the Prayer for the Church Militant, and say, ' Are you intending to receive ? ' and if the reply was in the negative, ' Then you are requested to leave the Cathedral.' This went on till, after one Trinity Sunday, I received a letter from a Cambridge undergraduate, saying that he and another had come to the Cathedral to see a common friend ordained. They had communicated early, and were much distressed by being interrogated by the verger, ' Are you intending to receive ? ' etc., and turned out of the Cathedral. I felt that this was an opportunity ; so I wrote to the undergraduate, saying that I was very sorry for what had occurred, and that if he would write me a suitable letter (for which I made some suggestions to him) I would bring the matter before the Chapter. The letter was accordingly written, and I read it at the next Chapter meeting. Thereupon the Archdeacon (*i.e.* Bishop Claughton) said he had fears of the reintroduction of the Mass, etc. I replied that the Archdeacon often insisted on the importance of obeying the Law, and, as far as I knew, the request which the vergers were ordered to make was a strictly illegal request, failing, as it did, to derive any support from the Rubrics. The order to the vergers was in consequence withdrawn."

In 1878 the twelve new bells for the Cathedral were being put in their place, and Liddon spent hours in the north-west tower, watching each step of the work with the greatest interest. But he felt that something was yet needed to make the outer voice of the great Cathedral fully expressive of all that it ought to announce to the world.

To the Dean of St. Paul's.

"3, Amen Court, August 17, 1878.

". . . The bells are arriving from Loughborough. The tenth is to-day just going into its place, as I am writing. The eleventh is half-way up the tower, and will be fixed on Monday. Then two little bells will come, and the twelfth or tenor bell about Wednesday. The Lough-borough workmen seem to be a very efficient and well-behaved set of men. The whole thing makes me wish more than ever for a huge Bourdon, which should cost some £3000, and be worthy of the Cathedral. There is plenty of room for it. Stainer, with whom I have had much talk, says that the existing big bell in the clock-tower, together with the two quarter bells, would melt down into eight and a half tons of metal, worth about £1500, and this would help us a good way through our enterprise. But I would rather leave that bell as it is, for the Lord Mayor, the Royal Family, etc., else they will get the control of our new bell, by a very natural process. The new big bell ought to have a Christian name, which, I am sorry to say, none of the Loughborough ones have. What do you say to ' Paulus, Doctor Gentium,' and for a motto, ' Væ mihi, si non evangelizavero ' ? "

This proposal was adopted; the City Corporation and the City Companies supplied a large amount of the money, and Dr. Stainer gave all his skill to assist those who cast the bell; and in the early days of December, 1881, great public interest was excited by the progress from Lough-borough up to London and through the City streets, of a great bell weighing just seventeen tons, which took its place with the others in the north-western tower of the Cathedral. On the Sunday after it had been raised to its position, on December 18, Liddon took for the text of his sermon the motto which at his own suggestion had been put on the bell. To him it was no mere noise-making addition to the Cathedral; it had its subordinate place in the work of the great Church.

" A church bell," he said, " is not a vital or a saving truth ; it is not a purified or consecrated heart. It belongs to the world of matter and not to the world of spirit. . . . But it is not therefore without its due measure of importance. Anything that, though itself matter, proclaims and advertises the reality of a higher and spiritual existence, has a certain value which cannot be overlooked. It acts insensibly upon the public imagination; it moulds and sways the less conscious processes of popular thought. No religious man will assign too much importance to this; no prudent man will altogether neglect it.[1] . . ."

Of all his friends the most likeminded on the Eastern Question was Mr. E. A. Freeman, who was abroad during the winter of 1877–78. Liddon kept him informed of what was happening in England on this absorbing topic.

To E. A. Freeman, Esq.

"Christ Church, November 25, 1877.

". . . Before this, I ought to have acknowledged your letter, written on the eve of your leaving England. You are, I heartily trust, beginning to feel the benefits of the change, or, at any rate, of the escape from an English November. The great event, since your departure, has been the fall of Kars, which will, I trust, soon involve the fall of Erzeroum. The home-Turks—so far as my observation goes—were at first stunned; but they have now recovered sufficiently to talk very violently about the renewed necessity for a war against Russia, in order to protect English interests. The *Standard* and the *Pall Mall* —the latter especially—shriek. The *Daily Telegraph*, more comically, has tried, within the last day or two, to attempt 'thoughtful remonstrance' with those of us whom the others describe as madmen or traitors. Of what is passing in high quarters I know nothing; but I cannot think that at least two members of the Cabinet would continue to sit in it, if Lord B. should insist on war with Russia. Probably his game is to wait for the negotiations for peace, and then to discover that the Russian demands are inconsistent with Lord Derby's definition of English interests. But it is this delay which makes some of the Anglo-Turk papers so exceedingly angry; they say that everything is being decided now, and that when Russia has crushed Turkey, intervention will be useless.

"You will see by the papers that Mr. Gladstone has answered Forbes, and, in particular, has answered that topic about the Turkish 'generosity' in leaving the Bulgarians alone when falling back before the Russian advance, very tellingly. As he is reported, he does not seem to have said all that might be said on behalf of the Bulgarians.

[1] "Advent Sermons," vol. ii. p. 116.

Of course, like other populations, they have a per-centage of roughs—
the number and quality of whom have not been diminished by four
centuries of cruel oppression. Such a war as this is the opportunity
of these people ; but Forbes' injustice—unintentional, no doubt—lies
in confusing them with the high-minded men who are to be found
everywhere in Bulgaria, and who have contributed, by all accounts,
the largest number of victims to that wretched Ibrahim Pasha at
Philippopolis.

"People here are too charged with suppressed feeling, on both
sides, to discuss this matter in Common Room ; although sometimes,
in private society, there is an allusion to it. From what I can hear,
the majority of those who are most violent against Russia are not yet
prepared for war. It requires a good robust conviction to overcome
British objections to an increased income tax ; and the Christian party
is sufficiently widespread to impair, although it cannot destroy, the
pro-Turkish enthusiasm."

His intense anxiety on this question in the early part
of 1878 finds expression on page after page of his diary.
His regular visits to Hatfield, Highclere, Longleat, and
to Sir Robert Phillimore were filled with talk on the one
absorbing topic. Three letters only can be quoted out of a
great mass of such correspondence ; they show the reasons
for his attitude, and the extent to which he would go in
supporting it.

To ———

"3, Amen Court, St. Paul's, January 15, 1878.

". . . To me the cause of Russia in this struggle appears plainly
to be the cause of Righteousness. She entered upon it unwillingly, the
generous instincts of the people forced the hand of the Government to
attempt something for their suffering fellow-Christians. Would that
England had taken the lead in forcing Turkey to respect her own
solemn engagements to deal justly by the Christian races of her
empire ! But we left the task to Russia ; and the 'crime' of Russia
is that she has succeeded. . . . Between Russia or England, taken
at their worst, and Turkey, the difference is enormous. It is the
difference which Christianity alone can make. Christianity always
carries with it the germs of a progressive improvement ; whereas
Mahommedanism condemns the races which it curses to stagnate in
evil. You are, as I think, misinformed as to some of your illustrations
of Russian cruelty ; I believe that you are right in what you say
about corruptness in Russian administration. It is deplored by the
best men in the country. But Russia contains the true secret of

improvement, and her advance in Central Asia has been as great a blessing to humanity as has our own in India. Each has limited the area of triumphant brutality. Certainly the Gospel is not to be propagated by war. The object of the present war is not to propagate the Gospel, but to vindicate elementary human rights against an oppressive and cruel despotism. And yet, incidentally, it is more than possible that one result of the war will be to place the Church of Christ in South-Eastern Europe in a new position of freedom to carry out its mission. I do not at all subscribe to your description of Russian Christianity as 'the very worst and most corrupt possible form of "Czarism."' The Czar is not more powerful in the Church of Russia than Louis XIV. was in that of France ; he is not so powerful as was Joseph II. in that of Austria. There is no Court in Russia that places the final settlement of questions of Faith in the hands of men who may make no secret of their rejection of Christianity altogether.

"We, alas, are in no condition, as a Church, which entitles us to complain of the Czarism of other Churches. But the Christians who have been oppressed for four centuries by the Turks, and whose agonies in 1876 roused the generous indignation of all who had hearts to feel, have nothing to do with the Czar of Russia. They are the spiritual descendants of Churches older than ours by some centuries ; and we owe them all the sympathy and assistance that it is in our power to give, if we care aught for the name of Catholic, and do not limit it to those Communions which owe allegiance to the Pope. I cannot believe that God will allow us to plunge into so frightful a crime as a war against Russia on behalf of Turkey, under pretence of upholding British interests. But if a majority of the people of this country should be so blinded as to force on this grave calamity, there will be a day of rude awakening, when men and Churches who have advocated it will be called to a stern account. At any rate, we can only do, each of us, what we believe before God to be His Will, so far as we can ascertain it, in this and in all other matters. 'Patriotism' is a sacred word, but it is terribly abused. It means, for me, the desire and prayer that my country should obey before all things the laws of moral Truth, which do not by any means sanction those wild appeals to unreasoning passion and selfish greed, which too often are described as patriotic. In the long run, as I believe, Church principles will succeed in such measure as men discover that those who hold them are loyal to a moral code higher and deeper than that of any patriotic party; and England will take her true place among the nations when she ceases to be jealous of their material prosperity, and endeavours to co-operate with them in promoting the happiness—temporal and eternal—of the largest possible number of human beings.

"Pray forgive my inflicting on you all this. But we have, I rejoice to think, so much in common on the most serious of all subjects, that I was unwilling to take only a cursory notice of your letter."

To ———

" 3, Amen Court, St. Paul's, April 18, 1878.

" . . . I can only answer your question by saying, that if I were a soldier or sailor in Her Majesty's service, I should feel obliged to retire, if I could, from the service, in the event of a war with Russia under existing circumstances. In ninety-nine cases out of a hundred a man would gladly leave the responsibility of deciding upon peace or war entirely and cheerfully in the hands of the Government ; but there are cases when, however reluctantly, one cannot help seeing that one's own country, under the conduct of a particular Government, may be hopelessly in the wrong ; and a conviction of this kind seems to make it necessary to avoid any personal participation that can be avoided in the destruction ot human life for an unworthy or insufficient reason."

To E. A. Freeman, Esq.

" May 16, 1878.

" . . . The General Election cannot be very distant. Lord Beaconsfield will not wait until the taxes which the war demonstration has rendered necessary have begun to pinch. He will, perhaps, dissolve this very summer, if he gets a diplomatic success, or anything that can be represented as being one before the end of the Session.

" The ' Turk ' papers have been more furious than ever of late ; the *Pall Mall's* correspondents suggest that I should be imprisoned—so I am told. There must be a reaction from all this nonsense ; my only fear is that it will carry us too far. But I shall rejoice at emancipation from the diseased opinion of London ' Society.' It is utterly artificial, and will astonish those who come after us. What an article that is in the *Quarterly !* Who, in his senses, that wished well to the Monarchy, would raise the questions which it inevitably raises?

" Before leaving town I had a long talk with the Bishop of Salisbury about Eastern matters : it was sad to see how the House of Lords had taken his old fire out of him. On the whole, he was for supporting the Government. The only Bishops who are not are—Oxford, Ely, Exeter, and Manchester. The rest go in for ' patriotism,' which has been debauched of late more than any word that I know."

In the autumn of 1878 he had great hopes of the consequences of the Berlin Treaty, because of the results which it actually achieved, as well as the promises which were made in it.

George Richmond, R.A. pinx.   Emery Walker, ph. sc.

Henry Parry Liddon
(1878)

To C. T. Redington, Esq.

"Glamis Castle, Forfarshire, N.B., July 25, 1878.

". . . Your kind note of the 21st reaches me here, in the castle of King Malcolm, where, in fact, he was murdered by Macbeth. It is one of the oldest buildings in Scotland, and is full of the most varied interest. My host, Lord Strathmore, is a thorough Churchman, living in the midst of a Presbyterian tenantry, but keeping up in his private Chapel the old ways and faith of his ancestors. Two cannon before the front gate were 'out' with Charles Edward at Culloden; and the Chapel in the castle was the last building consecrated by a Scottish Bishop before the Church was 'suppressed' by William III. in 1688.

"Yes, I did think of you at Iona. It is an island of rare interest, in which Ireland has as large a share as Scotland. Before visiting it, one ought to read over Montalembert's 'Monks of the West,' which I forgot to do. . . . Such scenes make me often very sad, when I reflect how greatly we are wanting in the heroic spirit of those pioneers of the Faith. By 'we' I mean average people, and not the Cowley Fathers in India, or the missionaries in Zanzibar. But, for myself, I am always uncomfortable in presence of the heroism of early Christianity, for reasons which you, who know me, would easily understand.

"I am more hopeful about the East than at any time yet. The Treaty of Berlin has carried out Mr. Gladstone's policy, or a great deal of it. It has destroyed the independence and the integrity of Turkey. But it has not done justice to Greece, or rather to Crete; that will come by-and-by. As to the Anglo-Turkish Convention, I do not agree with the mere Liberals in quarrelling with it because it is likely to be costly. Morality is often very expensive. The real question is, whether the good government of Asia can be made a reality? If it can, I am content with the Convention; but everything depends on that 'if.' . . . Looking at the Convention as a mere defiance of Russia, I have, of course, no sympathy whatever with it. . . . The wrath of the *Pall Mall* with the Treaty of Berlin is amusing, and reassuring too, is it not?

"As to Farrar's Gnosticisms about Eternal Punishment, they are an old story in a new rhetorical dress. To me they are very repulsive, and I believe they do enormous harm to souls. Of course, the Revealed doctrine is an unspeakably awful one; the imagination recoils from it. But it is revealed; and there is no more to be said. . . . Farrar and his school exaggerate one attribute of God at the cost of another—His Benevolence at the expense of His Sanctity and His Justice. His book may do indirect good, by reminding *us* of our neglect of the truth of an‖Intermediate State, which does much

Q

to relieve the difficulties of the problem on its practical side. . . . But, if only Satan were lost eternally, the difficulties which Farrar insists on would remain in force; and Farrar does not imply an ἀποκατάστασις for Satan."

To Miss Mirehouse.

"3, Amen Court, E.C., August 20, 1878.

". . . 1. The Association of Prayer for the Conversion of the Moslems would, I fear, be considered just as 'political' as anything else by the 'Jingo' party. Their interests are not moral or religious in any sense, and they cannot understand such interests in other people.

"But I do not doubt that, since the question has come to the front, much prayer *has* been offered for the conversion of the Moslems to the true Faith. Indeed, I know of a good many cases.

"2. We have had a most interesting missionary from Zanzibar staying here. He has lived for three years quite alone among the Africans, carrying his life in his hand. He can now preach in three languages, and has baptised a great many natives, including some Mohammedans. He seems to have a most remarkable influence over the kings and chiefs in that part of Africa, who regard him as having a charmed life. At Magila he has built a mud church, in which Lord Penzance is not exactly obeyed, but a great deal of good is done to souls, nevertheless. He really is a person of Apostolic proportions, quite a refreshment in all ways. In January he goes out again; his health *obliged* him to get a few months' change.

"3. Mr. MacColl was right, I think, in not drinking Lord B[eaconsfield]'s health. At least, I should not have done so, even for the sake of the wine of Cyprus.

"4. But I hope with you that God will bring good out of the occupation of Cyprus. To the Cypriotes the relief from the horrible presence of the Turkish officials must be a great blessing. I fear that the Asia Minor part of that Convention is a sham. The resistance in Bosnia, apart from the suffering which it entails, will do good. It will oblige Austria to put out all her strength, and to break down with a strong hand the social system which entails Moslem supremacy. Had the Beys submitted, they would have been left in the enjoyment of their privileges. Nor am I sorry that another European Power is finding out what the Turk is, by actual experience of his ways; or that a Roman Catholic army is learning what the most implacable of the enemies of Christ have been doing towards their Eastern brethren. Probably Rome will be less Turkish after this Bosnian episode. The new feeling towards Turkey in Vienna is very edifying. Prince Bismarck (as all through this question) is behaving well; I hope he will force the Turk to give their new position to the Greeks."

As the year closes Liddon's diary is full of anxious references to the wars in Afghanistan and Zululand, though the fears lest Lord Beaconsfield should plunge England in war with Russia on behalf of Turkey had passed away. His letters also to Mr. Redington show how largely his mind is occupied with political questions, especially with the vote of censure about the Afghan campaign.

To C. T. Redington, Esq.

"3, Amen Court, E.C., Christmas Eve, 1878.

". . . There is a lull just now. Lord B[eaconsfield] has carried Parliament with him, and is reposing on his laurels, while English and Afghan blood is being shed—for what *moral* object it would be hard to say—in a distant land.

"I feel about Russia, as I have always felt, that her worst aggressions may be paralleled in our own Indian Empire, while her general policy has been less selfish and degraded than that of Great Britain. As Lord Beaconsfield said in the House of Lords some time ago, it is not the business of Parliament to take care of the cardinal virtues, but of the 'interests' of the Empire, the phrase implying very vividly that these interests are something quite distinct from morality.

"I admit that in Asiatic politics there are unknown elements which ought to make one hesitate as to matters which, if Europe alone were concerned, would be plain enough.

"Mr. Gladstone is not in low spirits about his defeat. He told me last week that, for the first time, the 'go' and 'enthusiasm' of the House was on the side of the Opposition, and that the 'terrorism,' which the Jingo party had indulged in so largely during last year, had entirely ceased. In fact, the Conservative members have learnt from their agents that the country is no longer with them, and many of them voted for the Government with the greatest reluctance. The tide, I think, has turned.

"I wish I could look forward to the reaction with unalloyed pleasure. But I cannot. It will bring disaster to many interests which are very dear to me, and—not least to the Church, which has, alas! so largely closed her eyes to the *moral* bearings of recent questions, and has supported the personage at the head of the Government.

"But no more, except to wish you again a very happy Christmas."

To C. T. Redington, Esq.

"Longleat, Warminster, January 13, 1879.

"I do not say that the Russian statesmen are angels. Certainly Ignatieff is not one ; and probably Gortschakoff has too sharp an eye to what he would think ' business.' But the Russian *people*, which forced the Czar's Government to engage in an enterprise for the relief of the oppressed Christians in the Balkan provinces of Turkey does contrast favourably, as it appears to me, with the selfish bearing of the majority of Englishmen throughout the crisis. As to Bessarabia, it may be pleaded that it was taken from Russia by force in 1856, and that any other State would have used a successful war, if it could, to restore *forfeited* territory. The only *moral* plea for the Armenian annexations, is, that they secure safety of life, honour, and property to a large Christian population, without risking that of their fellow-subjects, who are Mohammedans. But *I regret* both the annexations. They soil the hands of men, who at first set out to achieve a disinterested and noble work ; and I explain this moral misfortune, by supposing, that before the period for making Treaties, first at San Stefano, and then at Berlin, had come about, the control over events had passed from the hands of the people into those of the diplomatists.

"We English, on the other hand, in this matter, did not so much as begin well, and only fail to do well to the end. We might have freed the Bulgarians ourselves, or have helped Russia to do so. We have stood aside, sneering, or screeching, or even threatening war. We have happily not been able to prevent the liberation of eleven millions of Christians ; but we *have* at Berlin, forced back some large populations which might have been free, into the claws of the Turk. And the cynical contempt for everything of the nature of virtue, when politics are in question, which is paraded by the *Pall Mall Gazette*, does, I fear, represent the temper which has dictated our policy.

"Patriotism is a virtue, no doubt : and it is a duty to cherish patriotism in ourselves and others. But patriotism means wishing well to our country, and the question is *what* is this ' well.' Lord Beaconsfield would say ' material prosperity, grandeur, increase of power and territory ;' Mr. Gladstone would say ' that our country may act virtuously.' If patriotism is an extension of the feeling which we have abou our relatives, Mr. Gladstone is surely right ; we wish our relatives to be good men in the first instance, and then successful men, if success is compatible with goodness. I cannot understand how many excellent people fail to feel thus about their country too ; it would seem to me that exactly in the proportion in which we realise the fact that a nation is only a very overgrown family which has kept open house for some centuries—will be our anxiety that this country should act as a good man would act ; and that patriotism consists in wishing this.

"I have not seen the Article to which you refer. But the objection is an old one. Tyndall, I suppose, does not believe in the first article of the Creed, else he would see that to accept a creation of the Universe out of nothing, and to object to the doctrine of the resurrection of the body on the grounds you mention is not very rational. And yet, the alternative to our faith in a creation out of nothing is an hypothesis about Matter which is surrounded with far greater difficulties—which, however, for the time, are ignored by the physico-non-theistic school.

" They say that the material of every human body is entirely changed in the course of seven years ; this has, I believe, been demonstrated. It follows that *I* must have changed the substance of my body exactly seven times ; you, not yet, quite so often. But I have no doubt about the identity of my present body with that which I had as a schoolboy ; this identity, in fact, is somehow independent of the identity of the matter composing it. This may afford a clue to the solution of Professor Tyndall's ' difficulty ;' a body may be the same body yet differently composed, as indeed being what St. Paul tells us it will be, a ' spiritual ' body, though it is difficult to say *exactly* what is and is not included under that term.

" I have been staying at Hatfield, and have come on here, where Lord Granville and several other people of that kind are staying. Lord Granville is not much in my way, though he can be brilliant and amusing ; the only Liberal I really trust is Mr. Gladstone, and he is often, like Lord Salisbury, damaged more or less seriously by his political associates. . . .

" Liberalism itself, is, on all matters connected with Church and Education, only a kind of corporate and ' respectable ' ungodliness ; and I cannot forget or forgive its misdeeds in this way (because it has largely, though not by any means entirely, gone right about the Eastern Question) so easily as MacColl does."

CORRESPONDENCE, 1876–1878.

In Reply to a Criticism on his Sermons at St. Paul's.

" 3, Amen Court, E.C., April 9, 1877.
" 1. The unjustifiable dilemma of which I was thinking was this : ' You must either believe in Papal Infallibility, or you must give up Christianity.' The dilemma *has* been pressed, and upon persons who have chosen the infidel alternative. You would probably agree with me that it is as fallacious as it is violent, but when people know little of history, it is imposing enough.

" 2. I was not thinking of any such dilemma as ' You must either receive the full Sacramental system of the Church, and in particular the doctrine and practice of Confession and Absolution, or you must give up Christianity.' I do not believe *that* to be a necessary alternative, *except* in the sense that the logical consequence of the rejection of any one fragment of Truth ought to be the rejection of all Truth which rests on the same basis. Clearly, however, Sacramental doctrine is related to the Christian Faith as a whole, in a very different sense from that in which the Resurrection is related to it.

" And I do not think that in the majority of cases such a dilemma would succeed.

" People would say, 'Very well, *if* Christianity involves all this, we cannot continue to accept it.' And as I think, they had better continue to believe what they do, however illogically, than to be logical at the cost of the faith which they still retain.

" 3. When you ask me, whether I think you right when you teach that 'if A or B is a Christian he is bound to accept the living voice of the Church, *in re* the Sacraments, and specially as to the forgiveness of sins,' I should first have to ask you what you mean exactly by the *living* voice of the Church. It is not a phrase of any great authority, and it easily covers false conclusions. It would be more practical to say 'the teaching of the Prayer-book.' If you ask me, ' Do I think that all persons are in any case bound to go to confession? ' I cannot, with the Prayer-book in my hands, say that I do. It has been a great help to me for *thirty* years, but I believe that thousands get to heaven without using it, now, as in the first ages of the Church.

" 4. As to the best way of presenting Christian Truth to a mixed multitude like that at St. Paul's, many of them on the frontiers of Christian faith, and many beyond them, I am likely enough to have made grave mistakes.

" But alas ! at the Day of Judgment, no one else can answer for what I say or have left unsaid; and, meanwhile, I try to think of that Day, and pray God for grace to enable me to help the greatest number as best I may."

To C. T. Redington, Esq.

The Inevitable Demand for a Religion.

" Powderham Castle, Exeter, June 27, 1877.

" . . . What you say about the educated class throughout Europe is sadly true, but there are large exceptions almost everywhere, and, meanwhile, the conditions of life and death do not accommodate themselves to the opinions of successive generations. So long as men die, life will reassert its tragic interest from time to time with fresh energy, and to this interest Christianity alone can respond. If the scientific people could rid us of death, they might indeed hope to win over the heart and conscience of the world, permanently, to some form of non-theistic speculation. As it is, the tide ebbs, as I believe, only that it may flow again."

To Dr. Newman.

On the *"Via Media."*

" 3, Amen Court, St. Paul's, December 17, 1877.

" Once more I have to thank you for your goodness in thinking of me. The second instalment of 'Via Media' is, in some respects, more interesting than the first.   Excepting the Letters on the Church Missionary Society, I had already possessed all the Papers in it; but I recollect that many years ago I had much difficulty in getting a copy of that on ' Suffragan Bishops.'

" To most men of this generation, the greater part of the volumes will be quite new.   Tract 90, of course, has been republished, and has been the subject of later controversy and apology.   English High Churchmen have never cordially accepted the symbol ' Via Media,' although in a certain sense it describes their relations to Rome and to general Protestantism.   This may be partly on account of the criticisms, which we are all taught to make on Aristotle's theory of the virtues.   But it is, I suppose, still more due to a feeling that in matters of Revealed Faith 'Via Media' implies deliberate compromise, as opposed to thorough-going loyalty to principle.   I have often thought of what you say—I think in the ' Apologia '—about semi-Arianism and Monophysitism being phenomena anticipatory of the Church of England.   Yet it always occurs to me that the Monophysites would have considered themselves the representatives of *principle* as against Nestorianism, and would have treated Catholics as compromising and inconsequent.   Is it not the case, too, that the recent Vatican Definition about Infallibility is itself a kind of 'Via Media' between the opinions of thorough-going Infallibilists, and what used to be called Gallicanism?

" I do not know why we should be sensitive about the word, but somehow it has never taken root."

To Professor Max Müller.

On his " *Lecture on the Origin of Religion.*"

" 3, Amen Court, April 8, 1878.

" . . . I am very greatly obliged to you for sending me your Lecture, and I have read it through, I need scarcely say, with great admiration, and, generally speaking, with complete assent.

" For, as you observe, it does not approach that region of discussion at which I feared there might be room for misunderstanding.   Perhaps I ought to say two things about it.

" First, that in your anxiety to construct a definition of ' Religion ' sufficiently wide to include all the uses to which the word has been applied, you seemingly include some uses of the word which are, at best, adaptations of it, as, *e.g.*, that of the 'recent philosopher' (p. 8, line 3). Would it not be more accurate to say that he had abandoned the idea that any Religion, properly speaking, was possible? and had addressed himself to the next best thing within his reach?

"Again—and this is a more serious point—your arrangement *appears* not to allow for any original knowledge of God which was gradually forfeited by unfaithfulness to moral light, such as St. Paul seems to contemplate in Rom. i. 18, *sqq.* I say 'appears,' because, of course, you might very well say, 'That doctrine or theory may be true; but if so, it belongs to an earlier stage of human history than any with which I have anything to do. I take human history as I find it, in India and elsewhere, and describe the process which *may* be a recovery, or an original discovery of knowledge of the Infinite.' But a single sentence which glanced at this would remove a great deal of misapprehension. May I say that I am especially struck by the truth and force and beauty of the argument, pp. 19–22?

"When I wrote to you the other day, I did not indeed mean to suggest that you should go out of your way to do the duties of a Bampton Lecturer. I only ventured to point out how some misunderstanding might be avoided. I for one am convinced that in drawing attention to the pathetic interest of struggles after light among the heathen, and to the substantial value of the truths which they attained to, you are doing us a very real service.

"You have the Alexandrians behind you; and the modern Church has too generally forgotten them. And when you say that 'Christianity influenced the world without protection,' I more than assent. All that I am anxious about is that Christianity, if it is noticed at all, should be noticed *as claiming*, at any rate, to be something more than the results of a spiritual evolution which has been going on for centuries. I have looked hard at it for many years, and have felt increasingly that if Christ's Resurrection is not a fact, true in itself, and important, as warranting the claim of Christianity 'to have come from heaven,' we must admit that Christianity, as taught by St. Paul, and believed in ever since his time, is a counterfeit. The attempts to connect the name with some ethical extracts from the New Testament, after all its distinctive features have been abandoned, do more credit to the heart than to the head of those who make them.

"Pray do not think that because I say this I am insensible to the work you are doing, in showing that Religion is, as you say, 'inevitable,' or to the command of historical and other knowledge bearing on this point, in which no Englishman that I know of could at all rival lyou. But I am thinking of what will happen when you have won your battle, at least, in honest and good hearts, and when your captives, convinced that Religion is essential to any true estimate of life, ask, as they must ask, 'What do *we* really know about its Object?'

"You will, I know, forgive me for writing to you with this boldness, or rather, for trying to say what I mean within so short a compass."

To Professor Max Müller.

"3, Amen Court, E.C., April 16, 1878.

" . . . It is indeed very good of you to answer me as fully and as patiently as you do. When we speak of 'knowledge of God' do we not always mean something very far short, from the nature of the case, of comprehension? Surely we do. In one sense we never 'know' God. In another, as all Christians believe, 'This is Life Eternal, to know Thee, the only True God.'

" Knowledge of God, in the sense of comprehending Him, is always impossible. Do we really comprehend even each other? Do we not feel each other just as we feel God? and then take our feelings to pieces and find that they include, or are based on, a recognition of certain qualities in the person who excites them?

" And is not this recognition really knowledge—such knowledge as may be expressed in propositions? And if so, how does it differ in kind—I admit that it differs enormously in degree—from the know-ledge that we have about God? Certainly our highest knowledge of God is only apprehensive, yet it is knowledge, as far as it goes, and it may be set forth in propositions. Even the most shadowy Theism includes at least one tremendous affirmative proposition—however this may be qualified. And this proposition makes this Theism a Theology as well as a Religion.

" Nor can I see any *à priori* difficulty in supposing that God may have furnished the mind of primitive man with some feeling or instinct about Himself—a feeling which would be irrational if not based on knowledge of some kind. Why should He have done this less easily than He has given *all* men the sense of right and wrong? Does not this sense of right and wrong itself imply God? Is it not a law? and does not a law imply a Law-giver?

" I could accept your formula about Christianity being one language out of many—but one mother-tongue, if I might differentiate Chris-tianity more clearly than you do. God *has* spoken to heathen souls, though His Voice is lost well-nigh among the echoes of surrounding errors. But He has spoken through His Son as never before : Πίστιν παρασχὼν πᾶσιν ἀναστήσας αὐτὸν ἐκ νεκρῶν.

" Pray do not think of writing again, but allow me to look forward to a renewal of our conversation at Oxford, if you have time."

To ———

On Renan's "Origin of the Gospels."

"Annecy, September 9, 1878.

" I am reading Renan's book on the 'Origin of the Gospels.' It is more ingenious, I think, than any of his other productions, but more suggestive of the insuperable difficulty of his task, which is to show

how anything of the kind could have grown up in the soil of the human mind without a Divine Subject to describe, and without superhuman aid in writing the description. Like some of Baur's books, it does one an indirect and unintended service by calling attention to features in the Sacred Text, which are often not noticed by believing writers, and which, when examined, throw new light on a great deal beyond. In literature, as in other things, the Evil one has to do God's Will in spite of himself, and when he least intends it."

To the Rev. A. M. W. Christopher.

On Baptismal Regeneration.

"3, Amen Court, E.C., January 2, 1879.

", . . I am much obliged to you for sending me a copy of Dr. Mozley's 'Review of the Baptismal Controversy.' I shall value your gift, although I have been more or less familiar with the book for many years, and have talked parts of it over with its author.

" Of course, it is marked by the great ability which distinguishes everything that he wrote. But the method of explaining the language of the Baptismal Service by the theory of a 'charitable hypothesis' appears to me to belong to that family of theological solvents which is apt to do more destructive work than is at all intended by the writers who employ them for a particular purpose.

" You would be acquainted with theories of accommodation by the aid of which the great texts in the New Testament, which, as we both believe, teach the doctrine of the Atonement, are emptied of their natural meaning, by Socinianising writers.

" If Baptismal Regeneration is not the doctrine of the Church of England, the language of the Baptismal Service is very misleading for plain people. When administering Baptism, we are instructed to pray that 'this infant' coming to this Holy Baptism may receive remission of his sins by 'spiritual regeneration ;' and that God would 'sanctify this water to the mystical washing away of sin ;' and then, when the rite is complete, to announce that this child 'is regenerate.' And we teach our little children to say that in Baptism each one was 'made a member of Christ, the child of God, and an inheritor of the kingdom of heaven.' It seems to me that the natural sense of this language will outlive the subtleties upon which the Gorham Decision was based ; and that if the Church of England had desired to leave the matter an open question, or to deny the revealed doctrine of Baptismal Grace, she would have done better to omit from her Formularies passages which, to ordinary apprehensions, seem to affirm the doctrine more explicitly than does the corresponding language of the Church of Rome.

" If, unhappily, I did not believe in Baptismal Regeneration, I should lose my faith in more than one Revealed Truth besides. The

Rationalism which denies Sacramental grace is the same Rationalism (only happily less consequent) as that which rejects the Atonement and the Holy Trinity ; and the arguments which enable it to achieve the one result are serviceable enough for the other.

" It is a great blessing that people don't see this, in many cases : it is better far to be illogical than unbelieving. But—Truth has exigencies which are beyond control.

" If, too, I rejected Baptismal Regeneration, and yet consented to use the Baptismal Service of the Church of England, I should not feel at liberty to denounce Ritualists or any other persons, on the score of unfaithfulness to the *natural* sense of our Formularies.

" In saying this, I hope not to be thought insensible to the kind spirit which dictates, I am sure, your New Year's gift."

To ———

On the Proposal to erect a Statue to Tyndale, one of the First Translators of the Bible into English.

" Longleat, Warminster, January 14, 1879.

" I entirely agree with you, that the Authorised Version of the Bible is one of God's greatest gifts to our Church and people ; and that Tyndale's share in contributing to its ultimate production was a magnificent one. But he has other aspects, which can hardly be separated from his claims as a scholar and a man of great honesty of purpose. It may have been a necessity of his position, as one of the early pioneers of the Reformation ; but his relation to the Church and Hierarchy appears to have been almost purely negative, and he might probably, as far as this goes, be claimed more justly by the Independents than by ourselves. What he would have been had he lived under Elizabeth, it is difficult to say ; but there is nothing, I think, to show that he would not have sympathised, *e.g.*, with Cartwright rather than with Hooker. If, then, he is to stand alone, as a representative of our Reformed Church, the representation will be at least a one-sided and distorted one ; but my difficulty would be at an end if his statue could be part of a larger scheme, more adequate in itself as an expression of the facts of our religious history, and thus capable of giving him his rightful honour without implicitly obscuring any parts of the Will of God, to which he did not bear witness. If, *e.g.*, Tyndale, Taylor, Ken, and Butler could be honoured in the way proposed, as representing scholarship, eloquence, devotion, and religious philosophy, I should gladly join the committee to promote such an object, and should subscribe what I could afford. But I had feared that any such proposal as this was out of the question ; and I felt that in promoting a statue to Tyndale *alone* I should not be quite loyal to my own religious convictions.

" P.S.—The Roman Catholics, I think, would see in Tyndale only the Reformer—not the scholar—and the *burnt* Reformer too. Archbishop Laud was a great patron of letters, but I fear that modern Puritanism would not welcome his statue on the Embankment—it would always be thinking of Tower Hill. Persecutors in all ages have a kind of conscience which makes the forgiveness of a victim well-nigh impossible—I suppose on the *odisse quem læseris* principle."

To Professor Max Müller.

On his " Lectures on the Origin and Growth of Religion."

" Longleat, Warminster, January 14, 1879.

" Long since I ought to have thanked you for your goodness in sending me your ' Lectures on the Origin and Growth of Religion.' It seemed better not to do this until I could find time to read them through with attention. The book is indeed full of the highest interest ; and, for me, it is full of instruction too ; knowing, as I do, alas ! almost nothing of its proper subject-matter except what I have gathered from other works of its author.

" If I might do so without being impertinent, I would say that when the world reads these Lectures, it can have but one opinion as to the beauty of their literary form, the wealth of knowledge which they imply, and, not least, the moral and religious enthusiasm which abounds in them.

" But I feel I cannot go along with you—when you propose, at the end of your last Lecture, to take refuge ' in the crypt.' No doubt the crypt has its beauties : have you not taught us to admire them ? But surely it is a bad place to live in. And, for my part, I must remain absolutely upstairs, in the sunshine, at least, except on those rare occasions when I join an archæological excursion. If Religion is to be a power with the mass of mankind, it must be, at any rate, something like historical Christianity ; that is to say, positive in its faith, practical in its requirements—above all and always, definite. While men are only ' feeling after God,' a Religion of this kind is, from the nature of the case, impossible ; it is, as I believe, only legitimately possible as the result of a Supernatural Revelation. Whether such a Revelation has been given or not, is a question for discussion ; but Christianity would seem to be ' nowhere,' except on the supposition that the existence of such a Revelation is a proved certainty.

" Probably your subject, or the prescribed number of Lectures, did not readily admit of any adequate reference to the sense of moral evil, considered as a prominent contributor to the growth and form of Religion. But surely some of the least lovely features of pagan religions have been due to man's passionate efforts to satisfy this imperious sense. And that Christianity *does* satisfy it, is a main secret of the power which Christianity does and will wield over the hearts of men.

" To people like myself, the great and lasting value of your book will be that it recalls to us what we are too apt to forget—the religious function of Nature, the services which Nature has actually rendered to man in fostering and guiding the sense of an invisible world, and in suggesting, however dimly, its Ruler and Author. If, as I believe, Christianity is the absolute Religion, and therefore cannot take rank even as *prima inter pares* among these earlier rudimentary Faiths, in the crypt or Church of the future, yet, assuredly, watching under your guidance man's struggle for a satisfaction which the Christian Revelation has given us, we Christians have much to learn. In particular, I can truly say for myself, that, since reading your book, I have been saying the Canticle, *Benedicite, omnia opera*, almost with a new mind and heart, and that I am correspondingly grateful to you."

CHAPTER IX.

WORK AT OXFORD—THOUGHTS ON ACADEMICAL MATTERS
—RELATIONS WITH PUSEY AND NEWMAN—DANTE
SOCIETY — REREDOS AT THE CATHEDRAL — THE
FUTURE OF CHRIST CHURCH—"RECENT FORTUNES
OF THE CHURCH IN OXFORD"—LIFE AT CHRIST
CHURCH.

1870-1881.

LIDDON'S heart was naturally full of the great problems
of Church life and work with which London brought him
into immediate relation. But he was far from being
indifferent to the many important questions which agitated
the Oxford world, with which, as Professor of Exegesis,
he still had much to do. Still, he had never been able
to regard the work at Oxford as his life's work. To Pusey
it was all-important ; his life was entirely devoted to it.
In Liddon's mind it had never had the same prominence,
and, but for Pusey's sake, he would have given up all his
academical positions when he was appointed to the
Canonry at St. Paul's. The recent legislation for the
University had also diminished the Church's influence
within it, and proportionately increased Liddon's disinclination to spend his time in working in it. But he would
not resign any of the work which, for the sake of the
"great Doctor," he had undertaken. He still retained his
seat on the Hebdomadal Council, and did his utmost there
to uphold the cause of the Church at the cost of a great
expenditure of time and labour ; and unless excused on the
ground of ill health, he delivered his Professorial Lectures
regularly until 1882. The chief memorial of these most

successful Lectures is the " Analysis of the Epistle to the Romans," which was published after his death, and contains the notes from which he delivered his Lectures on that Epistle. Any details of such work would command little general interest ; but this chapter is intended mainly to give his general ideas about the changes at the University, together with some account of his private life at Oxford. The following letters throw light on his thoughts on Academical matters :—

To Dr. Bright.

"Brislington, January 11, 1872.

" . . . I think that you scarcely do justice to the *commercial considerations* which enter so largely into modern Oxford Liberal calculations. They would have been profoundly repulsive to the men of 1833–45, but they dominate now. Oxford is more and more a great shop, trading on the tastes of the British public, abandoning to public prejudices its own best traditions, but in turn feeling that it cannot trifle with the general tastes of its customer. To a considerable extent Convocation represents this public, and a demonstration in Convocation would therefore awe the commercial instinct not to alarm popular religionists, while it might no doubt exasperate the speculative sensibilities of the typical Liberal. Myself I wish, now that matters have gone so far, that they could be worse, *i.e.* seen as they are. *Yes :* I *do* wish, if we cannot undo the work of last Term, that we could eliminate the religious element from the Examinations altogether. It would be the preferable alternative. We *must* in the end come to that, and if we did it speedily, there would be better chance of serious efforts to supply what the University failed to do by other means."

To C. T. Redington, Esq.

"Brislington, Bristol, January 24, 1872.

" There is, of course, a difference in the bearings of the moral and historical sciences on the one hand, and mathematics or philosophy, or physical science (in itself, as distinct from its bearing on psychology) on the other, in their relations to the religious element in education. It is impossible to teach history or ethics without ' taking a side ' as to the great questions which underlie them, and which are too importunately asked in the thought of every thinking man or boy to be passed over in silence. Something of the same kind may be said about physics, I suppose. But, even in the case of pure mathematics, where the subject-matter does not suggest Religion (except it be the relationship between mathematical truth as necessary and eternal, and the Life of the One Eternal, Self-existent Being), the ability of the teacher cannot but recommend his opinions on other subjects to his pupils, and on Religion as the subject of the greatest interest. You see, it is not a question of contract between grown-up men with developed minds, but of bringing boys and young men, at a time when their minds are particularly open to influence for good or evil, under the influence of powerful intellects, which religious men at heart believe to be enlisted in the cause of serious error. I am well persuaded that the recent changes at the Universities will, in a couple of generations, quite necessarily lead to an increase of downright Infidelity in the educated class of which we can at present form very little idea, and this will certainly be followed by grave social consequences. . . . However, what one feels is, that having done and said what is possible, we must leave these things in the Hands of God, Who sees beyond our own narrow horizons, and means, it may be, in His mercy, to bring new order and unity out of the intellectual chaos which is, to all appearance, threatening us, as a nation. But if I were an Irish Roman Catholic, I should certainly stand by Cardinal Cullen; and nothing but inveterate prejudice prevents Englishmen, who in different ways wish well to the cause of Religion, from seeing that in this matter the Cardinal represents the profoundly Christian truth that education without Religion is worse than barbarism. Fawcett, of course, is perfectly consistent; but he is oddly supported by a great many people who *say* that they believe in a Divine Revelation."

To C. T. Redington, Esq.

"3, Amen Court, E.C., December 23, 1872.

". . . Yes, Bismarck appears to me to have put himself quite in the wrong with the Jesuits. They may be dangerous politicians and much else; but, in the absence of some proof of guilt, they have the rights of citizens, which cannot be trifled with without giving a shock to society. The theological bearings of the Vatican Decree, and its civil, social, political aspects, are very different things. *I* deplore the former in the interest of our common Faith; the latter have been exaggerated, as it seems to me, by Canonists and Statesmen. The Jesuits have a long history, and will beat Bismarck. They recover, and more than recover, by being persecuted, the moral power which they forfeit by their diplomacy. Besides which, a man, however able, rarely has any chance against a highly organised, historical Society.

". . . The Oxford 'Rurals,' after whom you ask so affectionately came up to oppose Stanley's nomination to the Select Preachership

My heart was with them, but my judgment as clearly the other way. It was a discreditable nomination ; but, having been made, ought, in the interests of the Faith, to have been allowed to pass *sub silentio*, for, if opposed, it must be either defeated or affirmed by Convocation, a choice, *me judice*, of nearly balanced evils. To have defeated it would have been to invest Stanley with the cheap honours of a petty martyrdom. To have affirmed it is, I fear, to have given a new impetus to the barren, unspiritual negations which he represents. However, it was impossible to get Burgon, etc., to see this ; so Dr. Pusey and I retired, and—you see how Convocation has settled the matter. Alas ! it is merely one among many anxieties of the kind.

"In other ways I have reasons to be thankful for the last Term, having had a large number of men who took thorough interest in my subjects, which is a great assistance, in the way of a lower motive, towards trying to do one's duty—*licet indignissimi*.

"I hope you will have read Mr. Gladstone's remarkable speech at Liverpool on Saturday. His mind is just now very full of the subjects touched on at the end of it. He was much shocked by Strauss' 'Alte und neue Glaube,' which is the most outspoken infidel manifesto we have had for a long time. I do not think you can ever have met 'Scrutator,' but whenever you come to see me here, and give me timely warning, he shall come to dinner. He is full of matter, and of mental agility in dealing with it, in very many subjects, and he is a downright Christian into the bargain."

One of his holiday letters of a later date shows that he saw the struggle at Oxford being reproduced throughout Europe.

To C. T. Redington, Esq.

"Stromness, I. of Orkney, N.B., July 18, 1876.

". . . This [delay] has enabled us to see this island pretty thoroughly, and especially Kirkwall, which would interest you very greatly. It is the most perfect of the surviving Cathedrals in Scotland. It is in Presbyterian hands, and the internal arrangements of the building are all that this predicament implies. But the shell is remarkably intact, and its details are very beautiful. The red sandstone of which it is built gives warmth and beauty to it ; and £20,000 would make it one of the nicest churches in Christendom again. The Church of the Middle Ages in these islands, when they were under Norwegian rule, must have been very powerful and very enterprising, considering the very slender resources of the people to which she ministered. I sent you a small photograph of the Cathedral of St. Magnus by the post yesterday—before receiving your letter, and from Kirkwall.

R

". . . What you say about the attitude of the Church in Southern Europe towards Liberal culture and thought is true enough. It is a subject on which the Munich School is always insisting, and it would be better for the Church—better certainly for 'culture'—if the fact were otherwise. Still, I cannot help feeling a certain sympathy with the instinct which is at the bottom of this attitude. Christian ecclesiastics, all the world over, are, if they are good men, incessantly conscious of the presence and antagonism of a vast body of hostile thought and feeling, which is called in Holy Scripture 'the world.' As to the true frontier of this 'world,' they may and do often make terrible mistakes ; they often identify with it a pure and disinterested enthusiasm for Truth, which has lost its way, and which would, if it knew how, be the best friend of Religion ; and they ignore its subtle and penetrating commixture with the action of the Church, or of her representatives. Still, they are right as to the broad fact that this portentous phenomenon, 'the world,' is still what it was in the days of our Lord and His Apostles ; and it is better that they should cling to this major premiss, even though they misapply it, than that they should abandon or lose sight of it. The real difficulty about modern culture, as it seems to me, is to distinguish the subtle, cunning enmity to Religion and the Supernatural which undoubtedly pervades a great deal of it, from the truthful and healthful element, which is among God's best gifts to us in the order of Nature, and which is intended to enable us to serve Him more intelligently and fruitfully than we could without it.

"This distinction, I hope and believe, will be made out 'all along the line' during the remainder of this century, and then Christendom will be able to 'use the ear-rings of the Egyptians' without wishing for the fleshpots of Egypt.' For the present, as you say, the two things are confused in very exalted quarters.

"I have not seen *any* recent numbers of the *Dublin ;* the preparation of Lectures and Sermons, and other business, leave one greatly behind in all these respects. But the line it takes would, I think, only command the *entire* sympthy of those who, in their devotion to religious paradox, close their eyes to fact. The same thing is observable, *mutatis mutandis,* among the English 'Evangelicals.'"

In 1875 he had to seek re-election to the Hebdomadal Council very unwillingly ; but to Pusey's great regret, and to his own sincere relief, he lost his seat.

To the Dean of St. Paul's.

"Christ Church, October 21, 1875.

"Yesterday we had a great fight in Congregation, and I was turned out of the Council. I had only consented to stand in order to please

Dr. Pusey, and cannot but think that the majority did their duty, not only because I do not represent their religious or non-religious opinions, but also because I am not a good man of business. However, the Doctor is greatly put out, although the matter is quite beyond repair for six years. It will be a good thing when the University has passed through the transition phase into the completely secular condition of things to which everything tends now, logically and as a matter of fact. These struggles don't help study, although, while there are still more sets of principles than one in the place, they are inevitable."

To C. T. Redington, Esq.

"Christ Church, October 26, 1875.

". . . I was not surprised at being put out of the Oxford Council ; indeed, I should not have stood again unless for Dr. Pusey's sake. Theological Liberalism no doubt is a rising tide, but I suppose that in all generations the 'chances,' so to put it, have seemed to be against Religion, and the courage of faith and love has ignored these real or apparent probabilities. I am no prophet, and do not venture to forecast the future of Oxford. That it was logically lost to the Anglican Church by the legislation of 1870 I never doubted, but we are so illogical a people that it is at least conceivable that the event may defeat anticipations. However, of this I am not very sanguine. All that one can do, I suppose, is to take care not to have made the task of the Egyptians easier than it is."

At this moment the See of Brechin fell vacant by the death of Bishop Forbes, and Liddon was pressed by many of the late Bishop's friends to allow himself to be nominated for election as his successor, promising him a unanimous appointment. His diary records one of the interviews.

"*October* 26.—In the evening Mr. Nicholson, the Dean of Brechin, came here. He was most anxious to persuade me to accept the Bishopric. He said that I should be elected unanimously by clergy and laity. He had written out several arguments to move me. I said 'No'; (1) on the ground of nationality ; (2) on that of its being necessary to abandon my stall at St. Paul's, and my Professorship to Puritan and Rationalistic successors. Wrote to Lord Kinnaird to the same effect."

In all the work at Keble College, and in all the meetings of its Council, he took the warmest interest. In

1875 he strongly and successfully opposed the Consecration of the new Chapel, which had been built by the munificence of Mr. W. Gibbs. He maintained that if it were consecrated it would have to follow the fortunes of the Church of England, and might be entirely alienated from the purposes which the Founders of the College had most at heart.

His relation to Dr. Pusey not only retained him in Oxford, but it gave him also work of varied kinds, sometimes humorous, at others very serious.

To ——

" Christ Church, February 13, 1878.

" At present there is a difficulty with the great Doctor about the Board of Studies. He and Bright are at literary war, and I am being reproached, gently but firmly, first by one and then by the other. The question is the epochs into which Ecclesiastical History is to be divided. I cannot feel so strongly about it as either of them does, but while the matter goes on it is favourable to interior edification rather than to perfect enjoyment, within or without."

At the close of March, 1878, Pusey was very ill, and Liddon kept Newman informed about his state. As the illness seemed serious, Newman felt bound to make a last effort to win Pusey to the Roman Church.

From Dr. Newman.

" The Oratory, March 31, 1878.

" Your letter, so kindly sent me, has, of course, troubled me much. I fear Pusey cannot last long, and I am troubled, first, on that account, and next, as to my own duty under that anticipation.

" I know you will do me credit for honesty of purpose, as I do you. If his state admits of it, I should so very much wish to say to my dearest Pusey, whom I have loved and admired for above fifty years, that the Catholic Roman Church solemnly lays claim to him as her child, and to ask him in God's sight whether he does not acknowledge her right to do so.

" Were I now writing to an ordinary Anglican, I should expect you to answer, ' If I do ask him for you, he will be sure to make a strong declaration of his fidelity to the Church of England, and so you would be baulked, as you ought to be.' This would be the answer of a controversialist, but you will understand me quite otherwise. Should he make a simple avowal of his confidence in the Anglican Church, as part of the Church Catholic, at least I should gain this comfort from it, that he died in simple good faith.

"I cannot let him die, if such is God's Will, with the grave responsibility lying upon me of such an appeal to him as I suggest; and since I cannot make it myself, I must throw that responsibility on some one else who is close to him as you are; and this I do.

"Oh, what a world this is, and how piercing are its sorrows!"

The next day an anxious report from Christ Church caused Liddon to pay a hurried visit to Oxford, and in the evening he wrote to Newman.

To Dr. Newman.

"3, Amen Court, April 1, 1878.

"I have spent more than an hour with Dr. Pusey this afternoon. I found him on the whole much better than I had expected. He looked reduced by illness, but he was very bright and joyous, and even energetic. He spoke of his illness as a great subject for thankfulness, and when I alluded to his difficulty in breathing, said that each hard breath, like the flakes of snow to St. Francis when he was shut out of his convent, was part of the Will of God. He talked chiefly about unfulfilled prophecy, and especially about Damascus, which 'George Williams used to cite as a difficulty,' of which Dr. Pusey thought lightly. I told him that you had asked for him, and he desired me to write a loving message. But I did not say more about the contents of your letter. He has not a shadow of doubt as to the entire consistency of his position with the Revealed Will of God. Only two days before he became ill (he told me to-day) he 'quieted' a person who was unsettled about the Roman question; and on Saturday last, when he was in bed and too ill to see any one, he sent another for the same purpose to Dr. King. Only the week before last he told me how completely Mr. Allies appeared to him to have failed to answer his own book, 'The Church of England cleared from the Charge of Schism;' and how inconsistent the history of the African Church, under St. Cyprian and St. Augustine, was with the modern claims of Rome.

"I mention these things only, as you will believe, to show you how completely his mind is at rest on the main question; though he is, of course, very keenly alive to the evils which result from the language and action of living authorities in the Church of England.

"When the Athanasian Creed was attacked four years ago, he had made up his mind, if it was withdrawn from her, to resign his preferments ; but he had no thought, so far as I know, of secession. He always of late spoke as if the Definition of the Immaculate Conception and the Vatican Council had made that step *impossible*.

"You will, I am sure, forgive the explicitness with which I write this ; but you would, I think, say yourself that his clear and strong convictions were inconsistent with his being anything else than an English Churchman. Yet his vivid sense of the fundamental verities which bind the whole Body of Christ into one, always made him speak of Rome in tender and respectful language, and without the conventional asperities of Anglican controversialists.

"He is certainly somewhat better, and may rally for a time if the weather should improve. But I feel that he cannot be with us for long, and that each opportunity of seeing him is increasingly precious.

"Ever, my dear Dr. Newman,
"Yours most truly and respectfully,
"H. P. LIDDON."

In 1878 there was a bye-Election for one of the two seats by which the University was then represented in Parliament, when Mr. Gathorne Hardy was raised to the Peerage.

To E. A. FREEMAN, Esq.

"Christ Church, April 22, 1878.

"The resident Liberals have resolved, it is said, on putting up Professor H. Smith for Oxford. They are wasting their powder and shot. Oxford, as a constituency, is still largely clerical ; and what inducements has an ordinary clergyman to vote for H. Smith? Certainly he is a brilliant and accomplished man, but on religious subjects his mind is, I suppose, either a blank or abandoned to somewhat energetic negations. The only chance of doing anything lies in combining as much of the religious feeling of the constituency as may be with opposition to the Government policy. The right thing to have done would have been to have brought forward Mr. Gladstone ; but he is almost as much hated by *some* of the anti-religious Liberals as by the war-preaching Conservatives. Still, I think we ought to keep him in view for the next General Election. If a large number of men would plump for him, he might possibly be carried. And I know that *nothing* would give him greater pleasure, even now."

To E. A. Freeman, Esq.

"Christ Church, Oxford, June 12, 1878.

"As to the Oxford Election, I did not vote at all. To vote for J. G. Talbot was to vote for Lord Beaconsfield and his Eastern policy. To vote for H. J. S. Smith was to vote for that variety of Liberalism which, as *you* said, I think, is too academical to care about questions of right and wrong. J. G. Talbot is a very old friend ; and nobody can know H. J. S. Smith without liking him personally, besides admiring his brilliancy and accomplishments. But this is not the point."

One of the Oxford connections in which he always found the greatest pleasure was the Dante Society, a small club which dined together once a Term and discussed subjects connected with Dante. He was elected a member on the proposal of Dr. Moore, the Principal of St. Edmund Hall, at the end of 1878. Every meeting of the Society he records in his diary with evident interest and pleasure, although he thought that he could contribute but little to its discussions.

To the Dean of St. Paul's.

"Christ Church, March 4, 1879.

"We have a Dante Society here, which I am bold to wish you might some day illuminate with a Paper. I am a mere listener, as I know nothing really about him. But I am reading him through again by snatches. It is impossible while doing so not to make in one's thoughts all sorts of *modern* arrangements for the great worlds which he describes. But this is not always edifying."

He contributed three Papers, in 1881, 1883, and 1888, to the discussion of this Society ; the first two were on the relation of Dante to St. Thomas Aquinas, and the third on his relation to the Franciscans. After his death these Papers were prepared for publication by Dr. Moore, and were printed at the end of a small volume which was published under the title of "Essays and Addresses." In connection with this Society he also took great delight in making a large and valuable collection of books on Dante, which he had most elaborately bound.

Early in 1879, Liddon, as a Student of Christ Church, joined with Dr. Bright as Canon of Christ Church in offering to present a Reredos to the Cathedral at Oxford. Bodley had supplied a plan, to which the Chapter had raised some objections on architectural grounds; and Dr. Bright, fearing that between the artist and the Chapter the proposal might be wrecked, asked Liddon to see Bodley about it, and drew from him the following very characteristic reply :—

To Dr. Bright.

" March 31, [1879].

" I do not think that I should do much good by seeing Bodley. First of all, he would talk at great length about what we ought to do in St. Paul's ; and this, however interesting, would be unpractical. Secondly, he and I should both feel that the real decision about Christ Church lies elsewhere, and that our negotiations could not lead to very much. In all such matters, it seems to me, it is best to be decided, and as to this, I should be decided in two directions. To Bodley I should say, ' If you think that you cannot carry out the modified Reredos on which the Chapter of the Church insist, we must go elsewhere.' He would yield at once to this kind of language. And to the Chapter I should say, ' We offer you a Reredos, and we do not intend further to modify our offer so as to make it mural or mosaic decoration.' Unless something of this kind is said, the proposal will drift before the kind of half-captious criticism with which such proposals are invariably greeted, and you will end by putting up something which at heart you will only half like, or less than half.

" The first thing is to deal with Bodley, and this will be best done by letter. He must accept the decision of the Chapter of Christ Church as to the elevation of the Reredos, and modify his design so far. And then his modified design must be presented as an ultimatum. *Experto crede.*

" I should not be able to concur in any mural and mosaic substitute for relief Figures, or in any subject other than the Crucifixion."

The following interesting note deals with the details of the Reredos :—

To Dr. Bright.

"Christ Church, Oxford, February 27, 1880.

"I should quite agree with you in preferring that (1) our Lord's Face should be living, and (2) that the faces of the Blessed Virgin Mary and St. John the Evangelist should be looking upwards, although this is, I suppose, an open point.

"(3) It would seem to me better to keep Jerusalem behind the Cross. The representation is a very common one—I have it in a picture dated 1534. Probably Jerusalem is a type, for the moment, of the world, as in the Apocalypse 'where also our Lord was crucified.' As to the declivity, etc., the whole representation is too conventional to discuss any questions of exact topography.

"(4) And I prize the Angels and Chalice. They connect the Passion with the Holy Eucharist very vividly. For this reason they will be disliked by Puritans, etc., but if they can be had, they will preach wholesome doctrine for many a year to come."

Whilst the correspondence about the Reredos was still going on, the proceedings before the University Commissioners drew from Liddon a proposal of a very different kind.

To Dr. Bright.

"3, Amen Court, St. Paul's, E.C., December 4, 1879.

"You force my hand—but I must tell you what I think, and you will bear with me.

"If I were a member of the Chapter, I should endeavour to persuade my colleagues at least to *consider* the advisability of separating the Cathedral and Chapter of the Diocese of Oxford from Christ Church as it is to be.

"The union of the Chapter and the College has, in my opinion, been always very much more to the advantage of the latter than of the former. As a place of education, Christ Church has a history of which it is justly proud. As a Cathedral Body, it has scarcely ever made itself felt in the diocese to which it belongs; at the present moment we none of us think of the Dean as the Second Clergyman in the diocese, and he is true to traditions which his predecessors have bequeathed to him.

"But so long as Christ Church had in its hands the great and responsible work of educating two-thirds of the governing class in this country, and did after its fashion, as in Cyril Jackson's day, educate them in Christian principles, the loss to the diocese of a

Cathedral by its being buried within the walls of a house of education was not purchased too dearly, especially as in those days Cathedrals had no idea of being or doing anything of practical value to the spiritual life of the people.

"The Christ Church of those days has passed away for ever. Until this last revolutionary change, and so long as a majority of Students were in Holy Orders, there was reason for hoping that the unbelieving elements might be kept sufficiently under control—or, at any rate, at bay—to warrant the further hope that something of the old confidence on the part of those families who have traditionally belonged to us might yet return, and that it might be welcomed from within the walls, by a revived religious feeling such as —— and —— represent now—a feeling which might recover the best side of the past and might add something to it.

"But to look for anything of this kind, since the announcement of last Wednesday, is surely to play deliberately with shadows. . . . And what will be the position of the Chapter when the new 'lay' majority created by the Commission has carried out those further changes which will be in its power? The Chapter will have forfeited, religiously speaking, all the advantages, while it retains, religiously speaking, all the disadvantages of the connection. Early Celebrations open to all Oxford, Sunday evening Services, a due diocesan observance of Lent and Advent, the use of the Cathedral all the year round for diocesan purposes, will be as impossible as now, or more so. On the other hand, the already scanty attendance of undergraduates at 8 a.m. will have been reduced to zero ; and a 'lay' censor will have separated the maintenance of discipline from 'sectarian' or 'theological' interests, pretty completely.

"For myself, when (or before) matters had reached this pass, I should desire a separation, not in the interests of Christ Church, but in the interests of the Church of Christ. If it were promoted by the Bishop and Chapter and within the next few years, it is possible that you might save income enough (I *hope* your full £17,000 a year) to work a Cathedral with great advantage to the diocese and the University. Alas ! the present *buildings would* have to be surrendered ; but you would be entitled to adequate compensation ; and though much which you would give up could *never* be replaced, you *may* pay too dearly for retaining it.

"A strong Bishop, such as was Bishop Wilberforce, would know how to take the necessary measures for making St. Mary's the Cathedral Church of Oxford. The University Sermons *must* go before long ; in an undenominational Oxford they are untenable, on liberal grounds, and they do too little good to make *us* Christians care much for retaining them. The residences of the Canons could not, I fear, be near their Church ; but St. Mary's would give them an opportunity which might win an altogether new place of influence for the Church of Christ in the Oxford of future years. The Divinity Professorships might still go with the Canonries ; the only real objection to this is that it still gives the University a fatal purchase over the leading ministers of the Church.

" I do not dogmatise ; I only tell yo my thoughts. And as having belonged to the list of Students of the old Foundation for thirty-three years this Christmas, and loving every stone of a place with which I associate the happiest moments and memories of my life, and being sure that its greatness *has* been mainly due in the past to the associa-tion of the College and the Chapter, *but* under *religious* conditions, I should treat such a suggestion as I have put before you as even *profane*, if I did not try to look at matters as they will appear a hundred years hence, when we are in our graves, in the light of the announcement of last Wednesday, which will then be realised.

" Leave things as they are, and the separation *will* come, *but* under very different conditions."

To Mrs. Sidney Lear.

" December 22, 1879.

". . . Of late my mind has been chiefly occupied by the pro-ceedings of the Oxford Commissioners. Though appointed by a Conservative Government, they are completing the work of destruction which was begun in 1854 and carried forward by the Act of 1871. . . . Lord Selborne has satisfied the demands of the most extreme and destructive section of the anti-Christian Liberals—not, I apprehend, meaning to do anything of the kind, but yielding at each step to pres-sure, and quieting internal misgivings, if he has them, by the plausible arguments whiçh you get, in a distorted form, in the *Guardian.* As regards Oxford, I really see no future whatever on which a Christian can look with any approach to hope. At Oriel, with its splendid history of 1833–45, there is in future to be one Clerical Fellow, and he is retained in spite of urgent remonstrances. The rest are laymen, *i.e.* persons of whom nothing whatever is known, except that they are not in Holy Orders, and that the probabilities are in favour of their rejecting Christianity altogether."

To Dr. Bright.

" Christ Church, November 11, 1880.

" We are not likely, I fear, to agree ; but you will forgive the freedom of an old Student of Christ Church of thirty-four years' standing.

" I do not think that I deceive myself as to the future of the

Common Room. As soon as the 'lay' Students become strong enough, they will demand a large share of the revenues now assigned to the Chapter, for purposes of 'education.' That they will succeed nobody can doubt who remembers the history of the struggle which resulted (i.) in the establishment of the present Governing Body, and (ii.) in the radical alteration of the relation of Students and Canons. I advisedly held aloof, but I saw and heard what went on. Do you think that the Chapter will be relatively stronger in time to come?

"This step will only lead to a step beyond, which I need not describe.

"It is possible that nothing can be done, and that you have only to wait for the inevitable. If so, you have no responsibility towards those who will succeed you, and I at once admit that unless there was a considerable agreement in the Chapter, nothing *could* be done. Only, if I were a Canon of Christ Church, I should feel that I incurred far less responsibility towards the real interests of Christ and His Church in Oxford, by making a well-considered effort to save something out of a spiritual wreck, than I must incur by doing nothing at a critical moment when things are shaping themselves.

"The Cathedral Body can do little good by its connection with the [members] of our future Common Room; but all the disabilities which cripple its diocesan usefulness will remain in full force without the compensating considerations which there were when the Students were clergymen and Christians, as a matter of course.

"I do not go further into detail, not (you will believe) out of disrespect to you, but because I gather from your note that the very idea of the thing seems inadmissible, and life is too short, and we are both too overworked, to engage in fancy discussions. Nothing but a very strong conviction as to *duty* would enable any man to grapple with the difficulties that would present themselves; but having said to others what I have said to you, I felt it more honest to say my heart out to a very old friend who is a member of the Chapter, than to have to say to him, if we should live some years hence, 'I thought at the time it would be so.' There are times when a Revolution is the truest Conservatism."

To Dr. Bright.

"Christ Church, November 11, 1880.

"I am grateful to you for your letter, because I thought you might suppose I was writing, either solely out of vexation at what is passing or in a spirit of paradox. As far as I know my own heart, it is not so indeed. The Students of the present day (and this is likely to be still truer of their successors), with one or two bright exceptions, have nothing, or almost nothing, in common with their predecessors but the name. The only part of the Foundation which still commands the affectionate enthusiasm of my boyish years is the Chapter ; and the motive of my suggestion was the wish to save the Chapter, or such parts of it as can be saved, from a future which appears to be strictly inevitable, if matters are allowed to take their course.

"But in saying this, I only desire to explain myself, and not to refer to a matter which is naturally painful to me, and which you think beyond the region of what is practicable."

This correspondence shows the depth of his feeling about his own College ; about the University as a whole, he poured out all his mind in an anonymous Article in the *Church Quarterly Review* for April, 1881, which he entitled, "The Recent Fortunes of the Church in Oxford." The authorship of the Article was known immediately to all who knew anything of Oxford, not only by its style and matter, but also by the entire omission of any allusion to the Ireland Professor of Exegesis in an enumeration of the chief religious forces of the Oxford of the day. The Article thus sums up the recent history of the Church in the University—

"In all the centuries of her history Oxford has been nothing if not the handmaid and home of the Church. Before 1854 the Church was still everything and everywhere. That she failed during even long periods to make due use of the splendid opportunities which her rela-tion to the University placed at her disposal must be sorrowfully admitted. . . . Catholic-minded Churchmen have serious complaints to make of Oxford such as the Church Movement of 1833 found it ; but they are complaints not of the system, but of its administration. The Tractarian Movement was the day of grace for the old system of the Church in Oxford : a spirit was abroad ready to make all things new ; justifying old institutions by invigorating them with the enthu-siasms of youth ; reanimating the moral convictions which had made Founders and Benefactors lavish their work on the Church of Christ ; breathing into work as well as into prayer, into literature as well as into philanthropy, into art—whether music or architecture or poetry —as well as into scientific theology, a reality and vigour that had long been wanting. . . .

"But the Heads of Houses left no stone unturned to make the Tractarian position untenable. The opposition triumphed ; it 'made a solitude, and called it peace.' . . .

"Then followed the Gorham Decision and the University Legisla-tion of 1854. This legislation was nothing less than an Academical

Revolution, which is slowly advancing to its final logical issue, through the Tests Bill of 1871 and the Commission of 1877. . .

" Of all her ancient inheritance in Oxford the Church now retains the use of the College Chapels and the Faculty of Divinity ; and what is called 'the logic of justice,' with its bold and fallacious assumptions, renders her hold of these remaining fragments most precarious. . . .

" True, the Church still exercises considerable influence on some of its undergraduates, and many of them offer themselves for her Ministry ; and there are also some practical religious forces at work in Oxford, some Churches, some Divinity Professors—notably Dr. Pusey, Dr. King, and Dr. Bright—and the whole system of life of Keble College. But these forces are transient so far as they depend on persons ; and even as regards Keble College, it is difficult to be sure that in Modern Oxford the general atmosphere of the University will not sooner or later be fatal to its present distinctively Church spirit. The question before us is not the cause of truth and virtue in the universe at large, but the present and apparently future circumstances of the English Church in Oxford. We cannot be insincere. The prospect is, to a great extent, a dark one. The days are gone when those who knew the real state of the case could talk of Oxford as one of the 'eyes' of the Church, or could do other than smile when they read the conventional, or sometimes the almost mystical, utterances of Episcopal and other authorities on the subject. The plain truth is that henceforth Oxford will belong to the Church of England just as much and just as little as does the House of Commons. It is still a centre of social and intellectual interests ; but as a centre of religious force it is no longer what it was, and is unlikely in its future to be what it still is. God can take care of His own cause, no doubt ; but it is our business to note what He permits to traverse it, and to act accordingly."

The religious needs created by this Academical Revolution would, he thought, be most effectually supplied by a College of Priests, living in community, but under no strict rule, and in houses having no connection with the Colleges or the University. When, as will be seen, Pusey died in the following year, his last tie to academical Oxford was broken ; he resigned his Professorship, and threw all the great weight of his influence into the task of collecting funds for providing such a College of Priests in memory of his revered friend.

Certainly his thoughts about the future of the Church and her prospects in Oxford were sad enough ; and much of his life was clouded by this sadness. Yet it would be a most untrue presentation of his Oxford work to dwell on these losses and forebodings as if he thought of nothing else. There was, indeed, another and a very different side to the months that he spent at the University ; and it is associated in the minds of those who knew him with the brightest memories. It was admirably described, shortly after Liddon's death, in the following most interesting account of his life in Christ Church, written for this volume by his friend and fellow-Student, the Rev. E. F. Sampson :—

" I am sure that those who never knew Dr. Liddon as a member of Christ Church can have had no idea of much that was very real and deep in his character ; especially they can never have fully understood what I may call his home side. With us he was emphatically at home. Strange as it may appear to many to say such a thing, yet it is true that he was at home in Christ Church in a sense in which he was not in London or at St. Paul's. We saw sides of him which must have been quite hidden from people who only knew him as the great preacher, the kindly, sympathetic counsellor, the ready, generous helper in any case of necessity or of distress ; who regarded him first of all, naturally enough and with perfect justice, as one, and certainly not the least prominent, of the band of devoted clergy, who, through the twenty years of his tenure of the Canonry at St. Paul's, had done so much to set our Metropolitan Cathedral in its rightful place in the life of the Church of England. For with all his kindliness and graceful, winning courtesy, there was always a certain reserve about him ; something that, however it may be explained, fenced him round and kept him apart from the life of men about him. With us this reserve entirely disappeared. He had come to Christ Church when he was only seventeen years of age ; in connection with Christ Church, in many instances within its walls, he had formed his most enduring friendships ; almost without any break from the date of his matriculation, he had continued to hold his rooms ; and all through his life it had been his habit to spend a considerable portion of each year in residence with us. Christ Church was emphatically his home, and he lavished on it all the wealth of affection of which so deep and genuine a nature was capable. With men in general his entire truthfulness and sincerity made him somewhat reserved—made him hesitate to admit to close intimacy people whom he did not know or of whom he was not sure ; but when he gave, he gave royally, and out of a royal abundance. When you were once admitted to his friendship, he placed himself unreservedly, if one may use the word, almost recklessly, at your disposal ; I feel sure that any who had the privilege of close intimacy with him will agree that they learned from him, as from no one else, what the possibilities of friendship are.

" The Common Room is the centre of the home life of a College, and he was for many of us the life of the Christ Church Common Room. If we found Liddon was to be with us, the interest of the evening before us took a new and special colour ; something attractive was sure to be said—some sparkle of that delicious humour and fun of his give us new delight. He had a great affection for cats ; consequently the Common Room cat came in for a large share of his attention. He was in the habit of nursing it upside down, *i.e.* like a baby ; when the cat, not unnaturally, grumbled at this proceeding, he used to assure us that it was a complaint got up on purely fictitious grounds, with a view to enlisting our sympathy : cats, he declared, always desired to be the object of special and peculiar attention from every one near them ; and, therefore, while the tail (called the 'catometer') waved furiously, we were expected to believe that 'Tommy' was thoroughly enjoying himself.

"And then there were those stories of his—they were wonderful, inimitable—who that has heard them can ever forget them? or how can one possibly convey any idea of them to those who have not heard them?[1] They were

[1] How real the difficulty is, is shown by the attempt made by Sir M. E. Grant Duff, in his last volume of "Notes from a Diary," to tell one of Liddon's stories. The story has lost so much by passing through more

epics. Dean Gaisford, Bishop Philpotts of Exeter, Dr. Barnes, Dr. Ogilvie, Mr. Buckland, besides other old Oxford and Christ Church men, were brought into almost living contact with us. In later years it was difficult to get him to tell them: but if there was a small House party, and one or two younger members of our Society were present who had not heard some particular story, then, with a little management, he could be got to tell it— some wonderful history of past days of the House, brimming over with fun, told with a quick sense of humour—it was all astonishing and delightful. We lived with the older generation; everything, no doubt, coloured by the strong individuality of the reciter—but through the narratives there ran personal characteristics that obviously belonged to one or another of the speakers represented, and bore witness to the substantial truth of what he told us. In losing him we lost one of the links that bound us to the Christ Church of the past; he lived, however, with us of a younger and different generation long enough to impress upon us a picture of the older days: in the changes he lived to see—revolutionary as he and others thought them

than one hand, that it is worth while to re-tell it.

In 1865, just after the General Election, when Gladstone lost his seat as Member for the University of Oxford, Liddon was in Devonshire, and went to call on Bishop Philpotts. He was shown into a room where the old Bishop was lying in a comatose state, propped in a chair. His daughter was there, and welcomed Liddon, saying, "Oh, Mr. Liddon, if you will wait a little, my father is sure to wake up, and I know he would like to see you." So Liddon waited, and after a while the old man moved a little, and one eye opened. Gradually he became conscious of Liddon's presence, and recognised him. "Ah, Mr. Liddon," he said, "you come from Oxford: is anything happening there?"—"Yes," Liddon replied, "we have just been through the excitement of the election."—"Did you," the Bishop asked, "take any

part?" [The Bishop all the while, of course, knew perfectly what had happened.]—"Yes," Liddon replied, "I was a member of Mr. Gladstone's committee." — "And pray, Mr. Liddon," said the Bishop, "what reasons do you think it well to allege in excuse for your conduct?"—"I," Liddon used to say, "of course made some general reply, that I felt great confidence in Mr. Gladstone, and thought him quite the best representative the University could get."— "Ah," said the Bishop, "I am a very old man, Mr. Liddon, and old men, you know, have not many words at their disposal; but when I think of Mr. Gladstone, there is only one word —only one word, Mr. Liddon—remember I am a very old man—that expresses what I feel; and that is— Rascal!"—the last word almost shouted, with a vigour that all but shot the old man out of his chair.

to be, serious and far-reaching as we must all allow they were—he did something to ensure that historical continuity which it is to be hoped we shall never lose ; so that while we work under greatly altered conditions, we may never forget 'famous men, and our fathers that begat us.'

"Liddon was no respecter of persons ; he had learned to 'honour all men ;' because he had learned to look quite simply and directly below the surface of things, and to recognise each man whom he met to be a living soul. In nothing was this more evident than in the friendly, affectionate interest he took in all that belonged to the College servants ; especially in his peculiar care for any whose position he thought at all difficult or unpromising. He saw our under-porters must find the time hang heavily on their hands when watching the gates in the heart of the Vacation, with very little to occupy their attention or give employment to their minds ; so he bought some books and started a small library for their benefit. This is but one instance out of many ; in sickness, or in any time of difficulty, his purse was always at the disposal of those in need ; quietly, unostentatiously, generously, and we sometimes thought lavishly, he was always ready to help. But money was not all he gave—it was indeed only the less important part ; there was his bright, winning smile, the sincere and unfeigned interest he always took in people, the fun and humour that were never long below the surface ; these latter men valued, as they always will, far beyond any material gift: here, indeed, was the source of the deep affection that was felt for him—an affection which manifested itself during his last illness and after his death in unusual ways. Men not much given to emotion or to tears could scarcely trust themselves to speak of him in the days when the shock of his loss first came upon them.

"He was wonderful with undergraduates—'the young,' as he affectionately called them ; their ways were full of continual interest to him. As he held no official position in the House, he always felt he could move about among them without being in any way a restraint upon them.

' Oh, you know, dear friend,' he used to say, ' they regard me only as a part of the ancient architecture of the place ; ' so at night, if his head became troublesome and would not let him sleep or work, he was in the habit of wandering about the quadrangles and cloisters, an amused spectator of undergraduate life. He knew a large number person-ally ; fathers and guardians, indeed, all who knew Liddon, and some, I think, who did not, would write and ask him to be kind to a youth in whom they were interested ; there must be many men now in all sorts of positions in the world who owe, perhaps more than they know or suspect, to the response he made to such requests. Where he found he could be really useful, there was no trouble he would not take. As a younger man he gathered large crowds of undergraduates on Sunday evenings, in the Hall of Queen's College, to his Lectures on the Greek Testament. After-wards, his duties at St. Paul's and as Ireland Professor at Oxford, and, alas ! far more seriously, the continual strain of ill health, interfered with this ; but to the last, when he was not positively prevented by illness, and often when his friends knew that he was not fit for any exertion, on such Sundays in Term as could be found for the purpose he invited undergraduates to the Hall or the Common Room at Christ Church, and, after an hour's talk on the Greek Testament, gave them tea and coffee, and let them weary him with endless questions on all conceivable subjects. In the last year or two of his life, when this got too much for him, he gave up the Lecture and showed them photographs of his Egyptian and Palestinian journeys ; and talked to them about all the matters of interest connected with the scenes, which had taken so strong a hold of his imagination and thoughts, since his visit to the East in the winter of 1885–86.

"As a member of the Governing Body, he attended our meetings very rarely ; he belonged to the older generation, and had never approved the changes that transferred the government of Christ Church from the Dean and Canons exclusively, to the Dean, Canons, and Students. He never ceased to look back with regret to the old Oxford before the days of Commissions and Reforms. There were few of us who could not understand and sympathise with this affection for a past which, however it may be criticised, had produced illustrious men, and had in so many ways a special interest and attractiveness for Churchmen. But some of us thought the picture presented to us a little ideal—a representation of Oxford as it might have been rather than as it really was; at all events, we recognised that we could not go back to those old days; nor, indeed, were such a return conceivable, did we wish for it; much less were we prepared to make any attempt to bring it about. But none of us can forget how true and loyal he was to us; and this must be specially the case with those who have taken any share in supporting and forwarding changes which were distasteful to him, or which he thought mistaken or even disastrous. If, however, any scheme was attempted, in which he saw signs of hopefulness for the things he had most deeply at heart, he rose at once from his regrets and despondencies to welcome it; such movements as those which resulted in the Christ Church Mission to East London, or the founding of the Pusey House in Oxford, were to him sources of true and sincere happiness.

"He suffered terribly from rheumatism. I have often seen him come out of the Cathedral after our early Morning Service limping in his walk from pain and discomfort; in reply to any word of sympathy he would say, 'Yes, I am a sort of living barometer; I register every change of atmospheric conditions, and to-day I am down to " much rain."' Then, as often as not, he would push the subject aside with an amused smile, and one could see that he had got hold of what he called 'a pearl;' some one had sent him a cutting from a newspaper, or he had received one of those astounding anonymous letters which people are found capable of writing—some ridiculous attack had been made on him for what he had done or been supposed to have done, or for what he had left undone or been supposed to have left undone. 'Woe to the man who saith to the

dumb stone, It shall speak,' was the sentence of final condemnation hurled at him by one ingenious assailant, who in
these words summed up his views on the Reredos in St.
Paul's Cathedral. I do not know whether the people who
write this kind of thing are ever troubled with any qualms
of regret, or feel any distress, after such wild expenditure
of misdirected energy ; in his case, I think, apart from the
natural feeling of sorrow that there should be men who
could be so silly or so ignorant, these letters afforded considerable amusement ; the humorous side of it all took his
attention, and banished almost entirely any feeling of
irritation or annoyance. If any serious controversy started
that was sure to bring a full crop of such things, a large
envelope was at once labelled ; into it went all kinds of
letters, paragraphs out of newspapers, etc., referring to the
subject ; and very astonishing productions some of them
were. When he was very unwell, or had had, as too often
happened, a sleepless night, such attacks were hard to bear ;
but, as a rule, beyond the mere amusement, he was quite
unmoved.

"He had the great advantage of knowing what he was
doing and what he aimed at, and why he did what he did
and desired what he desired. A narrow mind, some will
say ; well, he used to say this of himself ;—but it was out of
the question for us who knew him intimately to speak
of a mind as narrow which commanded so large a range of
subjects, and was so entirely master of all the material
with which it dealt. He had his fixed premisses, of the
truth of which he was immovably convinced, and from
which he would not swerve ; but for that very reason he
could talk more freely and unreservedly all round any subject ; in this sense only is it possible even to think of his
as a narrow mind. But, after all, here was one of the
secrets of his strength : he was not flabby, or undecided,
or weak ; he was not one of those who, as he used to say,
'set their faces as a pudding ;' he was not overburdened or
confused by the wealth of detail which he had at his command, or by the extent and fulness of his knowledge ; his

T

was a strong, clear, vigorous intellect, which could afford to be amused, and make fresh collections of 'pearls;' he could be quiet and steady under any attack or any opposition, whether serious and earnest, or merely bad-tempered and spiteful.

"It has often been said that Liddon never convinced you if you did not agree with him—and there is truth in the statement. He was so entirely uncompromising in his way of putting things, so ruthlessly incisive and complete in his arguments, and withal so brilliant and so captivating, that you could not but have an uneasy suspicion that such wide knowledge and such versatile power could, had occasion called for it, have made an equally triumphant display on a different side of the subject. But if this was the case in purely speculative discussions, there was another line of thought in which he was and could not but be our master, one whose authority it was all but impossible to question. We learned this if we went to him in a difficulty, or put to him some hard question in moral or spiritual things, such as most men are, at some time or other, called upon to answer practically. Without a moment's hesitation, he would go straight to the point, and we could but follow his guidance; the one aim which he set before himself and others was that God's Will should be done; all the subtleties by which we would escape unpleasant duties, or refuse to face unwelcome facts, vanished like mists before the sun; we learned the strength there was in a life that was lived in the presence of the Eternal Truth. 'One would wish to act now in this,' he would say, 'as one will wish to have acted when one comes to die;'—this was the rule by which difficulty was tested, and by which conduct was governed. He did, in short, what he could to cut straight through the roots of those subtler forms of selfishness which blind the spiritual sight; and so to lead men to do their duty, simply and fearlessly, as in the sight of God.

"I know that much that I have written may appear exaggerated—as the natural, perhaps necessary, way of speaking of a lost friend, as only one more example of what is called hero-worship. But this is not so; all that has been said must give but an inadequate portrait of the figure that lives in our thoughts, or of the character we would, if we could, describe. We had not learned, with all our love and veneration, *jurare in verba magistri;* nor did he expect us to do so. This may well be insisted on for two reasons : first, that those who read about him may not make large deductions for what is called 'the personal equation,' and so blur what at best is but an incomplete outline of a most gracious personality ; and secondly, because enough, and more than enough, was said, at the time of his death, about his relations to those who were very near him, but differed from him about questions which he and they alike regarded as of very serious importance. That subjects were growing into prominence which were a cause of great pain and anxiety to him, and with regard to which he held very strong and very decided views, is certain ; none knew this so well as those who were continually with him, and whom he admitted to the closest intimacy with his hopes and fears ; but only those who did not know him as we did, could suggest that, whatever the distress or anxiety may have been on the one side or on the other, his deep affection for his friends was ever dimmed or even clouded ; rather, it grew more tender and more winning as he understood all that was passing in their minds. 'Ah, dear friend, you are one of those people that read all sorts of books and think all kinds of things ;' and the half-playful, half-reproving smile and warm handshake that would accompany these words, only those that have seen and felt can quite understand. For any one who knew him well and honoured him truly, to differ from him lightly was impossible ; difference on serious matters was of necessity pain to them as well as to him ; but it never clouded their friendship—it rather tested its truth, and gave it, if possible, even stronger life. We know we have not been hero-worshippers ; God gave us in him one of His noblest gifts—close and constant intercourse with a rare and beautiful character, with a mind of the very highest order, stored with varied information, and endowed with singular and most gracious courtesy ; while all the possibilities of these natural gifts were rendered more winning and more attractive by a pure and saintly life.   We cannot speak of him as one 'we have loved and lost ;' friendship such as this is not bounded by time and space ; over it death has no power."

CHAPTER X.

1879–1883.

IN January, 1879, the Chapter of St. Paul's lost one of
its most distinguished members by the appointment of
Dr. Lightfoot to the See of Durham.   Popular rumour
suggested many undesirable successors to his Canonry;
but to Liddon's great delight, his old friend and tutor,
Professor Stubbs, the Regius Professor of History at
Oxford, was chosen to be his new colleague. "It is too
good," he writes to the Dean, "to think true, and it softens
my heart towards the great person" (Lord Beaconsfield).   At
the same time, he received a letter from Père Hyacinthe
(who signs his name "Hyacinthe Loyson, prêtre"), begging
him, on the score of their long friendship, to be present
at the opening of his church in Paris on February 9.   The
Primus of Scotland and the Bishop of Edinburgh were
unable to be present, but, Père Hyacinthe urged, "Vous
diriez à tous, par votre seule présence, que le caractère de
nos relations avec l'Église Anglicane est éminemment
catholique."   Of course, he could not possibly be present,
but the appeal made him feel keenly the difficulties of
the divisions of the Church.

To the Hon. C. L. Wood.

"Christ Church, Oxford, February 8, 1879.

" . . . We have reason to be very thankful for Stubbs's appointment.
Lightfoot's will not help Church principles except in *this* way, that he
will be *just* to everybody; and justice towards High Churchmen will

have all the charm of novelty in the Diocese of Durham. But his convictions will not allow him to make High Church appointments, or to carry High Church principles into the counsels of the Church. He is essentially 'broad,' with generous and—pious—instincts to boot. Of course, the possession of the Episcopal office may lead a very honest mind to ask itself the question, 'What are the principles upon which the Episcopate is to be justified, at all seriously, before God and man?' Let us trust that this will be so. But, for the present, we must read his Essay on 'The Christian Ministry' in his book on the Philippians, and limit our expectations accordingly.

". . . I wish we could do something about the poor P. Hyacinthe. He is not at all in the same boat with the people who take him up in this country; he wishes to fall back on old lines, and abhors religious revolution. Rome demands submission pure and simple; but he would have fared better than he does at the hands of the present Archbishop of Paris, if Mgr. Darboy had lived. Pray read the enclosed, and return it to me. Are we to say to the French, 'Either believe in Papal Infallibility or go on without the Sacraments, as best you can'? Yet that is the dilemma.

"His position in Paris is anomalous, no doubt, but it is an anomaly for which other anomalies are responsible."

In reply his correspondent told him of the difficulties which some clergy in the English Church felt in what they thought a yet more defensible position than that of Père Hyacinthe. If a French priest, so it had been urged, sought the help of Scotch Bishops when his own Archbishop pressed Papal Infallibility upon him, why should not an English priest make a similar appeal when pressed by an English Bishop with the Infallibility of the Privy Council? And there were some English Churchmen who seemed ready to add, "Of the two Infallibilities we prefer the Papal."

To the Hon. C. L. Wood.

"February 16, 1879.

"Surely these epigrams about the two Infallibilities and the like are not wise. We really have to deal with two fallibilities. And, of these, Hyacinthe is unlike the 'other,' in that he has been forced into the difficulties of his present position by the speculative activity of the other 'Infallibility,' if it be one.

"He appeals to me, I own, by his theological conservatism, maintained, too, in a position of grave difficulty. If he would publish a purely Protestant programme, he might easily make his fortune in the worldly sense. If, too, just on the eve of his marriage, he would have submitted to Rome, he might have commanded a Cardinal's Hat. He is singularly free from both the vulgar forms of Ecclesiastical ambition, and though he may make grave mistakes—probably *has* made them—he does not mean to do so. Nobody ever impressed me as being less of a self-sufficient adventurer.

"The Primus's letter, I think, gave a false impression of his work, however unintentionally. He has no wish to 'supersede the Church of France.' He only wishes to provide a refuge for those who cannot believe in the Infallibility, etc., and cannot get on without the Sacraments. He hopes, too, that while doing this he may help to lead those who bear rule in the Western Church to see if nothing can be done in the direction of retreat and reform. His position is, no doubt, in itself anomalous; but then it is the product of a much greater anomaly.

"I doubt his judgment very often. He is a monk still, without any moderately accurate estimate of the forces which govern the world. He undertakes all sorts of things, from which characters less simple, less enthusiastic, less trustful, would altogether shrink. His marriage was dictated by a wish to raise a question of Church discipline in a practical form, and his career at Geneva was a series of tilts against the impossible. But all this does not make one like him less; at least I reproach myself for not doing him more justice in some practical way.

"People compare him to Luther. The correspondence is only outward. He is quite without Luther's incurable coarseness, a quality which was really fatal to his theology. As to Justification, he and Luther are in two entirely different boats."

To the Hon. C. L. Wood.

"February 26, 1879.

"Friday will do admirably. On Fridays from 6 to 8 is always devoted to the Dr. [Pusey]. But from 8 onwards I am again at your service. What a happiness it is that Lent has come—to save time—besides other things! I rejoice in it more and more each year."

The case which Dr. Julius brought against the Bishop of Oxford (Dr. Mackarness) for refusing to allow a prosecution of Canon Carter of Clewer for Ritualistic practices, had just been heard in the Queen's Bench, and the Bishop had appeared in person to defend his action. The Bishop's conduct did not appear to everybody as courageous as it did to Liddon.

To the Hon. C. L. Wood.

"March 7, 1879.

". . . I do not quite follow your judgment of the Bishop of Oxford. Do you not invest him with ideal attributes, and then feel disappointment at his not corresponding to them? Certainly his language about the E.C.U. was regrettable, both in itself and as inconsistent with his own past career ; but in order to do justice to his appearance in court the other day, we have to ask ourselves, Which of the Bishops would have stopped proceedings at all? Possibly Ely ; but who else?"

To Mrs. Sidney Lear.

"March 22, 1879.

"The Hyacinthic question is a trouble. The Bishops are, I suppose, right in looking cautiously round them before they commit themselves and create precedents ; and, in any case, great care would have to be taken to say that any assistance or recognition was provisional and solely due to the painful character of recent Ecclesiastical events. But this Hyacinthe is much misunderstood in England ; and if he were better known, the Bishop of Meath would not be on his committee, and others, whose names are absent, would be there.

"I have said nothing about it publicly, for *this* reason among others, that at the present time I do not wish to be in any way seeming to oppose Mr. Carter, who is dealing with the young lion and the dragon, and has enough to do with them on his hands. Besides which, we have another matter nearer home—I mean the 'Higher Education of Women' question. Talbot, and even dear King, have gone in for it, and are engaged in establishing a Hall for these young persons here in Oxford. Think of sending —— and —— to places like Oxford or Cambridge, where there are 2000 young men—to be met out for walks, in Lectures, at Church, to be discussed and observed, and everything else ! It seems madness to Christian common-sense. Dr. Pusey deplores it every day, but his influence has had no weight in checking the enterprise. The Liberal enthusiasm has turned people's heads quite. There are now *mixed* Committeees of both sexes, mixed Councils for these new Halls. And as to Religion, while Somerville Hall will recognise all denominations equally or not at all, the Church Hall itself is to make provision for Dissenters. You see what we have come to. . . ."

The following letters show the light in which he regarded the more recent phases of the Ritualistic controversy, including the imprisonment of clergy, and the manner in which he represented to his friends the need of an ecclesiastical Final Court of Appeal, consisting of Bishops only.

He found it hard to get a hearing for this plan, but at a later date he developed it at great length in his Evidence before the Royal Commission on Ecclesiastical Courts in 1885.

To the Right Hon. J. G. Hubbard.

"Christ Church, March 2, 1880.

". . . What the Church really needs is to get this whole question of Ritual relegated to its true position of *relative* insignificance. At present Newspaper Articles and Episcopal Charges combine to invest it with a supreme importance, and the consequence is that those who are identified with a pronounced ceremonial imagine its exact maintenance to be a matter of far greater intrinsic importance than it really is. Besides which, they are men—often very disinterested and brave men—and they feel as a soldier would feel about beating a retreat when under fire.

"While these prosecutions go on, there is no chance of anything but impassioned resistance (1) to what is felt to be a hypocritical appeal to only so much of the Law as is wanted for the purposes of fanatical and party prejudice, and (2) to Rulers who would appear to have lost sight of what is meant by justice towards their spiritual subjects.

"I do not wish to be 'fierce;' but to say less than this is to understate the case."

To ———

"3, Amen Court, St. Paul's, E.C., December 3, 1880.

". . . I do not think that a Bishop's authority depends upon the manner in which he is appointed. It inheres in his See. The modern 'representative' doctrine about Bishops which one often sees in the Papers is really a modern political conception imported into a higher sphere. It would help us, no doubt, in present difficulties, if it were true ; but I have yet to learn that this is the case.

"In these grave subjects, theoretical and abstract Truth often looks one way, practical aspirations another.

"P.S.—Of course, a Bishop abdicates his claim upon conscience if he tells you in so many words that he is enforcing State law as distinct from Church law. But if he claims to be enforcing Church law and referring to its principles and precedents, I do not see how to disobey him. And if a Court of Bishops does this, after being elected by the entire Episcopate of the English Church, obedience seems imperative —or departure. I have no love for Ministerial appointments ; but *that* does not touch the question."

To the Hon. C. L. Wood.

"3, Amen Court, Christmas Day, 1880.

"I must send you and Lady Agnes a word of truest Christmas wishes. . . . You see that the *Church Times* throws the Episcopal Court of Final Appeal overboard. It should propose something instead. I fear that Littledale is not alive to the *moral* difficulties of obeying nothing and nobody ; or, at least, not sufficiently so."

To ———

"3, Amen Court, St. Paul's, E.C., January 1, 1881.

". . . For many years I have been convinced that, upon ancient principles, the custody of doctrine does reside in the Episcopate, and that much of the language that has been used among ourselves will not hold water. I know, of course, only too well what this *may* mean in practice. Our actual Bishops have done all that man could well do to make it impossible to say the truth about their office without inviting a catastrophe. And you will not suspect me of holding a brief for them. No single Bishop has written to me since this controversy began ; and since Bishop Wilberforce's death there is no Bishop to whom I could write with perfect frankness on Church subjects. I know Bishop Fraser intimately as an old friend ; but his line in this matter has been more distressing than that of anybody else.

"Still, it is a great thing, if one can, to forget the personal and immediate bearings of a question, and to look to other ages and to abstract and enduring principles. Bishops, no doubt, are bound by the Canons of the Universal Church, and they may admit presbyters, as experts or consulters, to their debates. But I take it that our modern conception of a Lower House of Convocation related to the Higher, much as the House of Commons is to the House of Lords, would have made an ancient Christian hold up his hands with astonishment.

"The form of Convocation, as you know, is due to the royal necessity or wish to tax the clergy, and not to any theory of what would be most naturally suggested by the constitution of a Catholic Church. And since the Reformation the form has fitted in very well with the semi-Presbyterian conception of the Episcopate that has largely prevailed, as well as with the independent temper which belongs to an Englishman as such, whether he be priest or layman. There is room for a good Essay on 'the unconsciously felt influence of politics on Theology and Church life.'

"You see, I have not come yet to your texts or to the Apostolic Fathers. But that the executive of Church administration is in the hands of the Episcopate, and that presbyters are only admitted to a Church Legislature (rightly), as consulters, appear to me to be true propositions, however unpalatable in their practical results to you, and not less assuredly to me under present circumstances.

"Pray read again Dr. Pusey's ' Councils of the Church.' I have been careful *not* to bring this matter into the foreground in the *Guardian.* Union just now is of the first importance ; and if our friends say that they will have a Church Court composed partly of presbyters, I shall hold my tongue, though I cannot second them without violating my historical conscience. The present state of things is pretty well unbearable."

To the Hon. C. L. Wood.

" 3, Amen Court, January 13, 1881.

". . . Dr. Littledale and I evidently do *not* agree as to the relative force of principle and expediency. The Bishops are the only *de facto* governors of the Church who can show a commission from our Lord. They may, of course, wreck the *Church of England,* if they are inspired by the Evil One to do so. But the probability is that they will do better if they have real power than they do now. All men are better for being trusted. Even our cats do not scratch, except when they are afraid of people, or when they think that people are afraid of them. I do not think that we have much, if any, chance of an Episcopal Final Court. But I am quite sure that in some shape or other the principle of government by the Episcopate is the only thing we *can* go for, on grounds of principle, and that we ought not to be diverted from this by the misdeeds of many Bishops."

To Liddon's great joy, the General Election in the spring of 1880 returned the Liberal party and Mr. Gladstone to power.

To Dr. Bright.

" 3, Amen Court, April 12, 1880.

". . . Yes ! I *am* glad to have lived to see Mr. Gladstone's triumph. So far as the Election is *his* triumph—and to a very great extent it is—I rejoice at it quite unreservedly.

" There are, of course, rocks ahead. First of all, no peace of mind is possible until we know that Mr. G., and *not* Lord Granville or Lord Hartington, will be Premier. For these last are Whigs of the least lovely kind, with the traditional suspicion and dislike of the Church —making the most of her fetters, and stinting her means of spiritual self-expansion in all possible ways. Just at present these things are ignored, but they will come to the front.

"Lord Granville was in favour of the P.W.R.A. [Public Worship Regulation Act], and he introduced a very mischievous Burials Bill. And he has followed Mr. Gladstone in the Eastern question with a scarcely disguised reluctance.

"He is, of course, a very polished gentleman in society; but we must not deceive ourselves. . . . However, I hope that Mr. Gladstone's leadership is inevitable. *He* will be forced to do much that we shall not like, but the general spirit will be very different. . . .

"How miserable is all this culture of Renan! Any blasphemy, it seems, is forgiven to a good style."

In a few months another "Burials Law Amendment Bill" was before Parliament. Instead of the compulsory use of the Church of England Services at all burials in Churchyards, it proposed to allow the use of any "Christian service" or of no service at all.

To the Hon. C. L. Wood.

"Gmunden, June 20, 1880.

"This is only to say that I hope you will try to get the word 'Christian' out of the Burials Bill. It will do us no good, and may do a great deal of harm.

"1. It will be construed (and that in the Law Courts) as including Socinians, who really are as far off from Christ our Lord as the Mohammedans are.

"2. It will enhance the danger of the fabrics. If Atheists, etc., are let into the Churchyard, the difficulty of allowing anybody not of the Church to use the fabric will be much greater than it will be if the line is drawn at the 'orthodox' Dissenters, or even between the Socinians and the Deists (where, however, so far as I can see, there is, theologically, no room for it). Public opinion might too easily sanction the extension of the one principle, but it is a long way off sanctioning the other.

"3. Lord Selborne's argument is surely open to the charge of insincerity. He begins by basing the Bill on the ground of *civil right*, and then proceeds to limit the application of this right in accordance with a religious prepossession. If it *is* a civil right, every citizen, as such, has a share in it. We ought now to try to get up private Church cemeteries, vested in trustees, such as the Jews and the Roman Catholics have. They might be made very edifying, and would soon become popular among Church-people. If such are created, I shall leave a direction that I may be buried in one.

"If, in your charity, you answer this letter, you would catch me about a week or ten days hence at Hôtel de France, Ringstrasse,

Vienna. I have been seeing a good deal of Dr. Döllinger ; *he* is quite where he was in 1870. He teaches me more about men and books than anybody else I meet with now."

To the Hon. C. L. Wood.

"Vienna, Hôtel de France, July 6, 1880.

" I have seen no English papers since arriving, or indeed for a week past ; but the Burials Bill is now, I suppose, in the House of Commons. Thank you for writing to Mr. Gladstone. The more I think of it the clearer it seems to me that the word ' Christian ' will only throw dust in people's eyes now, and enable Gebal and Ammon and Amalek to get into the Churches more easily hereafter.

" The Votive Church here, which was built by the Emperor as a thank-offering for his escape from an assassin, and which I have just visited, is the sort of thing which we ought to build in memory of the μέγας [Dr. Pusey]. It is on the scale of a Cathedral, and seems to have corresponding Services, etc.

" Some of the details, painted glass, etc., might be improved on ; but altogether it is a splendid offering to Almighty God in acknowledgment of a great mercy. If you could bring Lord Beauchamp and Shaw Stewart to see it, they would have no doubt as to the propriety of our future course.

" Since writing to you we have been running about in the Tyrol and Styria.

" The Vienna papers are mainly written by Jews. They accompany Mr. Bradlaugh with great interest, and would be enthusiastic about Mr. Gladstone if it were not for the Eastern question and ' Hands off.' Ah ! they never forget."

To the Same.

" Lavington House, Petworth, September 24, 1880.

" . . . Gregory is always impulsive, and the Burials Bill, which *I* too do not like, seems to *him* to be nearly on a level with questions that touch the Faith, such as the Athanasian Creed or the Gorham Judgment. I do not see how Disestablishment would save the Churchyards, if it did not indeed forfeit the fabrics. It would do good by getting the Bishops out of the House of Lords ; but what would it give us, under present circumstances, in the way of a Church Synod ?

" Do you observe that in the Durham diocese *all* the parishioners vote for the lay members of the Conference, and Bishop Lightfoot actually speaks of this as a great venture, upon the success of which he congratulates himself. That the idea of a Church has been sacrificed to the pagan conception of a National Religion made up out of every kind of error, does not appear to occur to him."

Many allusions have already been made to the relations between Liddon and Dean Stanley. They had been friends for thirty years ; and each saw in the other very much that compelled affection, but very much also that compelled them always to be in complete opposition to one another on Theological questions. The Dean died in July, 1881, and Liddon was greatly pained at some of the unfair estimates that were made of his character by those who had not had the advantage of knowing him personally. In two private letters he endeavoured to state what he felt about him.

To ———

"Christ Church, November 12, 1882.

"I cannot agree with you about Dean Stanley. I knew him from 1849 or 1850 onwards, when he was a young tutor at University College.

"Every man who holds strongly to opinions which have no sanction from authority must be, in appearance, a conceited man ; and yet the fault lies in a radically vicious theory or method of which he is the victim. Stanley had another side, in which he showed himself in a very different light from that of the essay-writer, lecturer, and general declaimer with whom we are familiar.

"Still less do I agree about the 'disingenuousness.' Stanley had two intellectual deficiencies which flourished in his mind with a vigour that was extraordinary; he was hopelessly inaccurate, and he was more entirely destitute of the logical faculty than any highly educated man whom I have ever known. On the other hand, he had a very strong will and a very rich imagination which was under the guidance of an odd collection of impulses mostly negative, and which were incessantly capering all over earth and heaven.

"Under these conditions it was inevitable that he should talk and write in a manner which often seemed dishonest—which would have been dishonest in a person differently constituted.

"In these matters one cannot distrust one's own instinctive judgment of character. I have had many dealings with Stanley—most of them hostile ; but it never occurred to me that he was or could be capable of writing or saying that which he knew to be untrue.

"Your letter, however, shows at least this : that my assertion was too wide, and that other people are of a different mind in the matter.

"Stanley's theology is quite a different affair, and it can only be reconciled with honesty of purpose when we remember the two great intellectual deficiencies to which I have referred."

"Beziers, September 22, 1881.

"Stanley was two men. Personally he was one of the most attractive and unselfish people whom one could ever meet; but theologically he was almost everything that a theologian ought not to be. His curious want of logic prevented his seeing the real drift of a great deal of his published language; but it had disastrous effects upon younger men, who took him at his word. As Vinet says, no separation of the Ethics and Doctrines of Christianity is possible; the whole stands or falls together. This is well understood abroad, on the infidel as well as on the believing side; and minds like Stanley's—whatever their attractions in other respects—have no place in either camp, though I fear there is no doubt of the real result of their activity. Alas that one should write this of a man in so many ways admirable!"

A few extracts from the diary for 1882 will show how great a change came over his life in that year, besides illustrating the many interests that filled his mind.

"*January* 21.—Wrote a great many letters: one to Dr. Morgan Dix of Trinity Church, New York, who begs me in the most pressing way to accept the invitation to lecture at the Lowell Institute at Boston. Alas! this is impossible.

"*January* 22.—Went with Barff to the Dedication Festival at St. Agnes, Kennington. King preached beautifully on 'The Valley of Achor as a door of hope.' The ceremonial very elaborate. The people joined heartily in the hymns. But I was too crowded between two chairs to say my prayers in comfort. N.B.—To see that this is not the case in St. Paul's.

"*April* 22.—In afternoon, preached [at St. Paul's] on Professor Darwin, but with discomfort and misgiving.

"*April* 25.—A quantity of letters: one from the Duke of Argyll, referring to my Sermon in the kindest terms; another, anonymous, abusing me as a Rationalist for what I said about Darwin.

"*May* 3.—Correcting proof of my Sermon on April 22. Dined with Mr. Gladstone at 10, Downing Street, to meet the Prince of Wales. Sat between Miss Gladstone and Mr. Goschen. A talk with Lord Rosebery, and a great deal of talk with [John] Bright. Certainly he is a man for whom I can understand a warm affection.

"*May* 4.—Saw Dr. Pusey. He said that he should not join the Committee of a Darwin Memorial; but that they would not apply to him, and that my responsibilities might be different. He struck me as being weaker than last Term, and much less able to seize my meaning, and more wandering in what he said. In evening, dined with the Duke of Argyll, whose conversation about Darwin most interesting. He thought the Darwinian view of the world too mechanical—not room enough for the action of a living mind. There is much in Nature not otherwise explainable.

"*May* 10.—Spent some hours in writing a Preface to my Sermon on April 22 on Mr. Darwin. Wrote to Mr. J. Spottiswoode, declining to join the Darwin Memorial Committee ; put it on the true ground— a wish not to vex Dr. Pusey, at his age, to whom I owe such respect and affection. If I had only to think of my own convictions, I think I should join, as we owe Darwin much for his courageous adherence to Theistic truths under a great deal of pressure, as I cannot doubt.

"*June* 18.—Went to St. Gregory-by-St. Paul in the morning. The Church Service hearty. To St. Martin's, Ludgate Hill, in the afternoon. No organ or choir. Nothing could be more dreary. Until the *Magnificat*, Louisa and I alone ; afterwards nine people came in by driblets. In evening visited Bow Church, Bishopsgate Church, St. Ethelburga's, St. Magnus', St. Saviour's, Southwark. At this last an evening Communion was going on : about forty-three communicants. They administered to two at a time.

"*June* 24.—Dined with Mr. Hubbard ; a fierce discussion with him about the City Churches. He evidently was in favour of the Bishop of London's Bill. I had to convince him that when a majority of the City clergy had been for a long time neglecting their duty, it was impossible to form a true opinion of the real wants of the City from the attendance at the Churches."

As soon as his August residence was over, he went abroad to rest.

"*September* 15, *Turin.*— . . . On returning to the hotel at 5, I received a telegram from Mrs. Brine [Dr. Pusey's daughter] to this effect : 'My father is sinking fast ; could you return to England at once?' Telegraphed to Acland to know if I could arrive in time, and to Mrs. Brine to say that I had telegraphed to Acland. A very miserable evening ; no telegram arrived before bedtime.

"*September* 16.—A telegram from King, begging me to return to England at once. Decided to do so to-morrow morning, on finding that all the places in the sleeping-carriages are engaged to-night. In a most anxious state of mind about Dr. Pusey all day. The *Times* and *Daily News* of yesterday both speak of the seriousness of his illness. The *Times* says that Archbishop Tait is greatly interested in his case, and has sent him a message of sympathy from his own sickbed. *Must* start to-morrow for England.

"*September* 18.—Reached the P. L. M. terminus in Paris at 5.50, and drove to the Hôtel Windsor. Very tired, and lay down for some time. Telegraphed to King to know how Dr. Pusey was. No answer. Walked about the streets, and then came back to the hotel and lay down again for some time. Had a terrible presentiment of what might be. In afternoon to Rue d'Arras to see Père Hyacinthe, but he was not there. After dinner, walked out and bought to-day's *Standard* at a kiosk. On opening it, saw the beginning of an obituary notice, headed 'Dr. Pusey.' Had not the heart to look on, but walked about the streets rapidly for an hour, before I came back to the hotel. Then was enabled to read it, and also the *Times.* So he has left us, most dear and revered of friends, of whose friendship I have been all along so utterly unworthy. How little I can realise it ! Though I have been looking forward to this day for twenty years at least.

"*September* 19. *Calais.*—. . . Arrived at 7.6 p.m. The afternoon entirely wet. I never saw more steady and heavy rain continuously pouring down. In harmony with my feelings. After dinner, went to a café in the Place, as last year, and saw the same black-and-white cat. How things have changed since then ! Now that dearest Dr. Pusey is gone, the world is for me no more the same world. The whole past seems torn up by the roots. I feel the danger of disbelief in God the Holy Ghost. He Who created and trained Dr. Pusey can train successors, if He wills.

"*September* 21.—Left London at 9 for Oxford. Many old friends. . . . The coffin lying in the large study, E. and W. The whole place so natural ; the books and pictures just in their places. At 12.45 went to the Deanery, where I joined the Dean and the Bishop of Oxford. We then all walked to the W. door of the Cathedral. I read the Sentences and all the Burial Service after the Lesson, which the Dean read. The Cathedral crowded with people of all kinds. Mr. Gladstone one of the pall-bearers. In the afternoon, a meeting at Bright's about a Memorial. Lord Beauchamp for a Theological Appendix to Keble College, in which B.A.'s might be taught Theology. I advocated a College of Clergy, designed to act under a Provost. The latter carried, at least provisionally. Difficulty of believing that his dear body is really beneath the floor of the Cathedral.

"*September* 23.—A long talk with King about resigning my Professorship. He said that I must do it, if I attempted to write Dr. Pusey's 'Life,' and that to do this seemed to be a plain duty.

"*September* 29.—Pretty well made up my mind to resign my Professorship in order to write the 'Life.'

"*September* 30.—Wrote to the Vice-Chancellor to resign my Professorship.

"*October* 4. *Highclere.*—A short walk with Lord Carnarvon before lunch. Was very glad that I was going to write the 'Life.' Advised me not to put too many letters in it, but to write *currente calamo*, giving my own impressions as vividly as possible.

"*October* 5.—Felt very depressed in the evening. Cannot think how I shall manage Dr. Pusey's 'Life.' *Deus in adjutorium meum intende.*

"*October* 9.—My resignation of my Professorship of Exegesis is announced in the *Times* of to-day.

"*October* 12.—A very kind letter from Jowett, regretting my resignation of my Chair.

"*October* 13.—Went over to see the Dean [Church], who said that I

U

had better take Stanley's 'Life of Arnold' for a model as to form, and make a good deal of use of letters.

"*October* 19.—Dined in Hall for the first time after Dr. Pusey's death. Everybody talking and laughing just as though nothing had happened.

"*November* 5 [*Sunday*].—Began my Lectures in Christ Church Hall. Epistle to Ephesians. A very large attendance, about two hundred men; which made me feel that I ought to have prepared myself better.

"Rev. S. F. Green let out of Lancaster Prison to-day, having been there since March 19, 1881.

"*November* 16.—Wet, snowy, cheerless morning. At 3 p.m. went to Dr. Pusey Memorial meeting in Arlington Street. The most hearty speeches were Lake's and the Bishop of Ely's. The room was quite full. The enthusiasm less than I could have wished, but our plan of a Pusey Library was fairly floated. There was no opposition. Lord Beauchamp most generous; he simply endorsed what I said in order to avoid an appearance of difference. Dined at Sir R. Phillimore's. Could see that Lady —— was vexed at what I had said about Bishop Wilberforce's language respecting Dr. Pusey. She never knew Dr. Pusey, and cannot measure the relative greatness of the two men."

To C. T. Redington, Esq.

"Christ Church, Oxford, November 2, 1882.

"Yes, I have resigned my Chair. For many years I had felt the difficulty of combining a satisfactory discharge of its duties with those of my Canonry in London; and of late years the London correspondence and other work had greatly increased, and had made it more and more difficult for me to keep abreast of the ever-increasing literature of the serious subjects, for an adequate knowledge and treatment of which I was responsible to the University. Some years ago I mentioned the subject to Dr. Pusey. But he, in the kindness of his personal feeling, was so much distressed by it that I made up my mind not to reopen the question during his lifetime. But when he had left us, I felt that, as has indeed been the case, a great deal more work would shape itself for me, and that I could no longer hope to hold my Chair without grave moral discomfort. So I resigned at once. I shall hope to keep my rooms here, and shall try if I am spared to write his 'Life,' or something about it. Oxford is indeed to me a sad subject. The effect of the recent changes is to cut out almost by the roots the old religious provisions and associations of the place, and there is only one appropriateness—that those who think these changes good should be at the head of affairs. As yet, of course, men who like myself are products of the old system linger about their ancient homes, but death will soon do its work. . . . It is astonishing to me how little people generally seem able to realise the inevitable effects of such a momentous change."

To E. A. Freeman, Esq.

"3, Amen Court, St. Paul's, E.C., December 13, 1882.

". . . If I can, I shall come to you in January. It would be a true pleasure to do so. Just at present I do not reap the full advantage of being 'one instead of two;' indeed, there is some risk of my being resolved into 'many instead of one,' but in time this will, I hope, improve.

"What you say about Eastern Europe is more dark to me than I could wish, looking upon you as I do as a kind of director in all foreign politics. Yes; it is hard to give up 'the apostolic king.' The said king's ancestors did good service against the Turk, and the Hungarians may, I suppose, one day manage the apostolic king less completely than they do now. By the way is not 'the people's William' remiss in the matter of the Turk? Once or twice of late he has fondled the Turk more or less unbecomingly. . . .

"How could we help having the Pusey Memorial meeting at Lord Salisbury's house? We were obliged to have it in some house; 10, Downing Street, would have welcomed us if it had been anywhere else. But would Lord Granville, or Lord Hartington, have welcomed us? Is it not the fact that, except the Prime Minister (and it *is* a noble exception), every Liberal minister (perhaps I wrong Mr. Childers) is, if not *anti*-Church, at least *un*-Church. Why should this be so? Why does the Liberal *party* throw cold water on all serious efforts for Religion in the Church? . . . Lord Salisbury was careful to insist on the unpolitical character of the meeting, and W. E. G. and Lord Selborne have each given us £100."

At the same time, and within a few weeks of Dr. Pusey's death, the Archbishop of Canterbury passed away. As will have been seen, Liddon was never able to view with any favour the policy which dictated the acts of Archbishop Tait. He always believed that the Archbishop took a wrong measure of the Ecclesiastical position of the Church of England, as well as of the intellectual requirements of the moment for the proper defence of the Faith of Christendom. But, at the very close of his life, one act of the Archbishop's did much to conciliate those who had for years differed widely from him. With great courage and wisdom he succeeded in effecting an arrangement which put an end to the most painful tension that was caused by the tedious and unhappy litigation in connection

with St. Alban's, Holborn.   In admiration and gratitude
for that act, many of Liddon's friends wished to subscribe
to a Memorial which was being raised to him.   Although
Liddon had a high opinion of the Archbishop's sincerity
and genuineness of character, and had never found anything but kindness from him when he came into contact
with him, he hesitated about assisting this proposal.   Of
course, he fully admitted the great value of his latest act,
and was truly grateful for it : yet he could never forget
other official acts with which Dr. Tait's name was un-
avoidably associated in his mind.   He felt that to join
in a Memorial to him would be to compromise his own
convictions about the past.

To the Hon. C. L. Wood.

"Brislington, January 10, 1883.

" I wonder what you are thinking about the 'Tait Memorial Fund.'
That the late Archbishop's friends, and the general public, which looks
at these matters from the point of view of the daily press, should wish
to promote an enterprise of the kind is perfectly natural.   And we
High Churchmen must feel grateful to him for what he did on his
death-bed to promote the peace of the Church in the matter of
Mackonochie and Suckling.   But is this a reason for a 'Memorial'?
Was not the act on his death-bed an attempt to undo one part of the
wrong which he had done to the Church—I do not say intentionally—
in his life ?   Can we rightly forget the history of the Poole prosecution,
of the 'Essays and Reviews,' of the Colenso case, of the Divorce Bill, of
the attack on the Creed of St. Athanasius, of the Public Worship
Regulation Bill ?   Was not the whole drift and purpose of the late
Archbishop's life hostile to principles which we hold dear ?   And if so,
what is the moral value of our share in a Memorial to him ?   Is it not
a mere piece of social good-nature—just as much as leaving a visiting
card on a person with whom we have little in common, but with whom
we wish, for whatever reason, to keep on good terms ?   And will not
a Memorial of this sort destroy the *moral* value of other Memorials
which are intended to express deep and heartfelt gratitude to God for
the works and example of the saintly dead ? "

The effort to found the Pusey Memorial in Oxford,
or to watch over it when founded, took the same place in
Liddon's heart and life during the years that followed

Pusey's death as did the foundation of Keble College from 1866 to 1870. It was his greatest delight to labour for it ; for the Pusey House in Oxford was designed to carry on the most valuable part of Pusey's work. In his own words, it was to be, amidst the ruins of what he loved best in Oxford, a

"home of sacred learning and a rallying-point for Christian faith, and thus it will strengthen all that is dearest to a sincere Christian at what, so far as we can judge, must always be one of the chief centres of the mental life of this country. . . . It will form a centre of moral and intellectual and spiritual enthusiasm, in which all that is solid in inquiry and learning, and all that is lofty and aspiring in moral effort, shall find encouragement under the consecrating shadow of a great name." [1]

And it was a true happiness when one of the most valued of his younger friends, the Rev. Charles Gore, Fellow of Trinity College and Vice-Principal of Cuddesdon Theological College, undertook the great responsibility of inaugurating the work. When preaching to a congregation which Mr. Gore had once served as Curate, he said of him—

"You know something of his devotion to truth and duty, of his high and varied capacity, of the unstinted charity which has spent, in the service of your souls, year after year, the few weeks of leisure which could be spared from exacting labours. To others who have had opportunities of studying his mind and character, he has seemed to combine a lofty simplicity of purpose with that insight and know-ledge of the things of Faith which makes him not unworthy to represent, even in Oxford, the great name of Dr. Pusey." [2]

Liddon hurried back from the Continent early in October, 1884, to be present at the opening of the Memorial.

"*October* 9.—. . . At 11 the Pusey House opened by the Bishop of Oxford [Dr. Mackarness]. The Bishop celebrated, and after the Nicene Creed addressed and admitted to their offices the new Librarians. His Address was much tenderer and more effective than I should have at all anticipated ; indeed, one cannot be too grateful to him for his kindness and generosity throughout."

[1] "Clerical Life and Work :" Sermons by H. P. Liddon, D.D., Serm. xiv. pp. 372, 375.

[2] *Ibid.*, pp. 376, 377.

CORRESPONDENCE, 1879–1883.

To the Rev. J. Oakley.

On the Proposed Church and Stage Guild.

"Christ Church, May 15, 1879.

"C. L. Dodgson told me some days ago of the substance of the Paper which you are so good as to send me, and for which I am very much obliged to you.

"Certainly we must all of us agree that if the Stage could be enlisted in the cause of Religion and Morality, or even so influenced as not to oppose that cause, it would be an immense gain to the Church of Christ and to mankind at large.

"But at the risk of seeming faint-hearted, I must avow my belief that this happy result is quite impossible ; and that, while there always have been, are, and always will be, excellent people who devote their lives to dramatic representation, the Stage, as a whole, is and will be against us.   It may be that the conditions of dramatic representation make this inevitable—human nature being, upon the average, what it actually is.

"Speaking for myself, there is no form of entertainment which I should so entirely enjoy, as good acting.   But I have never been inside a theatre since I took Orders in 1852, and I do not mean to go into one, please God, while I live.   I have always felt that public opinion requires so very little of an Anglican clergyman in the way of self-restraint, that we are, in a manner, bound to respect its scanty demands somewhat scrupulously.   And there can, I apprehend, be no sort of doubt that a clergyman who goes to theatres forfeits moral influence to a certain extent with all classes, and quite irretrievably with some.   We cannot make war upon the partly irrational and partly just public sentiment which condemns clerical theatre-going, without exposing ourselves to the suspicion that we are really anxious to procure public approval of clerical participation in a form of enjoyment open to the lay world ; and this, of course, would go far to ruin any religious—as distinct from merely social—influence which we may yet, as an Order, retain among our countrymen.

"As I get older, I feel less and less sympathy for that singular misrepresentation of the real mind of St. Paul and St. John which, by a strange abuse of language, is called ' Evangelicalism.'   But whatever is to be said of the ' Evangelical ' theology, the strength of the Movement in its early days lay in its renunciation of the 'world.'   Judging from my own memories as a boy and a young man, *that* was the secret of its power, and its renunciation of the world was felt to be a reality, because it involved the giving up not merely a temper of mind, but acts and enjoyments which are its food and its expression.   It has been the fashion to call this Manichæism ; but I do not know that it was ever really associated with any speculative doctrine of the two principles, while it does harmonise very strikingly with a great body of teaching in the writings of St. John.

" A Churchman like myself has to ask whether he will really help the Cause of Jesus Christ, or win a larger number of people to accept those portions of Divine Revelation which the popular Puritanism and Latitudinarianism reject—if he engages in an enterprise like this. And to that question there can, I think, be but one answer. When the world at large hears of our 'asserting the right of Churchmen to take part in theatrical amusements,' it will say that the real motive of the æsthetic element in Church Services is at last apparent. It will argue that Religious Ceremonial had been all along—not an aid to enable the soul to mount to the Unseen and the Supersensuous—an aid to be used and then forgotten—but an indulgence of a taste which is only and really to be satisfied in the theatre. It will insist on the justice of its scornful epithet ' histrionic,' and perhaps it will add a few civilities about our being liberal and unpharisaic only because it will instinctively feel that we have made it a present of the little moral power that we had.

" There would be a great deal to be said for a Guild, composed of theatrical people, having for its object the promotion of a high aim in their profession and of purity of life. But it would be no part of the business of such a Guild to 'assert the right of Churchmen to take part in theatrical amusements ; ' human nature is quite strong enough to assert ' rights ' of this sort without being aided by Guilds. The Church and Stage Guild proceeds upon a different estimate of the true service which might be rendered to the theatrical profession from that which I am thinking about.

" You ask me to say plainly what I think, so I have written plainly, and I fear at too great length. But you will forgive me, I trust."

To the Rev. R. W. Dale.

" Christ Church, Oxford, November 11, 1879.

" I cannot help acknowledging and thanking you for your very kind letter.

" I ventured to send you the volume of Sermons ['University Sermons :' Second Series], because, although I knew that as a whole they could not hope to command your approval, I was at the same time sure that, within the very large area of our common convictions, they would meet with a kindly and generous greeting.

" They have no relations to each other, and no pretensions to form a treatise, however loosely compacted. Much too that is in them would appear to be flat and pointless to persons who have not had some sort of knowledge in detail of what has been passing in the University, or in particular sections of it, during the last ten years.

"Had I been quite free to follow my own judgment, I should probably never have published them at all. But there they are—full as I know only too well, from any point of view, and most of all from His Who is first to be thought of by any of His ministers, of human imperfections and errors.

"Still, it would be a great happiness to me if they should help to draw together hearts which are one, at least in the sincere desire to promote His glory ; and though there are only one or two allusions in them to the most recent events (as they were for the most part preached before the Eastern Question became prominent), I cannot help saying to you how greatly the history of that question in England has affected my own feelings towards those who are not members of the Church of England ; I have often and often wished that we, as a body, could have been as true to what was morally as well as theologically the Cause of Christ in Eastern Europe as were the English Nonconformists."

To ———

On the Church and Stage Guild.

"Christ Church, June 8, 1881.

" I am sorry to be conscientiously unable to help you in the way you suggest. I say ' sorry,' because I am entirely satisfied that your motives in supporting the ' Church and Stage Guild ' are those which oblige me to decline to support it, or to make it easier for others to do so.

"The reason is, because I am convinced that the influence of the theatre, in the case of *average* human nature and character, lies in the *direction* of sin.

"No doubt there are actors and actresses who lead even saintly lives—saintly because victorious over temptation—and certainly higher than that, *e.g.*, of a Clergyman who is never tried as they have been. And there are also, I do not doubt, many people in each generation who attend the theatre regularly, and only derive from it a pleasure which is elevating and pure.

"But the real question is as to average human beings. And here I cannot but think that the experience of generations and centuries is too plain to be mistaken. The Church, at any rate, has never had much doubt upon the matter. It is, I know, sometimes thought that the feeling against the theatre is a creation of the Low Church party, and that it originated at Clapham. But I learnt it from Dr. Pusey, from Mr. Keble, from others who have passed away, and who spent their lives in combating the errors of Puritanism. It has been said too that the theatre against which Tertullian wrote and the Council of Arles legislated was a very different thing from the modern theatre ; but, then, the theatre about which, *e.g.*, Bossuet wrote two centuries ago, or Bouvier, to take one moralist out of several, in our own days, is the modern theatre. In a practical matter like this, the instincts of the Church are likely to be right ; especially as she has every reason for enlisting the sympathies of so powerful an agent as the drama, if—morally and spiritually—she can afford to do so.

"It is quite unreasonable to say that it is sinful either to take part in or to witness a dramatic representation that is perfectly moral. But practically the theatre maintains its popularity by trifling with subjects which are on the other side of the line ; and it is urged to do so by the instinct of self-preservation—average human tastes being what they are. This tendency on the part of the theatre would appear to me to be too radical and imperious for the Church to hope to resist or even modify successfully. She can only save her children by warning them against that which she is powerless to prevent. And it is surely much better that young people should not go even to Mr. Irving than that they should gradually learn a taste for performances which would be as unwelcome to Mr. Irving as they are to ourselves.

"It does not appear to me that, because a man conscientiously keeps away from theatres, he is obliged to think harshly, or pharisaically, of everybody connected with them. A Christian will think and hope the best of every one until he is obliged to think otherwise by the evidence of facts. But, on the other hand, I cannot think it a duty to go to theatres merely in order to show that you do not suppose everybody connected with them to be leading immoral lives.

"I am not sure how far you will agree with me when I add that, as to this matter, the clergy and laity do not appear to me to be in the same case.

"Even if it were clear that all Christian laymen might and should go to theatres, I should still hesitate, or do much more than hesitate, about the clergy. A priest cannot do many things which, in themselves indifferent, are yet fatal to his spiritual influence or efficiency. There is no necessary harm in dancing, but a dancing priest becomes invested with grotesque associations of which, unfortunately, he cannot rid himself in the pulpit or before the Altar. There is surely no doubt that a clergyman who goes to theatres forfeits a great deal of power of doing good to others, and I cannot myself think that the 'prejudices' which involve this forfeiture are wholly without value. On the contrary, they appear to me to point to a popular ideal of the clerical state, which Puritanism and unbelief between them have well-nigh destroyed, as implying a real commission from Heaven, and exacting at the hands of those who hold it a different sort of life from that of the layman on whom no such burden has been laid.

"In writing this I do not forget that some of the clerical names connected with the Guild are among the most saintly and self-denying of the London clergy, and that they lead lives much more worthy of a priest than I do myself. But the question is as to average men who will quote and follow their example. Is it for us clergy to break down one of the last remaining traces of a feeling among our fellow-men that we have received more, and are bound to more, than others?

"I must trust to your indulgence for the length of this letter, and for what you may well deem its dogmatic tone. You will, however, I think, forgive me for telling you quite unreservedly how the matter presents itself to me."

To the Hon. C. L. Wood.

On the Church and Stage Guild.

"3, Amen Court, St. Paul's, E.C., September 10, 1879.

". . . In what you say about Greek life I quite agree. It was elegant and detestable. When the Renaissance tried to revive it in mid-Christendom, the Church looked hard at it. She smiled on it in Leo X., but she would have none of it before the sixteenth century had closed. It was the paganism of Italian Renaissance-life which gave its main strength to the Reformation Movement in the south of Europe. Only think of what a gospel Mr. J. Addington Symonds's would be!

"The clerical promoters of the Theatre Guild movement mean well, I am sure. But I am sure, also, that from a *religious* point of view they are gravely mistaken. They will never raise the tone of the stage. . . . The Theatre Guild will only break down, if it can, the dislike of the more serious clergy to go to Plays; and in doing this it will lessen their moral power proportionately. People talk of Manichæism, but the early Church knew how to excommunicate the Manichees, and to keep clear of *spectacula* at the same time. There can be no evil in dramatic representations as such; but practically they are found in all countries to imply associations which are evil. . . .

"The one good thing which the early 'Evangelicals' did was to recover the idea of the 'world' as we get it in St. John's Gospel, and to aim at a stricter life. They made mistakes in this, and their successors have long since made friends with the 'world' in order to crush good Churchmen; but it would be a sad thing if *we* should help to undo in any minds the one bit of positive moral good which they succeeded in achieving."

To the Dean of St. Paul's.

On the Discussion about Eternal Punishment.

"Christ Church, Oxford, October 28, 1879.

". . . I agree with him [Dean Goulburn] in his anxiety that something should be done to meet the general and increasing scepticism on the subject of Eternal Punishment, and, indeed, of the future state as a whole. Farrar is a symptom rather than a cause ; he represents the passion rather than the logic of the attack on the old doctrine. Indeed, as to logic, his book and its preface presuppose two different sets of premises, apparently, too, without his being aware of it. But he is eloquent, and has a great reputation, and probably carries a great deal of 'Society' with him, as Goulburn says.

"You might well say to me, or to any other of the Chapter, 'Why do not you do something?' and this has been pressed on me from other quarters. I have hesitated chiefly on *this* account: that I am sure that the true and adequate reply to Farrar, etc., lies in a very full statement of the doctrine of the Intermediate State, with its practical corollary of Prayers for the Faithful departed. The mass of people do not think about the texts of Scripture which, *pace* Farrar, do prove that lost souls are punished eternally. They ask what has become of A., B., and C., whom they have known in life, and who have died, and who cannot be thought of as at once either in heaven or in hell without moral violence. The popular Protestant doctrine, with its two categories of the dead, gets into endless difficulties when applied to the facts of life ; and Farrar is on strong ground when he urges this. But unless the graduated relief afforded by the belief in a state of suspense and training for heaven be granted, the majority of modern men *will* resolve hell into a purgatory—probably into a very brief and endurable purgatory—and will persuade themselves that Scripture allows them to do this, or that it must be done whether Scripture allows it or not."

To ———

On judging Public Men.

"Christ Church, November 22, 1879.

". . . You asked me, you will remember, to tell you 'frankly' what I thought about your allusions to Lord Salisbury ; and I thought it due to your past kindness to myself, to my respect for you, and to our common sympathies, that I should do so. No doubt I expressed myself awkwardly ; but I meant to say that you would have judged Lord Salisbury differently, if you had known him personally and for a long term of years. For you would have known that he is quite incapable of knowingly saying what is untrue or doing what is dishonourable. All the world knows that, in 1867, he left the Government rather than acquiesce in what he deemed wrong ; and he is indeed governed by a higher motive than what is vaguely called 'honour;' namely, a desire to do what is right so far as he knows it.

"And this is quite compatible with his making great mistakes, and, on subjects of the gravest importance. And, as I cannot but think, he has made such a mistake in relation to the Eastern Question. But political error is one thing, and want of moral principle is another. If Lord Salisbury has been controlled by the subtle genius and imperious will of Lord Beaconsfield, I deplore the thraldom in which he is held, but I do not therefore think him a bad man. We must be, before all things, just. Mr. Gladstone used the sternest language about Lord Palmerston, and afterwards accepted office under him ; . . . but I have not therefore ceased to love and respect Mr. Gladstone. In judging of public men and of their public acts, it is necessary to remember that much which influences them can never be known to their contemporaries ; and therefore the opinion which we form of them must be largely influenced by what we know independently of their characters. I know Lord Salisbury well enough to be sure that, if you knew him too, you would not alter your opinion of the merits of the Eastern Question, but you would appreciate his relation to it somewhat differently."

"3, Amen Court, St. Paul's, E.C., December 16, 1881.

". . . So far as I understand the subject, I have no doubt that the Decision against the Vestments was a bad Decision, and that those who wear them are obeying the true law of the Church. But I have also no doubt that a man like Lord Selborne entirely believed it to be a good Decision, and that he is quite as incapable as you or I would be of giving a false Judgment, believing it to *be* false, or of knowingly playing any tricks whatever with his sense of truth. But, on the other hand, I know, in my own case, how difficult it is for me sometimes, under the pressure of strong bias or feeling, to see facts as they really are ; I misread their real import in perfect good faith, and discover my mistake some time afterwards. . . ."

To Mrs. Sidney Lear.

On the First Volume of the " Life of Bishop Wilberforce."

"3, Amen Court, St. Paul's, E.C., January 24, 1880.

". . . Everybody has been reading Mr. Ashwell's 'Life of Bishop Wilberforce.' It does not allow sufficiently for his development ; he springs out of the earth a full-grown 'Bishop Wilberforce,' whereas he learnt a great deal by experience ; and the Hampden affair, by making him unpopular at Court, was probably the greatest blessing of his life. But for it he would have been a mere courtier without any moral interest whatever attaching to him. As it was, he never altogether got over the immense drawbacks of his Puritan bringing up ; but his life towards its close had a nobility and pathos about it which more than redeemed its earlier weaknesses. . . ."

To the Hon. C. L. Wood.

On the Same.

"Christ Church, Oxford, February 17, 1880.

". . . The letter [from Bishop Wilberforce] to Miss L. Noel about Dr. Pusey would be mischievous if it were not grotesque. But for the Bishop's sake I am sincerely sorry that it was ever published ; it shows that he had much less fear of hasty judgments, and much less of an eye for the real outlines of character, than I had supposed to be the case. But long before his death he would have regretted writing anything of the kind. He was when writing it in a fair way to be spiritually ruined outright, and was saved by the consequences of the Hampden matter. It cut him off from the Court, and from ambitious visions which had overclouded his soul ; and it sent him back to his conscience and to his diocese. . . .

" However, after the Hampden matter, the Bishop *did* make great efforts ; and his later life, notwithstanding elements that disappointed one, was noble and lovable in very many great respects. *I shall always love him dearly,* though perhaps I had as much experience of that side of him which is regrettable as anybody. . . .

" Nevertheless, I agree with you entirely about that letter to Robert J. W[ilberforce] touching the Ordination Sermon. It is deplorable. I have not seen the *Month,* which, in spirit and temper, belongs to the same unlovely family as the *Record* and the *Rock,* though its creed is very different."

To a Young Man.

"3, Amen Court, St. Paul's, E.C., August 10, 1880.

". . . I cannot sympathise in any sense whatever with your notions of 'studying' all sorts of subjects before you have even passed the examination for your Degree.

" You tell me in one letter that you are studying Icelandic ; in another, that you are reading Señor Castelar ; in another, that you are investigating questions connected with the Early Celts ; in another, that you think Dr. Newman's arguments unanswerable (from which I have to suppose that you have read them carefully all through, thought about them, and read and thought about what is said on the other side as well) ; in another, that you are reading Delitzsch. And so on. How can this do your mind any kind of good ? If you were an Aristotle, you would have to give time and concentration to one subject before you entered upon another ; as it is, you *must* enfeeble and dissipate whatever powers God has given you, while you deceive yourself by thinking that you have a wide range of intellectual interests, and that (as you wrote to me the other day) your father ought to 'endow research in your person.'

"Your letters to me, especially during the present year, have made me feel that your father may have good reason to complain. . . . If you have written to him at all in the terms in which you have on former occasions written to me, I cannot be surprised at his displeasure with you. He must either think, as I do, that you have no idea of the value of language, or that you do not know what is due in the way of respect to older people than yourself.

"If, as you say, your father's objection was mainly against Church principles, I would ask you whether you have done what you might have done to remove it. Has your Oxford life been that of a consistent Churchman? What has been your practice in respect of attending the Daily Service, or of receiving Holy Communion, or of cultivating that temper of self-distrust and consideration for others which marks a man who is trying in earnest to lead a Christian life? And have you not gone far to justify his suspicions of your loyalty to the English Church, by your language and practice in the direction of Rome, while at the same time, with odd inconsistency, you play with infidelity? Is it not so?

"To me you have seemed to live upon the surface of things, mistaking a power of talking about all sorts of subjects for knowledge of them, and caring more for being acquainted with persons of reputation of whatever kind, than for ascertaining the exact worth of the principles which they represent. Such a life must, if it lasts, be a wasted life ; and when you tell me in your last letter that you 'mean to use your pen,' I am obliged to say that I do not think that it will be to any great purpose, unless you undergo a very great change of character. . . ."

To a Roman Catholic proposing to join the Church of England.

"3, Amen Court, St. Paul's, E.C., September 19, 1880.

". . . The case, as it stands in your mind, seems to be a balance of difficulties. On the one side there is the Vatican Decree, with no probability, so far as we can see, of its being reversed or seriously modified by authority. On the other, there are the shortcomings, practical, and, to a certain extent, theoretical, of the Church of England. As it seems to me, these last may be shown to involve nothing organic, while the practical may be lessened in the future, as they have been lessened in the past, by the revived Church spirit of our day. And, of course, the Church of England cannot claim finality for anything that dates from the Reformation period ; and that was settled, for whatever good reasons, on her own, *i.e.* a local authority, and therefore, from the nature of the case, provisionally. The Roman Catholic claim to represent the *entire* Body of Christ, makes revision of later language almost, if not quite, impossible.

". . . Practically speaking, I suppose, the change from the Latin Mass to the English Communion Office would be more felt than any other. I hardly see how this could be avoided. Yet here, I should say, that while our Office has suffered, especially in 1552, in some important respects, there is the undoubted fact that it contains all that is necessary to a valid Eucharist, while perhaps it has gained *devotionally* in the transfer of the *Gloria in Excelsis* to the end of the Service. And as life goes on, the soul becomes less dependent upon the very words of the Service. Our Lord's Presence is the great fact which throws all else into a relative insignificance, or, perhaps, it is that the ever-accumulating associations and experiences of life cover up the devotional framework which supports them in these most solemn moments, like ivy burying the trunk of an old tree."

To ———

On Agnosticism.

"3, Amen Court, St. Paul's, E.C., December 12, 1881.

"An 'Agnostic' is a person who maintains that *we have no means of knowing* that the great facts of Religion are true ; *e.g.* he does not, like an Atheist, deny that God exists, but he maintains that we cannot know that He does exist. It comes practically to the same thing, as the Agnostic takes as little account of God in his daily life as does the Atheist.

"Agnosticism seems to be a less 'blasphemous' state of thought than Atheism ; it wins our sympathy by pleading ignorance, and not insisting upon knowledge. But it is, I fear, often more hopeless. The Atheist is committed to a position for which he is intellectually responsible, and from which he may be dislodged by argument. The Agnostic is committed to nothing except to the lazy theory that we have no means of knowing anything which is really worth knowing in this life. Perhaps I ought not to have troubled you with this. But, next to *prayer* for your friend, the best thing would be to get him to read, *e.g.*, as to the Being of God, Professor Flint's book on Theism, which disposes of Agnosticism while it replies to Atheism."

To ———

On the Title " Episcopal Church of Scotland."

" Christ Church, May 21, 1882.

" DEAR SIR,—I am sorry to be unable to send you more than the enclosed small contribution (£5).

"Will you forgive me for saying that I must beg you to remove my name from the Committee, unless the word ' Episcopal ' is omitted from the documents for which it is responsible ?

"To talk of an Episcopal Church is like talking of a two-legged man. Apart from the Episcopate the Church of Christ does not properly exist; and when in Scotland she consents to call herself 'Episcopal,' she implies that the self-organised Presbyterian communities, whether established or non-established, are really parts of the Catholic Christian Church, which only differ from herself, as the phrase goes, in the question of Church government. If this were the case, the position of 'Episcopalians,' so to call them, in Scotland would be a sinful because a schismatical one; they would be making an uncalled-for division in the Fold of Christ. The only justification for the continued existence of what I must call the Scottish Church since 1688, as a body separated from the established community, is that, by the destruction of the Episcopate in that community, the conditions of true union, through the Sacraments, with our Lord Jesus Christ, were forfeited, and that it thus became a duty to supply the means of grace independently.

"You will, I trust, forgive me for saying as much as this. If I lived in Scotland, and thought that the Presbyterian body was a portion of Christ's Church, I should belong to it as the larger body, and as a matter of course, in order to avoid the sin of unnecessary division among Christians."

To ———

On the Permanence of Gifts in the Church.

"3, Amen Court, St. Paul's, E.C., January 14, 1881.

". . . I should answer your first question by saying that a Church, like a man, may do a great deal that is wrong without dying. I share your feelings very largely indeed as to what is involved in submission to the existing Courts. But if, *e.g.*, you consider the degree in which the Eastern Church submitted to the Emperors, and at a time when the communion between East and West was still unbroken, you will see what I mean. Probably, too, we should both agree that the claim of Supremacy on the part of the Pope has no sufficient grounds in Scripture or in primitive tradition; while, on the other hand, it is certain that submission to it has entailed a great many mischiefs, both in faith and morals, on the Roman Church. Yet I should be sorry indeed to say that the Roman Church was on this account dead or dying.

"As to your second question, I cannot think that Orders can be rendered invalid by any misconduct of ordained persons. The 'character' conferred by Ordination is an objective fact, which as such is independent of the conduct of the ordained man. I agree with you that the validity of Archbishop Parker's Consecration is certain. And it follows that there can be no doubt whatever as to the Orders of English Bishops and Priests at the present day.

"A remarkable illustration of this principle is afforded by the case of Talleyrand, who was Bishop of Autun, and then became a Minister of State under the first Napoleon.

"Talleyrand, even while he continued to administer his diocese, openly professed Infidelity (I think Atheism) in Paris. And the consequence was that, some years afterwards, the question was raised whether his Ordinations and Confirmations at this time had been valid. The question was referred to Rome, and it was decided that his Episcopal acts *were* valid, notwithstanding his professed convictions, and on the grounds that there was no doubt about his Orders, and that, apart from personal convictions, he 'intended to do what the Church intended.' This is a very extreme case, and you will, I think, agree that it more than covers any case of Episcopal unfaithfulness to Truth of which there may be reason to complain among ourselves.

"I would beg you to consider that the evils in our own Church do not by their existence remove the evils in the Church of Rome. And we have a *greater* responsibility before God for the evils of a Church which we adopt, than for those of a Church in which He, by His Providence, has placed us. . . ."

To ———

On the Constitution of a Parochial Council.

"3, Amen Court, St. Paul's, E.C., December 6, 1882.

"The only point on which I ventured to express an opinion was as to the bearing of the question of being a communicant on the proposed Parochial Councils. And I certainly cannot but hope that no one will be elected or will vote at an election who is not a communicant.

"The alternative is really to abandon the religious and Scriptural idea of the Church for the profoundly irreligious fiction—which would have been shocking in the eyes of St. Paul—that every Englishman as such is a member of the National Church. I sometimes fear that nothing but Disestablishment will rid us of this nightmare.

"Why not constitute the Council independently of the church-warden, if unhappily he is not a communicant? No doubt there would be grave practical inconveniences, but the Church would gain in moral power by being true to the principles which alone warrant her existence. The question is largely one of detail, but a practical dead-lock would be a better thing for a parish than a formal recognition of the Anti-Church theory, by incorporating Dissenting or non-communi-cating churchwardens with the Parochial Council.

"If the Parochial Councils became strong, they would live down the opposition of non-communicating churchwardens. But better oppose the whole plan than inaugurate it with a conspicuous act of disloyalty to the very idea of 'the Body of Christ.' The danger lies, no doubt, in the direction of sacrilegious Communions, made with a

X

view to getting parochial influence. This could only be guarded against by insisting on, at least, a *three-year* test—I should like more —as a precedent condition for either vote or candidature."

On a Proposed Protest against the Ill-treatment of the Jews in Russia.

"3, Amen Court, St. Paul's, E.C., January 12, 1882.

". . . I cannot, I fear, altogether follow you in what you say as to our responsibilities in 1882 as compared with 1876.

" What a ' technical ' responsibility may be, I do not understand. A responsibility, if it exists, must be moral ; but there are degrees of moral obligation, and it is upon the difference between a greater and a less degree that I was laying stress.

" England has nothing whatever to do with the position of the Jews in the Russian Empire ; she has in no way contributed to bring that position about, or to maintain it. But it was English diplomacy which, for its own objects, upheld the Turkish power in the Danubian provinces, and this, after being warned of the inevitably brutal character of Turkish rule.

" When, therefore, the outrages of 1876 took place, every reflecting Englishman knew that outrages had taken place which but for the public action of England would have been impossible. This consideration appears to me to establish a very wide difference indeed between the two cases. I do not say that we ought not, as a country, to use our influence with Russia, just as Russia might retaliate by representations on behalf of Mr. Parnell (of course, *I* don't think these cases parallel). But, in the Bulgarian matter the English people had to prevent the perpetration of wrong which England had made possible ; in the present case England is no more responsible for what is done in Russia than for what is done by any independent Power, all the world over, within its own territory, and for the main-tenance of whose empire England has in no way exerted herself. . . .'"

On the Parliamentary Oath, and Mr. Bradlaugh.

"3, Amen Court, St. Paul's, E.C., August, 1880.

" You are probably right about the Oath, and certainly I have no business to be deciding upon the measures which the House of Commons should take with its own members. Only it seems to me as an outsider, that the Oath notoriously breaks down, if considered as a protection of the Theistic belief of the House : and this quite inde-pendently of Mr. Bradlaugh. We both know, or have known, members of the House who are not Theists, but who have no scruple about taking the Oath.

" I see nothing to differentiate, *e.g.*, the late Mr. J. S. Mill's doctrine of the categories in his ' Logic ' from Mr. Bradlaugh's perormances in the *National Reformer*, except that the latter is coarse and repulsive, while the former is interesting to every educated man. Our modern society tolerates any amount of blasphemy against the Being and Attributes of God,—still more against His Revelation of Himself in and through Christ our Lord—if only the blasphemy be thrown into good literary form.   Mr. Bradlaugh's real offence is not his Atheism, but the coarseness which accompanies it; and yet this coarseness is surely a service which he unintentionally renders to Religion.

"When I say that the religious character of the House of Commons is a 'fiction,' I do not forget that it contains a great many excellent Christians.   But it also contains misbelievers and unbelievers in large numbers ; and, alas ! as matters stand, these latter interest themselves quite as actively as do the Christians in the sacred interests of the Church of Christ.   Mr. Bradlaugh's presence in the House will not really add much to the Anti-Christian and Anti-Theistic elements of it ; but it will bring vividly before the mind of the people of this country the unfitness of a legislative body to which he belongs to handle the truths of Divine Revelation and the concerns of the Christian Church. He reduces to a positive absurdity a state of things which for sincere Christians has long been well-nigh intolerable.

"You will say, perhaps, that this is a narrow issue on which to decide a great question.   But there is another point, which I own has great weight with me as a clergyman.

"If Mr. Bradlaugh had been admitted to the House of Commons without any delay, he would have found his level, and in all probability his baneful influence with the people would have been materially lessened, as Mill's certainly was.

"But, as matters have gone, he has made himself a name and a power beyond his wildest expectations.   He has, as somebody said, become part of the history of England ; and he will pose as a Confessor all through this autumn.   His wretched books have now an enormous circulation ; I have had a great many letters from people who have taken to reading him solely in consequence of the vast advertisement which he has secured for himself and for his productions.   The longer the resistance to his entrance to the House goes on, the keener and wider will be the infidel propaganda—a propaganda which is not less serious from a social point of view than from a theological and religious one."

To the Hon. C. L. Wood.

On "John Inglesant."

"Highclere Castle, Newbury, September 2, 1881.

"I have been reading 'John Inglesant'—indeed, have nearly finished it.   The writer knows a great deal about the seventeenth century, though I should suppose that some of his knowledge was unbalanced, while it seems to me that he might perhaps have written a more interesting book if he had known less ; for both plot and characters suffer from the apparently dominant necessity of showing that he is well up in the period. The book is full of antiquarian irrelevancies, and the characters talk, as they never possibly could have talked in life, in order to show that certain districts of feeling or of speculation are familiar to the writer. They talk very like each other ; sentences, cadences, and turns of expression constantly repeating themselves, just as in the speeches in Thucydides, and they cease to talk when the author has said what he had to say, but to the disappointment of the reader who wants to know how the conversation ended, or what is going to happen next. The book gives one the impression of being written by a man who had taken up the study of the classics (especially Plato) and of theology late in life, and was overpowered by his acquisitions, or, at any rate, unable to digest them. He further appears to me to welcome with an indiscriminating crudeness all sorts of foolish mysticisms, and he lets John Inglesant become a novice in a monastery near Florence, and come out again (apparently from and into the English Church) as if these transitions were the easiest possible thing for an English Churchman in the middle of the seventeenth century. The book has unquestionable merits."

"September 5, 1881.

" I am leaving for Dover at 12.30, but send one line of good-bye and of modification of what I said about ' John Inglesant.' I still think that the writer's learning is too much for his digestion, and that he must have read Plato, etc., late in life, and without succeeding in perfectly assimilating them. Besides which, in the descriptions of the Renaissance (life and art), upon which he has expended much pains, and which I like *least*, I trace the influence of J. A. Symonds and Pater. But his description of the converted Malvolti is very fine, and sets one quite aglow, and he has a fair idea of intellectual justice towards Religious Orders and Churches. Only I cannot understand how John Inglesant himself springs about, out of one Communion into another and back again, like a young goat upon the hill-tops."

On the London City Churches.

" 3, Amen Court, St. Paul's, E.C., January 26, 1883.

" I sincerely sympathise with the effort to insist, while there is yet time, upon 'the importance of the City churches.' This importance by no means depends only on their historical or religious associations. They might be made, I believe, of great practical service to the vast population which is crowded into the City of London during the working hours of week-days, while the attendance in them on Sundays is not a real measure of the needs of the resident population.

"The first necessity of the Church in the City is that the clergy should reside, should visit their parishioners constantly, and should be at their call whether by day or by night. As a rule, whether in town or country, a well-visited parish means a well-attended church. I do not forget that some of the City clergy—as, for instance, the Rev. W. Rogers, of Bishopsgate—are most constant residents ; and in such cases, I believe, there is always a good attendance at the parish church. In some cases, too, there is no residence within the parish, but too often the Rectory or Vicarage is let for purposes which have no other relation to Church work than that of augmenting the income of the incumbent. If the clergy generally resided in the City, as they do elsewhere, and it was still found that the existing number of City churches was larger than is needed by the parochial population, some of the superfluous buildings might still be preserved and applied to the work of special Missions to different classes of the population of London. Thus the cabmen, the police, the telegraph and postal services, might each have their own church, with a clergyman devoted to the spiritual charge of them. Such 'parishes' would not be 'territorial ;' they would be created and secured by the *esprit de corps*, which is generally found among those who have a common occupation. If, after all, some churches were still thought to be superfluous, they would be removed with a better conscience when a serious effort had been made to make the best use of them. Until this is done, we do not know how many churches the City population really needs. Nobody would have his measure taken for a new suit of clothes at a time when he had been reduced by neglect of the plain rules of health to something like a skeleton."

CHAPTER XI.

ROSMINI'S "FIVE WOUNDS"—LIFE IN LONDON—DE-
SCRIPTION OF HIS PREACHING AT ST. PAUL'S—
PROPOSED FOR A BISHOPRIC—"NOLO EPISCOPARI"
—TOUR IN EGYPT AND THE HOLY LAND.

1883–1885.

THE change that came over Liddon's life after 1882 was
very great. All his London work was as it had been
since 1870 ; but his Oxford work was radically altered.
When he resigned his Professorship he gave up all relation
to Academical work, even refusing to have a place on the
Board which regulated Theological Studies. He still retained his Studentship at Christ Church, and resided there
for the same length of time as before ; and as a rule he
gave his Sunday evening Lectures to undergraduates. But
the heavy correspondence about the Pusey Memorial and
the claims that Pusey's "Life" made on him had the
first claim on the time he spent in Oxford. Hence he fell
out of touch with the ordinary Academical life ; he did not
meet his fellow-Professors or his pupils as before, and
the "Life of Pusey" naturally caused his thoughts to
dwell far more on the literature and the needs of the first
half of the century than of the second.

That he might devote himself exclusively to the great
biography, all other literary work was laid aside as soon
as possible. From 1880 to 1882 he had spent a very
long while in preparing an edition of St. Augustine's
"De Doctrinâ Christianâ ;" this he never looked at
again after Pusey's death. For years he had been committed, by a promise that he made to Bishop Forbes

of Brechin, to publish a translation of Rosmini's "Five Wounds of the Church," and long before Pusey's death he had asked a friend to translate it for him. This translation he received in 1882, and spent many laborious hours in endeavouring to correct it into a more exact reproduction of the original. From such a weary waste of his time he was relieved, to his very great joy, by another friend, "one of our best Italian scholars," whose able assistance enabled him to publish the book early in 1883.

Bishop Forbes's hope in laying this burden on Liddon was that the book would have its bearings on English Church life, while it would also show what some of the best minds in the Roman Communion were thinking of their own Church. But Liddon is careful in his Preface to point out that the writer is not an author whom an English Churchman can accept unreservedly; for he is an "unfaltering" and "a conscientious" Ultramontane; and not only his phraseology but also his historical and moral estimates are coloured by this radical defect. This necessary reserve in dealing with Rosmini, combined with the pressure of work much nearer his heart, made the whole task most unwelcome and wearisome. In his diary he repeatedly laments over such a way of using his time. He resolutely refused, at the risk of whatever misunderstandings, to enter a single step into the intricacies of the heated controversy respecting his author, but he persevered in strictly fulfilling his promise to his friend. At last he sent the translation forth, to his own great relief, and not without some hope that his toil would be of real value; for he was certain that, when all allowances had been made, Rosmini's readers would find themselves "in communion with a sincere and beautiful mind which those who come after us will not improbably deem one of God's greatest gifts to Western Christendom in the present century" (Preface, p. xxv.).[1]

[1] In an elaborate passage in Lord Acton's published Letters (pp. 184–186) he severely criticises Liddon for translating this book. He says, "My real difficulty is that he speaks of his author with great respect, and evidently thinks his doctrines sound and profitable." The first charge is

He was now at liberty to devote himself to the preparation of "Dr. Pusey's Life," and this he did with characteristic thoroughness. He received from Dr. Pusey's daughter, Mrs. Brine, an immense mass of papers, private letters, manuscripts of books, published and unpublished, sermons, pamphlets, notices of meetings, University papers—all in hopeless confusion. In addition to this, Pusey's letters were sent him from every side, pages of a minute and almost illegible hand. All these had to be sorted, arranged, and in many cases copied. He had at least a hundred bound volumes of copies of letters and papers which were made for the purpose of the "Life." The letters which Pusey had received were also carefully arranged, and bound if they were from any one whose influence was of weight in the Oxford Movement or who was high in Pusey's friendship. There were some fifty of these volumes, besides a large number of bundles of letters sorted carefully for reference. He made elaborate notes of every conversation that he had with Pusey's old friends, whom he travelled far to see. He ransacked all the family records for traditions of the Pusey family; he travelled to Lille, Douai, Liège, Brussels, Ghent, and Bruges, to find traces of the Bouverie family, from which the "great Doctor" was descended. The preparations were indeed most lengthy and elaborate, and some of them he allowed others to do for him; but the work of writing which fell on himself alone, was a burden, lovingly borne indeed, but a very heavy burden, until the end. Every fact had to be stated most exactly and minutely in order to satisfy his scrupulous sense of what was due to his subject; and the length of his analyses of Pusey's works and early Sermons was beyond all possible proportions for a biography. When Pusey died it certainly seemed as if Liddon were the proper person to write his

true; and no one could attack Liddon for it unless he joined with this distinguished Roman Catholic writer and many extreme Protestants in an indiscriminating condemnation of all Ultramontanes. The latter charge is not altogether true, for Liddon's recommendation of the book is qualified by his Preface and his Notes.

life. In one sense he was, not only because of his literary
power, but because no one else was more intimate with
Pusey, or more full of devotion to his memory ; nor did
any one possess more fully the confidence of all who could
contribute materials for the " Life." But we may well wish
that the burden of the work had been entrusted to some
other hand. It seems strange that it did not occur to any
of his friends that to a mind so exact and subtle as Liddon's
the work of such a biography would be of necessity endless ;
and, as will be seen, the attempt to complete it compelled him to refuse far more important work for which
his singular powers specially marked him out, and to wear
away his strength in a drudgery which a less gifted person
might well have borne in his stead. Beyond any other
one cause, the attempt to write Pusey's " Life " led to
Liddon's comparatively early death.

His daily life in London, when he was in residence at
St. Paul's, admits of little description. His house at No. 3,
Amen Court, was brightened by the companionship of his
sister, Mrs. Ambrose, who lived with him there for the
twenty years that he was Canon. Not only did she enter
most keenly into all his interests, but her presence bound
up all his work in London into the closest connection with
his early home life, which had always such a deep place in
his affection. His mornings were filled with letter-writing ;
in the afternoon he took a walk on the Embankment, either
with his sister or with some one who wished to consult
him. In these walks he made acquaintance with many
of the police, and with poor people, especially with the
"gamins," who used to wheedle pennies from him by
making "wheels" for his amusement. For many years
every Saturday, when he was in residence, he gave up his
afternoons to taking parties of men over the Cathedral,
explaining carefully every detail, and making it as interesting to them as he could.

The Cathedral was, of course, the centre of all his
work. There was no part of its life in which he did not

take the warmest interest.   Not only important Chapter business, and great questions about the music, the Services, and the more worthy decoration of the building, but every question of arrangement and order, and any detail about choir boys and vergers always commanded his interests.

His sermons took up, of necessity, a very large portion of his time and of his strength.   Preaching had always been a great strain to him.   When he went to St. Paul's as Canon, he gave up preaching without notes, as had for very many years been his regular habit except when he was preaching before the University ; and he carefully wrote out every word of his sermons, and delivered them as a rule exactly as they were written.   A comparison between his manuscripts and his sermons as printed in newspapers from the shorthand notes of reporters, show how closely he adhered to what he had written.   As one of his reasons for giving up extempore preaching, he used to say that he found that the constant effort to control his voice so as to suit the acoustic conditions of the Cathedral distracted his attention and made clearness of thought more difficult. Certainly the change must have given him some real relief, but still the delivery even of the written sermons always greatly exhausted him, and after he had preached in the afternoon he could do little for the rest of the day except read the Lessons at the great evening Service.

It was very seldom that he would undertake to preach anywhere except at St. Paul's in his later years ; in fact, after 1870 he greatly disappointed friends who felt that they had a real claim on him and whose claim he was ready to admit, by refusing to accept their most pressing invitations.   He felt that he owed all his strength, such as it was, to his London and Oxford work.   The following letter is one of very many which he had to write :—

To _____

"Christ Church, June 16, 1881.

". . . As to preaching at ——, I am in the same difficulty with I know not how many other places and friends.   My work here and in London can only be done by myself ; I can never transfer any part of it to a curate. And in both places much of it is very undemonstrative, but very engrossing, so that, at the end of Term, as now, I feel quite tired out, and have had lately, as I told you, to give up my public Lectures owing to a succession of violent headaches. Within three weeks of writing to you I had declined invitations to preach from three Bishops, and from I know not how many friends and pupils, who have in all senses a first claim on me. I should not write this, except with the object of showing that 'coldness and contempt' have nothing whatever to do with my not accepting your invitation. The fact is, you and others, in your kindness, make a great mistake about me ; you give me credit for unlimited resources both of mind and body, whereas I am in reality a poor creature who has soon got to the end of his tether, and ought to make way for younger men who have not lost their energy and freshness.

" Besides which, as we get on in life (I am now well on the wrong side of fifty), we have to ask ourselves how we can do the best for God's glory with what may yet remain of time and strength. And, speaking for myself, I used to believe more in the value of single sermons, preached about the country to congregations of whom I knew nothing, than I have of late years. Even if I were more at liberty and stronger than I am, I should doubt whether this was the best way of working, *if* the only end of work that we shall think anything about hereafter is to be kept steadily in view. With others, of course, it may be different ; God gives us very dissimilar capacities and gifts ; and I am speaking only of myself.

" However, no more. Only, dear ——, do not think me unfriendly because I am less of a hero, and much more useless, than you have hitherto supposed."

The characteristics of his Sermons at St. Paul's are sketched in the following passages by men who were well qualified to judge of them. The first estimate is from a letter by Dr. Benson, afterwards the Archbishop of Canterbury. It is printed with the date that is given in his " Life " (vol. i. p. 403) ; but the sermon to which it refers was preached at St. Paul's on August 27, 1876 :—

" July 26, 1876.

" I have been hearing Liddon at St. Paul's. Very beautiful and very eloquent, yet the *art* part of it does not seem so unattainable. But he unites many charms. His beautiful look and penetrating voice are powerful over one, and then his reasoning is very persuasive. He does not make leaps, and dismiss one with allusions, or assume that one knows anything. He tells it all from beginning to end, and seems to assume nothing. But all his physical and intellectual structure is quite swallowed up in spiritual earnestness,[1] and he is different to other preachers, in that one feels that his preaching in itself is a self-sacrifice to him—not a vanity nor a gain. I do not mean that one feels others' preaching to be these, but with him one is conscious that it is the opposite. He does not look as if he were in pain, yet you can't help thinking of it. I gather from his sermon that there is no danger, as has been thought, of his taking up Disestablishment. The subject was the feast at Levi's. Besides the more obvious applications, he said the Church, too, must be like her Master in order to do His work ; must eat with publicans and sinners —cannot leave the world to itself, as Donatists and Puritans would, but must sit down at its feast of art, literature, society, government, legislation—not always unhurt by it, for she is not sinless like her Master, but still she is bound in this way to work out His scheme for the world."

In one of Dr. Bright's note-books[2] in the Keble College Library, there is a striking passage on one feature of Liddon's Sermons—

" One of the signal excellences of Liddon's preaching was his power of *vitalising* Scripture events, and bringing them into close relation with the present. Thus, in the volume of Sermons on the Old Testament, we find vivid sketches of the trials of a clergyman in an unpromising parish, where he cannot expect to live long enough to produce an effect ; of invalids trying to make out that they are not so ill as their friends suppose ; of women encouraged to rival men in the sphere of professional or public life ; of those who talk about spiritual religion while mainly intent on buttoning up their pockets. (Here comes in the ironical alteration of David's words about the Temple ; the modern spirit would say, 'Of course we must have a temple, but it must be *exceeding cheap.*' The 'old Prophet of Bethel' reminds him of a worldly old incumbent cynically discouraging the enthusiasm of a young curate ; Ahab objecting to consult Micaiah is like a man who suspects he has a mortal disease, but will not follow the doctor's advice. Naaman's ' Behold, I thought,' is illustrated by the craving for a more imposing Church authority, or a brilliant philosophical theory, or by preference of a ' scientific lecture' to a sermon ; or Solomon's cosmopolitanism in religion by the unbalanced eagerness to be in 'sympathy' with other creeds, etc. ; or ' How shall we sing the Lord's song?' suggests the anomalousness of making sacred music 'the amusement of an infidel audience.' There surely never was a preacher who, in dealing with the past, had his eyes more thoroughly and practically

---

[1] A writer in the *Saturday Review* of August 24, 1889, expressed the same feeling about Liddon ; he said that in his sermons the whole argument is steeped in emotion. "The light is never dry."

[2] "Sylva" [see "Letters and Memoir of W. Bright, D.D.," p. lxxvi.], xxxv. pp. 367–371.

H. M. Paget. Pinx.   T. & R. Annan & Sons. Pho. Sc.

Henry Parry Liddon.

(1885)

open to the present, who felt more intensely the 'solidarity' between human nature in modern England and human nature in the days before the Incarnation. What made Liddon so *vitalising* a preacher? What but his supreme devotion to a Christ *alive for evermore?*"

In the *Guardian* for July 24, 1889, there is a masterly estimate of the points of excellence in Liddon's sermons— of "his characteristic ways of thinking and working," which were some of the contributory causes of his remarkable influence. It is, unfortunately, too long to be quoted here in full; the following passages give its chief points :—

"1. It is often said that there is 'something very French' in Dr. Liddon's preaching ; and, apart from certain superficial traits which may commonly suggest the criticism, there is an important group of qualities in which it may find real justification. They are the qualities which are summed up fairly well in the word *lucidity*. Dr. Liddon sees clearly what he wants to say, and no capable person who really attends to him will fail to see it also clearly and accurately. . . . One knows that beyond the hedge there are vast tracts of country stretching into untraversed distance ;[1] but the road is in faultless order, the sign-posts are frequent and explicit ; and, while for the most vigorous the interest of the walk never flags, the simplest and least imaginative are in no danger of losing their way. . . . But lucidity requires sustained watchfulness at many points ; and in Dr. Liddon's work one can see some of its conditions admirably illustrated. For, in the first place, his sermons are always methodical in structure. He is frank even to shamelessness in telling his hearers when they are to gird up their attention to a new point of departure. He is far too wise to forego the old-fashioned *firstly, secondly, thirdly,* and *in conclusion.* In the second place, lucidity is guarded by the precision of outlines. Whether the subject is described at length, or gathered up into an epigram, there is no mistake as to the lines and no wavering in the hand that draws them. . . . His work has also a third characteristic of the highest value for the attainment of lucidity. It is always deliberate ; nothing is done *per saltum* or allusively ; nothing is left unexplained ; hardly any knowledge is presumed. With polite adroitness, he manages respectfully to convey to a critical congregation the most elementary, but by no means unnecessary instruction [*e.g.* he explains in detail what a covenant is ; and that the ark was 'an oblong chest or box, made out of shittim wood, a variety of acacia,' etc.].

"2. Closely connected with this is his singular power of leading a large and diverse crowd through the course of a careful argument. . . . His arguments certainly are not superficial ; they are often very thorough and exacting ; they always rest on real learning. But he

[1] One of his reasons for this " hedge " is given in a letter on p. 230.

is a master of the art of so wielding logic that the mass of men can see its drift and outcome, and . . . lay hold on the conclusion with a fresh grasp, as a real acquisition that they have made their own.

" 3. It is probable that much of Dr. Liddon's power depends upon a third characteristic : . . . his sincere and unfailing respect for those to whom he preaches. It is not often that one whose gifts are so rare and brilliant . . . can refrain so steadily from any sign of conscious superiority in their exercise. He cannot be unconscious of his remarkable gifts ; but he is much more vividly conscious of certain other things, about which he is quite sure that they matter infinitely more than the advantages of intellect and training. The supremacy of goodness ; the issues that are within sight when Divine Truth is being presented to immortal souls ; the tremendous gravity of any work that is done in God's Name ; the beauty and the greatness and the severity of the Gospel ;—these are vivid and dominant in his mind, and they make it as inappropriate and impertinent to be thinking of intellectual advantages or natural ability as it would be to presume on good looks or high connections in a storm at sea. Men may not always like what Dr. Liddon says to them ; they may sometimes say he is too confident ; but no fair critic can deny that all his confidence rests wholly and simply in his message, and none of it in himself or his ability.

" 4. Analogous to the use of logic without stiffness is the wielding of learning without pedantry. There is not to be found in all his sermons nearly as much pedantry as many a young man has assumed after a hasty glance at the ' Dictionary of the Bible.' . . .

" 5. One more characteristic . . . is peculiarly clear in the sermons he has preached at St. Paul's, as the years were drawing to an end— the note of steady and resolute reference to the plain duties of life. Practice, conduct, character—these are never out of sight when Dr. Liddon preaches. People may not be prepared to link their daily life with the great truths of which he speaks ; but they are made to feel that it might be done. . . . All along the sermon protests against being treated as anything but practical ; it is wholly bent on getting at the conscience . . . If a man is really wanting, among the difficulties and temptations of London, to live, by the grace of God, a pure and honourable and religious life, he is fairly sure to feel the reality of Dr. Liddon's insight into the practical trials which beset the effort. [In listening to him, men] learn from one who is much more than a great scholar, theologian, and orator : one who knows them with a strangely penetrating sympathy and insight ; one who seems somehow quite naturally to take his stand with them in their temptations, and who, for all his understanding of their lives, or for all his undisguised severity, is not afraid to point them to the very highest hope that can enter into the heart of man.

" Such seem to be some of the elements of Dr. Liddon's power as a preacher. They are qualities of a very fine order ; and when they are controlled and animated by an intense conviction of the absolute certainty of the Divine Revelation, by an absorbing zeal for the salvation of men, by a fearless trust in God, and by a constant recollection of our Saviour's Presence, and of the Day of Judgment, it is not strange that they should hold a great place in the life and hope of England."[1]

Whilst Liddon was still collecting the materials for Pusey's biography, some of his most influential friends were planning for him a very different occupation for the remainder of his life. In July, 1883, soon after Dr. Benson had been translated from Truro to Canterbury, the Dean of St. Paul's had, with some insistence, laid before him his reasons for thinking that it would be a great mistake if Liddon were not soon made a Bishop. A few days later he followed up his conversation by a letter.

The Dean of St. Paul's to the Archbishop of Canterbury.

"The Deanery, St. Paul's, July 23, 1883.

". . . Will you let me return to the charge about Liddon? Of course, knowing him as I do, I know what all the world sees and knows of him. He is a man of strong opinions, and he is a man who has the courage of his opinions, and would, if the occasion arose, make every sacrifice rather than surrender what he held to be vital truth. This, which ought to be said of any man, is eminently true of him. He has, too, the dangerous gift of epigrams, and an incisive tongue to give them force; and, from natural disposition, he is inclined to look on the darker and more anxious side of things, and has done so too much at Oxford. But the course of things in Oxford has been such as to tempt less desponding men to doubt sometimes whether the fight was worth fighting. There has been great cause for over-powering distress to a man who feels so deeply and so keenly as he does. But I do not think he has deserted his duty there. He has fought valiantly, though it would have been much better if he had not fought so sadly. But I quite admit that there might be risks in putting him into high place. Occasions might come, as, *e.g.*, if Parliament were to deal roughly with the Prayer-Book, when he would retire rather than submit, though I do not think any occasions would affect him which would not affect me as much. But, though this is a danger, it must be remembered that there are dangers on the other side. There is danger in ostracising such a man as Liddon. My own experience in life has made me feel the mischiefs of distrust and over-fear of powerful men, who, if they had been welcomed and trusted,

[1] *Guardian*, vol. xliv. pp. 1125–6.

might have been a strength instead of a worry and something more mischievous. And then it must be remembered what Liddon has to bring to the counsels of the Episcopate. He is an accomplished theologian, even of European reputation. And, further, I believe that there are few men in England so much in touch with the deeper and more alarming forms of the anti-religious movement, both in England and abroad, more alive to its dangers, and who could tell so much about it from personal acquaintance, both with literature and persons. I cannot help thinking that the knowledge which he could impart might often prove most valuable.

" Of course, we all wish that our friends had just some one or two qualities which would make their other gifts more useful, and there is more than one point in H. P. L. which I could wish otherwise. But I think they are, for the most part, those points which are tempered and harmonised by the elevating and sobering influence—to a man of his calibre—of great place. It is more than you can say of any man, that he may not make great mistakes. I dare say Liddon would make them, as Archbishop Tait made them. . . . But I don't think that Liddon would make irretrievable ones. If he accepted a Bishopric, of which I am not sure, he would do it with a statesmanlike knowledge that he could not have everything that he could wish, or according to his mind. And I cannot but think that he would be a great Bishop, and one who, if he did not always agree with all his brethren, would be of the greatest help and value to them."

At about the same time similar arguments were being laid before Mr. Gladstone from a very different quarter. All the allusions to Liddon in the " Letters of Lord Acton to Mary Gladstone " (George Allen, 1904) have a special interest. Lord Acton met him first at Dr. Döllinger's house at Tegernsee, in June, 1880. " I have made Liddon's acquaintance at last," he says. " Nothing but Tennyson prevented me from seeing more of him, for I found in him all that I love Oxford for, and only a very little of what I dislike in it " (p. 21).

This "very little" is perhaps partly explained a few pages later, where Lord Acton, in enumerating the traits of Mr. Gladstone's mind, includes " the microscopic subtlety and care in the choice of words, in guarding against mis-interpretation and in correcting it, which belonged to the Oxford training, which, even in such eminent men as Newman and Liddon, is nearly a vice."

In March, 1884, Lord Acton very eagerly pressed the

claims of Liddon on Mr. Gladstone for elevation to a vacant
Bishopric. He admitted—

"I am not in harmony with Liddon, and scarcely in sympathy.
He has weak places that nobody sees and resents so sharply as I do ;
and he has got over or swallowed such obstacles on the road to Rome
that none remain which, as it seems to me, he ought logically or
legitimately to strain at. . . . Nothing steadies a ship like a mitre.
And as to his soundness, his determination to work in and through
the Church, and not on eccentric courses, I satisfied myself with the
supreme authority of Dean Church on my last night in town. One
cannot help seeing that Liddon is a mighty force not yet on its level.
He knows how to kindle and how to propel. Newman and Wilberforce may have had the same power ; but one was almost illiterate,
the other knows what he might have learnt in the time of Waterland
or Butler ; whereas Liddon is in contact with all that is doing in the
world of thought" (p. 180).

Three months later, in June, 1884, he writes again on
the same subject, but with far more knowledge and insight
than is shown in the reference to the "road to Rome" in
the last extract.

"It was not my purpose to depreciate Canon Liddon. I came
over with the highest opinion of him—an opinion higher, perhaps, than
Dr. Döllinger's, or even than Mr. Gladstone's, whose ostensible preference for Divines of less mark has sometimes set me thinking.
Impressed by his greatness, not as a scholar to be pitted against
Germans, but as a spiritual force, and also by a certain gracious
nobleness of tone which ought to be congenial, I tried, at Oxford
and in London, to ascertain whether there is some element of weakness that had escaped me.

"Evidently Liddon is in no peril from the movement of modern
science. He has faced those problems and accounted for them. If
he is out of the perpendicular, it is because he leans the other way.

"The question would rather be whether a man of his sentiments,
rather inclined to rely on others, would be proof against the influence
of Newman, or of foreign theologians like Newman.

"On the road Bishops and Parliament were taking a few years
since there would be rocks ahead, and one might imagine a crisis
in which it would be doubtful who would be for maintaining the
National Church and who would not. I have chanced to be familiar
with converts, and with the raw material of which they are made, and
cannot help knowing the distinct and dissimilar paths followed by
men like Newman himself, Hope, Palmer, R. J. Wilberforce, Ward,
Renouf, many of whom resembled Liddon in talent and fervour, and
occupied a position outwardly not far from his own. . . .

Y

"Putting these questions not quite so crudely as they are stated here, I thought that I obtained an answer. At any rate, I was assured that Liddon is made of sterner stuff than I fancied, that he knows exactly where he stands, where others have stood before him, and where and why he parts with them ; that the course of Newman and the rest has no secrets and no surprises for him ; that he looks a long way before him, and has no disposition to cling to the authority of others. In short, it appeared very decidedly that he is—what Bishop Forbes was not—fixed in his Anglican position.

"Under this impression I could not help wondering why Wilkinson, Stubbs, and Ridding are judged superior to Liddon. I could have felt and have expressed no such wonder, if I had not taken pains to discover that he has tried and has rejected the cause of Rome, and that neither home difficulties nor external influence are at all likely to shake him" (pp. 182–3).[1]

At the very beginning of 1885, while the See of Lincoln was waiting for a new Bishop because of the resignation of Dr. Wordsworth, the See of London also suddenly became vacant. Bishop Jackson preached in St. Paul's on Sunday, January 4, and died on Tuesday, and was buried at Fulham on the Saturday following. Liddon was at this time paying one of his regular visits to Sir Robert Phillimore ; but this was to be his last, for his friend died in less than a month after the date of this letter.

To the Hon. C. L. Wood.

"The Coppice, Henley-on-Thames, January 8, 1885.

"This morning I had the great happiness of administering the Blessed Sacrament to Sir Robert Phillimore ; but ever since have been shut up in my room by acute neuralgia, which, if it does not mend, will prevent my being at the Bishop's funeral on Saturday. What a sudden call from an active life his has been ! and what a warning it is to us all to be, by God's grace, ready ! I own I think of him with pleasure. He was not a strong man ; but he was, according to the tenor of his convictions—a servant of our Lord, and not of the world. We, at St. Paul's, may find in his successor a less friendly Visitor by far—possibly a King Stork.

"Since October, Sir Robert has gone down the hill. He moves with greater difficulty, and takes less part in conversation. When he

[1] This is followed by a long passage written from the point of view of a "close student of Roman pathology," in which he severely criti-cises Liddon for translating Rosmini's "Five Wounds." This criticism has already been alluded to (see note, p. 299).

does speak about matters long past, or of abstract, as distinct from immediate, interest, the old mind is there quite unimpaired. To me his removal when it comes, will be a very great loss; I have learnt to feel for him a very great and always increasing affection and respect, and he has been closely mixed up with others, like Bishop Hamilton, who have left us."

As soon as Bishop Jackson died, Lord Acton and many others began at once to urge on Mr. Gladstone that Liddon ought to be appointed either to London or to Lincoln. A few days later, on January 14, Lord Acton describes the arguments with which he had been pressing the Prime Minister.[1]

". . . It is clear, very clear to me, that it would not be right to pass Liddon over now that there are two important vacancies to fill ; and one asks one's self why he should not be chosen for the more important of the two ; and who is manifestly worthier to occupy the greatest See in Christendom ? The real answer, I suppose, is that his appointment will give great offence, and that he is a decided partisan, and a partisan of nearly the same opinions as the Prime Minister himself.

"No doubt there would be much irritation on the thorough Protestant side, and in quarters very near Downing Street, and I feel myself more strongly than most people that partisanship in Liddon runs to partiality, to one-sidedness, to something very like prejudice. And with all that strong feeling, I cannot help being agitated with the hope that the great and Providential opportunity will not be lost.

"Assuredly Liddon is the greatest power in the conflict with sin, and in turning the souls of men to God, that the nation now possesses. He is also among all the clergy the man best known to numbers of Londoners. There must be a very strong reason to justify a Minister in refusing such a Bishop to such a diocese. . . .

"So eminent a representative of Church principles has not occupied the See of London within living memory, and there is a balance to redress. When I think of his lofty and gracious spirit, his eloquence, his radiant spirituality, all the objections which I might feel, vanish entirely. . . .

"One qualification ought to be remembered. He is more in contact than other Churchmen with questions of the day. Not only Politics and Criticism, but Science. Paget delights to relate how Owen was discoursing on the brevity of life in the days of the Patriarchs, and how beautifully Liddon baffled him by asking whether there is any structural reason for a cockatoo to live ten times as long as a pigeon. . . . The Dean assures me that Pusey being gone, Liddon will be under no personal influence, that he has more confidence in himself and more backbone than I was able to discover for myself."

[1] "Letters of Lord Acton," pp. 201–204.

At the same moment, letters of a very different character were of course reaching Mr. Gladstone ; and even before Bishop Jackson's funeral, he had written to the Dean of St. Paul's to inquire from one who was above all the best qualified, both by wisdom and by personal knowledge, to speak on the subject, what weight he attached to the objections which were alleged against Liddon. The Dean replied in a long letter addressed to Mr. Hamilton, the Prime Minister's private secretary, covering much the same ground as his letter to the Archbishop eighteen months earlier, and ending in the following words :—

"The Deanery, St. Paul's, January 8, 1885.

" As to his willingness to accept [a Bishopric], that is really a point on which I cannot say that I know anything. I do not think that his work or his likings would weigh with him if he felt it the call of duty. But although he must have heard people for years talking all round him of this kind of thing, he never to me made a sign,—with all his interest in such appointments, and his interest is always very great.

" I earnestly hope, for the honour of the Church of England, that it will be possible, in some way, to recognise a man who is not only her greatest preacher, but, as I believe, her most learned theologian, and whatever criticisms may be passed on him, one of the most brilliant intellects and most attractive characters among her clergy."

The Dean's reply was quite convincing to Mr. Gladstone ; he sent it at once to Archbishop Benson for his opinion.

THE RIGHT HON. W. E. GLADSTONE TO THE ARCHBISHOP OF CANTERBURY.

"Hawarden Castle, Chester, January 9, 1885.

" . . . The Church of England has suffered heavily within my recollection from the unnatural suppression of men who were in themselves great powers. I cannot but feel that that definition (of a great power, not of suppression) strictly applies to Dr. Liddon. He has been nearly the first to associate a great thinking force with the masteries of a first-rate preacher. To hear him is, I apprehend, the advice [that] would be given to, or the course which would be spontaneously taken by, an inquiring unbeliever. May he not perhaps be called the first champion of belief ? It is in this light that he appears to me so strong as to be entitled to have his claims *considered* carefully. Should your Grace's judgment be favourable, I should think it well to learn, if possible, privately what his own inclinations are."

The Archbishop entirely agreed. "There is nothing," he said, "I so deeply lament as the miserable policies of exclusion." His great and only fear was lest Liddon, "*liking* (as the Dean of St. Paul's had said) to feel the courage of his convictions, and having the spirit of the resolute fighter in avowed controversy," might not, as a Bishop, "some day find some uncompromising protest dearer than the love of unity" within the Episcopate. The Archbishop was sure that, as a rule, Liddon's gentle and winning nature would make for peace : and "a fresh responsibility might make sad steps strengthen themselves." If Mr. Gladstone should decide that it was right to appoint him, "he would be one of the foremost undoubtedly of all English Bishops of all time," and would have the most warm welcome from the rest of the Episcopal Bench.

Accordingly, on January 23, Liddon received this letter from the Dean of St. Paul's—

From the Dean of St. Paul's.

"January 22, 1885.

"I hope I am not venturing on too great a liberty with you, but I am asked this question, which I cannot answer of my own knowledge or even surmise. 'Do you think that Dr. Liddon would take a Bishopric if it was proposed to him?' You see I am asking an unusual and delicate question in every point of view, and it is desirable that I should have some grounds on which I could give an answer. It must not be understood that I am conveying to you any proposal ; but it would be very convenient if I was able to give even a qualified answer.

"You will, I believe, not doubt what I hope the answer would be, which you would enable me to give. We must, I suppose, make up our minds to very varying elements in the Episcopate. But there seems more disposition to work together in a wise and just direction than there has been for a long time, and any additional contribution of strength is a great gain. I should be thankful for an answer as soon as it is possible for you to give it, even by telegraph if possible, to save time."

The entry in the diary (January 23) mentions the letter, and adds—

"I telegraphed that Dr. L. most earnestly desired never to be obliged to consider the subject. On reaching London I had one and a half hour's talk with the Dean of St. Paul's.[1] The Dean urged me to reconsider my answer, and to say that my name might be submitted to the Queen, but I could not make up my mind that this would be right. So that nightmare is, I trust, at an end. This most anxious question has given me a great heartache. *Domine, miserere.*

"*January* 29.—It is announced this evening that Dr. Temple, Bishop of Exeter, accepts the See of London.

"*January* 30.—At Mr. Ellis' shop in Bond Street, I met ——, who asked me if I was not going to be Bishop of Exeter. He had heard all about it, what the Queen said, what Mr. Gladstone said, what I said. He 'did not generally believe these stories.'

"*January* 31.—Heard from King to the effect that he has accepted the See of Lincoln. 'I dared not refuse. I could not face the men here, if staying from my own choice, against God's Will.'"

A note in the diary of the same day records also the appointment of Dr. Bickersteth to the See of Exeter. It was a great personal relief to Liddon that all the vacant Sees were now filled; and as he had agreed with the Dean of St. Paul's that something must be said in general terms about what had happened, he felt at liberty to tell his story in strict confidence to his most intimate friend, in reply to some complaints against Mr. Gladstone's Ecclesiastical appointments.

To the Hon. C. L. Wood.

"Christ Church, February 3, 1885.

"Here, in justice to Mr. G., I must tell you something, *in entire confidence.* Some days before Bishop Temple's appointment was announced, he sent me a message through the Dean of St. Paul's, to inquire whether I would take a Bishopric! He said nothing about any particular See. And while I should have had great and sore misgivings in answering *any* specific proposal, I could not but answer the general question in the negative. To have done otherwise would have been to be false to the whole Tractarian (*i.e.* the Patristic and Catholic) tradition on the subject. What would St. Ambrose have said to a willingness to accept a Bishopric *in the abstract?* What would Dr. Pusey or Mr. Keble have said? My reply was that I earnestly hoped to be spared the great anxiety of answering such a question. This put an end to the matter for good and all: but had I given an affirmative reply, I should have been offered, not Exeter,

---

[1] See p. 152.

but Lincoln. So at least the Dean of St. Paul's thinks, in the light of what has since happened. . . .

"Had I accepted, King would not have been a Bishop. I should have been at Lincoln, only, it *may* be, balanced against something more decidedly Puritan than Bickersteth at Exeter. Surely they are much better as they are? I feel so *ex intimo corde*.

"I must implore you to consider this as *strictly confidential*, but I cannot bear having secrets with you on these matters. Not a soul in Oxford knows what has passed. It will, I think, convince you that in one respect at least Mr. G. has not acted as you suppose. He is, as to that matter, in the greatest difficulties. But also—I think you must not think of Salisbury. As far as I am concerned, *res finita est*, in virtue of what has taken place.

"And surely this is not other than well. I am much freer than I ever could be as a Bishop. I doubt whether I should not be a bad administrator, and so get Churchmanship and the Episcopal Bench into discredit; and most assuredly I am altogether wanting in the sympathy and lofty spirituality of character which are so full of the highest promise for the Episcopate which is about to begin in the throne of St. Hugh. It is better, far better, as it is."

His correspondent really knew far more about what had been happening than Liddon did, and took a very different view of it. But Liddon was quite clear that he could not have acted otherwise; and with great happiness, at Dr. King's request, preached the sermon at his Consecration on April 25. In it he described the origin and claims of the Episcopate, and maintained that it is both organically necessary to the structure of the visible Body of Christ, and also a part of the revealed Will of God for the government of the Church. Historically, he argued, the Episcopate is in years the most venerable of public institutions in modern Europe, "older than any secular throne," and "by some centuries older than the Papacy." The sermon was published under the title "A Father in Christ." On all sides it was vehemently attacked by Evangelicals, Nonconformists, Scotch Presbyterians, and Roman Catholics. The "war" went on for twelve months, and Liddon would point with much amusement to a bulky volume of the pamphlets and letters which were hurled at him in the course of it.[1]

[1] Some letters in defence of the Sermon will be found at the end of this chapter.

The loss of Dr. King from Oxford left a great gap in the rapidly diminishing circle of his most intimate friends there. "Everything desolate without dear King!" he notes as soon as he returns to Christ Church. "His house now quite empty." But it was soon filled again, and that by one whose departure from Oxford for a country living he had sorrowfully recorded but two years before. In his diary on March 14, 1883, he writes, "F. Paget left Oxford to-day. What a blessing he has been to me during the last four years! And how greatly I shall miss him!" The return of this friend to Oxford, early in 1885, as Professor of Pastoral Theology, following so closely upon the foundation of the Pusey House in the preceding autumn, was a real joy to him amid all his anxieties and his ill-health.

Before he preached the Sermon at the Consecration of Dr. King, he found that he would have to face the question of accepting a Bishopric as a definite proposal, and not merely as a general proposition.

"*April* 7.—After afternoon Service, the Dean said that Salisbury would soon be offered to me. He hoped that I would not put it aside. Said that there never was such a case of clear call. His eyes filled with tears, and he begged pardon, in his characteristic way, for mentioning the subject. I said that I had hoped this ghost had been laid by what happened in January. But he said, No, it had been all along intended, and he was surprised that nothing had yet been said.

"*April* 10.—The Dean called. He did not see any difficulty about my accepting a Bishopric arising from ' Pusey's Life.' I should find time to finish it. I assured him that this would not be the case."

As the Dean was going away at the end of the month, Liddon made up his mind, and wrote to him before he started.

To the Dean of St. Paul's.

"3, Amen Court, E.C., April 28, 1885.

" You will forgive me for troubling you just as you are starting on your holiday ? But I am asking you to do me a very great kindness. What you said the other day about Salisbury, combined with reports from other quarters, has obliged me to think that matter over as carefully as I can. And I have come to the conclusion that, if Mr. Gladstone were to offer me the See, I ought to decline it.

" My main, although not my only, reason is, that to accept it would be to give up the plan of writing ' Dr. Pusey's Life.' If I were more versatile than I am, this consequence need not follow. But interruptions in a work of this kind trouble me sorely. And, indeed, I have often thought of late whether it might not be a duty to resign my Canonry, so as to get long, uninterrupted periods of time for serious work. I could not attempt such a book as a πάρεργον to the work of a Bishopric. I should have a bad conscience on the one score or the other, and should probably end with a ruined diocese and an unfinished book.

" My choice then lies between the book and the See. And although in itself the work of a Bishop may be far higher, yet *for me* the humbler task seems to have been marked out Providentially. If I resign it, I see many who would do it far better than I, but few, if any, who would undertake it. Nor am I sure that I could persuade those who have given me their correspondence and their confidence to pass it on to some one else.

" Then I have no belief that I have the aptitudes for a useful Episcopate. I am about fifteen years too old ; only three years younger than Bishop Hamilton was at the time of his death. His real work was quite done before he had reached my age. And Salisbury, surely, needs a young man, who will throw into the administration of the diocese the full energy of the best years of life.

" The upshot of all this is to ask you, while you are abroad, to write a few lines to Mr. Gladstone, apprising him of my real feelings, and begging him not to submit my name to the Queen. It would be a great relief to me to know that nothing of the kind was hanging over me, and to be able to go on my way rejoicing. A very few lines to Mr. Gladstone would suffice. And this letter needs no sort of acknowledgment. I meant to say it all to you to-day, but my courage failed me."

But there were many others who were just as urgent in this matter as the Dean ; and Liddon was obliged to repeat the argument of the preceding letter to one friend after another, although he found that he convinced no one that his refusal was right.

" *May* 16.—Walk with Bright ; much talk about Salisbury. He thought I ought to accept it, if offered ; that the book could be somehow provided for. Feel miserable about it.

" *May* 20.—Letter from F. Paget, urging the Bishopric question on me strongly, as from the Dean. I said what I could in reply.

"*May* 27.—The *Guardian* of to-night announces that the Bishop of Salisbury [Dr. Moberly] is going to resign his See.

"*June* 3.—Wrote to the Dean, telling him that my mind about Salisbury was still what it had been ; hope that he will write to beg Mr. Gladstone not to submit my name to the Queen."

But the decision did not lie with Mr. Gladstone, for a few days later his Government was defeated, and the appointment to the See of Salisbury was left to be made by his successor, Lord Salisbury.

In June, 1885, the continued strain of work and anxiety compelled Liddon to take a prolonged holiday, partly at Standish and partly on the Continent. But this rest did not improve his health ; and he at last yielded to the advice of his friends and medical advisers, and determined to spend the winter and the spring in Egypt and the Holy Land. As he was too ill to travel alone, his eldest sister, Mrs. King, and one of her daughters, went with him. A most interesting and graphic account of their tour has already been published in the form of Mrs. King's letters to her family.[1] His own record of his journey fills two thick volumes, containing a minute account of everything that he saw and experienced every day. Here it will be sufficient to give a few letters describing visits and other matters of special interest or recording reflections on what he saw.

To Dr. Bright.

"Alexandria, Hotel Khedival, Christmas Day, 1885.

" . . . This afternoon I went out to the Monastery of St. Saba, a little to the east of the city, where the Orthodox Eastern Patriarch resides. The monastery has externally a very humble and modern look ; but the columns in the small Church look as if they might have belonged to a pagan temple ; they are certainly very old. Vespers was being said, the congregation consisting of four clergy and four laity besides ourselves. You would remember that it is still twelve days to the Greek Christmas. After this I asked to be allowed to see the Patriarch Sophronius, and was admitted without much difficulty. He is an old man, apparently nearer eighty than seventy, with a beard, partly brown and chiefly white, and a prominent nose, and a strong

[1] "Dr. Liddon's Tour in Egypt and Palestine in 1886 " (Longmans, 1891).

mouth, and a voice rather harsh than pleasing, and a sweet smile. He was clothed in a cassock open at the front, but lined with fur, and had the ordinary undress Greek clerical hat on. He was extremely courteous, and we all had to eat preserves and drink scented water on a divan, and then I had a conversation of about forty minutes. The subject was, of course, the importance and the probabilities of Reunion. He thought that it would come in time. 'People must not expect to hasten so great a matter.' He agreed that the *Filioque* question was not beyond the reach of explanation, and spoke with great respect of Döllinger. But he added that a great mistake had been made by those English who wished to promote this excellent work. They had applied to himself, or to one of the other Patriarchs, instead of applying to all at once. The effect of this method was that the unconsulted Patriarchs were more concerned with their being unconsulted than with the merits of the questions submitted to their colleagues. What ought to be done was this : English theologians must decide under authority what explanations, etc., they were prepared to submit to the Orthodox Patriarchs, and they must submit them to all four at once. No Patriarch could act independently of the others. Thus far the successor of SS. Athanasius and Cyril. I wish I could think that we were likely, as a Church, to make the necessary effort. . . ."

To Dr. Bright.

"Luxor, January 28, 1886.

". . . As to Worcester, I can have no secrets with you, though, as you will understand, what I write cannot be public. When I reached Cairo I found a letter from Mr. Egerton, the English Commissioner there, offering me, on the part of Lord Salisbury, the Deanery of Worcester. He pressed me for an immediate reply, so, having taken two hours to think it over, I begged to be allowed to decline ; and this reply was telegraphed back to England. The refusal was not accepted, and I had letters of undeserved kindness from Lady Salisbury and Lord B[eauchamp] and the Dean of St. Paul's, advising me to reconsider it. These I did not answer so quickly. But after trying to look at the subject from all points of view, I finally have decided. . . . My chief cause of dissatisfaction with the decision at which I have arrived is the fear that it may have grieved so true and old a friend as Lord Beauchamp, and that it may appear to imply insensibility to the generous kindness of Lord Salisbury. Most assuredly the present Government was under no sort of obligation to notice me in any way, and I feel deeply how much is implied in its having done so.

". . . One of the great pleasures of being in the East, as I find it, is the extraordinary relish, if I may use the word, which all that one does and hears gives to the Old Testament. The habits of the people, their whole bearing and aspect, suggest the Bible. Egypt, I suppose, is more Arab than it is Egyptian ; the Oriental world is in full force. Hebrew reads more pleasantly here than in England ; its simple, rich ideas seem in keeping with all around, just as the modern languages of Europe are more enjoyable in countries which talk them than in England, where an effort is necessary to enter into their spirit and genius.   Here the Bible is enacted day by day before one's eyes in its familiar features : Pharaoh's daughters, generally *very* dirty, coming down to the Nile to wash ; Israel, in bondage in the peasant fellaheen, 'watering the land with his foot,' as Deuteronomy, I think, has it ; the Patriarchs driving long processions of cattle of all sorts, over the desert wastes of sand that here and there fringe the Nile for long intervals ; Rebekah watering the camels, as well as the men. The very donkey-boys, whom we constantly employ in our visits to tombs at a distance from the river, when they are—as they often are —Copts, reproduce in a wonderful degree the very features of the Pharaohs, as given on their mummies in the Bulak Museum. We call them Rameses, or Thothmes, or Sethi, or Menephthah, as the case may suggest.

" I have said nothing, I see, about this wonderful place, the hundred-gated Thebes.   Here for the first time one understands what Egypt must have seemed to Israel. . . . Only think of my seeing three mummies, discovered a fortnight since, waiting on the sand to be shipped for the Museum at Bulak, and learning that one of them was Rameses III., the Rhampsinitus of Herodotus !   After remaining at peace for all these centuries, he was discovered about a fortnight ago !   It seems almost tragical."

To Dr. Bright.

" Below Asyoot, March 7, 1886.

" . . . I do not wish you to misunderstand me about Worcester. I have no fanatical feeling against accepting preferment ; nay, I quite admit that, when conscience recognises a particular offer of preferment as an opportunity of doing better work than at present, it is a duty to accept.   But I do not think that an offer of mere preferment to higher dignity and larger income constitutes any claim upon the conscience ; and on this point the old Tractarian feeling, as on so many others, is profoundly opposed—at least as I have understood it—to that commercial view of the higher offices in the Church which was very sincerely held by the old Latitudinarians.   In the army it is natural enough that a Captain should be uneasy until he is a Major, and a Major until he is a Colonel, and a Colonel until he is a General. 'But ye shall not be so' is surely our Master's rule ; and the craving for preferment which prevails so largely among the English clergy, is one of the secrets of our moral weakness as an Order.

" If Lord Salisbury had offered me the See of Salisbury in the autumn, I had, with much misgiving and after long hesitation, made up my mind that it would be a duty to accept it. I knew the diocese at one time well, and still have many friends among the clergy. As you know, he did not offer it. . . . I can truly say that the settlement of the matter was a relief to me, as it enabled me to dismiss from my mind the whole question of a change of duties. When the Deanery of Worcester was offered some months afterwards, I could not think it necessary to reopen the question."

From Cairo, on his return journey, he sends Dr. Bright a long letter on the state of the Church in Egypt.

To Dr. Bright.

"Cairo, Shepherd's Hotel, March 29, 1886.

"Since I last wrote to you I have seen something of the Coptic clergy here, which would interest you and dear Paget, and—if you should think right to forward this to him—the Bishop of Lincoln. Yesterday I sat for some time with the Coptic Patriarch Cyril, who lives in Cairo, although taking his title from 'the holy metropolis Alexandria.' He is about fifty-three or fifty-four years of age, and looks younger than that. Several people were waiting for him in an ante-chamber ; but he was good enough to take me into an inner room, and talk for some time. He expressed a very earnest desire for the union of Christians ; agreed to what I said as to the Providential symptoms in the modern world which appeared to make for it, and as to the weakness in presence of Islam and unbelief which resulted from our divisions. When I went into topics connected with the Council of Chalcedon, my Arabic interpreter, Simiaka, begged me not to do this, as it would 'disturb' the Patriarch, who has a dread of controversy on this particular question. He was, however, very courteous and kindly, rather of the cautious Episcopal type with which we are so familiar in England, and, as I should suppose, rather a good man of business, than one of much learning or thought. A much more remarkable and influential person is the Aboonah Felthâus (φιλόθεος) who is Dean, as we should say, of the Coptic Cathedral here. He is a great Arabic preacher, and at two of his sermons I observed a great many Moslems among the congregation. He is probably not much above forty, but is a natural theologian, with the added instincts of a practical man of deeply earnest piety. His sermons on the Prodigal Son, and on our Lord's conversation with the woman of Samaria, which were translated, or rather condensed to us, paragraph by paragraph (I only understood bits of donkey-boy and sailors' Arabic), were indeed beautiful, sparkling with many pearls of thought and feeling, which one would be thankful to have uttered. This morning I have been talking with him for nearly two hours on the Monophysite question. He, of course, defended the formula that out of the two

Natures arise a single Nature; insisted that the Copts only repeated the language of Athanasius and Cyril, and was not disposed to enter into the question of the different senses of the word ' Nature,' or into the consideration that a formula which might be harmless at one epoch may be mischievous at another, when brought into relations with a new heresy. He said, however, that the Copts condemned Eutyches as a heretic, and that *practically* they held the Faith of the whole Eastern Church. . . .

"*March* 31.—Yesterday I had a second interview with the Aboonah on the subject of the education of the Coptic clergy. In this cause, the [late] Patriarch Cyril, who must have been a very remarkable man, was very enthusiastic. He used to assemble the Coptic clergy at Cairo at the Patriarchate, and give them lectures and addresses : and he had large schemes for clerical education in his mind, when the end came ; since then nothing has been done. The Patriarch is chosen from among the monks, and these in Egypt now are generally uneducated, and at heart unwilling to promote a generally higher education in the priesthood. The consequence is that the clergy are very deficient in legitimate influence ; as the Coptic laity is by far the most educated class of natives. The Aboonah discussed plans for the improvement of the monasteries, but the subject is evidently beset with difficulties.

" There are, by-the-by, three Coptic Sisterhoods in Cairo, obeying, so far as I could understand, some adaptation of the Rule of St. Anthony. I had an interview with the Mother of one—a very intelligent person, with obvious capacities for management, entirely wrapped up, like the Arab women, in a black mantle, with only two large eyes looking out. She and her twenty-five Sisters work incessantly among the poor, a good number of children were being taught, washed, combed, and variously administered, in the courtyard of the nunnery. She showed me some Arabic sermons and prayers, dictated to the Sisters by Macarius, Coptic Bishop of Khartoum, who, since the fall of that place, has been unable to return to his diocese and is resident in the Dayr. With him I had a long talk about Khartoum and General Gordon of the most interesting description. He said that Gordon was his best friend, that he frequently prayed in his church, that he did all he could to encourage the eight hundred Christians in Khartoum to persevere in their Faith, and that he was so much liked, nevertheless, by the Mohammedans, on account of his virtues, that ' the very Mahdi desired that he should on no account be injured.' He was killed, the Bishop added, 'as Khartoum fell, by treachery.' Altogether, I feel sure that my earlier impressions about the Copts, which I believe I mentioned to you, did not do them justice. In recognising this, I sympathise with Mr. Greenwood's effort : only I wish I could be sure that he, and those whom he represents, are fully alive to the importance of the Monophysite question, and to the need of a settlement of it before anything can be done. The English Church is not strong enough in the matter of adherence to ancient and Catholic dogma to take any liberties with her safeguards, and she unhappily contains within her fold a very powerful party which would be too glad to commit her to some step which would imply repudiation of the general principle by tacit or implied acquiescence in an error which has been condemned by the Universal Church. The peril is here to reconcile practical loyalty to this vital consideration with due attention to the difficulties and great claims upon us, of the Copts. Greenwood is as good and kindly as can be.

"The other day as I was riding out on a donkey in one of the by-streets of Cairo, a camel that passed suddenly gobbled and spat at me—a curious variation of the look of tranquil disdain with which these beasts generally regard everything, as if they were Heads of Houses of the old type. Said Hassan (my donkey-boy), 'That camel has been at Mecca, on the Hadj ; all that go there learn to know Christians when they see them.'"

He landed at Joppa from Alexandria on April 4, 1886, and travelled leisurely to Jerusalem, and lived in tents on the Mount of Olives. The distance from Jerusalem was a great drawback, but—

"the association of the Sacred Hill and the constant view of the Holy City counterbalance *all else*. Only one feels that breakfast and dinner are a sort of desecration : it is like eating in the Choir of a Church."

He took an early opportunity of presenting his introductions to the Patriarch of Jerusalem, and records the visit at length in his diary, and in a letter to Dr. Bright.

"*April* 13 [*Monday*]. *Mount of Olives.*—After breakfast I went to see the Orthodox Patriarch. I was late, but he kindly accepted my excuses. I sat with him for two hours ; he began by thanking me for my Bampton Lectures, and by saying many more kind things about them than they deserved. The Divinity of our Lord was, he said, the central truth of Christianity, which was now, as it always had been, opposed, but the constant reassertion of which was of vital importance. This led to some conversation on the aggressive attitude of modern Infidelity throughout Europe, and on the resulting necessity for greater union among Christians. He referred to the Bonn Conferences ; thought that Union would come about in time 'on the basis of the Seven Mysteries,' but, that in order to promote it, constant intercourse between the English and the Eastern Churches was desirable. In reply to my saying that we felt all this and longed for Unity, he said that 'The English profess to desire Unity, but they sometimes act very inconsistently with the profession.' He referred to the Church Missionary Society church now served by a son-in-law of Bishop Gobat's. 'It was established to convert the Moslems; it really only unsettles our own people, or detaches them from the Church of their Baptism. It is useless to wish for Unity and send a brigade to break up the congregations of the Church with which you wish to unite. Yet this destruction of our Churches is carried on by the Church Missionary Society here, which professes to act under the sanction of the English Church.' I pointed out that the Church Missionary Society only represented an extreme party. 'They claim,' he rejoined, 'to act under the sanction of the English Bishops, and we have to look to what the English Bishops allow or disallow. We want the moral support of the English Bishops in resisting attempts to break up our Churches if we are to think of unity with them.'

"I suggested that he should write to the Archbishop of Canterbury and protest against the schismatical and unchristian action of the Church Missionary Society. 'I have done so,' he said. The Archbishop replied very kindly, and said that he would write to the Church Missionary people. But the Patriarch had not heard that anything had been done to stop or undo the mischief. 'Methodists, Bible Christians, Quakers, and other sects from England and America prey' he said, 'upon our poor people, and in this work they are joined by the Latins, who make no converts from Mohammedanism, but only try to destroy the ancient Eastern Church.'"

To Dr. Bright.

"Tent on the Mount of Olives, Good Friday, April 23, 1886.

"I have, indeed, seen a good deal of Nicodemus, the Orthodox Patriarch. He is a very striking person, who would make himself felt in almost any position. He is physically a big man, with great hands and feet, and a great mouth; and he sits in a chair like Julius II. according to Raphael, or Cardinal Wolsey, waiting for the world to come to him, and addressing it with tranquil authority when it does. Not that this comparison does him justice; there is an unworldliness and sincerity about him which were not always conspicuous in the two Prelates I have named. He delights to talk of the Greek Fathers: for him the three great ones are Chrysostom, Basil, and Gregory the Theologian. 'Humanly speaking, they had saved Christianity.' I pleaded for St. Athanasius and the two St. Cyrils, especially as one of these last had been among his predecessors. He agreed, but without enthusiasm: of course, St. Athanasius was beyond discussion; the Alexandrian St. Cyril was a great theologian, but 'very pugnacious' (here the Patriarch clenched his fists, and appeared to be striking out at me). Of the Westerns he had little to say: I doubt if he knew much of them, but did not like to ask. He was loud in his praise of Photius—rather, I suspect, for my benefit. Photius was all sorts of things—pious, orthodox, above all κριτικὸς. And then a fat Bishop from Cyprus, who was present, dutifully echoed all the Patriarch's epithets, and added others of his own. I talk Greek with difficulty, and so had no chance with these Prelates ; nor could I forget what the μέγας always used to say about this same Photius—as you would very well understand, nor do I know enough of him to venture upon anything very decided of my own : though I feel after this that I ought to read him up. The Patriarch had received your letter, and was delighted with it. He talked freely about English Church matters, and asked why the Archbishop of Canterbury, whose photograph he showed me, was not dressed in the same way as the Bishop of Aberdeen, whose photograph he also showed me ; the latter being arrayed in a magnificent cope and mitre. To which I could only say that the tradition of the ancient Episcopal dress was found in certain parts of the English Church and not in others—a statement which he evidently thought odd. . . . He is much troubled, too, by the proceedings of the Church Missionary Society here.

"You ask me about the Greek Services. Their length is, according to our Western ideas, excessive. Indeed, the Patriarch said that this was a practical mistake, due to the ascendency of the monks in the fourth and fifth centuries, who did not sufficiently allow for the inability of ordinary Christians to conform to monastic standards of piety. He should never wish to see Eastern devotions introduced into, *e.g.*, England ; we might unite with the Orthodox Church on the basis of the Orthodox Faith 'and the Seven Mysteries.' . . .

"N.B.—At Bonn we never got to that grave question about the Unction of the dying.

"*April* 24. *Easter Eve.*—Last night we went to the Patriarchate and accompanied the Patriarch to the Church of the Holy Sepulchre for the ἐπιτάφιον. It was a long Service, made up of psalms and hymns, and we went in procession with candles to every part of the Church, Latin as well as Greek. A Service was held at every altar by the Patriarch ; it began at 10 and ended at 3.15 this morning. I was afraid that my sister and nieces would be crushed to death in two places ; and I fear I had my pocket picked on the stairs of Mount Calvary. There were three sermons—one Russian, on Calvary ; one Arabic, at the Stone of the Deposition ; and one Greek, before the Sepulchre. This last was preached by our friend the good Archimandrite Stephanos ; and he burst out at the end into an English epilogue, to the astonishment, I should suppose, of a large part of his audience, but to our edification. It was indeed 'for our benefit.'

"To-day at twelve we went to the Service of the Holy Fire. . . . The eagerness of the people to get and keep the fire was astonishing. The Archimandrite told me that the Patriarch does all he can to disabuse them of the notion that it comes from heaven every Easter Eve : ' It is only the old fire, always burning at the Sepulchre and rekindled thus annually as a symbol of the quickening of the spiritual flame

Z

which should be a result of Easter.' Thus understood, it is an edifying ceremony ; and the Roman Catholic sneers at it are undeserved as levelled against (at any rate) the present authorities of the Church in Jerusalem, while they are not altogether appropriate in the mouth of a religious system which has not always been careful of the question of truth in matters of this sort.

"The enjoyment of Jerusalem is dashed by the ever-recurring question about the sites. As to the Holy Sepulchre, I do *not* believe in the only serious proposal about an alternative. The hill called ' Hill of a Skull,' outside the Damascus gate, and having a garden and a tomb at its base, is much too striking and picturesque to have been overlooked, unless the tradition of the local Church had run powerfully in favour of the much more prosaic traditional site. It (this ' new Calvary ') has all the attractions, and it incurs all the suspicions of a ' very good' reading in a MS. The actually received site is in many ways disappointing, almost shocking to prepossessions formed at a distance ; and yet on reflection this unwelcomeness is surely evidence in its favour ! I can hardly doubt that St. Helena really acted on some earlier local tradition, although, of course, the question will never be finally settled until the ' second wall' is excavated, at a distance of some seventy or eighty feet below the soil in a thickly populated part of the city. General Gordon seems to have taken up this ' new site of Calvary' with great fervour, and this settles the question with all those many persons who think that a good man, a good engineer, and a brave soldier must necessarily be an antiquarian and Biblical critic to boot."

To Lord Halifax.[1]

"Damascus, May 23, 1886.

". . . At Jerusalem I saw a great deal of the Orthodox Patriarch Nicodemus. A very remarkable man, who would be remarkable in any country or position. Quite unlike the ordinary type of higher Eastern ecclesiastics — timid, cowed, unenterprising people, whom Moslem dislike of Christianity imposes upon the unfortunate Church. Somehow the Evil One made a mistake as to Nicodemus. He is a power in Jerusalem ; treated with great respect, but not, I apprehend, by the Pasha, and exerting an influence beyond the limits of the Orthodox Eastern Church. He knows a great deal about the West generally, and in particular about England. . . .

" He allowed me to celebrate in the Church of the Holy Sepulchre, in the Chapel of Abraham, which is on the Hill of Calvary, and parted only by a thin screen from the Chapels of Calvary, Greek and Latin. He gave me introductions to the Patriarchs of Antioch and Constantinople, and to several Bishops and Hegumens and Archimandrites.

[1] The Hon. C. L. Wood succeeded to this title in 1885.

" There is a *nescio quid* about people like this Patriarch which one misses, I know not why, in average English Bishops—a decision, an unworldliness, a reticence and humility as to *everything* personal, and a tranquil confidence in a heavenly mission and office, which is what the Bible leads us to expect, and what we so often look for in vain at home. I have often felt it to be a great privilege to have seen so much of him.

" *May* 25. *Damascus.*—This morning I called on Geronimus, the Œcumenical Patriarch of Antioch. He received me in the great hall of the Patriarchate, where he was sitting with two Archbishops, to whom I was introduced—one of them the Archbishop of Edessa. He looks like a man under fifty, in weak health, who has seen much sorrow. He speaks French fluently, and is more European than his compeers of Jerusalem and Alexandria. He had been a delegate to the Congress of Berlin on the part of the Patriarchs of Constantinople and Alexandria. . . .

" He entered warmly into what I ventured to urge respecting the Reunion of the Church. He longed and prayed for it daily. He spoke much more cordially about the English Church than the Patriarch of Jerusalem had done. The Archbishop of Canterbury, Edward, had written him a letter about the Mission to the Nestorians that had greatly delighted him, and had convinced him that the English Church would co-operate loyally with the Eastern Church—would not prose-lytise from them ; would work, in short, in a truly Christian spirit. He was going to write to the Archbishop to thank him. . . .

" Like the Patriarch of Jerusalem, he talked a good deal about the ' Erasmian' pronunciation of Greek ; but thought that there was a stronger case for sacrificing accents to quantity than the Patriarch of Jerusalem would allow."

From Damascus they rode through Lebanon to Beyrout, and thence by sea to Constantinople. On reaching his hotel there, he found " a telegram from the Dean of Edinburgh, announcing that I had been elected Bishop of Edinburgh —*Deus misereatur mei.*"

To Dr. Paget.

" Hotel Royal, Constantinople, June 11, 1886.

" Before receiving your letter, or indeed any letter on the subject, I had answered the Dean of Edinburgh's telegram. I took twenty-four hours to think it over ; but cannot say that I ever had any doubt about the right answer to give. The Bishops of the Church of Scotland should be Scotchmen. So long as they are Englishmen that Church will always wear the appearance of an English importa-tion in the eyes of the Presbyterian majority, whose conversion will

thus be rendered more difficult by a sense of slighted national feeling.
The Italian appointments to English benefices which were made by
the Papacy (in the thirteenth century) were not without their influence
on the events of the sixteenth century. . . .

" The freedom from State Courts (in Scotland) is a powerful
attraction to me. . . . And the Scottish Bishops are none the weaker
for being without the unmeaning trappings of feudalism which still
hang around our English Sees.   But I should not forgive myself if I
were in my own person to aid an evil tradition of seeking Bishops for
Scotland south of the Tweed, which I have deplored ever since I
have been able to think about these things seriously at all.

" The heat here is considerable, and we feel it more than in Syria,
because the air is damper.   The Ramadan is going on ; and the
mosques are illuminated every night.   Last night I saw St. Sophia
lighted up in this way ; it was full of people.   One could not but wish
to see the day when the Liturgy of St. Chrysostom will again be
heard within its walls, instead of the miserable parody of serious
religion which the impostor of Mecca produced.   The pathetic thing
is the number of truly noble and generous natures who are and have
been victims of his delusion."

He was greatly disappointed that he could not see the
Patriarch of Constantinople.   He had, as has been recorded,
visited the occupants of three Patriarchal thrones ; but when
he presented his introduction at the house of the successor
of St. Chrysostom, he found that he was too ill to see
any one.

On his return to London, the offer of the See of Edinburgh was again pressed upon him from many quarters,
but he never saw any reason for doubting the validity of
the arguments which made him telegraph from Constantinople to refuse it.

CORRESPONDENCE, 1883–1885.

On the Right Estimate of Ritual.

" 3, Amen Court, St. Paul's, E.C., August, 1883.

"ₜ . . . I agree with you in regretting the prominence which is
given in modern discussions to questions of Form and Ceremonial.
But I observe that this prominence is not only or mainly due to people
like Mr. ———.   Surely those who make silly objections have something

to answer for. As a matter of religious feeling, I myself dislike the way in which the Service is conducted in churches which belong to the Puritanical party : it seems to me often, though unintentionally, somewhat irreverent and grotesque. But to make a fuss about it would be at issue with charity and common sense ; when men know what the Revelation of God in His Blessed Son really is, all else follows in due time—reverence on one side and charity on the other."

On the Plan for a Reredos at St. Paul's.

"3, Amen Court, St. Paul's, E.C., September 4, 1883.

"I ought to have returned Mr. Bodley's report before this, but it will meet you on your return to London.

"I have read it over two or three times, and like it better the more I think it over.

"Referring to the two points which you mentioned in conversation, Bodley is, it seems to me, right in asking that two of the columns should be twisted and wreathed. He forcibly urges that Wren contemplated this ; and such columns do give a great impression of richness—not to speak of their association, even in popular art, with the fittings of the Temple. Then he has almost, if not quite, made me a convert to his Statues on the top of the Reredos. They belong, as it seems to me, to the general conception of the work, and indeed to Bodley's theory of a religious effect in Art.

"His idea is to take captive the mind of the spectator by some composition of great beauty in detail—beauty in detail which extends throughout the composition, and does not allow the mind to escape from its effect by anything on a lower level than its own. It seems to me that the exquisite treatment of the background of the Crucifixion, and of the frame of the picture, and of the columns adjoining, demand something not less elaborate than Statues would be at the top. In short, I credit Bodley with an instinct of symmetry which I trust ; and I trust it at the cost of sacrificing a more simple ideal of the general frame of the Reredos. For this simple ideal, however beautiful independently or in other hands, would not be natural to Bodley ; and I doubt whether it would be in keeping with the central feature of his work. He is eminently a man who has a good reason for what he suggests ; and I shrink from the attempt to modify his proposal if it be accepted at all.

"As to the Figures chosen—that is a theological or historical, not an artistic question. I should anticipate a much happier result from this effort of Bodley's than from the Committee's more ambitious scheme for decorating the Dome, about which I feel less and less comfortable."

To THE HON. C. L. WOOD.

On the Luther Commemoration, and the Rejection of a Proposal to affix the University Seal to a Congratulatory Address to the German Emperor.

"3, Amen Court, November 14, 1883.

" I am most thankful that that Address touching Luther was thrown out. I did not at all expect it ; as the Puritanical party and Jowett's ordinary supporters were allied in its favour, and —— led the motley host. But the victory was *not* purely a Church victory. Two other forms of opinion contributed to it : (1) one, those extreme anti-Christians who regard Luther as representing a sort of Theology, and will have no Theology of any sort if they can help it ; (2) another, those purely academical people, who do not think that subjects of this kind should be brought before Convocation, as they do not help the proper work of the University. Still, these *nuances* are not understood at a distance ; and if the Address *had* been carried, we should never have heard the last of it from the Puritan party. As it is, they are greatly put out. How thankful I am that this Luther Commemoration has nearly come to an end ! Such Sermons as that of Archdeacon Farrar in the *Guardian* of this week make one sick at heart at being a Priest in the same branch of the Church. Luther had some great personal qualities, no doubt ; but unless it is right to reject all Scripture that does not bear out your private views, and to make feeling instead of conscience the test of your state before God, his general influence upon Christendom must be deemed to be a grave misfortune."

To ——

On the Value of Belief in a Future State.

"3, Amen Court, St. Paul's, E.C., January 8, 1884.

" I should be sorry to say that progressive improvement in the condition of this world has nothing to do with the future state of existence. On the contrary, I believe that the *true* improvers here will be greatly distinguished hereafter. Still that 'hereafter' is one thing, and this life, however 'improved,' is another. As to the monks and the hermits, everything seems to me to depend on what sort of monks and hermits they were. A lazy monk or hermit, who is in fact a sham, is deplorable in the ratio of his high and forgotten professions. But, believing as I do in the power of prayer, I do not think that a monk or hermit, who lives up to his calling and intercedes for a world which generally forgets God and the true philosophy of existence, does waste his time.

"He may bring about a great deal that goes on in public affairs more really than people think. And, of course, there have been monks, like Roger Bacon and Peter the Hermit, whose achievements would be thought considerable even by your Cambridge correspondent.

"At least I cannot but feel that it is a loss of time to debate the value of motives, drawn from a world in which —— does not believe, with him and others like-minded. For him, Heaven and Hell are what the 'Arabian Nights' are for you and me. He *cannot* understand the elevating, purifying, chastening, stimulating force of a conviction to which his intellect is implacably opposed; and, on the other hand, it is no real objection to our faith on the subject, at least in my eyes, if here or there the true influence of a future life on this has been misapprehended or forgotten.

"The real question is one of facts. Shall we live after death, or not? If I could imagine that we shall not, I should not care to discuss with —— the moral value of a precarious hypothesis. But if we do, the influence of such a future upon this present life is the least important among the many and tremendous considerations connected with it. Yet this influence is very real indeed."

On "*Sectarianism*."

"3, Amen Court, January 26, 1884.

"I must, I fear, own to you that I am not at all frightened by the word 'sectarian.' Christianity *is* sectarian as against the non-Christian world; and so is Truth as against Error, and Virtue as against Vice. Everybody who is not indifferent to Truth and Virtue draws a line somewhere to exclude from unreserved sympathy and co-operation those who reject them, and he thus becomes a 'sectarian.' The question between 'sectarians' such as Dr. Martineau and Cardinal Manning is only one of degree. The only escape is in Pantheism, which means, among other things, in the last resort, indifference to morals."

On Good Friday Celebrations.

"Christ Church, March 23, 1884.

"Thank you for the pamphlet on 'Good Friday Celebrations.' I have read it through with much interest.

"Mr. Wilson no doubt is right as to general *post*-Reformation practice among ourselves. His inference from Tunstall's language would appear to me less certain. Tunstall would have had something strong to say about our practice of disallowing Reservation (in view of Primitive Antiquity, to which we appeal), and also about *consecrating* on Good Friday. And his language about the practice of Christendom is probably to be interpreted by the *theory* of its practice. As a matter of fact, I doubt very much indeed whether there were any lay communions on Good Friday in England before the Reformation.

"Mr. Keble used to say that Good Friday Communion was a tradition which had come to us from the Lutherans, like the late age of Confirmation.   I suspect, however, though I cannot be sure, that he himself did celebrate at Hursley on Good Friday, out of consideration for good people who had always been accustomed to it.

" Is not the question *this*—whether to deny people the opportunity of communicating on Good Friday involves a larger departure from ancient practice than to consecrate on Good Friday?   On this I should be sorry to have to pronounce ; although I myself have never communicated on Good Friday for more than thirty years.   But then, it has never been my business to consider whether I should run the risk of shocking good people by denying them the Communion on a day when they have been accustomed to communicate all their lives.

"The Prayer-book would appear to me to leave the question sufficiently open to make it wrong to charge either practice with disloyalty. We cannot say that when a Collect, Epistle, and Gospel are appointed, a Celebration is *obligatory*, so long as the Rubric immediately before the Church Militant Prayer remains in the Prayer-book.   On the other hand, we are still less able to say that when Collect, Epistle, and Gospel are appointed, a Communion is contrary to the mind of the Church of England.

"There is a larger question behind, as to the relation of the Eucharist to the Passion of Our Lord—but upon this I will not enter.   Only I do not think that everybody who shrinks, as I do, from communicating on Good Friday is wishing to imitate Rome or thinking at all about Roman practice.   The question *is* one of feeling—but of feeling clearly allied to the apprehension of dogma, and entitled, as I think, to consideration, *unless* the Church of England leaves no choice in the matter.   And this I do not—for the reason above given—suppose to be the case.

"But I have never taken part in this controversy ; to do so would require more knowledge of a special department of inquiry than I can pretend to."

To ——

On the Work of Father Benson.

"3, Amen Court, St. Paul's, E.C., April 3, 1884.

". . . To weaken Father Benson's hands would be to weaken one of the few strong and beautiful things in the Church of England. High Church principles are more widely diffused than they were ; but they are held in a much feebler and less emphatic form than was the case some years ago. . . . It differs alike in intellectual consistency and in moral intensity ; but in virtue of this it is much more popular.   Before his death, Dr. Pusey noted the change with sorrow ;

and since he has left us, as was natural, it has become more marked. If you lived in Oxford, you would see what I mean. The change is far-reaching ; it promises to become—as far as the Church Movement is concerned—little less than universal.

" . . . Now, Father Benson is one of the few elements of resistance to the new order of things—unconscious resistance, of course, for it may well be doubted whether he has realised it. But the isolation of his work, the odd severity of his character, his absolute unworldliness, not to speak of the authority which belongs to him as dating from what is now a previous generation—all combine to invest his enterprise, at least so it seems to me, with increasing importance. Any clever man who believes in Christianity and can understand the bearings of a book like the Duke of Argyll's, can give lectures which will impress a great many people. I do not depreciate this sort of work—far from it—but it is infinitely lower work than that which is achieved by merely belonging to a Society in which everything has been given up for God, and the silent eloquence of whose Rule is worth a thousand Sermons. . . ."

To the Hon. C. L. Wood.

"February 3, 1885.

"George Eliot's 'Life' is very heart-aching reading. Such an abuse of so rich a genius ! The easy way in which she throws off her Christianity, as if it were an old bonnet, without any trace of moral or intellectual anguish, is terrible.

" I met her two or three times, and with me her conversation took a turn which did not prepare me for such scenes as that to which you refer—translating Strauss's odious account of The Passion before a Crucifix.

" And yet there is something which makes one read the book with a pity that outweighs all other feelings whatever. Beneath all that is most revolting, I seem to hear an undertone of deep sorrow, . . . which makes one think what she might have been had she not been what she was."

To ———

On the Ministerial Commission.

" Standish House, Stonehouse, Gloucestershire, May 12, 1885.

" . . . I have no doubt whatever of the excellence of many Dissenting ministers. I know many of them—men worthy of all honour. But their personal character, and the mentally beneficial effect of high personal character upon those who come into contact with it, proves nothing as to the question of their Ministerial Commission. Some, too, of my dearest friends are laymen in the Church of England. They are much better men than some clergy whom I could name, and have a better influence on those around them. They bring more men to the knowledge and love of our Lord. But this does not prove that He has commissioned them to celebrate and administer the Holy Communion. Personal character is one thing ; a Ministerial Commission is another.

" The converse to my position is not that Dissenting ' ordinations ' and 'sacraments' are valid, but that no Ministry whatever is necessary in the Christian Church.

" The Threefold Ministry is clearly before us in the Pastoral Epistles, and until the middle of the sixteenth century no Ordinations that were not Episcopal were known in the Church of Christ. The Episcopate was received in the early ages much more unanimously than several Books of the New Testament ; and I am unable to understand the mind of those who, if they are fairly educated, have no hesitation, *e.g.*, about believing the Second Epistle of St. Peter, or the Epistle to the Hebrews, to be parts of the Inspired and Infallible Word of God, and yet think that Presbyterianism or Congregationalism will do as well as that one Ministry which has existed in His Church from the beginning."

To the Rev. R. W. Dale.

On the English Ordinal.

"Christ Church, June 23, 1885.

" My Sermon ['A Father in Christ'] was not meant for any who do not belong to our Church, but for *ourselves*. It seems to me that to say that the Prayer-book or Ordinal proceeds on a mistaken view of the Will of our Lord, must be less ungrateful to Him than to employ its solemn language in a perfectly unreal way, and to profess indifference to the only conceptions of the Ministerial Office which make such language justifiable. Alas ! I can understand only too well how naturally people are alienated from the Church of England by those of us who accept her Formularies and Organisation for no better reason than that they are recognised by the State, and in combination with religious theories which make them unintelligible or erroneous. You will think me paradoxical when I express my belief that a more general acceptance among us of the teaching which I tried to set forth in my Sermon would, *in the end*, bring us much nearer religious Nonconformists. . . ."

To the Rev. R. W. Dale.

On the Ministry of the Church.

"Christ Church, Oxford, August 15, 1885.

" On returning for a few days to Oxford, I find another kind present, which reaches me from the Congregational Union, but for which I find I am indebted to you. I am ashamed to have to confess to you that I have never before read the 'Jubilee Lectures,' and I am more than glad to be introduced to them in so pleasant a way.

"I have just been reading your own on 'The Early Independents,' and if it were not impertinent to say so, am greatly struck by the sympathy and justice which run through it, and which, as it seems to me, Dr. Allon is less able to command in his effort to understand Laud. Of course, I cannot subscribe to what you say about Baptismal Regeneration [p. 29], or in the estimate which underlies your account of what was retained by the Reformed Church [pp. 29–30]. But, for all that, if I may make bold to say so, I do feel that we agree in our major premises much more nearly than I can with some others who, ecclesiastically speaking, are more nearly related to me. We neither of us have much heart for a Church polity which professes itself to be a matter of indifference, and does not claim the authority of our Lord ; and this is my quarrel with that estimate of the Episcopate among ourselves which would keep it up, for historical or social reasons, without feeling or professing any serious belief in its relation to the Divine Will. That such a representation of the Church's Ministry should have been so actively repellent to religious souls, as to have produced much of the Dissent from the Church, I can more than believe from what I know of my own feelings towards it. And people will only understand the moving principle and the strength of the High Church School (as it is called) when they see in it an effort to insist that the estimate of the polity of the Church shall be a religious and not a worldly one. You would not agree in the Scriptural or historical considerations which appear to us to warrant this higher view of the Episcopate, but you would heartily agree in the necessity which all religious people must feel of seeing God's Will, and not some earthly substitute for it, in the laws and organisation of His kingdom upon earth."

To the Rev. R. W. Dale.

On the Use of the Crucifix.

"Hôtel Windsor, Paris, October 3, 1885.

"Your kind letter of September 25 only reached me here and to-day. I know only too well how little the Sermons [1] deserve some of the terms which you so generously apply to them : they were published with a practical object, and under some sort of compulsion. But it is a true delight to me to know that—as I ventured to hope—they express the vital truths which we hold in common, in terms which, in the main, you approve.

"As you say, our Lord's *present* Life is the life of His servants ; and the daily, hourly realisation of this is at once our safety and our joy.

[1] "Easter Sermons."

" I have often thought of what you say as to an effect of the Crucifix—in withdrawing our thoughts from our Lord's present Glory to His *past* Sufferings and Death.

" On the other hand, the disproportionate length, if one may write this, of the narrative of the Passion in the Four Gospels seems, like such passages as Gal. iii. 1 and Heb. xii. 2, to suggest that Christians are to give especial consideration to our Lord's Sufferings and Death. And I have sometimes thought that in reading the Gospels the mind escapes from the sense of time into a world of thought for which time does not exist. (You would remember Kant's speculation as to the purely subjective character of time and space.) Such an expression as, 'the Lamb slain from the foundation of the world,' might seem to warrant this ; many Christians, I apprehend, live over in thought the events of our Lord's earthly life, as if there were not eighteen centuries between us and it. . . . I am arguing against myself, and trying to suggest the balance of the subject. For, to me the great protection against a false subjectivity is the thought, ' What is our Lord doing now ? '

" Through God's great mercy, my illness, I hope, *has* been a blessing. . . . I have been idle ever since the middle of June, and since early in August have been out of England. After staying in the mountain air of Switzerland, I went to Tegernsee on a short visit to Dr. Döllinger, who spends his holiday there in a small villa of Lord Acton's. He is eighty-six, but his mind and his sympathies are as keen and fresh as ever."

To C. T. Redington, Esq.

On Theology and Science.

" Standish House, Stonehouse, October 13, 1885.

". . . Certainly I did read M. St. George Mivart's article. The mistake that was made by Rome about Galileo arose, I suppose, from not sufficiently considering where lies the frontier between Theology and Physics. In that age the distinction could hardly have been realised, as we realise it. The idea that, when the Bible speaks on popular topics, it was popular, and not scientific, or objectively true language, belongs to a later time, although something similar had· been recognised in ancient interpretations of the anthropomorphic language respecting Almighty God, which is to be found in the Old Testament. I do not know that a *consensus Patrum* can be claimed for the theory which Galileo disputed, except in the sense that the Fathers would naturally have taken the Ptolemaic, or some cognate, theory of the universe for granted, and have applied this—the stock secular knowledge of the time—to the interpretation of those passages of Holy Scripture which seemed to bear on it. One can hardly see how any such collision as that of the new and the old Astronomy is possible within the limits of pure Theology, because within these limits there is no place for a theory based upon experience ; and the last word has surely been said upon the great passages in which the Nature, Attributes, and Acts of God are propounded to us on Divine authority. Modern unbelief does not trouble itself greatly about the interpretation of these passages ; it saves itself this effort by rejecting them—on whatever grounds."

To C. T. Redington, Esq.

On Irish Politics.

" 3, Amen Court, St. Paul's, St. Stephen's Day, 1885.

" I return with all my heart your kind and welcome Christmas greetings. Each year one finds fewer friends on this side the veil, and values them more, without forgetting those who have passed beyond. With you the Festival has been, I fear, dashed by much inevitable anxiety and sadness ; but I hope you have been able to enjoy the sunshine which is always to be had beyond the clouds. As to Home Rule, I have what the Liberals call 'an open mind,' although I find it difficult to see how, if granted, it will not create more troubles than it relieves. Arthur Balfour's line is a strong one, but hardly likely to succeed unless it be supplemented by some conciliatory and remedial legislation, of which I wish I could hear more than I do. But next week I am going to spend four or five days at Hatfield, and may get better informed The real misery of our times is that Party Politics are constantly blinding even our best men to the true bearings of great interests ; although I feel sure I should be worse than any of them in this respect, if I were a politician.

" I cannot understand M. Mivart's position ; he does not seem to me to have at all realised the very serious bearing of the new School of Old Testament destructive criticism on the authority of our Lord as a Religious Teacher, to say nothing of His higher claims upon us. This is a very vast subject, but it has pained me to see how little the writers in the Reviews entertain it."

To Dr. Paget.

On the Use of the Bidding Prayer at the University Church.

" November 15 (?), 1885.

" In using the Bidding Prayer before a sermon at the University Church, I always leave out the name of Henry VIII., contenting myself with 'the Founder of Christ Church ;' and I always change the phrase which implies that the Universities are places of religious and useful learning, which is obviously not the fact, since they have been made head-quarters of Infidelity.

"Except in these particulars, I go on, I believe, in the old-fashioned way, not, however, without some inner qualms."

To ———

On the Unity of the Church.

"Christ Church, Oxford, November 20, 1885.

". . . 1. It does not seem that the unity of the Church has always and everywhere been such as is implied in the Roman Catholic contention. As a matter of fact, it has constantly been less satisfactory to abstract logic, and more waiting upon disturbing facts, *e.g.* in view of Antiquity, the proposition that not to be in communion with the See of Rome is necessarily to be outside the pale of Catholic Communion cannot be maintained except by interpreting Antiquity by the exigencies of a theory of the principle of Unity which is relatively modern.

"Those Christian bodies which preserve a public profession of the Faith committed by our Lord to His Church, and which retain the Commission which He gave to His Apostles, are one through their union with Him, even although, through human sin, on whichever side, they are not at present one in purpose, or in visible communion with each other.

"This may be illustrated by the Meletian schism : by the separations between the British Churches and the rest of the West in Saxon times : by the mutual excommunications of the Popes and Antipopes in a later age (no one supposes that the nations which took part with the 'Antipopes,' were outside the Church of Christ), and still more by the Division between East and West, which can only be described as the 'Eastern Schism,' or (as the Russians do) as the 'Western Schism,' by begging all the questions which have to be proved. These and other passages in Church history accord best with the opinion which lies at the basis of the English Church posiion, viz. that although strictly visible, and unimpaired unity of will and communion best accords with the Will of God, yet that unity is not altogether forfeited when portions of the Church are, for a while, separated from or opposed to each other, provided that they retain a hold upon the Faith and structure of the Church, as our Lord has revealed them.

"2. To answer your second question would take a volume. Each of the *dicta probantia*, which are cited in favour of Papal Claims, must be separately studied, and in the light of (1) the context in which each occurs, (2) the personal or other circumstances which may illustrate or account for the language. When this has been done to any considerable extent, it will be seen, as I cannot but think, that the language of

Antiquity falls very far short indeed of proving what is required for the Roman position. Such language, equitably interpreted, illustrates, sometimes the deserved and wide influence of a single Bishop of Rome, sometimes the authority which belongs to a See founded by an Apostle, and in many ways illustrious, sometimes the personal relations of the writer with the reigning Bishop of Rome, sometimes the psychological characteristics of the writer himself, as distinct from anything *de fide*. It is checked by such facts as the absolute independence of the Eastern Churches in the Ante-Nicene age, and still more by the conduct of the African Churches—themselves founded by Rome—under St. Cyprian and St. Augustine. As Dr. Pusey used to say, ' If St. Augustine had believed about the Pope as Cardinal Manning does, his conduct would have been very sinful.' And if it be said that the Papal Supremacy has been ' developed ' since St. Augustine's days, the answer is that this is an abandonment of the principle upon which, *e.g.*, St. Irenæus confuted the Gnostics of his day, and that ' Development ' is a dangerous guide which may lead us as easily to Infidel conclusions as to Roman ones.

" This is little enough on a vast subject, but it is possible to be ' honest ' with Dr. Bright—to concede to Rome all that a true interpretation of documents obliges us to give her, and yet to share his absolute conviction—that the Supremacy, and still more the Infallibility, of the Pope, *cannot* be defended on grounds of Antiquity.

" 3. As to divisions, etc., in the English Church, they are, of course, sinful and deplorable. But they do not touch the organic conditions of life. I may ade that they are not peculiar to the Church of England. If, *e.g.*, you would study the history of the French Church during the Jansenist and Jesuit controversies, you would see separations as wide and antagonisms as bitter as any in the Church of England to-day. About what you say about your being ' out of touch ' with the general run of the parochial clergy, is what most of the monastic clergy in England would have said, often and often, during the fourteenth and fifteenth centuries ; yet that did not make them distrust their position.

" If I might do so, I would make bold to beg you to reconsider your doubts in the light of the past annals of Christendom. Your difficulties seem often to turn on points of which you exaggerate the real importance. Perhaps I am a bad person to advise you, because I am obliged frankly to own to you that, *e.g.*, in view of the whole history and attitude of the Eastern Church, it does not seem to me possible that the Roman idea of Catholicism can be adequate or true. Whatever may be the logical defects (so to call them) of a wider conception of the Kingdom of the Divine Redeemer—such a conception seems to be imperatively necessary, unless we are to get into much more real trouble with the general sense of Antiquity than you would seem to be thinking of.

" And, as you know, the Church of England is not concerned to maintain that she is perfect or infallible, or other than a loser by the loss of visible unity. She has plenty to say in favour of the position that [there] are demonstrable faults and innovations upon ancient Christianity elsewhere, while she makes no pretensions to have escaped others of a different character.

" I pray that our Lord may restore to you peace of mind, and confidence in your present position and work for Him.

" P.S.—Until you are, by God's grace, a little more settled, do not expose yourself to the trials which come from advising other people in questions of this kind, or from contact with other priests who unhappily do not know what is to be said for their being where they are. Contact with a restless mind may do what no argument ever could do, by the mere force of irritating friction.

" Pray remember, too, that the very suspicion that the tendency of other minds with which you are in contact ' calls ' you to Rome begs the question. God cannot call any of us to that which it is not His Will that we should do ; and we are not right in allowing an apprehension of this kind to take the place of proof. I see around me many more minds which are moving in the direction of unbelief than in that of Rome. But I do not suppose that this tendency—whatever the excellence of many of the persons who share it may be—is a ' call. Before I trust it as such, I must be satisfied that the arguments for this or that sort of unbelief are valid."

CHAPTER XII.

ALMOST as soon as Liddon returned from the East, he heard a rumour that the "Jerusalem Bishopric" was about to be revived. The origin and history of this Bishopric had been equally unfortunate. It dated from 1841, and was the result of the proposals of Chevalier Bunsen for making a head for all Protestant bodies in Syria, and of Lord Shaftesbury's enthusiasm for the restoration of the Jews to Palestine. According to their plans, a Bishop of Jerusalem was to be selected alternately by the King of England and the King of Prussia, and was to be consecrated by English Bishops, although the nominees of Prussia would be Lutherans. To the minds of the English supporters of the scheme it was, in their own words, "the revival after long centuries of the diocese of St. James at Jerusalem;" and by the Chevalier Bunsen himself, the new Bishop was called "the successor of St. James," and under him was to commence "the restoration of Israel."[1] As a means of supervising the English congregations in the East, many good Churchmen at first approved of the proposal that an English Bishop should, with the consent of the Greek Patriarch of Jerusalem, be stationed either in that city or at Beyrout; but when the full story of the ideals of Bunsen and his English friends became known, this momentary support was changed into unmitigated hostility. It was

---

[1] "History of the Church Missionary Society," vol. i. p. 420.

not to be expected that High Churchmen could consent to the entire disregard of the historical constitution of the Church, which was involved in this intrusion into one of the great Patriarchates of the East, and to this compromising alliance with German Protestantism ; nor could they tolerate the proposed formation of a separate Jewish Church. Besides, they had grave fears lest the work of the Bishop should, as a matter of fact, consist chiefly of proselytising from the Greek Church.

Mr. Alexander, who was consecrated on November 7, 1841, to be the first " Bishop of Jerusalem," was, in Bunsen's words,

> by race an Israelite, born a Prussian in Breslau, in confession belonging to the Church of England, ripened [by hard work] in Ireland, Professor of Hebrew and Arabic in England [in what is now King's College]. So the beginning is made, please God, of the restoration of Israel." [1]

Newman, in his " Apologia," shows that the fact of Mr. Alexander's Consecration was a turning-point in his life, and had very much to do with his secession to the Church of Rome. Liddon knew of other less distinguished persons who, whether logically or not, had also alleged this alliance with the Lutherans as their reason for leaving the Church of England.

Matters were made very much worse when Bishop Alexander died, four years later. The selection of his successor lay with the Prussian Government ; and they chose Samuel Gobat, a Lutheran pastor, who had been in the employment of the C.M.S. in Abyssinia and in the East since 1825, and whose diaries of his work in Abyssinia had raised doubts about his orthodoxy on the doctrine of the Incarnation. It was only in August, 1845, that Mr. Gobat had been ordained deacon in order that he might be head of the Malta Protestant College ; and now in March, 1846, he, while still a deacon, was nominated to be the successor of Bishop Alexander. He had to be ordained

---

[1] " History of the Church Missionary Society," vol. i. p. 420.

priest privately at Fulham to avoid a public protest against him for unorthodoxy, although the Bishop of London had taken pains to receive from him privately explicit confession of the full faith in the Incarnation ; and he was consecrated at Lambeth four days later. When he went to Jerusalem, he allowed his clergy to receive proselytes from the Greek Church ; and thus Bishop Gobat, to use the words of Archbishop Benson,[1] "violated the provisions" which had been made in 1841 for the due recognition of the rights of the Patriarch of Jerusalem.

When Bishop Gobat died, in 1879, Liddon did all he could privately to prevent the appointment of a successor ; but an Englishman, Mr. Barclay by name, was consecrated. He died in 1881, and then the appointment lay, for the second time, with the Prussian Government. For five years they did nothing, and Liddon and his friends had begun to hope that nothing more would be heard of this " Bishopric." If anything could have increased his natural aversion to the whole plan it was that the news of its revival should reach him soon after his return from the East.

He at once tried to influence the Archbishop and his own friends at Oxford. The character of the Archbishop's rule was beginning to inspire a feeling of confidence in the Primate which those who did not know him had not felt at first.

To the Archbishop of Canterbury.

"3, Amen Court, St. Paul's, E.C., October 19, 1886.
"May I ask for your Grace's kind indulgence when I venture to trouble you with this letter?

"A report has been in circulation for some time to the effect that the appointment of anotherBishop to the 'Anglican See of Jerusalem' is seriously contemplated. This report seems to gain some countenance from Lord Lichfield's recent letter to the *Times*. It probably rests on no foundation. But the subject itself is very serious, and already causes disquiet to many minds. It would be a great relief if the report could be contradicted.

[1] "Life of Archbishop Benson," vol. ii. p. 167.

"When I was in Jerusalem in May last, I ventured to say to the Patriarch that, so far as I knew, no new successors to Bishop Gobat would be appointed. And he was pleased to express his great thankfulness and satisfaction at the news.

"For some time Churchmen have been hoping that we had at last quietly escaped from the unhappy experiment which was inflicted on us at the suggestion of a foreign *doctrinaire* like Bunsen, and at the heavy cost of losing Newman's allegiance to the English Church. The intrusion of a Bishop into a See already occupied by a Bishop of an ancient Church, with which we desire to be at least on friendly terms, cannot be defended by the example of Rome, who treats the Orthodox Patriarch as schismatic and therefore sends her own, or of the Copts and Armenians, who differ from the Orthodox on the grave questions that were ruled at Chalcedon. In the eyes of the Easterns an English Bishop at Jerusalem means that we English are wanting either in intelligence or honesty when we appeal to primitive rules and ways, and it involves our professions of a desire for a good understanding with them in a fatal suspicion of insincerity.

"Your Grace will, I trust, forgive me for venturing to say thus much. I should not have done so, unless I were convinced that the measure referred to would be hardly less disastrous in its effects upon many minds at home than upon our improving relations with the Apostolic Church of the East."

To the Rev. C. Gore.

"October 26, 1886.

". . . If you can say anything to —— as to the exceeding mischief which will arise if the Archbishop fills up the so-called 'Anglican Bishopric of Jerusalem,' pray do. One had hoped that that unhappy result of Bunsen's meddling and pedantic influence on English religion had been allowed to die quietly. . . . For all really spiritual purposes it [the Puritan party] sincerely believes that a Presbyterian or Baptist minister will do just as well as a Bishop ; and, indeed, it resents, as we know, any attempt to show that a Bishop has any spiritual faculties with which the Christian Church cannot dispense."

The Archbishop replied that the Foreign Office could not obtain any answer from the authorities in Prussia ; if they should wish to give up their part of the contract of 1841, it would be then necessary to consider what the statutory position of the Church of England would be with regard to the money which had been collected for this purpose. Liddon replied—

To the Archbishop of Canterbury.

"Christ Church, Oxford, November 8, 1886.

"Pray allow me to thank your Grace for your very kind letter. You will believe that I should have shrunk from adding to your many and overwhelming burdens, unless I had been exposed to a pressure which I could not well resist. Your Grace's letter will enable me to give reassuring explanations without in any way betraying your confidence. If I may venture to say so without being too bold, your Grace's rule has been most happily distinguished by the disappearance of many irritating questions which, in former years, have kept minds in constant disquiet, even when not provoking them to disaffection towards the English Church. And to this I trace the fact, for which it is impossible to be too thankful, that—at least within my own experience—there is now much less tendency to go to Rome than at any time within the last twenty years. But the Jerusalem Bishopric is a spectre of the past, associated in many memories with a long history of religious perplexity, and, putting the Eastern Church for the moment out of the question, we should be much stronger, because more satisfied, as well as more united at home, if it could be quietly buried out of sight. The Patriarch of Jerusalem struck me as a man seriously alive to the help which we might afford him by helping him to promote religious education among his clergy and laity, and by other means which a sincere and respectful sympathy would suggest. But, as your Grace would feel, we must do any good we can—and we may hope to do a great deal of good—*through* the authorities of the Eastern Church, and not independently of, or in opposition to them. It is a case in which practical wisdom and Ecclesiastical order point in the same direction. If hereafter it should be discovered that any funds now devoted to the maintenance of a Bishop at Jerusalem are placed at your Grace's disposal, that they may be devoted in some other way to the furtherance of Christianity in Palestine, might I suggest that they might furnish a yearly grant to the Patriarch, with the object of enabling him to print LXX. copies of the Old Testament, the New Testament in Greek and Arabic, and perhaps some of the early Fathers at the Press of the Holy Sepulchre? Books imported from Europe, even though printed on better paper, and textually identical, encounter a certain amount of suspicion among the Eastern clergy ; they are reassured by a title-page, and a type, which shows that the book is offered them by their Ecclesiastical superiors, and through channels to which they have been accustomed. The ' Press of the Holy Sepulchre ' has published a good many volumes and very creditably ; I brought back some twenty from the Holy Land, and have a copy of the works of St. Cyril of Jerusalem and an Arabic-Greek Christomathy lying before me, which would not discredit the Pitt or the Clarendon Presses.

Your Grace will forgive me saying thus much, and will believe that I shall be delighted to be allowed to talk with you on the subject, whenever you may command it."

Liddon had tried to prevent newspaper correspondence on the subject ; but the Archbishop requested him to send a short paragraph to the *Guardian*, stating the facts, and at the same time to suggest that correspondence should be allowed. Several letters from Low Churchmen at once appeared, pleading for a revival of the Bishopric. Liddon and others unwillingly were obliged to reply ; and there was, of course, the usual controversial turmoil, for which, however, Liddon was in no way responsible.

At the same time, he received news from Jerusalem, which did not agree with the impression which he had formed during his visit there.

To Sir Edmund Lechmere, Bart.

"Christ Church, November 23, 1886.

"Pray let me thank you sincerely for your letter. To get one from the Holy City is always a privilege. In April, I understood the Patriarch to be opposed to the plan of sending another Anglican Bishop to Jerusalem. The history of Bishop Gobat's Episcopacy would make this feeling on his part very natural. But I gather from your letter that, if I then rightly understood him, he must have changed his mind. Nothing could exceed the generosity and kindness which I experienced at his hands, and which I do not doubt was the expression of his general feeling towards the English Church. I own that, in view of the unhappy history and associations of the Anglican See of Jerusalem, I had most earnestly hoped that no more Bishops would be sent there. The enterprise is bound up with two humiliating memories —the loss of Newman, and Bunsen's pedantic effort to amalgamate our branch of the Church of Jesus Christ with the Lutheran body in Prussia. So far as my experience goes, few mistakes of later years have done more to recruit the ranks of the Roman Church from among us than the ' Jerusalem Bishopric.' Of course, when we are free—if we do get free—from the Prussian alliance, the whole thing will be on a better footing. But still, the question will arise, What business have we to be there at all ? My objection would be largely removed, if any future Bishop would be content to call himself ' The Chaplain-Bishop of the English residents at Jerusalem.' This would describe accurately his real and only legitimate position ; and it would avoid all appearance of invading the jurisdiction of the Patriarch. And it would be an additional gain if the Patriarch could be induced to issue some public Letter, stating that the Chaplain-Bishop of the English comes to Jerusalem with his own full sanction and welcome."

His correspondent reassured him by saying that the Patriarch had most positively expressed his willingness to welcome an English Bishop at Jerusalem, and wished both the Archbishop and Liddon to know this. " He said," added Sir Edmund Lechmere, "that he should like a Bishop like you."

On February 16, 1887, the Archbishop wrote to Liddon, enclosing a lengthy Memorandum,[1] signed by himself, the Archbishop of York, and the Bishop of London, and stating that the Prussian Government had finally withdrawn, and the alliance with the Lutherans was thus at an end. But since the Patriarch had expressed a strong desire that an Anglican Bishop should reside at Jerusalem, he was about to appoint one. The new Bishop would set his face against all proselytising among the Christians ; the title, " Bishop of Jerusalem " would be dropped ; the new Bishop would only place the word " Bishop " after his usual signature. "If he has to describe himself more fully, it will be as Bishop of the Church of England in Jerusalem and in the East." Liddon immediately replied—

To the Archbishop of Canterbury.

" Christ Church, Oxford, February 18, 1887.

" Pray allow me to thank your Grace for your great kindness in writing to me so fully, and in sending me the Memorandum which I have received from your Grace this morning. I shall, of course, obey your Grace's desire that your communication should be treated as absolutely confidential.

" Your Grace does not invite, and it might well seem disrespectful in me to offer, any observations whatever on a decision which appears to have been already arrived at by your Grace. But I crave your pardon, if I make bold to add a few words on a subject which has, indeed, caused me much anxiety and distress, not only, or mainly, on my own account. It is difficult to reconcile the Patriarch's Letter to your Grace with what I certainly understood him to say to myself. But I may have misapprehended or missed something in the course

[1] The document is published in the " Life of Archbishop Benson," vol. ii. pp. 165–167.

of conversation. Or he may have of late been led to hope that an English Bishop of sound Church principles may be able in some measure to restrain the English missionaries in Jerusalem. Whether this expectation is likely to be justified by the event would appear to be at the best very doubtful, and especially if £600 a year of the proposed Bishop's income is to be paid by the very Societies whose schismatical activity he is to repress. Nothing short of a solemn and public assurance, made to your Grace on the part of the Committees which direct the operations of the Societies in question, that they will neither make nor receive 'converts' from the Church of Christ in Palestine, would really avail to put a stop to a course of action so discreditable, and, indeed, so ruinous to our Church, both in Syria and at home.

"If an English Bishop is to live at Jerusalem, I would plead that the word 'Jerusalem' might disappear altogether from his title, and that his permanent spiritual superintendence should be restricted in terms to persons of English descent. Your Grace would feel that converts from Mohammedanism or Judaism, on the soil of Palestine, by whomsoever they may be made, are rightfully the spiritual subjects of the Patriarch and Bishop of the historical Church of Christ in that country.

"And if English clergy and missionaries are honestly and consistently to assist the Patriarch, they will work with a view to promoting this and no other result ; avoiding, therefore, the formation and organisation of congregations of native Christians permanently severed from the local and Orthodox Church.

"For more reasons than I can well state, I could most earnestly have wished that it had been possible utterly to cut off the entail of the unhappy history which is associated with the presence of an English Bishop at Jerusalem. But your Grace is surrounded with such difficulties in arriving at any decision as may well make others very unwilling indeed to say anything that could add to a burden of anxieties which they cannot share."

In arriving at his decision the Archbishop had evidently hoped that his action would be interpreted in the light of his dealings with the ancient Christian Church in Assyria, where he had taken every care, when sending some English clergy to Assyria, to respect the jurisdiction of the Patriarch of Antioch and the local Bishops. But the Jerusalem Bishopric had so long borne so evil a name in the ears of many English Churchmen, and the proceedings of Bishop Gobat had so fully justified their worst fears, that the reverse of what the Archbishop hoped was happening. His action towards the Assyrian Church

was in danger of being interpreted in the light of the
lamentable history of the Jerusalem Bishopric. To prevent
this, he sent to Liddon, through Mr. Athelstan Riley, a
further statement of his own intentions with regard to the
new Bishop and his work. He wished the work to be on
the model of the work among the Assyrian Christians ;
and the new Bishop would be the bearer of a Letter to the
Patriarch of Jerusalem similar to that already sent to the
Patriarch of Antioch by the hands of the Assyrian Mission.
The C.M.S. would in no way control the Bishop ; he would
act as the vicar or representative of the Archbishop, who
would alone control his policy, and who was against any
form of proselytism. This courteous communication Liddon
immediately acknowledged, pointing out where it failed to
satisfy him :—

To Athelstan Riley, Esq.

"Christ Church, February 25, 1887.

" Pray accept my very sincere thanks for all the trouble you have
taken on behalf of myself and other people ; and, if any opportunity
should occur, pray make my respects to his Grace the Archbishop,
and thank him for the confidence he has shown me in allowing me
to see the Paper which you have enclosed. It has been seen by
Dr. Bright, Dr. Paget, and the Warden of Keble. This, I think,
would have been in accordance with the Archbishop's intention, as,
unless they had seen it, nothing practically valuable could have
resulted from your sending it. The Archbishop's assurances that the
new Bishop will be under his Grace's control, and not that of the two
Societies, is all that we could wish as regards his own feeling in the
matter. But I hope it will not seem petulant or obstinate if I am
unable to set aside the broad consideration that you cannot take
people's money and ignore their wishes. And the wishes of the C.M.S.,
whether at home or abroad, are not doubted : (1) what I saw and
heard for myself in Jerusalem ; (2) the last C.M.S. Report ; and (3)
the articles and correspondence in the *Record* newspaper during the
last six or more weeks tell exactly the same story.

". . . This must be borne in mind when weighing the Archbishop's
kind words. The only chance of keeping the C.M.S. even moderately
in order lay in being perfectly independent of them. And with this
independence the £600 a year is surely incompatible.

" I very gratefully recognise the importance of the opening sentence
of the Memorandum that the policy pursued with reference to the

Patriarchate of Antioch will be followed at Jerusalem. My fear would have been that co-operation with the two societies made it impossible. The most practical thing I can suggest is some Declaration on the part of the Archbishop as to the principles which will guide him and the new Bishop—a Declaration much more explicit than that of the Memorandum published in the *Record* of last week. It is a matter fo consideration whether this had better be elicited by a Memorial addressed to the Archbishop or in any other way. But it should be in a form which can be pointed to hereafter. We are dealing not with men, but with institutions which survive them. We cannot forget that Archbisbop Howley was succeeded by Archbishop Sumner, and the revival of the Jerusalem Bishopric almost inevitably makes a renewed Puritan aggression probable sooner or later, do what we may. But a clear Declaration would not be without its effect. I have written to you with much greater freedom than would be respectful if I were writing to the Archbishop. But people *feel* very deeply indeed on this subject. Let me acknowledge most warmly your own most generous and clear-sighted line of conduct in dealing with it.

" P.S.—You should read the *Record* of yesterday. Its satisfaction will give the reason for the feelings with which both the revival of the Bishopric and the appointment to it are regarded by good Churchmen."

It was strongly felt by Liddon and those who worked with him that some influential Memorial ought to be addressed to the Archbishop, which might afford him a good reason for making further provisions, than those contained in the Memorandum of February 16, against any action which would infringe upon the prerogative of the Patriarch of Jerusalem. It was not that they in any way mistrusted the Archbishop's intentions, but rather that they were full of fears lest his intentions should be frustrated by powers which he would in the future be unable to control. The following Address was therefore drawn up and sent to him, signed by a number of the leading Clergy of the High Church party. The concluding Clauses contain the real purpose of the document :—

" To His Grace the Lord Archbishop of Canterbury.

" We beg leave to approach your Grace with an earnest petition for some reassurance in regard to the grave anxiety caused to Churchmen by the conditions proposed for the maintenance of an Anglican

Bishop in Jerusalem. We do not venture on the present occasion to express any opinion with regard to the decision to appoint a Bishop for this position. We are sincerely grateful that we can trace, in the deference expressed to the wish of the Patriarch, the same principles of action in regard to the Eastern Church which have been defined by your Grace in respect to the Mission to the Assyrian Christians. Our anxiety is for the present directed to a feature of the proposed arrangement which seems especially to threaten the integrity of those principles ; for they are distinctly and avowedly violated by work which has been going on in Palestine under the name of the Church of England.

" It is natural to ask what will be the relation of the new Bishop to this work ; and it is impossible not to feel that, by the present pro-visions for his maintenance, a very serious public appearance of sanction is given to these proceedings in the past, and very little hope allowed that they will be uniformly repressed in the future. For it is proposed that the Bishop shall receive a large portion of his income from the Society whose agents have been eager in proselytising from the Orthodox Church (cf. ' C.M.S. Report,' p. 60), and whose Reports speak of the Patriarch himself as a chief hindrance to some of their operations (cf. ' C.M.S. Report,' p. 58).

" The ultimate, though perhaps gradual, result of this seems to us to be inevitable and disastrous. For it is necessary in regard to this new departure to think of consequences likely to ensue not only during your Grace's tenure of the Primacy, and while the matter is fresh and minds are alert, but also in the future under other Primates, who may be otherwise minded than your Grace, or less interested in the East, or much distracted by other affairs. Under such conditions watch-fulness at home might cease, and local and financial pressure might steadily encourage the work of proselytising from the Orthodox Church.

" We believe that your Grace will recognise that in this arrange-ment we have just grounds for disquietude, and warrant for humbly craving some definite reassurance and precautions : and we would, therefore, venture, encouraged by the admirable expressions which your Grace has frequently given to the true principles of our intercom-munion with the East, most respectfully to suggest, for your Grace's consideration, two safeguards by which it might seem good to your Grace to protect those principles in future relations between the Church of England and the Church of Jerusalem.

"(1) That your Grace might be pleased to inform the Patriarch, when commending to his Christian charity the newly appointed Bishop, that it is a part of your intention in sending him that he should use his Episcopal authority to check all proceedings on the part of English clergy which infringe on the rights of the Patriarch and his clergy.

"(2) That inasmuch as the residence of the Bishop has been fixed at Jerusalem, in accordance with the wish of the Patriarch, your Grace's intention might be declared to be that, at each vacancy of the English Bishopric the continuance of this arrangement for the Bishop's residence shall be dependent upon the continuance of the same wish on the part of the ruling Patriarch."

The purpose of this Address he explains fully to Lord Halifax.

To Lord Halifax.

'Christ Church, March 4, 1887.

". . . The Archbishop is committed (1) to the re-establishment of the See ; (2) to the nomination of Archdeacon Blyth, the day of whose Consecration is fixed ; (3) to the payment of the new Bishop out of the funds of the C.M.S. and L.J.S. It is useless to ask the Archbishop to reconsider steps to which he is publicly committed. But if he will promise to make the *residence* of each English Bishop at Jerusalem contingent *upon the wish of the Patriarch for the time being*, the sting will have been taken out of the measure, the Patriarch's jurisdiction recognised, and a very effectual means furnished for stopping the proselytism. Read the second of the two points at the close of the document. . . . I should think that the safest thing now for the E.C.U. to do is to promote Petitions to Convocation against proselytising in Jerusalem. If the Bishop—now unhappily an unalterable fact—could be reduced to the position of a legate or 'nuncio' from our English Primate to the Patriarch, we might in this way escape from the immense difficulties which have been thrown in the way of future Christian unity by this miserable mistake."

The Address was sent on March 12,[1] and on March 18 Liddon wrote to an intimate friend of the Archbishop's to explain more definitely the aims of the signatories.

To the Rev. Canon Mason.

"Christ Church, March 18, 1887.

". . . Many Churchmen object to the Address as a very inadequate expression of what they think and feel. As you know, it was constructed upon the principles (1) of not asking the Archbishop to reconsider anything to which he is publicly committed, and (2) of respectfully placing before him an opportunity of giving public explanations and guarantees which could not indeed reverse in any sense the decision at which he has arrived, but which might modify it

---

[1] It appeared with the reply of the Archbishop, dated the 19th, in the   *Times* of March 22, three days before the Consecration of Bishop Blyth.

in a direction which would be as welcome, as we hope, to himself as to his petitioners. But it is—in view of the situation—a *minimum.* I, who have been thrown in the way of knowing something of what Oxford Churchmen felt on the subject forty years ago, am not surprised at the survival of feelings of those days. If the Address had not been put out, the feelings would before this have taken other and—to the Primate—less welcome forms.

"Another remark is that it is hard to attach much importance to the distinction between the payment of the Bishop directly by the C.M.S. and the payment through the Archbishop. In any case the C.M.S. pays, and the moral influence which attaches to that fact is inevitable, however the fact itself is disguised. So again, if the *worst* language in the 'C.M.S. Report' is not the language of the Society itself, still it is language which the Society has deliberately selected for publication from the letters of its agents.

"(3) But, especially, may I express to you a *most earnest hope* that the second petition may not be set aside? It is indeed the *causa ob quam* of the Address. Grant that the Archbishop cannot 'bind his successor,' in any political, legal, or even Ecclesiastical sense. Is that really a reason for declining to accede to the prayers of the petition? Is it not equally a reason against sending a Bishop to Jerusalem at all, since if he is to be (as we hope, or more than hope) only a Bishop-resident with no pretensions to the jurisdiction attaching to a See, he may be removed from Jerusalem, or recalled altogether by a future Archbishop? What the Archbishop *can* do is *this*—he can establish a tradition with a great moral if not with a legal Force, a tradition which in all probability will guide and govern, if it does not coerce, the action of his successor. If the present Archbishop says that the residence of the Bishop in Jerusalem shall be dependent on the sanction of each succeeding Patriarch, it will be *difficult* for another Archbishop to say that it shall not : since to do so would be notoriously to reject a safeguard which was deliberately attached to the renewal of the Jerusalem Bishop by the present Primate. Pray forgive me for saying so much : and do not trouble yourself to answer."

The Archbishop's reply to the Memorial added nothing to his previous public assurances, and Liddon was specially distressed that he could not obtain any declaration of an intention to make the residence of an English Bishop at Jerusalem always contingent of necessity on the Patriarch's consent. He found the same fault with the Letters[1] in which the Archbishop recommended the new Bishop to the Eastern Patriarchs. The Archbishop had kindly

[1] These Letters were naturally dated March 25, the date of the Bishop's Consecration, but they were still only in draft on April 7.

requested Mr. Riley, who had drawn them up, to forward
the rough draft of them to Liddon, more than a fortnight
after Bishop Blyth's Consecration.

To Athelstan Riley, Esq.

"3, Amen Court, April 7, 1887.

" I thank you for these Papers, which I have read through.   They
are very well drawn up, and, as far as they go, are satisfactory.   Perhaps I should wish to see ἀειπάρθενος and Θεοτόκος attached to the
name of the Blessed Virgin.[1]   The latter especially ; because many
of the Low Church English clergy, from ignorance rather than from
heretical intention, do talk Nestorianism, which naturally shocks the
instructed and believing clergy of the Eastern Church.   The Letters
are satisfactory—so far as discouraging the C.M.S. agents and
other schismatical workers goes, although a stern word of condemnation of their conduct in the past would improve matters in the
eyes of the Easterns.   But the Letters contain no statement to the
effect that the presence of future Anglican Bishops in Jerusalem will
depend upon the approval of future Patriarchs.   And this is necessary
if the Anglican Bishop is to be a legate and not an occupant—or
rather a pretended occupant—of a See with inherent jurisdiction.   Nor
is there anything about the Mission to the Jews and Moslems.   If
the missions are to go on forming a Church distinct from the Orthodox
Church of Jesus Christ in Palestine, they will be engaged in a
schismatical work ; English missionaries have no business in Palestine
except on the condition of working for the true Church of Christ in
that country.   Surely the Letters to the Patriarchs ought to contain
some assurance on this head too ? "

The Patriarch was fully alive to all that was going on
in England, and had received also from Sir Edmund
Lechmere a copy of the Address to the Archbishop.   This
he acknowledged a month after the Consecration of Bishop
Blyth, in a letter of which the following is a translation :—

From the Patriarch of Jerusalem to Sir Edmund Lechmere.

"April 22, 1887.

" To the most noble and in Christ our Lord, well-beloved Son of
our Humility, Sir Edm. Lechmere, Bart., member of the House of
Commons of Her Majesty the Queen of Great Britain.

---

[1] *i.e.* in the subscription and date   of Archbishop Benson," vol. ii. p.
at the end of the Letter (see " Life   172).

" We, Nicodemus, by the Grace of God, Patriarch of the Holy City of Jerusalem and of the whole of Palestine, wish you grace, peace, and every prosperity from God Almighty. Having read with paternal solicitude your Nobility's filial letter of the 12th of April of the present year, we received with great joy the news contained therein. And in answering now, first we thank your Nobility for having seized every convenient opportunity to ensure that the appointment of the Anglican Bishop in Jerusalem should be made in accordance with the wish of our Humility, that is, that relations should be mutually kept up between the two Churches.

" Secondly, we request of your Nobility the favour kindly to transmit to His Grace Edward, Archbishop of Canterbury, our assurance, first, that we shall await the safe arrival among us of the Bishop before answering His Grace's official letter of appointment concerning the choice and consecration of the Bishop ; and secondly, that we have received with pleasure His Grace's promise to you that this Bishop is totally independent of and unconnected with any Missionary Society whatever ; and further, we have made it known to whomsoever it may concern as an everlasting pledge that the Anglican Bishop in Jerusalem will in every way act according to the wishes and instructions of His Grace the Archbishop of Canterbury, His Grace the Archbishop of York, and His Reverence the Bishop of London. The appointed Anglican Bishop whom your Nobility has kindly recommended to me has not yet arrived, and after his safe arrival among us we shall also write our impression concerning him, and will at the same time forward our own Patriarchal Letter of authority as drawn up in this our holy city.

" We have also carefully read the translation of the Memorandum which your Nobility has had the kindness to forward to us, and we rendered thanks and glory to our Lord God and Saviour, that under the leadership of our well-beloved Son in Christ, the Right Reverend Canon Liddon, there have appeared in the fold of our well-beloved Anglican Church honourable and worthy men, who, imbued with reverence and the spirit of Truth, while worthily upholding their just claims, recognise and support the sovereign and jurisdictional rights of our most Holy Apostolic and Patriarchal throne, according to our Catholic Orthodox Church of Christ. We declare, and the whole Orthodox Church will declare with us, that the most honourable and beloved Anglican Church has already given striking proof of mutual love in having decided that the Bishop among us shall not be called ' Bishop of Jerusalem,' but simply ' Bishop,' having control and guardianship over the [Anglican] clergy and laity in the East, and with instructions to oppose and denounce, when necessary, the unjustifiable proselytising proceedings of certain Protestant societies among Orthodox Christians. This testimony is further characterized by our Humility as a most important step towards the desired future union of the Anglican and Orthodox Churches, a result which does not seem impracticable if, on both sides, the minds of the clergy and laity are prepared beforehand, by means of earnest research and study of the mysteries and dogmas given to the Catholic Church of Christ by the Holy Writers of the Gospels, the Holy Apostles, the Holy Fathers of the Church after them, and the Seven Œcumenical Synods. And we, whilst striving our utmost towards this much-desired and Godly end, rejoice exceedingly that the opportunity is offered us of strongly declaring and noting the sisterly love of the Anglican Church towards our Orthodox Eastern Church ; and we further intend, very shortly, to publish the Letters of His Grace the Archbishop of Canterbury."

The Patriarch rightly saw that the worst features of the scheme of 1841 had disappeared. The Prussian withdrawal gave the Archbishop a splendid opportunity for some reform, and he availed himself of it eagerly and consistently. In his position he could not well denounce the past ; but condemnation of it from some quarter or other was really needed. Had the change been made without protest against the past, and *sub silentio*, people at home and in Jerusalem might well have supposed that, in spite of assurances, all the old abuses were to be continued ; Liddon and his friends alone openly condemned and repudiated what had happened since 1841, and on this account the Patriarch gave the credit of the improvements to their efforts. Their remonstrances had done much to efface the memory of Bunsen's eccentric and calamitous experiment.

But Liddon felt that he had failed ; an English Bishop had gone to Jerusalem in the pay of Societies in which he had no confidence, and there were no guarantees for the future. The controversy cost him dear. It was clear that he had spent in this effort a large portion of his recently recovered strength, and almost daily his diary records weariness and inability to work ; even his handwriting witnesses to the exhaustion that it produced.

CORRESPONDENCE, 1887–1888.

On the Eastern Church.

" 3, Amen Court, St. Paul's, E.C., August 25, 1887.

" I must not allow you to suppose that I accept your account of the Eastern Church.   I have spent some time both in Russia and in Syria, and have seen a good deal of its Patriarchs and Bishops, and Clergy and laity.   And I have read something of its literature—I mean since the period of the Separation of the West.

" And let me say, first of all, that to my mind there is no greater difficulty in supposing that the Eastern Church is alone the Church of God than in supposing the Roman Church to be alone the Church of God.   Either supposition is attended by difficulties, which appear to me to be insuperable.   But I should have no stronger reasons for ceasing to be a Christian if, like Mr. Hathaway, or Dr. Overbeck, I were to become satisfied that the Eastern Church was the ' One Body,' than if, like yourself, I were to think this of the Western Churches of the Roman Obedience.

" The Greek Church is 'local' in the same sense as the Latin. She is coloured by the language, thought, and civilization of the ancient Eastern Empire, just as the Latin is coloured by that of the West.   The Roman Church is really at home in the Latin countries of Europe, or in countries formed and influenced by them.   In the East she is just as much an exotic as the Anglican.   I have felt this in Jerusalem and St. Petersburg.

" And as regards formalism, or a low type of Christian life, there is not, as far as I know, much to choose.   In both Communions there are saints and great servants of God.   In both there are many who dishonour the Christian name.   No one whom I have ever met in this life impressed me more by his saintliness of character than Leonide, Suffragan Bishop of Moscow, who died Archbishop of Tver.   I should be thankful indeed to be anywhere near him in another life. And Innocent, the Apostle of Kamtchatka, who died Archbishop of Moscow, was as noble a Christian as any whom I have ever heard or read of in either division of the Western Church.   It is not yet twenty years since his death.

" No doubt there are bad clergy in the Eastern Church, some of them ignorant, some vicious.   Have we none in the Church of England ?   Are there none in the Azores, in South America, of the Roman Communion ?   A moderate knowledge of the real statistics of existing Christendom, and still more of its past history, enables us to throw stones all round, if we have a mind to do so.   But the wounds and diseases of one portion of the Holy Body are the wounds and diseases of the whole ; since, as the Apostle says, ' If one member suffer, all the members suffer with it.'

2 B

" The Eastern Church has few friends in the West. Puritanism dislikes her because she upholds Sacramental Truth. Rome, because she rejects the Papal Supremacy. As to the charge of ' formalism,' there is just as much and just as little justice in it as when it is urged, as it is popularly in England, against the system and worship of the Roman Church. As to Erastianism, a study of the reigns of the Emperor Justinian or of Louis XIV., but particularly the former, shows that Erastianism is not of one age or country. No Eastern Bishop has gone through more humiliations at the hands of the Civil Power than did Pope Vigilius in the latter phase of the Monophysite controversy."

On Matthew Arnold.

" 3, Amen Court, St. Paul's, E.C., August 18, 1887.

" . . . I cannot, I fear, quite agree with you about Mr. Matthew Arnold. He is a true poet, and a delightful person to meet in society. But these are not the most important things in life. His language on the most solemn of all subjects—the Being and Personality of God— makes it, as it seems to me, impossible for a sincere Christian to think of him with other feelings than those of the deepest regret that he is not a believer. Do we not live in days in which there is a temptation to think little of Religious Truth in comparison with literary or other eminence ? "

On Religious Differences.

" 3, Amen Court, St. Paul's, E.C., January 7, 1888.

" When you ask me why sincere people should differ so very seriously as they do in matters of religious belief, I can only say that I cannot confidently answer you. It is obviously impossible to say either (1) that one dissentient is not really sincere, or (2) that he has committed some sin which entails a penal spiritual blindness.

" I can only *suppose* that (3) the true answer to the question is to be found in a region which Divines associate with ' dispositions for faith,' and which you would perhaps say is the soil in which assumptions grow. Why one soil should have these dispositions, and another be without them, is one of the secrets of the Divine Predestination which would always be a difficulty if St. Paul had not written Romans chap. ix., and yet a difficulty which is beyond question, also, a fact.

" For myself, I cannot believe in a God Who is not merely a First Cause or a Supreme Intelligence, but also, and persistently, a Moral Being, without feeling profoundly the antecedent necessity for a Revelation—a necessity which is created by the actual circumstances of the world which He has made. This presumption or necessity appears to be strong enough to carry us through a great many difficulties,—imperfections in the evidence, as we may think them, of the Revelation which has been made, and this or that feature of the Revelation itself. When I look about me, I see nothing besides Christianity which at all satisfies the hope that God has not left us to ourselves ; while it is easy to understand that the many difficulties of Christianity are not without a moral purpose, in that they make our assent to its claims distinct from, and higher than, that of the understanding acting *apart from* the moral nature. . . ."

On the Later Position of the Old Catholic Body.

" February 20, 1888.

" . . . During the last ten years there have been considerable changes in the Old Catholic body. In more than one way they have abandoned the position in which they found themselves in 1870, after the Vatican Definition. Their abandonment of clerical celibacy has alienated Dr. Döllinger and Professor Reusch ; and the lay element in their Synods, in itself anomalous, is, for those who know something of the ingredients which compose it, a matter for anxiety. I should fear that it may mean that they are drifting, or likely to drift. I have never doubted that they were right in making the stand they did in 1870, but I confess I do not feel as hopeful as I then did about their future, and I should be sorry if the English Church were to consecrate a Bishop for them. But *do they* want one ? They have two already."

CHAPTER XIII.

THE "LUX MUNDI" CONTROVERSY—VISIT TO BISHOP LIGHTFOOT—CORRESPONDENCE WITH THE REV. C. GORE—DEATH OF BISHOP LIGHTFOOT—MESSAGE FROM THE QUEEN—CORRESPONDENCE IN THE *SPECTATOR*—OFFER OF THE BISHOPRIC OF ST. ALBAN'S—LAST SERMON IN OXFORD—ILLNESS AND DEATH.

1888–1890.

FOR many years a silent change which was nothing short of a revolution had been taking place in the attitude of the younger generation of the Churchmen in Oxford towards the question of Old Testament Criticism. Liddon, of course, was fully alive to all that the advanced critics were writing, and regarded their latest conclusions with the hostility with which Dr. Pusey had regarded the cruder statements of the earlier writers of the same School sixty years before. He held, with Dr. Pusey, that far more than the Old Testament was at stake. This form of Criticism was raising other and very serious questions with regard to our Lord's authority, and the intellectual atmosphere was in certain quarters becoming unsettled on even the most fundamental questions.

TO C. T. REDINGTON, ESQ.

"3, Amen Court, December 29, 1888.

"Dear X.'s move to Socinianism—a Socinianism, too, which would have shocked Priestley or Channing—has been a great sorrow to me. But I cannot think that it settles the question of the Old Testament. He is a good Hebrew scholar, and a man of high intelligence and mental integrity. But—at least as I used to think when I knew him more intimately in his younger days—he is much too facile in presence of new theory of whatever sort. Two-thirds of the questions about the Old Testament have nothing to do with Hebrew, and can be settled by the reverent common sense of ordinary Christians. X. has placed himself, with almost childlike trust, in the hands of Wellhausen. Well, I have no right to place my judgment against X.'s. But I have read Wellhausen, and have a robust confidence that he will go the way of other Rationalists before him. In September I spent four days with Dr. Döllinger at Tegernsee, and among other things we talked over Wellhausen's ' Prolegomena.' ' I could not get on with it at all,' D. said ; ' it is full of unproved assumptions.' Any one who takes the trouble to read it carefully will, I think, share this opinion. Is it not remarkable that our Divine Lord, as if in anticipation of the sceptical spirit of our day, sanctioned those portions of the Old Testament which are most strongly objected to by the modern Rationalists ? The Flood, Lot's wife, Jonah in the whale, are all used by Him in His recorded teaching. Was He referring to fables which He knew, or—worse still —did not know to be such ? Especially noteworthy is the prominence given in His teaching to the Book of Daniel—the *bête noire* of the Rationalising writers. I cannot think that any such change as you anticipate is before us. ' Heaven and earth shall pass away, but My Words shall not pass away.' You will think me old-fashioned. But I can't help the fashion of faith ; and, as for ——, I shall hope and pray that, D.G., *pleniores haustus ad religionem reducant.*"

But in his constant ill health and prolonged absences from Oxford, he had never noticed that many of the results of this Criticism were held by the younger men around him, of whose loyalty to the Catholic Faith he was fully assured. He knew well its prevalence in other circles, and he frequently spoke about it during the early months of 1889.

"*May* 27.—Long but unsatisfactory talk with —— about the new School of Negative Criticism about the Old Testament.

"*May* 30.—Long talk of an hour and a half in the evening with —— about the Old Testament. He—defending Driver and the young people who are attacking its trustworthiness—says that Gore goes a long way in the direction of Driver, though not exactly taking up his position."

Yet when he left Oxford in July, and paid a visit to Bishop Lightfoot before his August residence at St. Paul's, the subject is not mentioned, and it seems to have passed from his thoughts as if it had not been felt as a matter of urgent importance. His visit to Bishop Auckland, in July, 1889, was a very great delight to him ; it was a renewal

of intimacy with one whom he had known so well at St.
Paul's, and for whom, in spite of many differences, he
ever retained a deep and affectionate regard. He always
spoke of this meeting, and looked back to it with great
happiness. Three days after it had come to an end he
records in his diary—

"*July* 30.—Letter from Bishop Lightfoot, asking me to allow him to
dedicate his 'St. Ignatius' to me. What an honour ! Alas ! how little
I deserve the good things my friends say and think of me !"

This Dedication to the Second Edition of the Bishop's
great work ran as follows :—

"TO
HENRY PARRY LIDDON, D.D.
TO WHOM GOD HAS GIVEN
SPECIAL GIFTS AS A CHRISTIAN PREACHER
AND MATCHED THE GIFTS WITH THE OPPORTUNITIES
ASSIGNING TO HIM HIS PLACE
BENEATH THE GREAT DOME OF ST. PAUL'S
THE CENTRE OF THE WORLD'S CONCOURSE

THIS WORK IS DEDICATED
AS A TRIBUTE OF ADMIRATION AND AFFECTION
FROM A FORMER COLLEAGUE"

But as soon as he returned to Oxford for the Michaelmas
Term, he heard that the subject that had filled his thoughts
in the Summer Term was to be treated by one of his most
valued friends in a way which he felt convinced would be
disastrous to the interests of the Divine Revelation.

"*October* 23.—In Hall sat next to ——, who is now at Cuddesdon.
He says that it is reported that Gore's Essay in the forthcoming
volume of 'Studies' will make great concessions to the Germans.
"*October* 24.—Told Paget what —— had told me about Gore's
Essay. Begged him not to speak to him. But he did."

From the Rev. C. Gore.

"Pusey House, October 25, [1889].
"I hear from Paget that evil rumours have reached you of our
Essay book 'Lux Mundi.' I believe you will approve almost all of it.
What you will least like are a few pages at the end, I am afraid, of

my Essay. I send it herewith, so that if you wish you may know the worst. Only I hope if you read it you will read the whole Essay. . . . Whatever I have said there I have said times out of number to people of all classes in difficulties, and have found again and again that it helped them to a firm footing in Catholic Faith. Where you have found a certain method spiritually effective and useful, and you believe it to be quite orthodox, it seems impossible to refrain from saying it. Something had to be said on the subject. I do sincerely hope that if you read it you will not seriously disapprove. I think I should almost die of it if it did harm. But certainly experience has led me to hope otherwise. If you seriously disapprove, it would be a great misery. But, at least, I had better send it without delay."

Liddon wrote at once a lengthy criticism, of which, for the sake of brevity, the details are here omitted.

To the Rev. C. Gore.

"Christ Church, October 26, 1889.

"In speaking to Paget, I did not indeed wish to suggest that you should take the trouble you have so kindly taken. ——'s language in Hall seemed to make it a duty to ask whether there was any real ground for it ; and I hoped that if there were, the work might still be so far from publication as to leave time for reconsideration.

"I have read through your Essay, but nothing else in the volume. It is needless to say that with the drift of the earlier part of the Essay I am in hearty agreement. There are passages which command my warmest admiration.

"You will, in your kindness, forgive me if I add how much I wish that pages 345–362, or large passages in them, could have been modified or abandoned.

"May I go into details ? . . .

"Is there not a temptation in an age like ours to 'purchase the good-will of the barbarians by repeated subsidies' drawn from those treasuries of Revelation which we have no right to surrender ? I have felt keenly the pressure of this motive myself ; I wish I could be quite sure that I had always resisted it. For a time, no doubt, a concession may ensure a truce between Revelation and its enemies. But not for always, or probably for long. The *nexus* between Truth and Truth and error and error forbids this. —— I apprehend is as good a Hebrewist as Dr. Driver, while in the spheres of history or of abstract argument he probably is superior. His clear, strong mind has, alas ! pushed the premisses of the psychological Criticism of the Old Testament to its real conclusion ; and, in doing so, most assuredly a few years hence he will not have been alone.

"You will, I know, have thought as much, or more than I do, of

Cheyne ?

what may be due to Dr. Pusey's name, and to the confidence of good Church-people in the Pusey House for which you have done so much and so well, and to—what is much more important—the confidence of other minds in the Church of England. For you must know, as I do, that the one bit of ——'s contention which has told is the suspicion that, after all that has been done for us by the Oxford Movement to recover the authority of Catholic Antiquity, we have again begun to slide down the hill towards the pit of uncertainty or unbelief.

" I must not say more than ask you to forgive what I have written from my heart."

It was to Liddon alone that this attitude of his friend had for so long been unknown. In his Lectures, as Principal of the Pusey House, he had openly spoken of it for years ; and in his next letter he explains what he thought had been Liddon's attitude on the subject.

" I never doubted that you knew all this. I thought you never said the things I heard of your saying to others about the Old Testament to me, because you knew this. I thought you did not countenance it, but acquiesced in it."

To the Rev. C. Gore.

" 3, Amen Court, E.C., October 29, 1889.

" I am indeed sorry to have been adding to your burden of work when you are so busy. But what I am going to write now needs no answer. You will, I know, do the best you can. No doubt if I had been more observant, or rather less stupid than I am, I should have discovered what you were saying and thinking about the Old Testament. I had thought of you as keenly interested in everything that was said on all sides, but as holding tenaciously to the principles which underlie the trustworthiness of the Sacred Volume.

" Of course, I have never heard you lecture, nor had I been present at the other occasions to which you refer. And, as you would know, it does not fall in my way to hear much of what is going on. . . .

" When you accepted the Principalship of the Pusey Library, I remember your telling me—I thought it had been in conversation—that you could not always agree with Dr. Pusey about the Fathers. I believe I replied, that in so wide a field, within the bounds of which so many questions might be raised, anything like absolute agreement was not to be expected, and I instanced Tertullian, whom I knew you to have been reading very carefully, as a writer about whom people might differ widely on a great variety of points without doing any particular mischief. I do not now remember any allusion to the Old

Testament. But this may be due to my bad memory ; or, if we were talking, to my deafness ; or, if you wrote, to a careless way that I have of reading letters imperfectly ; or from my turning the subject out of my mind, from thinking at the time that all that you meant was that you could not bind yourself to every opinion of Dr. Pusey on matters of detail, or to every interpretation of particular passages of Holy Scripture which he has sanctioned. . . .

"We are not opposed in *this* sense, that I hold all Criticism to be mischievous, while you hold it to be generally illuminating and useful. For Criticism is an equivocal term, and is applied to very different kinds of Textual or Exegetical work. Dr. Pusey, in one sense, was a great critic ; in another, Strauss, and Bruno Bauer, and Feuerbach were. What the young 'experts,' such as Professor Cheyne, mean by Criticism now, is, I suppose, that kind of discussion of doctrines and of documents which treats the individual reason as an absolutely competent and final judge, and which has the most differentiating merit of being independent of Church authority. At least this would be, I fancy, the general sense of the term in that home of modern Criticism, Protestant Germany. Criticism with Dr. Pusey was, of course, something very different. It was the bringing all that learning and thought could bring to illustrate the mind of Christian Antiquity which really guided him. All Criticism, I suppose, *really* proceeds on certain principles, preliminary assumptions for the critic to go upon. The question in all cases is, Whence do the preliminary assumptions come ? A Catholic critic would say, 'From the general sense of the Church.' But a modern 'psychological' critic (if that is the right word) would say, 'From his own notion of the fitness of things, or from the outcome of literature at large.' Certainly these *placita* which abound in the new 'Old Testament Criticism' do not appear to come from the text itself ; they are imposed on it from without. When I saw Dr. Döllinger a year ago, we were talking about Wellhausen's 'Prolegomena.' I forget how many 'assumptions' he told me he had counted, when at last he could stand it no longer, and put the book down.

"Now, dearest friend, when you write about recognising the mythos as an ingredient of the Sacred Scriptures, or about our Lord's references to the Old Testament as *ad hominem* arguments, are you not assuming principles, in the one case out of deference to a supposed analogy of the mental and literary development of Pagan Greece, in the other as an expedient whereby to meet the difficulties which are presented by a modern estimate of the events or texts to which our Lord referred ?

"But Holy Scripture nowhere suggests that its narratives are mythical ; nor does our Lord, in the passages referred to, give a hint that His argument is only *ad hominem*. And Origen and one or two other names, when made the most of, do not go for much against the general *consensus Patrum* on the first point ; while I should doubt whether any Father is in favour of the modern view on the second.

" But I am writing without books, and may make mistakes. And the questions raised are much too vast to be discussed in a letter. The *immediate* point to be settled—though I fear I understand you to say it *is* settled—is whether all that you have printed should be published. You seem to me to underrate the gravity of publication.

" While a man lectures orally, he is relatively uncommitted, he is often swayed by his class, he can retract, or modify, or ' efface by silence,' without grave difficulty ; but if he publishes—*littera impressa manet*—then it is beyond his control for all time. How thankfully would Dr. Pusey, in the later years of his life, *not* have published his ' Theology of Germany ' ! And is it certain that Bishop Lightfoot has not sometimes wished that he could recall his ' Essay on the Christian Ministry ' ?

" And when you think of those who would welcome your publishing the passages in question, is not something to be said for others who love and trust you, and who would be perplexed and distressed by their publication ?

" Are we not bound, before taking a grave step, to look well on all sides of us, and consider, not only how it would affect those in whom we are immediately interested, but also how it would affect others, who, in the general scheme of Divine Providence, have other, but great claims on our consideration ? And might I make one closing suggestion ? To wit, whether it would be well to submit the passages in question to a Bishop—say the Bishop of Lincoln, whose Chaplain you are ; or the Bishop of Oxford, in whose diocese you are and who is one of our [the Pusey House] Governors ; or the Archbishop of Canterbury, as the highest official authority in the Church ; or the Bishop of Durham, who combines learning in these subjects with the Episcopal office ? If any of them should bid you publish, you would have something to fall back upon in the way of authority ; if they should hesitate, you would have a good reason for any inconvenience which delay in publication might cause to your publisher.

" For myself, I have no sort of authority, either in Church office or in virtue of special learning. I can only write to you as an old friend, begging you to consider some sides of the matter which you may have overlooked in the pressure of your work, but which cause me much real anxiety.

" P.S.—You would, I feel sure, recognise the difference between the claim of any particular intellectual presentation of Truth—however intimately bound up with one's mental history—and that of any certain part of the Catholic Faith. The former *may*, in time, be modified or abandoned, however improbable anything of the sort may seem to us *now*. The latter never, *i.e.* supposing us to remain in a state of grace."

FROM THE REV. C. GORE.

"[End of October, 1889.]

" I have consulted some one under seal of utmost confidence, whom you would really trust for age and wisdom and Catholicity—I am sure you would have approved of him as adviser in the matter—and he advises me decidedly (having read the Essay) to let it be. I feel I have done all I could. I did not feel that I could ask a Bishop in his official capacity to intervene at this stage. I feel absolutely that no Bishop could, as Bishop, claim the suppression of the Essay on Theological grounds. On the other hand, to ask him, even indirectly, to sanction it, would be to ask him more than I dared. I have done all I feel I can. But if *you* like to ask the Bishop of Oxford to consider the question, I should be most glad to send him the Essay. Of course, if he did desire to suppress it, as Bishop, I would do so. . . . I really could not tell you how much the discovery of what you feel has crushed me."

Liddon was too firm to be moved by even the most revered opinion, and on both sides the distress was as great as it could be. Liddon notes on October 31, " *Miserable* about Gore's Essay. It takes the heart out of all one's hopes for the Pusey House." On the day after the book appeared he wrote to a friend who had in September given £500 to the Pusey House on Liddon's assertion that he fully trusted its Principal, and offered to refund the sum out of his own pocket, because it might appear that he had misled him. And on the same day he writes to another friend—

To D. L. LATHBURY, ESQ.

" November 24, 1889.

". . . A matter which touches me more nearly is the appearance of the volume of Essays called 'Lux Mundi.' The writers are a remarkable group of men, and some of the Essays, or, at any rate, one of them, F. Paget's, is a real contribution to Christian Theology. But I have been more distressed than I can well say by the eleven concluding pages of Gore's Essay, which has come upon me as a thunderbolt out of a clear sky. It is practically a capitulation at the feet of the young Rationalistic Professors, by which the main positions which the old Apologists of Holy Scripture have maintained are conceded to the enemy, in deference to the 'literary' judgment of our time. Not only could Dr. Pusey never have written these pages, it would have been difficult to have written anything more opposed to his convictions. Gore's personal attractions are so great, and his ability and reading so considerable, that he has carried all before him, and I suspect I am very nearly alone in Oxford in feeling as I do on the subject. But I am quite clear that these pages will tell powerfully on many minds in the opposite directions of Rome and a more consistent unbelief.

"The whole thing shows, among much else, how little hereafter you ought to trust me, as I had no idea of what was going on in minds around me, and have been pressing the claims of the Pusey House in all sorts of quarters, on the ground of its continuing the teaching and work of Dr. Pusey.

"A less purblind person would have, at least, known what was coming."

His loneliness was, of course, only on this one subject ; his time in Oxford is full of engagements with all kinds of people, including undergraduates, to whom he was ever ready to show his photographs of Jerusalem and talk of Egypt and Palestine. Walks and talks with other friends are often recorded with the sad remark that he found them "more near Gore" than he had expected ; and from the moment of that discovery it was always felt that the cause nearest his heart must not be mentioned. In a P.S. to a long letter to Dr. Bright, who was heartily at one with him, he writes—

"DEAR BRIGHT, — I cannot tell you how miserable the whole thing has made me. It has destroyed very much of the confidence of my younger friends here. They avoid the subject—even dear Strong and Burrows do not speak of it. I see Paget every week, but there has not been one allusion, however remote, to 'Lux Mundi.'"

His December residence took him from the immediate pressure of Oxford troubles ; but he preached a Sermon at St. Paul's on "The Worth of the Old Testament," of which so much was said that he had to publish it, rather against his will. On December 21 Bishop Lightfoot passed away ; his loss, though not unexpected, was at such a moment a real addition to the strain and the loneliness which Liddon felt.

To C. T. Redington, Esq.

"3, Amen Court, January 2, 1890.

". . . The Bishop of Durham's death has been a personal sorrow to me. I only knew him slightly before he became a Canon here, but we sat together in the Chapter for eight years. And I soon learnt to respect his learning, and his character even more than his learning. We could not always agree, and our differences turned themselves upon points which I, at least, thought of grave importance. But he was ever generous and considerate, and life seems much poorer now that he has been removed out of our sight.

"As to the spirit of the age and education, I can only say that I do not attach such importance to the spirit of the age as the typical Theological Liberal does. One age has one spirit and another another, and, as I read history, the successive ages seem to change their spirit much as ladies change the fashion of their dress ; whereas the truths of Divine Revelation, whatever may be the attitude of a particular age towards them, remain as being the Voice of Him Who does not change. Am I not right in saying that the men who most profoundly represent the modern spirit are sad at heart at the desolation in which it leaves them as to the greatest problems that surround our lives? This is, I believe, evidently the case with Huxley. And sooner or later the sadness with which a non-Christian age contemplates pain and death will lead men to turn their eyes to a Faith which makes these inevitable facts of human life, not merely endurable, but welcome."

To the Rev. G. Marshall.

" The Coppice, Henley-on-Thames, January 10, 1890.

" It is a great pleasure to me to receive your New Year's greeting, which I return, though somewhat later in the day, with all my heart. *Fugaces labuntur anni;* and each year leaves one poorer in the matter of old friends, and more thankful to retain those whom God still spares. . . .

"At the end of last July I spent a week with Lightfoot at Auckland, and left it with a strong presentiment that I should never see him again in this life. He was hard at work on his ' St. Clement,' at all such intervals of time as diocesan business left at his disposal ; and now and then, but only now and then, he would talk as if he might have some few years still to live. But his general feeling was that his time was very short, but this he expressed as clearly, as, on such subjects, he would have allowed himself, when we parted. I made bold to try to get him, many years ago now, to reconsider his position about the Christian Ministry in his celebrated Essay. There were more reasons than one which made this difficult, or perhaps impossible. But I think he looked upon his edition of ' St. Ignatius ' as a corrective to inferences which Dissenters and others drew from his Essay ; he certainly has left that part of the controversy, and, to all appearances, unalterably, in a very different condition from that in which he found it.

" When you are next in town, do visit the Tudor Exhibition. It is very interesting, not only on account of the Holbeins, etc., but because it enables one to enter so fully into the by-play of the period. . . . It is difficult, after looking at portrait after portrait, to feel much moral joy in either Henry or Elizabeth ; but (even after all that has been written during the last thirty years) the Exhibition gives one a more vivid impression than could be had before of the remarkable people who surrounded them."

Two days after writing this letter, he wrote of the death of Dr. Littledale—

" How all one's contemporaries are packing up for the Other World ! Every month seems to impress the nothingness of this life more and more vividly on us."

In December, the Principal of Pusey House went on a visit to India. Just before starting he wrote a long letter of explanation to Liddon, who told Lord Halifax what he thought of it in the following letter :—

To Lord Halifax.

" The Coppice, Henley-on-Thames, January 14, 1890.

". . . Since we met there has been some public and a great deal of private correspondence about ' Lux Mundi.' In the first, for obvious reasons, I have taken no part. The second I cannot decline. The Archdeacon [Denison] has written to me, too, several times ; also Sir Walter Farquhar, and several other people.

" Gore, too, has sent me his ' Letter of Explanation,' leaving it to my discretion whether it should be published.

" I am quite clear that it had better not be published—better not even be printed for private circulation.

" While it is characterised by all the features which make Gore and what he says and writes as attractive as they are, it does not really recede from the position which is taken up in the Essay, nor does it offer any such explanation (how could it ?) as could reassure those who have been distressed by the Essay. Very little is said to the effect that the positions taken up in the Essay were only hypothetical, while a good deal is urged in their favour as though in the writer's judgment they were at least tenable. I do not resign the hope that hereafter, when the matter has somewhat blown over, he may voluntarily make some explanation that will relieve the difficulties of the present position.

" There is no getting over the fact that between Gore's position in that Essay and Dr. Pusey's teaching on these very subjects there is nothing short of absolute contradiction. The evidence of this is in the perception of the world, and it will take note of so significant a fact, do what we may.

" In view of this I agree with Walter [Phillimore] (who has been here) that it will be impossible to press the Pusey House Enlargement Scheme proposed by Wakeman, at our meeting on the 20th. To do so would be to raise the controversy about ' Lux Mundi ' in its most unmanageable form. We could not now put out an Appeal for a renewed effort to perpetuate the teaching of Dr. Pusey without being asked how far ' Lux Mundi ' is in harmony with that teaching. So very reluctantly I have come to think that nothing in this direction can be done without great risk of doing irreparable harm. I share your general feelings on the subject as to the need of patience and silence, though I am not sure whether I do not in my heart think more seriously than you do of Gore's line in the Essay. It involves—apart from its particular statements—nothing less than an abandonment of the ground won by the Oxford Movement in favour of Church Authority as against private or merely literary Criticism ; indeed, this characteristic is by no means confined to Gore's Essay.

" Since you left how busy death has been ! First the Bishop of Durham, then on Friday Dr. Döllinger, and on Saturday Dr. Littledale. I cannot say what the removal of a mind like Döllinger's means to me, but I cannot write about it. I constantly think of that pathetic description of the reign of Jeroboam II. : ' In those days the Lord began to cut Israel short.' "

He writes again in February an account of his life at Oxford during the Lent Term of 1890 to the same friend, who was spending the winter at Madeira.

To Lord Halifax.

"Ash Wednesday, February 19, 1890.

" . . . The ' Lux Mundi ' matter does not disappear from thought and discussion. It would do so if the contents of the book were alone in question, but the world at large thinks it *piquant* that such a book should have issued from the Pusey House. And certainly both friends and foes have a right to say that I ought to have known better what I was about than I did when I recommended Gore for the First Post in the Pusey Library.

" I knew and loved his general character, I knew that he was sound about the Incarnation and the Sacraments, and I did not suspect that he had constructed a private kennel for liberalising ideas in Theology within the precincts of the Old Testament, and so much of the New Testament as bears upon it.

" As it is I can only hope and pray that when he comes back from India he will do or say something that may set things, at any rate in part, to rights, though I scarcely yet see how he is to do it. Everybody is not a St. Augustine, to write two books of Retractations straight off and have them prefixed to his works throughout all time.

" The whole volume, as I read it, has a naturalistic and Pelagianising tone. The writers seem to think it a gain when they can prune away, or economise the Supernatural, or the great and awful doctrines of Grace, which are the heart of Christianity.

" The best view that we can take of it is that, like an eruptive disease, it was latent in the system of the modern Churchman, and is less dangerous now that it has ' come out,' and can be observed and dealt with. May God give us grace to do this wisely and unselfishly in some way or other !

" There is, I fear, no doubt that among all older Churchmen it has, at any rate for the present, destroyed confidence in the existing management of the Pusey House, and put an end to those plans for its enlargement upon which we had set our hearts.

" I wish I knew anything worth telling you about the Bishop of Lincoln's Case. The general impression seems to be that the Archbishop will devise some sort of compromise, which however will not satisfy the Church Association, so that there will be an Appeal to the Privy Council. At ' Nobody's ' on the 5th I had a long talk with the Dean of Windsor, who had been sitting at Lambeth all day. He did not say a word to me on the subject ; talked only of Archbishop Tait's ' Life,' and about the insertion in it of letters from Dr. Pusey and others.

" About Durham nothing has yet transpired. It is generally supposed—I know not whether correctly or not—that the vacant See was offered to Dr. Westcott, and that after long hesitation he refused it. I fear we cannot look for a sincerely good Churchman, though Lord Salisbury would wish to avoid a θηρίον.

" The most noteworthy event since my return to Oxford has been Mr. Gladstone's visit. He lived for a week in Wakeman's rooms at All Souls, and received all the world ; dined everywhere, and said nothing about politics. I had long conversations with him about the Old Testament, Dr. Döllinger, and the old Tractarians. Not a word about Ireland. He dined with me in Hall ; delighted the Common Room by his conversation ; and then came up to my rooms for a long talk afterwards. I am bound to add that he also dined at ' Mansfield,' though I think he would have made the enterprising Principal understand that the basis of their sympathy was political and not theological. The world at large, however, would not understand this. . . .

" We have indeed lost many whom we could ill spare this winter. Littledale, paradoxical as was his logic at times, was, for his knowledge, a tower of strength ; and his disinterestedness, his courage, his perfect good temper, made his help to the Church cause of the greatest value. And dear Aubrey Moore can—as it seems to human eyes—be still less spared."

In March, 1890, the Sees of Durham and St. Alban's had been vacant for some time, and there were many paragraphs in the newspapers suggesting reasons for the prolonged delay in filling them. In the *Guardian* of March 5 there was a report, quoted from a Manchester paper, that Lord Salisbury wished Liddon to go to St. Alban's, but had had to give up all hopes of it, as the Queen was "unalterably determined" that he should not be a Bishop. Other papers related stories of his Sermon at Windsor in 1868, and of the supposed displeasure of the Queen at his manner or at the matter of what he said. Liddon was not the only person who was pained at this thoughtless gossip.

From the Dean of Windsor.

"Deanery, Windsor, March 7, 1890.

"DEAR DR. LIDDON,—The Queen has enjoined upon me a somewhat delicate task, which I must perform as best I can.

"Her Majesty has been a good deal annoyed during the last few weeks by certain paragraphs which have gone the round of newspapers, culminating in a flaring Article in last night's *Pall Mall Gazette*, to the effect that she had (with reference to present Episcopal vacancies) been acting with personal disfavour to yourself. The story was sufficiently absurd, and might perhaps have been well left to die of itself, but the Queen, knowing the annoyance its circulation has caused to herself, has feared it may perhaps have vexed you also, and therefore bids me send you privately what will be, I think, an unnecessary assurance, that it has not a vestige of foundation. It is, I think, very hard upon the Queen that fabrications of this sort should obtain so ready a currency. With genuine apologies for this note,

"I remain, very truly yours,
"RANDALL T. DAVIDSON."

Liddon immediately replied.

To the Dean of Windsor.

"March 8, 1890, Christ Church, Oxford.

"If you should think it right to do so, I must beg you to make my most respectful duty to Her Majesty the Queen, and to express to Her my very deep and sincere sense of the great consideration and kindness of the message which she has sent me through you. Before last Wednesday I had not heard of late years any such rumours as those to which you refer. On Wednesday I observed a paragraph in the *Guardian* copied from a country paper, which appeared to me to be unworthy of the high tone of the *Guardian*, and to have been inserted through some mistake.

"Then I read in Common Room on Thursday the Article in the *Pall Mall Gazette*—an article about which it is scarcely possible to trust myself to write. Nor have I said or written a word about it to any human being, until now. My friends here, I suppose, must have read it too, but they have been too considerate to mention it. I could only hope that it might not have been brought under the notice of Her Majesty. That any folly connected with my name should be a cause of annoyance to Her Majesty must be to me a matter of very great regret.

"When I preached at Windsor, I think in 1868, the late Dean Wellesley said some kind words which I have always gratefully remembered, and which were inconsistent with the truth of the stories that were afterwards circulated. And although it is dangerous to make negative assertions on the strength of a bad memory, I do not think I have ever even referred to such stories except once or twice in confidence with my sister. You will believe, however, that all this does not lessen my very grateful sense of Her Majesty's great kindness in the matter, or of the manner in which you have conveyed it to me."

With regard to "Lux Mundi," Liddon felt that delay was imperatively necessary. Therefore he did his utmost to leave time for the issues which were involved in the controversy to get clear ; as he would say, " In order to see what propositions involve, you must have time ; in Theological matters time and delay are of the greatest importance." It was natural that the Head of Pusey House should propose to resign his position if he had not the full confidence of the Governors ; but Liddon did all he could to prevent the Governors from considering his offer to retire. He saw that, on the one hand, a vote of confidence from them would be impossible, and that, on the other hand, resignation would be disastrous ; so he managed to postpone the question at least till the end of the year. He had great hopes that Gore would be willing on his return to England to reconsider the statements in his Essay.

Hitherto, except for his Sermon in December, Liddon had taken no public part in the controversy. But when he had gone to London for his April residence, an Article in the *Spectator* compelled him to break his silence. He thus alludes to it in his diary—

" *March* 29.—The *Spectator* of to-day contains an Article on ' Mr. Gladstone and Dr. Liddon on the Bible,' attacking, although in kindly terms, my Sermon on the Old Testament. The writer thinks that I depreciate the reality of our Lord's Humanity."

This touched on a point on which he could not allow any misapprehension. And, on the following day,[1] he wrote a long reply, not mentioning " Lux Mundi," but showing the points at which the present discussion seemed to him vital, that is, with regard to the suggestion that our Lord was really ignorant of any matters on which He claimed to speak with decisive authority, and with regard to the loss of respect for the Old Testament consequent on a theory, which seemed to put parts of it on a level with the pseudo-Isidorian Decretals. This letter gave the Principal of Pusey House, who had just returned from India, an opportunity of explaining himself publicly and putting himself on Liddon's side on these crucial points. In the *Spectator* of April 12, he wrote in the name of " many of us who cannot go all the way with Dr. Liddon," to declare emphatically his thorough agreement with him on these central positions. He claimed, also, that it was quite possible and consistent to adopt the " main conclusions of the new Criticism as held, *e.g.* by the great Delitzsch," while at the same time repudiating the fancies of extreme critics. There was a great hope that Liddon would have replied by publicly welcoming this letter as containing the explanation he had longed for ; and for some time he hesitated, but at last he decided to let the public correspondence drop.

[1] He dated the letter " Palm Sunday," with a tacit reference, obvious enough to those who knew him well, to the Epistle for the day, Phil. ii. 5-11, which contains St. Paul's great assertion of the Divinity of our Lord, and of His Self-emptying.

To the Rev. C. Gore.

"Brighton, April 18, 1890.

"The *Spectator* of to-morrow contains no letter from me.

"I should like to have thanked you for your agreement in the two great matters which you specify.

"But I could not do this without discussing the epithets which you apply to Dr. Delitzsch and Dr. Driver—'great' to the former, 'moderate and reasonable' to the latter. From a merely literary point of view, eulogies of this kind, and probably stronger ones, are well deserved. But we are both thinking of something much more precious than literature. And to enter on the subject would only add to existing difficulties."

But as Liddon in his honesty could not accept the epithets, so also his correspondent could not honestly withdraw them.

"I wish," Gore added, in reply to Liddon's note, "you knew how very deep the pain is of having given so much pain to you. I would do all in the world I could to alleviate it."

By the same post Liddon received another letter equally perplexing, but of a very different nature.

"*April* 22.—Letter from Lord Salisbury, offering me the See of St. Alban's. Felt as though I had been shot. *Deus in adjutorium meum intende.* The Dean advises me to accept it if health permit. Wrote to Lord Salisbury, begging for a few days' delay.

"*April* 23.—In great distress and perplexity about Lord Salisbury's letter throughout the day. Ogle [his medical adviser] came to see me, and appeared rather to advise me to take the Bishopric, thinking that my health would improve with more exposure to the air.

"*April* 24.—Long talk with the Dean. It left me in greater trouble about the Bishopric than ever. I don't know *what* to do. Lord, guide me in Thy mercy!

"*April* 25.—Wrote to Lord Salisbury, declining to be nominated for the See of St. Alban's. Fear that it will vex him very much, but do not see how I could do otherwise."

To the Marquis of Salisbury.

"3, Amen Court, April 25, 1890.

"Already, I fear, I may have presumed too largely upon Her Majesty's indulgence in delaying my answer to the gracious message which your Lordship conveyed to me on Tuesday.

"I have, indeed, endeavoured to think it over with the best

attention I could give to it, and not to forget that no less responsibility attaches to declining an invitation to undertake new work than to accepting it.

" But after a great deal of anxiety, I have come to the conclusion that I ought to ask the Queen's permission to decline the offer of the See of St. Alban's. Ever since my illness of five years ago my health has been more or less uncertain, and at sixty I cannot reckon upon its improvement. Certainly Dr. Ogle tells me that he thinks an open-air life would suit me better than a sedentary one, but even quite of late I have had too much experience of such ill health as makes attention to duty more than difficult, to feel justified in undertaking an office for which nerve and strength are especially necessary.

" But, further, I am deeply and unceasingly conscious of other disqualifications, with which I ought not, perhaps, to trouble you ; while, on the other hand, I am embarrassed by having long since undertaken work, which I see no means whatever of transferring to others, and the prosecution of which would be inconsistent with what is due from a Bishop to his diocese. I have tried to look at the question of duty from the point of view of a disinterested observer, who had the good of the Church sincerely at heart, and who knew me as I know myself. Among the many attractions of the proposal which I owe to your Lordship, the prospect of being brought from time to time to Hatfield in the course of duty could not have been the least—no place in the world is so associated in my mind with the great and undeserved kindness of many years."

Among his papers Liddon left a statement of all his reasons for refusing.

" REASONS AGAINST TAKING THE SEE OF ST. ALBAN'S.

" 1. My age—60. I could only hope but for a very few years' good work. Then decrepitude, with the alternative of resignation or neglecting the interests of the diocese.

" 2. My health—very uncertain during the last two years, and especially this spring.

" 3. ' Lux Mundi.' It shows that I could not depend on the sympathy and support of the young High Churchmen, as I could not in any case have that of the Low and Broad ; I should be practically without friends.

" ' Lux Mundi ' is a proclamation of revolt against the spirit and principles of Dr. Pusey and Mr. Keble.

" 4. I can do more with what remains of life by working on in a private station. The Episcopate would mean the giving what strength remains to innumerable details.

" 5. If St. Alban's afforded any opportunities for governing the future policy and direction of the English Church, the case would be different. But of this there is no prospect whatever. It means merely absorption in the details of rural administration. This I should not do well, and it would prevent my doing anything else. —*April* 25, 1890."

But he was far from hearing the last of this offer. In his letter to Lord Salisbury, he had alluded to the fact that he had for many years been a regular welcome guest at Hatfield, and his relations with the whole family were most intimate. It was, therefore, a great personal disappointment to them that he should decline this offer. The day after he had written to refuse the Bishopric, his diary records the first attempt to make him change his mind.

" *April* 26.—Lady Salisbury appeared about eleven, to remonstrate with me about my ' very foolish letter to Salisbury.' She insisted on the smallness of the diocese, the certainty that I should recover my health by a change of air, the chance for the High Church party, etc. I pleaded my age and health ; it was 'too late.' . . . Miserable.

" *April* 27.—Lady Salisbury wrote a most kind letter, saying that no reflection she understood better than before the force of my objections, and that it might be better that I should remain on to strengthen the Church element in the Chapter of St. Paul's. Preached in the afternoon on John Howard. [It was his last Sermon in St. Paul's.]

" A great crowd of people in the Cathedral and at tea. Felt quite worn out at night."

There remained still one more great force that might possibly compel him to change his determination. He is asked to Lord Salisbury's house in Arlington Street, to meet Mr. Gladstone, " who is coming to tea."

The interview is most fully described in a letter to the Dean of St. Paul's the evening after it took place.

To the Dean of St. Paul's.

" Queen's Hotel, Brighton, Friday, May 2 [1890], 10 p.m.

". . . When I got to Arlington Street I found the G.O.M. and Mrs. Gladstone encamped in Lady Salisbury's boudoir. Lady Maud Wolmer and Lady Gwendolin Cecil were the only others present. Tea and muffins and conversation for more than an hour on every subject. The G.O.M. complained of Lady S.'s Radicalism, and she of his Conservatism. Among the subjects were Scottish Disestablishment, Deceased Wife's Sister, Sir W. Harcourt, ' Lux Mundi,' the Welsh language, the history of the Welsh Church, the qualifications of Welsh Bishops, etc. At last he had to go to the House, to speak, as I imagine, in favour of Scottish Disestablishment.

"As he went, he took me out into the passage, with the door open, and rated me soundly about St. Alban's. ' Was it too late ? ' etc., etc. Mrs. Gladstone joined him, and then they both dealt with me. . . .

" When they were gone, I returned to the boudoir, and talked to Lady Salisbury for ten minutes about Mr. Gladstone, a sufficiently inexhaustible topic. But she said not another word about St. Alban's. However, I listened to a conversation which was in some sense historical, and came down here with a lighter heart than I had anticipated as the fruit of the summons."

As soon as the offer of the Bishopric was known, the newspapers retailed again the usual gossip about the Queen's displeasure at his Sermon in 1868. One private correspondent drew a reply from him.

To ——

" 3, Amen Court, St. Paul's, E.C., June 3, 1890.

" Certainly I should advise you to believe very little of the personal gossip which is retailed to you from London.

" It is true that when Mr. MacColl was attacked, on the score of his account of the impaled man whom we saw on the Save, I thought it my duty to bear witness to his accuracy by writing in the *Times.* But I have no reason to suppose that the correspondence which followed ever attracted the notice of the Queen.

" Your correspondent speaks of my preaching before the Queen as ' subsequent ' to this correspondence. The only time on which I ever preached before Her Majesty was eight years before it. On that occasion I did not ' imitate Bossuet,' or use any such words as, ' And you, Madam, must also die ; ' nor did the Queen leave her seat before the conclusion of the Service. I have no means of knowing what She may have said to the late Dean of Windsor ; but I was staying with the Dean at the time, and what he said to me was quite inconsistent with the words your correspondent quotes as having been said by the Queen.

" I have the best reason for knowing that the Queen does not entertain towards me any feelings less kindly and gracious than towards others of her subjects. And your correspondent has probably discovered before this that since he wrote his letter Her Majesty has offered me the See of St. Alban's, and that I have had to decline it on grounds of health.

" I do *not* authorise you to publish this letter, because I think it better *never* to notice personal gossip of this sort in the newspapers. Sensible people attach no weight to it. Nobody is exactly responsible for the shape it takes ; it grows up in the atmosphere of a great capital, and is insensibly added to by passing from hand to hand. But, if left to itself, it soon finds its level, while any public discussion of its merits may secure for it an undeserved importance."

For some time Liddon had been under a promise to the Vice-Chancellor of the University of Oxford to preach the morning sermon at St. Mary's on Whit Sunday, May 25. When this became known as the time drew near, expectation ran high. The "Lux Mundi" controversy was in full flood. For many years Liddon had been the most brilliant and powerful of academical preachers at Oxford, but now he had not preached before the University for six years, and his return to the Pulpit of St. Mary's was naturally associated with the principal discussion of the day. But apart from the speculations of the mere seekers after excitement, few sermons that have been preached in that historic Church were ever awaited with such deep interest and anxiety by all parties of serious Churchmen in Oxford.

The *Oxford Magazine* described the scene at length:—

"The day, the preacher, the occasion, all combined to make a memorable, and, to the reflective or imaginative mind, a singularly suggestive scene. Dr. Liddon, *nolens episcopari*, the most finished preacher of our day, the Diadochus of the Tractarians, the Bossuet of the Nineteenth Century, the youthful friend of Keble, the biographer of Pusey, was to take his stand, and to adjudicate between the living and the dead, between the older and the younger High Church party, between the Tracts and 'Lux Mundi.' All Oxford, old and young alike, was pervaded with that indefinable sense of a great and central occasion. Every one was there : Professor Jowett and the Vicar of St. Mary's, side by side ; Canons from Christ Church and Lecturers from Mansfield ; Professors of Arabic and Moral Philosophy ; Readers in Biology and in History ; smart friends from London up for the Sunday ; parents and sisters from the country who had come to see the 'Eights,' and found themselves confronted with this solemn and at the same time exciting scene.

"Never has St. Mary's within recent years been so crowded. M.A.'s overflowed into the Proctors' thrones, strangers into the Doctors' stalls ; the Heads of Houses could hardly thread their way through the throng to their already crowded places ; ladies sat on cushions upon the floor, and a mingled press of those who could not find even extemporised seats, stood all through the long discourse in the aisles and porticoes.

" Of the Sermon in itself we will not attempt to speak, except very generally. That it was in the grand style and on a noble scale goes without saying. It was the Sermon of a preacher who is one in a generation ; a Master of Theology and of Scholarship, sacred and profane ; a Master of language and of eloquence, and gifted with a rare and impressive presence and bearing. Yet even he seemed overborne and clogged at times by the weighty responsibility and reserve which the difficulty of his high theme and the trammels of personal considerations imposed. But it was full of passages of the deepest interest and the finest and most forcible expression, and it will remain the permanent and memorable voice of a ' moment ' in the religious life of Oxford and of England, the importance of which it is impossible to-day to attempt to gauge." [1]

His text was, " He shall glorify me, for He shall receive of Mine, and shall show it unto you ; " and the subject was the work of the Holy Spirit in individuals and in the Church, and especially in inspiring men in the Church to write the Bible. He described the method of their Inspiration as a guidance to select what was true out of materials of varied character, and to interpret them in the light of the preparation for Jesus Christ. In some passages the sermon directly traversed statements in " Lux Mundi," though the book itself was never mentioned. His closing words describe, in contrast to the ever-varying spirit of the age, the true spirit of human life and the one hope of a clear understanding of all its perplexing questions—a spirit and a hope which filled his own heart, and which he knew to belong also to those who, to their great sorrow, were on one point at that moment separated from him.

" ' He shall glorify Me.' All that wins for the Divine Redeemer more room in the thoughts and hearts of men ; all that secures for Him the homage of obedient and disciplined wills ; all that draws from the teachings of the past and the examples of the present new motives for doing Him the honour which is His eternal due, may be

[1] The sermon was published at once, under the title, " The Inspiration of Selection."

safely presumed to come from a Source higher than any in this passing world, and to have in it the promise of lasting happiness and peace. And, for the rest—

> "'Sunt multa fæcis illita
> Quæ luce purgentur Tuâ,
> Tu vera Lux cœlestium
> Vultu sereno illumina.'"

They were the last words of his last Sermon.

His diary had for some time become only occasional, and far more scanty in its detail than in former years, and the pressure of controversial correspondence diminished the number of his letters to friends. Only a few throw light on this period.

TO LORD HALIFAX.

"Christ Church, June 2, 1890.

"The report about St. Alban's is quite true. It was a very great perplexity, about which I can only say that I tried as well as I could to put personal considerations out of sight, and to think of what was best for the interests of the Church, and of what I should wish to have done hereafter. . . ."

After giving all the reasons for declining, he adds—

"After all, the great question is, as Dr. Pusey used to say, How to do the best you can with your life, or what remains of it, for the glory of God.

"But I have been egotistical enough in all conscience, and should not have said so much (I have not written a page to any one else upon the subject), except to so old and kind a friend. You will, I know, consider what I have said confidential.

"Our Pusey House difficulty is delayed until October. Gore is going to write a public Letter to Canon Furse. I hope and pray, rather than expect, that it will be what one would wish ; but in the conversation which I had with him, on his return from India, I could not but see that he is more than ever under Dr. Driver's influence on all questions connected with the Old Testament, though he was, as he always is, anxious to do and say anything he could to lessen his divergence from the old and Catholic estimate of Holy Scripture, while he has actually altered for the better two of the more painful passages that bear on the Person of our Divine Lord.

"But the young generally are strongly on his side, and are 'keeping him up to the mark,' so that I do not venture to be sanguine.

"No reports have reached me about the Archbishop's decision in the Lincoln Case. Efforts have been made to get clergy, myself among others, to pledge themselves to submission to whatever may be decided. Of course, anybody would *wish* to submit to such a Spiritual Court, but in such a matter one 'might protest too much.' Such protests remove one motive which the Archbishop might have against inclining to the Puritan side, because they would assure him of the submission of Churchmen beforehand. And though I will not anticipate the application of the maxim in the case of all spiritual Tribunals, short of a really Œcumenical Council, there *may* arise reasons for refusing submission. Anyhow, the invitation seemed to me to be a mistake."

Once more Liddon appeared in public, at Cambridge, on June 10, to receive the honour of a D.C.L. Degree, walking up the Senate House side by side with the Master of Balliol, on whom the same honour was conferred. At the time it was noticed how ill he looked, and on his return to Oxford his health continued to fail rapidly. His last piece of literary work was the Preface to the fourteenth edition of his "Bampton Lectures," dated June 29. It is really a review of Dr. Martineau's "Seat of Authority in Religion," which had just appeared, and it contains a striking comparison between the old and the new Unitarianism.

On July 3, although feeling very ill, he went to Highclere for the funeral of Lord Carnarvon, and only managed to get back to Oxford with the greatest difficulty. He had to put himself at once into the hands of Sir Henry Acland ; and, in spite of all remedies, for a fortnight he suffered such intense pain from acute neuralgia in the neck that he could only call it "agony" and "unspeakable distress." "If it should please God that I should ever again preach at St. Paul's," he said one day, when speaking of that pain, "I shall try to tell them what life would be without God." He could see very few people. When he was first taken ill, he used every day to ask one of those who was allowed to see him if he had been to Pusey House ; and, if he had been there, he would add, "And did you see Gore ? How was he ? " One day, when he asked that question as usual, he was asked, "Shall I ask Gore to come and see you ? " "No, dear friend, I cannot bear it now. But give him

my love when you see him again." Then, after a pause,
he added very slowly, " Will you tell him that I am too ill
to talk to him ? But if he will come down and let me see
him without speaking to him, I shall be very glad." From
that day the Principal of Pusey House was one of his most
regular visitors. The following letter was written to one of
his oldest friends in the second week of his illness :—

To the Bishop of Lincoln.

" Sixth Sunday after Trinity, July 13, 1890.
Christ Church, Oxford. From my sick-bed.

" DEAREST BISHOP,—Many, many thanks. God has laid His
hand very heavily upon me ; and I have been through the fire—I
greatly needed it. Nothing [is] more wonderful in Him than His
goodness to such as I am. Pray for me, that I may learn how to be
humble and patient, and that this visitation (in the Day of Account)
may not be seen to have been as nothing—or worse than nothing—
instead of a great means of grace. I never before knew what pain
might be. Pray for and bless your devoted. . . .

" H. P. LIDDON."

On July 19 he was removed to Standish, in Gloucestershire, to the house of his sister, Mrs. Poole King.

Here he was in much better air, removed from the
scene of so much work and anxiety, and able to enjoy the
companionship of his sister and other near relatives. This
companionship was throughout his life a great refreshment
to him ; for within the circle of his own family the warmth
of affection, which his many friends knew so well, had
always found its fullest expression. Neither the unavoidable long absences nor the advance of years in any way
diminished this happiness. In the preceding November he
had dedicated his volume of Sermons on *The Magnificat*
" to my dear sister, Annie Poole King, in the joyful conviction that as our days on earth are drawing towards
their close, we are more and more united in heart and
mind with respect to those things which are of lasting
value." In her home on the hills in Gloucestershire there
was every hope that he would soon regain his strength ; and
though his nights were still full of pain and distress, he soon
began to enjoy his days, either in the garden, or sitting

at a window which afforded a beautiful view of the Severn valley. Scenery was a never-ending pleasure to him, and he would sit for hours enjoying this view, with his field-glasses by his side, while his sister or his nieces read or wrote for him. Every day he had the *Times* read to him, and, as a matter of business, he would most punctiliously dictate answers to every letter he received, of whatever kind, whether about his work or from people in want of help or advice, or from kind people in all parts of the world suggesting all sorts of remedies for his illness.

During these long days he found the same pleasure as in former years in Sir Walter Scott's novels ; all the characters came back to him as old and welcome friends. His chief favourites were " Waverley," " Guy Mannering," " Peveril of the Peak," " Ivanhoe," and " The Talisman," all of which were now read aloud to him again. He tried to read some of Newman's sermons, but found them too great a strain for his head. But he did manage a little serious reading ; and, in spite of his doctor's order, he also corrected the proofs of the Preface to the fourteenth edition of his " Bampton Lectures."

In one or two of his letters he speaks about his illness. When he had been at Standish for ten days he dictated the following letter to Dr. Dale, the Congregationalist minister of Birmingham :—

To Dr. Dale.

[Dictated.]

" Standish House, Stonehouse, Gloucestershire, July 30, 1890.

" I cannot yet write letters, but I must dictate a few words of sincere gratitude to you for your most kind letter. While my general health has much improved, I am still liable to recurring attacks of severe pain, which leave me very prostrate ; but, at least generally, this later pain is of a different character from that of three weeks ago. I then felt I had never before known what pain might be ; and that, though I have reason to believe that there was nothing organically wrong, it might crush life out of me by sheer violence. Such experience can only be sent to any of us for some especial purpose, and while I have good reason to know that I greatly needed the chastisement, it has taught me, I hope, more than I knew before of the

Justice and the Love of God. Your kindness, my dear Dr. Dale, emboldens me to venture on these private, and in some sense sacred regions, not without a hope, too, that you will remember me in your prayers, and ask that such a visitation may, at least, not turn to my loss in the great Day of Account."

A few days later he is able to write with his own hand to Lord Halifax, and speaks almost hopefully of himself.

To Lord Halifax.

"Transf. D.N.J.C., August 6, 1890.

"My DEAREST FRIEND,—I can only write a line (in defiance of the doctors) to thank you for your most delightful letter. But I must do that. Last week I had a relapse, but am again, by God's mercy, improving. I dare not, as matters stand, make any plans, 'One step enough for me.' At best my recovery must be a very slow matter, so it seems.

"I have read Mr. Lilly's 'Right and Wrong.' It is a well-written restatement of the old intuitional morality which they used to teach at Oxford before the rise of J. S. Mill. His quotations from Coleridge I recalled learning by heart before I went into the Schools. Certainly it is a book calculated in these days to do a great deal of good.

"I can write no more. How heartily I agree with you about dear Lord B[eauchamp]! He is the truest of friends. May God of His mercy enable Charlie [Lord Halifax's son, his own godson] to regain strength!

"Your most affectionate,

"H. P. LIDDON."

After his illness began he dictated his diary daily; only two entries are in his own handwriting. On his birthday he adds to what he had dictated, in a hand so weak as to be only just legible, "Domine, miserere mei peccatoris." And on August 12, he records the announcement of Cardinal Newman's death. "Found it impossible to think of anything else throughout the day. Dictated a letter to Father Neville." The letter was as follows:—

To the Rev. Father Neville.

"Standish House, August 12, 1890.

"I must, indeed, ask your pardon for intruding on you at all at this solemn moment. But I should like to be allowed to say that had I been well I should have hoped to be present at the Cardinal's funeral, in any way that might be permitted to those who are not Roman Catholics. Mr. Keble and Dr. Pusey would certainly have wished this, and, as you know, I am indebted to the Cardinal for many kindnesses continued through a long term of years.

"But during the last six weeks I have been prostrated by severe illness, and am still unable to walk, and confined to my room. I can therefore only ask you to allow me to associate myself in heart and mind with your sorrow. Of the event itself it is difficult to trust one's self to say anything."

When he was removed from Oxford, Sir Henry Acland left him in the charge of Dr. Edward Liddon, his brother. To him alone Liddon always said that he did not think that he should recover. Still, in the middle of August his brother thought that he had rallied sufficiently to profit by a change to the seaside ; but Liddon did not wish to leave Standish, and begged to be allowed to remain there a fortnight longer. He seemed to have a clinging to the place ; besides, he was now able to enjoy it so much more, and could even manage to see one or two friends. At last it was settled that on Friday, September 5, he should be moved to Weston-super-Mare. Two days before his leaving he received the Holy Communion ; and on the day of his leaving he insisted on seeing each of the servants separately, and saying "good-bye" to them, adding that he should never see them again. His brother and two of his nieces travelled with him, and his sister was to join him in a few days. He reached the lodgings that had been taken for them at Claremont Crescent without any discomfort. He notes in his diary with evident pleasure the good situation of the house—"not far from the entrance of the pier, and on a projecting piece of land that runs out into the sea. My bedroom window commands a view of the Flat and Steep Holms, Cardiff, a long line of the Welsh coast, and the Devonshire and Quantock Hills."

The next day he spent a good time in the open air, and astonished his nieces in the evening by walking upstairs into their sitting-room to pay them a visit. He preferred talking that evening to the usual reading aloud, and sat with them chatting about his coins and other things in a more natural manner than he had done since his illness began.

On the Monday morning, when his niece went to his room to write some of his letters for him, she saw by his face that something had happened ; and in answer to her inquiry he handed her a letter from Lord Halifax, announcing the death of his godson. The news so deeply affected him that he was unable to write with his own hand any message of sympathy, and could hardly even sign his name to the letter that he dictated. All through the day he was greatly depressed, and was conscious that he had lost much ground ; yet he listened with interest to all the articles in the *Spectator*, and insisted on hearing one on " Dr. Dale on Religious Authority" a second time, and on hearing the end of " Redgauntlet " in the evening.

The next morning, Tuesday, September 9, just before the time for dealing with his letters, his servant alarmed them all by a hurried call for help. His master, without being unconscious or faint, had suddenly become quite unable to move. He could not speak ; his eyes looked very large and bright, and were filled with an unnatural expression. A few minutes later he seemed to fall into a sound sleep ; and those who were with him thankfully noticed that his breathing gradually became less laboured, and then more and more quiet, until they could hardly hear any sound. It seemed to them like the deep sleep of a little child , they did not think what it really was. The doctor had been summoned as rapidly as possible ; but, before his arrival, the breathing had ceased altogether ; the pain-worn body was still, and the soul had passed through the gate of the Eternal World.

The news of his death came as a terrible shock to all who knew him. They had supposed that the improvement, when he was moved from Oxford, was permanent, and were in no way prepared for the great and sudden loss.

Of the many expressions of this sense of bereavement, two may well be quoted. The following Sunday, Canon Scott Holland, preaching at St. Paul's Cathedral, from the pulpit so inextricably associated at that moment with most

Photo.: The London Stereoscopic and Photographic Co., Ltd.

THE MONUMENT IN ST. PAUL'S CATHEDRAL.

vivid memories, spoke of him as the great single-hearted preacher of the Revelation of God.

"As the words of Scripture rang from his lips (and who ever could make Scripture ring as he did ?), their original force seemed to reach and touch us across all the dividing years. No insincerity withheld it. No half-hearted allegiance made them falter in their coming. 'The world,' with its worries, its disputes, its vanities, its beguilements, its pettiness, its greeds—the world threw no veiling mist between us and those Divine appeals. He who spoke to us had got past all that. He had pushed his way up through all the tangle. He was not afraid of what was involved in facing the Truth. He, at least, was ready for the sacrifice. He had counted the cost. And so, by virtue of that sincerity, of that purged eye, he, we felt, saw something of that Vision which the Apostle opens to us. That inner world was real and substantial to him. That fiery zeal had its echo in him. That ever-climbing life of grace upon grace had come within his ken.

"His life was a clear channel down which the news of it might pass to us without derision. Can there be a better test of the spiritual sincerity of a man than this—that we feel no shock when he speaks to us the Bible language? And was it not this which was the entire secret of Liddon's power over us when he preached? As we listened, that inner world that lies before the spiritual eye was once more felt to be laid bare. St. Paul became once more intelligible. Our world, which we collect together under the range of the outward eye—that world in which we creep about, whispering, muttering, nursing a faint hope, struggling to keep our hold on the Vision, trembling ever lest it should break and vanish; that world of shifting resolution, and bewildered.doubts, and miserable timidities, and haunting hesitations; that world of ours was parted asunder! It was pierced through and through by that vibrating voice, that shook us as it told of that which lay beyond, as it lighted on us like a flame, to sting and to stir.

"Ah, that voice! As I speak of him, as I recall to you his message, standing here in this place, where his presence was so familiar, it is I who should be dumb. It is this silent pulpit which speaks to you! It is he whom we still feel here, he under whose dear and remembered tones our hearts still tingle and our spirits burn, so that we cannot believe that we shall never hear them again!

"But at least he has bequeathed to us the solace and the succour of some imperishable memories—memories that you and I shall carry with us to our dying days, uneffaced by all that the coming years may bring us.

"To some here, it will be perhaps some memory of St. Mary's, Oxford, crowded with the black mass of gowned men, thick packed in gallery and on floor, the outburst of organ and of hymn, the quick passage of the preacher up the pulpit steps, the low Bidding Prayer with its delicate articulation, and then across our life, our young life, giddy with light gaieties, glittering and bubbling with all the fleet gossips of the changing hours, we shall for ever remember how there shot the voice, alive with passionate insistence, that told of the Eternal things that can never fade away !

" To others—to most who are here—it will be the memory of the motionless crowd of upturned faces in this great house of God, as the yellow lights flickered and shone through the illuminated haze of some heavy December afternoon, while all the walls were yet tremulous with the lingering music of the Service. And they will never forget how up and up there rose, higher and higher, filling all the misty hollow of the Dome, the piercing tones of that most beautiful of all voices, as with kindling figure and flashing eye, he 'reasoned of Righteousness and of Temperance and of Judgment to come.'"

At the Cathedral at Oxford, Dr. Bright, his gifted companion, and entirely like-minded friend for thirty years, described more in detail the character which he had so long watched and revered.

" One could not quite be silent under the oppressive sorrow of that immense loss which has unexpectedly fallen upon this House, upon Oxford, upon the whole Church of England, upon many who for years have counted his friendship among the chief blessings of this life. Something must be said ; but what? One cannot, here and now, attempt to dwell on the great career which has so lately closed, in what may be called its public aspects. Of course, we remember him as a preacher of supreme excellence, as a constructive Catholic theologian of the first order, as an unwavering defender of the spiritual character of the Church, and of the rights which that character involved. But now, while the grave in his own vast Cathedral has not yet opened to receive his corpse, we here in Christ Church may be pardoned if we think rather of the Henry Liddon whom we ourselves have known so long and have loved so admiringly, and, let me add, so gratefully. We recall the charm of that intense, unique personality, at once so commanding and so attractive ; the conversation, so enriching, so illuminating, with its brilliance and its humour, its fulness and energy of thought, its refined and perfect accuracy of expression. We think of what he was as a friend, how tender, helpful, and faithful, how pathetically generous in his estimate of the most trivial kindnesses. We remember the pains which he would take in answering questions even when he was well-nigh tired out. We think of the sympathy which he would expend on the difficulties or the anxieties of others ; of the exquisite old-world courtesy which flowed forth, simply and without effort, to persons of all sorts and conditions, on the principle of honour due to all men for the Son of Man's sake.

" Yes, and we must needs also be mindful of the responsibility incurred by frequent intercourse with one who could always be relied upon as an example of high unselfishness, of absolute superiority to the influences of what St. John calls 'the world,' which, in the words of this day's Epistle, was crucified for him through Christ. Even those who did not always agree with him must always have been sure of him on that point, and would have understood him had they heard him say, as I have heard him say more than once, 'Whatever happens, we must keep our loyalty to our Lord ; to compromise that would be the worst of all bargains ; nothing else will answer in the long run. The fact was that he had his eye fixed, more and more steadfastly fixed, on the end of life, on the World Unseen, on the Judgment to come.

"He of whom we are thinking did live, ever more and more consciously, in the presence of God, as it encompasses and dominates the soul that has learned to behold the Glory of the Father in the Person of the Co-eternal Son, Incarnate for us men and for our salvation. Yes, on this Holy Cross Day, we may well think of him as devoted to the Crucified Redeemer, the Infallible, Impeccable, Adorable Lord Jesus. All his thoughts about Religion, including his contention for the Catholic Faith as embodied in the Creeds of the Church, or for the operations of the Incarnate Life, by means of the Holy Spirit, through Sacramental Ordinances, and ultimately even all the convictions, which, as an English Churchman, he held so fast, ran up into, and took their force and meaning and sanction from the fact which for him was above all, beneath all, around all—the Reality, the Presence, the Rights, the Character of God as revealed in Christ."

He made his Will in 1885, before going to Egypt. It began with the words—

"First, I commit my soul into the Hands of Almighty God, trusting to obtain His mercy only through the Merits of Jesus Christ, and firmly believing the Christian Faith as held by the whole Catholic Church before the Division of East and West, and by the Church of England. Next, I desire, in case I should die in England, to be buried in the Crypt of St. Paul's Cathedral, if it may conveniently be arranged."

Even before this desire was known, every one felt instinctively that St. Paul's was the only appropriate resting-place for his body. Accordingly, it was brought to London from Weston-super-Mare on the Thursday after his death, and placed in his own study at No. 3, Amen Court. On the evening of the Monday following it was borne to the North-West Chapel in the nave of the Cathedral. There the Holy

Eucharist was celebrated the next morning, September 16, both at 7 and 8 o'clock. At the Burial Service at mid-day the vast area of the Cathedral was crowded, as for one of his Easter sermons in the preceding April. Every arrangement was as simple as possible. A guard of honour of the London Rifle Brigade, of which he had been the Chaplain, kept the line of the procession as the body was moved up into the Choir ; the Altar was vested in white, nowhere was there any conventional sign of mourning. The Lesson was read by Canon Gregory ; the Dean of St. Paul's—in a very few weeks about to follow his friend and colleague—uttered the Words of Committal ; and the concluding prayers were said by Canon Scott Holland. When the Service was over, there followed the Hymn which he so often chose when he was in residence, " When morning gilds the skies," which, in its constantly recurring refrain, " May Jesus Christ be praised," told of his deep and simple loyalty, and of the pure-hearted aim that inspired him and bore him up through all the toils of his life's work.

Immediately after the burial a Meeting was held in the Chapter House at St. Paul's, at which it was resolved that "a Fund be raised to do honour to the memory of Dr. Liddon, and that it be applied in the first instance to provide a fitting memorial of him in St. Paul's Cathedral, and that the remainder be invested to provide an annual fund for assisting graduate members of the University of Oxford in the study of Theology."

With the amount collected for this purpose, the beautiful Altar Tomb, with its recumbent figure in white marble (designed by Messrs. Bodley and Garner), was erected in the Eastern Apse of St. Paul's, and the Apse itself was most carefully decorated. The remainder of the sum was entrusted to the Warden and Council of Keble College for the foundation of " Liddon Studentships" at the University of Oxford.

CHAPTER XIV.

(*BY THE BISHOP OF OXFORD.*)

As one comes to the close of the story of a man's life, it is natural to ask what picture of him rises out of the successive scenes; what manner of man he seems to have been who did and said and suffered what the book has told. And those who knew him well bring with them to the weighing of that question much which no book can tell; they see more than others, and although they may be less impartial, it is in ampler light that they either judge or shrink from judging.

Such light they often long to share with those who did not know the man, or knew him but externally and slightly. And so it may be allowed to one who had for many years the happiness of Dr. Liddon's friendship to write in this last chapter what he can of the thoughts which seem to him as conditions for a just estimate of the life—conditions for seeing rightly the true character that did its work through the events and trials and conflicts told in the chapters that have gone before.

For it may be the case that some who read this book will have a certain feeling of disappointment as they think over it and try to get clear the impression it has left upon their minds; that others will reckon Dr. Liddon amongst those who have brought to the task of life brilliant and effective gifts rather than the qualities of temper and judgment which give lasting value to a man's work; and that others again will fall short of seeing the man as he was, just because they are wholly delighted with the telling phrases, the epigrams and comparisons and unflinching verdicts which exactly match their own opinions; just because they find an absorbing pleasure in the voice of echo, almost as though it were the voice of prophecy. For the hope of staying or moderating judgments such as these, the venture of this chapter is made.

The truth is, that it is a perilous thing to publish any man's letters fourteen years after his death; and most perilous if much of his life was spent in controversy. The world moves quickly nowadays, and as it moves the light fades off the old battle-fields, and the point of view shifts, and the standards of size and importance are other than they were, and the positions on which all seemed to turn may even be hard to distinguish in the broad, distant landscape. And thus, unless one is a connoisseur in controversies, it is difficult to do justice to any disputants save those who are of one's own time; and even among them one may be apt to think poorly of those who are not on one's own side, and, in those who are, to miss the real elements of greatness which lie beneath the obvious attraction of their agreement with one's self. Probably, almost every man who has been much employed in controversy suffers for it more or less in the judgment of those who come after him; even, perhaps, in the judgment of those who are glad to stand on ground which would have been lost but for his hard fighting. But there is one way of controversy which, more than any other, gives hostages to the uncertain future, and leads a man to write what it is easiest for a later generation to disparage. It is a way which Dr. Liddon often took; a way in which his eager, keen, unhesitating mind seemed almost to exult—the way of foretelling what would result from the acceptance, the prevalence of the cause, the movement which he was opposing. He liked to push a position further along the road than those who held it wanted to go. It was a phrase of his that if you begin to slide down an inclined plane, you cannot stop in the middle merely by wishing earnestly to do so; and he would recall how Bishop Lightfoot, when they worked together at St. Paul's, used to protest against his " Oxford logic." And with the same relentlessness, the same concentration on one line of inference, he was wont to foretell what must be the outcome of a policy, a change, which he thought wrong. He put his whole heart into the forecast ; the imagined future came to be to him nearly as vivid, as cogent, as the present ; at times he seemed almost to think of men as though they were saying and doing what he had convinced himself must come of what they said and did. Such forecasts were a large part of the cause of that despondency which, though he never let it stay him from doing all he could for the cause he served, yet brought much sadness and some feeling of isolation into his later years. His prophecies had power to lead him, generous and warm-hearted as he was, to be not wholly just to those from whom he differed ; they appear, sometimes directly, sometimes through their effect upon his judgments, in the pages of this book ; and so appearing now, when much time has passed, bearing its steady witness against all exaggerated estimates and hasty words, they may lead some to be not wholly just to him.

But it should be remembered that it is the rarest thing for a man to keep his exercise and habit of judgment simply unbiassed by the distinctive conditions of his life. We may learn a great deal as we toil or stumble along our course ; but insensibly we tend towards using our minds with increasing readiness and inclination in the way in which our work allows or forces us to use them ; and, so tending, we are all likely to think too little of the points which are not the most prominent in that way, the most often pressed upon us in our work. So one man lets his mind be swayed out of the strait and narrow line of justice by attending overmuch to considerations of one sort ; another is always thinking, in the stress and haste of business, of another sort, which his task gives him no chance of forgetting, and he too falters off after his fashion. We all make our mistakes, all get habits of judgment which are not quite the best ; and biographies must be written very quickly or very unscrupulously, if they are to

convey any idea that a man was always right. And
perhaps the most frequent manner of divergence between
minds, diversely used, is just this : that one man tends to
fasten on a single train of thought and inference, pursuing
it without regard to the surrounding facts that tell on it,
the laws and conditions that should check his confidence ;
while another, constrained, for his very work's sake, to
recognise all such conditions, laws, and facts, lets the
custom of deference to them grow upon him, till abstract
principles have less than their rightful power over him, or
the energy of whole-hearted confidence is but rarely his.
It is the latter way of harm and loss that they have most
to fear who bear great burdens of administration or of
government, in Church or State ; who cannot stand aloof,
or take action only when they choose, warning others meanwhile of the disastrousness of misdirected action ; who
must work with others if they are to work at all ; who can
do nothing if they ignore the limitations of what they can
do ; and who, if ever they resolve to have things their own
way, are almost sure to find things too many for them.
The way of life least like theirs has, naturally enough,
the opposite sort of perils hovering about it.

Now, Dr. Liddon's life was singularly free from great
burdens of administration or of government. In ability,
learning, and strength of will he excelled many who in his
day were charged with great tasks and overwhelming
responsibility, while he, in comparison with them, was
almost a free-lance. His splendid gifts were used indeed
with conscientious and persevering diligence ; few men
worked harder ; but the constant discipline, the haunting
constraint, the stubborn hindrance that belongs to such
offices as he should have held, he never knew. Had he
known them, he might have judged more leniently those
who had to do their best under such limitations ; he might
have realised the imperfection of deductive logic as a guide
of life. He was less laden with responsibility, less dependent upon others, less closely and inevitably hampered by
intractable conditions, than one so able should have been.

It is curious to look back and mark how strangely he was left free from the restraint that is involved in every charge of chief authority :—as a Curate at Wantage, with a Vicar unlikeliest of all men to put his primacy into commission ; as Vice-Principal of Cuddesdon, with a Bishop ready and resolute to determine the lines of growth for the newly founded College ; as Chaplain to Bishop Hamilton, rendering a reverent and willing deference; as Vice-Principal of St. Edmund Hall ; as a Student of Christ Church, never charged with the anxieties of a tutor, or a censor, never called to enter into the difficulties of sustaining, year after year, a discipline which must be real and never can be masterful ; as a Professor, teaching freely those who freely and gladly came to him, and unfettered even by any necessity of teaching for examinations ; as a Canon of St. Paul's, holding indeed an unique place in the attention and gratitude of thousands, yet bearing no unshared weight of responsibility, no lonely tasks of decision, bound by no imperative need of carrying others with him that he might do his own work. Why it was that he was left thus free, whether any one was to blame for it, whether after all it did not lead to his doing the most he could of that which he could do best, it is not relevant here to ask. The point is that such gifts as his, with such freedom as he enjoyed, escaped that discipline of insuperable difficulties and of dependence upon others which, while it brings indeed its own temptations, is none the less a safeguard of the exercise of judgment. Brilliant and eager as he was, placed as he was, he could ignore what otherwise he must have reckoned with ; he could pursue his course of inference, his insistence on a single principle, without always facing facts which, had the duty of government or a foremost place in administration been his, he would never have been suffered to ignore. The tide of change that nothing can arrest, the awakening of criticism that none can silence, the asking of questions that must somehow be openly and adequately met ; the real, exacting, penetrating claim which these bring with them is pressed inevitably, constantly on those

who have somehow to work with men of widely diverse
temperaments and views, under conditions which they cannot
change. The greater responsibility involves more com-
plexity, and less freedom. It may be well indeed to warn
men of the perils that are hidden in the tides of change,
and of the deep issues that may be affected by them ;
for irreverent haste and love of novelty are common
enough : but something more than warning, more than the
threatening forecast of a disastrous sequel, is demanded
of those who bear the great burdens of administration or
government : and high ability ought not, for its own sake
or for the sake of others, to escape those burdens and
that demand.

It was scarcely to be avoided that, in the picture of
Dr. Liddon's life, the scenes of controversy should form a
large part. In general, biography lies open to the same
causes of disproportion which are apt to make history seem
as though nations lived to fight. And he lived at a time
when there was much fighting to be done ; he had at command all the resources and powers for fine, effective fighting ; and, while he was too good a man to love anything
more than truth and peace, there were elements in his
character which made him peculiarly unlikely to hang back
when the claims of truth seemed to make it necessary to
forgo the enjoyment of peace. When he was a small boy,
there was a feud—if the story is rightly recalled—between
his school and another. It was agreed that the feud should
be fought out by champions from either side ; his schoolfellows discreetly chose him their champion, until further
notice ; and day after day when morning school was over,
he went out, ready to do battle with any boy who might
come from the other camp. The choice, and the acceptance of it, and the indefatigable fulfilment of the task which
it involved, all seem to find some representation in his later
life. And the consequences of a perpetual championship
when one is grown up, though they may be less obvious,
are more serious than those which attend the office at a
preparatory school.

But the friends who saw most of him, and saw him, it may be, when he was happiest, have a memory of him widely different from the impression which would be gathered from the history of his wars. The friend with whom he travelled year after year, who really, perhaps, was to him nearest of all, save his own kindred, and whose happiness it was to be constantly adding to the gladness and pleasantness of his Oxford life ; the friend who toiled with him hour after hour in the building up of Dr. Pusey's biography, and by whose loyalty and care both that great book and this have seen the light ; the friends with whom he dined quietly every Friday when he was at Christ Church —always coming late, always apologising after the same fashion, always disclosing, bit by bit, his most delightful ways ; the friends who will exactly recognise every trait in Mr. Sampson's sketch of him ; the friends whose lives were simpler than his, such as those who remember him as the kindest and most generous of masters ; the friends who walked with him along the familiar roads round Oxford, and hardly kept him from trespassing through Bagley Wood in quest of wild flowers, sometimes to be borne home in open triumph, sometimes to be stored precariously in his hat ; friends, again, such as those he had at the Deanery of St. Paul's ;—they know how far deeper and richer and nobler his nature was than all that can appear in controversy ; they hold and honour a remembrance of him which they may feel to be a greater thing than can be gathered even from the most brilliant parts of his correspondence, or from all his share in determining the course of affairs ; they may think that they can understand why it really was that he held a foremost place amongst men, and won the admiration and gratitude and trust even of those who on many points differed from him.

For they remember him as one who, possessing in extraordinary measure the gifts most perilous to simplicity and modesty, and so wielding those gifts that men of all sorts gathered round him in thousands and listened to him as to no other preacher, yet remained unmarred by admiration, and kept quite out of his heart all the degrading thoughts of what is called success ;—remained apparently one of the least self-conscious of men, ready to enter with undivided interest into anything that was of real interest to others ; as simply grateful as a child for the simplest kindness shown to him ; never talking about himself, nor talking as men do who, when they are silent, think much about themselves ; and making others somehow feel that it would not do to talk to him as though they thought him remarkable or great. Something of that restraining influence seems still to belong to the very thought and memory of him ; it makes one hesitate (not in doubt, but in reverence) about venturing to give him the deep praise of humility and simplicity ; but one can say that the constant tokens of a very humble, simple heart were there, through all his exercise of splendid powers and all the tribute rendered him by men. And as one so thinks of him, it does not seem strange that he held a high place and did a great work. For men are quick to see where the tribute of their admiration does no harm.

And then his friends remember (and the lines of thought, though they move on different planes, seem parallel) how unselfishly he used his wonderful ability in ordinary conversation ; though, indeed, no conversation into which he came was really ordinary. It is hard to imagine any one talking much better than he did. The voice, the look, the manner, the perfect flexibility of tone ; the phrases that summed up everything, the reticence that suggested more than any phrase ; the gesture, or something less obtrusive than a gesture, which came in when any word would have been clumsy ; the delicate enunciation that was always precise and never prim, that lent itself alike to earnestness and fun ;—these were but the accessory graces of a mind rich with knowledge of all sorts, and swift to bring out the aptest thought, and of an imagination so vivid that every detail stood at once before it, so discerning that it saw at once the detail that meant most. Indeed, most minds, as they move in talking, appear to be rather lumbering things in comparison with what one can recall of him. And yet all the wealth and keenness and vigour of his mind, and all the singular brightness that played round it in his talk, seem less remarkable, as one looks back, than his admirable aloofness from the besetting sins of a clever talker. He never (to use a curious but picturesque and sadly suggestive expression in common use) "absorbed the conversation;" he seldom seemed even to take a prominent part in it ; others found themselves unconsciously talking with the more freedom, the more enjoyment, because he was there ; his brilliancy was not like the warning and intermittent flashes from a revolving light ; it quietly lit up all around him, so that every one saw things the better for it. He seldom talked of people, and never talked of them in the petty, narrow ways of gossip ; he never scored off others, save where he knew that the victim of the score was just the one who would best enjoy it. And he seemed clear even of the last infirmity of good talkers with strong convictions about the affairs of Church or State ; for, as one recalls what he was in social life, it is very hard to imagine that he had any "ulterior aim," marring the simplicity of his pleasantness ; that he ever thought that anybody would be more likely to share his views because they had found him attractive as a guest or as a host ; that he ever wished thus to bring about what might be reverently left to Reason, and to Grace. When great questions came into the conversation, he spoke out, with as little hesitation as he would have shown under any other conditions ; and people who thought that nothing mattered much were apt to elicit, by a venture or a blunder starting from that hypothesis, a good deal more than they anticipated. But that was in a fair and open field, into which others, wilfully or carelessly, had called him out. It was a different matter from carrying under the colour of friendliness an unavowed aim ; it never warranted the feeling that one must still be on one's guard when hospitality had hoisted a flag of truce.

But in any adequate remembrance of him there is far more than has yet been touched to account for the strength and depth with which, over a wide range, his work told. For as those who knew him well look back, and recollect what it was to be with him, and how he seemed to regard life, they must recall the discernment of two thoughts as often evident in his bearing and his words ; two thoughts which enter, perhaps, more than any other secrets of power into the character which has, from time to time, made men leaders of their fellow-men in matters of religion : —the thought of the greatness and worth of every human soul, and the thought of allegiance to an ever-present Lord. They are indeed but the elementary thoughts of the pastoral office, the Christian life ; both are required from the outset in every man who is ordained ; both are pre-supposed in all the daily duties and privileges of every clergyman's work. And there is something terrible, not only in considering the clerical lives which it is difficult to regard as controlled at all by these thoughts, but also in marking the distinctive and peculiar power which accrues to those in whom they are the central force and fire that they should be, and in trying to imagine what the Church would be if they so ruled and so inspired all her servants. For it seems as though the dull and deadening tendency of routine and compromise were always loosening men's grasp on the axioms of serving God. And in truth it is these primary and elemental thoughts that are the hardest to hold with a real apprehension, to explore and fathom with a steadily advancing penetration, to guard in a supremacy which is unimpaired and carried loyally through the whole domain that such thoughts have a right to rule. They ask much of a man at every step forward in the recognition, the understanding of them ; he sees that they will go on asking more and more ; there is no discharge in the war for which they enlist him ; there is no telling what it may be found to involve. But in proportion as a man, heart and soul, acknowledges them, and sets himself to remember them in all his ways, and to bring all other thoughts into captivity to them, he can really teach and help his fellow-men in things pertaining to God ; he finds their unsought

trust setting towards him ; and so he draws near to the
burden of leadership in that sphere, on that level, where—
be it the leadership of many or of few—it means most.

It must sound intrusive and presumptuous to say of
any man that to him these thoughts were continually
recurring, and that his work, his will, were held ever ready
to be controlled by them. But that does seem to be the
true way of accounting for much of Dr. Liddon's singular
and characteristic power. He habitually regarded men as
the New Testament speaks of them ; the countless points of
difference which lead most people to be eclectic, not only
in their friendship, but also in their interest and sympathy,
he kept really subordinate to those universal elements and
aspects and conditions which give greatness to every
human being and infinite importance to every human
life. He fulfilled, with the further penetration of Christian
insight, the saying that the abler a man is the fewer
ordinary people he finds. Even the distinctions of intellect and culture did not stay his direct looking to the
real vocation of the soul. The roughest tramp upon the
road was in his eyes one who might come to be numbered
with Christ's saints in glory everlasting ; the most brilliant
and distinguished guest he met had no higher possibility
than that ; and there was a peculiar note of sadness and
of pity in the way he sometimes spoke of men who, with
splendid gifts and ample opportunities, seemed to have
declined their task in life or lost their way. And as he so
moved among his fellow-men, so thought of them and
approached them, he seemed as one who was often thinking
of the gaze of Christ lighting on him, the Hand of Christ
pointing to some act of service, the Voice of Christ prompt-
ing some witness to the Faith. There was a memorable
tone that came into his words when in preaching or in
argument or in conversation he spoke of that which he
condemned as slighting or disloyal to Christ. It was,
quite simply, like the way in which a man fires up when
any one has, even unawares, spoken rudely or con-
temptuously of his friend ; and there are parts of his

writings in which, for those at least who knew him, that same tone still sounds. It was but one sign of a real habit of thinking constantly of his Master; of a very attentive listening for His command; of an earnest, anxious desire to go straight forward in His cause, to live and die as His.

Of course, no claim is made for Dr. Liddon that he was peculiar in so thinking of human life, and of his own duty in it. But in the memory of some who knew him well he wears a certain distinction as having shown very brightly, very impressively, the character that is thus formed, the way that is thus learnt. They feel as they look back that it was he who most helped them on towards the fellowship of such thoughts, and they may wish that they had made more of the chance they thus had, and been apter and more willing to receive the best of all his teaching. And perhaps even those who did not know him, if they thus think of him,—as one who used, in unwearied industry, great learning and great gifts of heart and mind, with indifference to praise, with reverence for all men, with an eager allegiance to Christ,—may see how it was that, even had he made all the mistakes which criticism may be busy to discover in his life and in his letters, still he could not have failed to be among the foremost of his day, and to bear signal witness to the Faith he held, and to lead many to the knowledge and the love of God.

APPENDIX

LIST OF DR. LIDDON'S PRINTED WORKS.

The Repentance of Ahab. A Sermon (on 1 Kings xxi. 29) preached in St. Giles's Church, Oxford, on the Second Friday in Lent, February 26, 1858. Oxford, 1858.

Christ's Welcome to the Penitent. A Sermon (on St. Luke xv. 20) preached in St. Giles's Church, Oxford, on the Second Wednesday in Lent, February 29, 1860. Oxford, 1860. 8vo.

The Aim and Principles of Church Missions. A Sermon (on 1 Cor. ix. 22) preached, on behalf of St. George's Mission, East London, in St. Mary Magdalene's Church, Munster Square, London, November 27, 1860. London, 1860.

Our Lord's Ascension the Church's Gain. A Sermon (on St. John xvi. 7) preached before the University of Oxford, in the Cathedral Church of Christ, on Ascension Day, May 17, 1860. Oxford, 1860. 8vo.

On Penitentiary Work. Two Sermons (on St. Luke xv. 5 and St. Mark ix. 29) preached at the Opening of the Chapel of St. Mary's Home, Wantage, July 30, 1861, by the Bishop of Oxford and H. P. Liddon, with a short Preface on Sisterhoods, by W. J. Butler, M.A. Oxford, 1861. 8vo.

Our Lord's Example the Strength of His Ministers. A Sermon (on St. Matt. iv. 19) preached at the Ordination of the Bishop of Oxford, in the Cathedral Church of Christ, December 23, 1860. Oxford, 1861. 8vo.

Active Love a Criterion of Spiritual Life. A Sermon (on 1 St. John iii. 14) preached, on behalf of the Church Penitentiary Association, at St. James's, Piccadilly, London, May 15, 1862. London, 1862. 8vo.

Apostolic Labours an Evidence of Christian Truth. A Sermon (on Rom. x. 18) preached in the Chapel of Lambeth Palace, at the Consecration of the Bishop of Nassau, November 30, 1863. Oxford, 1863.

The Whole Counsel of God; or, The Duty of the Clergy as Teachers of the People, etc. A Sermon (on Acts xx. 27) preached at the Ordination of the Bishop of Salisbury, in Sherborne Abbey Church, February 21, 1864. Oxford, 1864. 8vo.

Witness for Jesus. A Sermon (on Acts i. 8) preached in St. Paul's Cathedral, April 17, 1864. London, 1864. 8vo.

Our Founder's Vow. A Sermon (on Ps. cxxxii. 3–5) preached at the Dedication of the Chapel of St. John's College, Hurstpierpoint, October 17, 1865. London, 1865.

Profit and Loss. A Sermon (on St. Matt. xvi. 26) preached in St. Paul's Cathedral on the Third Sunday after Epiphany, January 22, 1865. London, 1865. 8vo.

Some Words for God. Being Sermons preached before the University of Oxford, chiefly during the years 1863–1865. Oxford, 1865. 8vo.
—— Second Edition, 1866. This title was dropped and was replaced by "Sermons preached before the University of Oxford."
—— Eighth Edition, 1884. With further title, "First Series."

The Secret of Clerical Power. A Sermon (on Acts i. 8) preached at the Ordination of the Bishop of Salisbury, in Salisbury Cathedral, September 24, 1865. London, 1865.

Fatalism and the Living God. A Sermon (on Ps. viii. 4) preached at the Ordination of the Bishop of Salisbury, in Salisbury Cathedral, September 23, 1866. London, 1866. 8vo.

The Divinity of our Lord Jesus Christ. Being the Bampton Lectures for 1866. London, 1867. 8vo.
—— Second Edition. London, 1868. 8vo.
—— Fourth Edition. London, 1869. 8vo.
—— Fifth Edition. Oxford, 1871. 8vo.
—— Ninth Edition. London, 1882. 8vo.
—— Tenth Edition, revised. London, 1884. 8vo.
—— Eleventh Edition, revised. London, 1885. 8vo.
—— Thirteenth Edition. London, 1889. 8vo.
—— Fourteenth Edition. London, 1890. 8vo.

Love of the Parish Church. A Sermon (on Ps. xxvi. 8) preached at Madresfield, Worcestershire, November 12, 1867. Malvern, 1867. 8vo.

There is a Holy Ghost. A Sermon (on Acts xix. 1, 2) preached before the University of Oxford, at St. Mary's, on Whitsun Day, June 9, 1867. London, 1867. 8vo.

Personal Responsibility for the Gift of Revelation. A Sermon (on St. John xii. 47, 48) preached in St. Mary's Church, Oxford, on the First Friday in Lent, February 28, 1868. London, 1868. 8vo.

The Moral Value of a Mission from Christ. A Sermon (on St. John xv. 16) preached at the Ordination of the Bishop of Oxford, in the Cathedral Church of Christ, December 22, 1867. London 1868. 8vo.

The Honour of Humanity. A Sermon (on 1 St. Pet. ii. 17) preached before the University of Oxford, at St. Mary's, on the First Sunday in Lent, 1868. London, 1868. 8vo.
—— Second Edition. London, 1868. 8vo.

The Divine Indwelling, a Motive to Holiness. A Sermon (on 1 Cor. iii. 16) preached before the University of Oxford, at St. Mary's, on Whitsun Day, 1868. London, 1868. 8vo.

The Work and Prospects of Theological Colleges. A Sermon (on Isa. l. 4) preached at the Anniversary Festival of Cuddesdon College, June 10, 1868. London, 1868. 8vo.

Christ and Human Law. A Sermon (on St. John xix. 10, 11) preached before the University of Oxford, at St. Mary's, on the Third Sunday in Lent, February 28, 1869. London, 1869. 8vo.

The Power of Christ's Resurrection. A Sermon (on Phil. iii. 10) preached in St. Paul's Cathedral, on Easter Day, March 28. London, 1869. 8vo.

Sermons preached before the University of Oxford. Second Series, 1868–1879. London, 1879. 8vo.
—— —— 1868–1880. Second Edition. London, 1880. 8vo.
—— —— 1868–1882. Third Edition. London, 1883. 8vo.
—— —— 1868–1882. Fourth Edition. London, 1887. 8vo.

A Sister's Work. A Sermon (on Col. iii. 23, 24) preached in All Saints', Margaret Street, London, June 6, 1869. London, 1869. 8vo.
—— Second Edition. London, 1869. 8vo.

Christ and Education. A Sermon (on 1 Cor. iii. 11) preached in St. James's, Piccadilly, London, June 13, 1869. London, 1869. 8vo.

Life in Death. A Sermon (on St. Luke xxiv. 4, 5) preached in Salisbury Cathedral, August 8, 1869, being the day after the Funeral of W. K. Hamilton, D.D., Bishop of Salisbury. London, 1869. 8vo.

Walter Kerr Hamilton, Bishop of Salisbury. A Sketch, reprinted, with additions, from the *Guardian*. London, 1869. 8vo.

How to do Good. A Sermon (on Gal. vi. 10) preached in St. Paul's Cathedral, at the Anniversary Festival of the Sons of the Clergy, May 18, 1870. London, 1870. 8vo.

Pauperism and the Love of God. A Sermon (on 1 St. John iii. 17) preached at St. Paul's, Knightsbridge, on behalf of the Convalescent Hospital at Ascot, June 26, 1870. London, 1870.

The Model of our New Life. A Sermon (on Rom. vi. 4) preached in St. Paul's Cathedral, on Easter Day, April 17, 1870. London, 1870. 8vo.

The Day of Work. A Sermon (on St. John ix. 4) preached in St. Paul's Cathedral, on the morrow of the Funeral of the Very Rev. H. L. Mansel, D.D., August 6, 1871. London, 1871. 8vo.

St. Paul's and London. A Sermon (on St. Matt. v. 14) preached in St. Paul's Cathedral, January 29, 1871. London, 1871. 8vo.

The Purchas Judgment. A Letter of acknowledgment to Sir J. T. Coleridge ; together with a Letter to the writer, by E. B. Pusey, D.D. London, 1871. 8vo.

The Purchas Judgment. A Letter to the Bishop of London, by the two Senior Canons of St. Paul's, Robert Gregory and Henry Parry Liddon. London, 1871. 8vo.

Some Elements of Religion. Lent Lectures, 1870. London, 1872. 8vo.
—— Second Edition. London, 1873. 8vo.

Some Elements of Religion. Third Edition. London, 1881. 8vo.
—— Fourth Edition. London, Edinburgh, 1883. 8vo.
—— New Edition. London, 1904.

The Life of Faith and the Athanasian Creed. A Sermon (on St. John iii. 36) preached before the University of Oxford, at St. Mary's Church, October 20, 1872. London, 1872. 8vo.

The One Salvation. A Sermon (on Acts iv. 12) preached, on behalf of the Bishop of London's Fund, in St. Paul's Cathedral, May 18, 1873. London, 1873. 8vo.

The Moral Groundwork of Clerical Training. A Sermon (on Job xxviii. 12) preached at the Anniversary Festival of Cuddesdon College, June 10, 1873. London, 1873. 8vo.

Love and Knowledge. A Sermon (on Phil. i. 9, 10) preached in King's College Chapel, London, November 9, 1873. London, 1873. 8vo.

Penitentiary Work in the Church of England. Papers prepared for the meeting of the Association ; with a Preface by H. P. Liddon, D.D. London, 1873.

Bishop Samuel Wilberforce. A Sermon (on 1 Cor. ix. 22) preached at the parish church of Graffham, Sussex, November 2, 1875. London, 1875. 8vo.

John Keble. A Sermon (on Col. iii. 10) preached at Keble College, Oxford, on occasion of the Opening of the Chapel, April 25, 1876. Published in " An Account of the Proceedings at Keble College on the Occasion of the Opening of the Chapel." Oxford, J. Parker & Co. 1876.

Phœbe in London. A Sermon (on Rom. xvi. 1) preached, on behalf of the Parochial Mission Women Association, in the Parish Church of Kensington, June 10, 1877. London, 1877. 8vo.

Teaching and Healing. A Sermon (on St. Matt. ix. 35) preached, before the International Medical Congress, in St. Paul's Cathedral, August 7, 1881. London, 1881. 8vo.

Thoughts on Present Church Troubles. Occurring in four Sermons preached in St. Paul's Cathedral in December, 1880 ; with a Preface. London, 1881. 8vo.
—— Second Edition. London, 1882. 8vo.

The Recovery of St. Thomas. A Sermon (on St. John xx. 27) preached in St. Paul's Cathedral, April 23, 1882 ; with a Prefatory Note on the late Mr. Darwin. London, 1882. 8vo.
—— Second Edition. London, 1882. 8vo.

Of the Five Wounds of the Holy Church. By A. Rosmini. Edited, with an Introduction, by H. P. Liddon, D.D. London, 1883. 8vo.

Die Gottheit Unseres Herrn und Heilandes Jesu Christi. Acht Vorlesungen gehalten von H. P. Liddon, Domherr und Professor an der Universität, Oxford. Autorisirte Uebersetzung der 7 Auflage. Mit einem Vorwort von Ph. Fr. Mader, deutscher Pfarrer in Nizza. Basel, Bahnmaier's Verlag (C. Dethoff, 1883).

Edward Bouverie Pusey. A Sermon (on St. Matt. v. 19) preached in aid of the Pusey Memorial Fund, in St. Margaret's Church, Liverpool, January 20, 1884. London, 1884. 8vo.
—— Second Edition. London, 1884. 8vo.

Easter in St. Paul's. Sermons bearing chiefly on the Resurrection of our Lord. 2 vols. London, 1885. 8vo.
—— New Edition. London, 1891. 8vo.

A Father in Christ. A Sermon (on 1 Cor. iv. 15) preached in St. Paul's Cathedral, at the Consecration of the Bishop of Lincoln and of the Bishop of Exeter, on the Feast of St. Mark the Evangelist, April 25, 1885. London, 1885. 8vo.
—— Second Edition. With a notice of the Rev. Dr. Hatch's Paper in the *Contemporary Review*, June, 1885. London, 1885. 8vo.
—— Third Edition, revised. London, 1885. 8vo.

Devotion to the Church of Christ. A Sermon (on Isa. lxii. 5) preached before the University of Cambridge, in Great St. Mary's Church, October 28, 1888. London, 1888. 8vo.

Advent in St. Paul's. Sermons bearing chiefly on the two Comings of our Lord. 2 vols. London, 1888. 8vo.
—— Second Edition. 2 vols. London, 1889. 8vo.
—— New Edition. London, 1891. 8vo.

The Name of Names. A short Sermon (on Phil. ii. 9) preached in St. Paul's Cathedral on the Feast of the Circumcision, being New Year's Day, 1889. London, 1889. 8vo.
—— Second Edition. London, 1889. 8vo.

Religion and Arms. A Sermon (on 2 Tim. ii. 3) preached in St. Paul's Cathedral, before the officers and men of the London Rifle Brigade, on Low Sunday, April 28, 1889. London, 1889. 8vo.

The Vision at Corinth. A Sermon (on Acts xviii. 9, 10) preached in the Cathedral Church of Christ, Oxford, on behalf of the Christ Church Mission at Poplar, East London, May 12, 1889. London, 1889. 8vo.

Christmastide in St. Paul's. Sermons bearing chiefly on the Birth of our Lord. London, 1889. 8vo.

The Magnificat. Sermons in St. Paul's Cathedral, August, 1889. London, 1889. 8vo.
—— Second Edition. London, 1890. 8vo.

The Worth of the Old Testament. A Sermon (on Rom. xv. 3, 4) preached in St. Paul's Cathedral, on the Second Sunday in Advent, December 8, 1889. London, 1890. 8vo.
—— Second Edition, revised, and with a new Preface. London, 1890. 8vo.

The Inspiration of Selection. A Sermon (on St. John xvi. 14) preached before the University of Oxford, in the Church of St. Mary the Virgin, on Whitsun Day, May 25, 1890. London, 1890. 12mo.

Passiontide Sermons. London, 1891.
—— Second Edition. London (Edinburgh University Press), 1891. 8vo.

Sermons on Old Testament Subjects. London, 1891. 8vo.

Sermons on some Words of Christ. London, 1892. 8vo.

Essays and Addresses. London (Edinburgh), 1892. 8vo.

Explanatory Analysis of St. Paul's Epistle to the Romans. London (Oxford), 1893. 8vo.
—— Fourth Edition. London (Oxford), 1899. 8vo.

Life of Edward Bouverie Pusey. By H. P. Liddon. Edited and prepared for publication by the Rev. J. O. Johnston and the Rev. R. J. Wilson. With portraits and illustrations. Vols. I., II. London (Oxford), 1893. 8vo.
—— Vol. III. London, 1894.
—— —— Third Edition. London (Oxford), 1895. 8vo.
—— Vol. IV. London, 1897. Edited and prepared for publication by the Rev. J. O. Johnston and the Rev. W. C. E. Newbolt.

Clerical Life and Work. A collection of Sermons, with an Essay. London (Edinburgh), 1894. 8vo.

Sermons preached on Special Occasions. 1860–1889. London, New York, and Bombay (Edinburgh), 1897. 8vo.

Explanatory Analysis of St. Paul's First Epistle to Timothy. London, New York, and Bombay (Oxford), 1897. 8vo.

Sermons on Some Words of St. Paul. London, New York, and Bombay, 1898. 8vo.

Dr. Liddon's Tour in Egypt and Palestine in 1886. Being letters descriptive of the Tour written by his sister, Mrs. King. London, 1891. 8vo.

INDEX

———◇———

THE END

PRINTED BY WILLIAM CLOWES AND SONS, LIMITED, LONDON AND BECCLES.